The World Year Book of Education 1971/72

Higher Education in a Changing World

The World Year Book of Education 1971/72

Higher Education in a Changing World

Joint Editors:

Brian Holmes, B.Sc., Ph.D., A.Inst.P.
Reader in Comparative Education, University of London
Institute of Education

David G. Scanlon, Ed.D.
Professor of International Education, Columbia University

Associate Joint Editor:

W. R. Niblett C.B.E., B.A., B.Litt.
Professor of Higher Education
University of London Institute of Education

Published in the United States of America by

Harcourt Brace Jovanovich, Inc.
New York   Chicago   San Francisco   Atlanta

First American edition 1971
ISBN 0–15–598567–1

Printed in 11/12 Bembo (270) in Great Britain by
Western Printing Services Ltd, Bristol

The World Year Book of Education 1971/72

143442

Contents

Editors' Introduction

During the sixties and throughout the world the problems facing higher education have received a great deal of attention. This is not surprising since in this decade the immediate post-war population explosion hit higher education. It was accompanied by a new climate of opinion about access to higher education and by new industrial demands. Decision makers have had to face major questions. Could pressures to expand be contained? How should they be met? At what rate should expansion take place? Should existing institutions absorb the demand or should new institutions be established? What kinds of institutions were needed? In few countries has the growth of higher education taken place in an orderly fashion. Student unrest should not be exaggerated but it does reflect the crisis through which universities have been passing. It is by no means certain, even now, that lasting solutions have been found to the questions posed by post-war expansion.

It seemed appropriate to the Editorial Boards that at the end of this decade of controversy, developments in higher education should again be reviewed in THE WORLD YEAR BOOK OF EDUCATION. In 1959 the volume on *Higher Education* surveyed the field in articles dealing with the adaptation of university tradition, the position of professional studies, finance, academic freedom and the relationships between universities and other institutions of higher education. Since then higher education seems to have been examined from every conceivable angle. The literature is vast – and in this volume Thelma Bristow's bibliography represents only a selection of articles relevant to the topics examined. Now emerging from the turmoil are new policies and practices. Some relate to the reorganization of systems of higher education, other practices more particularly concern the internal organization of institutions of higher education.

The Editorial Boards agreed that the topic was too big to be covered adequately in one volume so they decided that in this first volume on higher education attention should be given to the problems of re-appraising and reorganizing systems of higher education in the light of changing social institutions. In the next volume, which has been planned in conjunction with the present one, articles will deal principally with individual institutions throughout the world – the problems they face, their aims and the new practices they are introducing.

This volume is divided into three main sections. In the first of these, articles analyse concepts of the university in society in historical perspective. They are intended to illustrate the direction of thinking about the universities and higher education in major regions of the world. In the second section, articles were commissioned which would show how socio-economic and political changes are forcing decision makers to re-think policy and devise new practices. Demographic, economic, social class and political factors are examined in case studies and comparative investigations. National solutions to the problems of reorganizing higher education are presented in Section III. As usual it has not been possible to achieve world-wide coverage, so that the articles are simply representative of approaches to reform.

When the volume was first planned it was hoped that major comparative studies based upon research could be commissioned. The time we were able to allow authors to prepare articles was too short to permit lengthy research. Consequently many of the articles are informed by long thought and experience rather than on new research. In some cases we were able to draw on comparative research already in progress and we are particularly grateful to the Higher Education Research Unit at the London School of Economics and Political Science and members of the Organization for Economic Cooperation and Development for their help. We should also like to thank colleagues everywhere who responded to our invitations to write articles at short notice in a field which has its own peculiar hazards.

Inevitably there are gaps. We regret them but remain confident that the volume will stand comparison with its predecessors in presenting a world picture of some major problems facing higher education in the seventies.

In conclusion we wish once more to re-state our editorial policy: that, while the Editors accept responsibility for the choice of writers for the volume (and some of them write about higher education in countries other than their own), we have left each contributor entirely free to write out of his own experience and knowledge with no suggestion of censorship whatsoever from the Editors. Accordingly, the responsibility for each article rests with the author under whose name it appears.

Brian Holmes
Institute of Education, London

David G. Scanlon
Teachers College, New York

Introduction

Universities, Higher Education and Society

Brian Holmes

Torn-up cobblestones, burning cars and barricades put up by French students were the immediate aftermath of the 1968 riots in Paris. They helped to bring an end to a political era. That year heads were broken at Columbia University when city police were eventually called in to deal with students who had taken over the administrative buildings. At Berkeley, Japan and elsewhere equally violent scenes took place during the sixties. Tragically one student was shot dead by police during a demonstration in Berlin, and the climax occurred in 1970 when four were killed by National Guardsmen at Kent State University in Ohio.

Countless examples of student unrest could be cited. In universities and other institutions of higher learning it is a world-wide phenomenon. Its causes are many. International conspiracy theories offer a simple and, to many, a comforting explanation. But why does conspiracy succeed? What conditions in higher education today provide fertile soil for revolutionary seeds? How can even sporadic outbursts of violence throughout the world be explained?

There are at least two issues. One is related to the internal management of institutions of higher learning: and it is not only students who are dissatisfied with the authority structure in university communities of scholars. The other issue goes deeper and is the theme of this volume. Unrest in the universities is more the reflection or result of an unsettled world than the source of a new social revolution. In the post-war world expectations have been raised for a vast number of people far beyond the possibilities of satisfying them. Among these expectations were promises of a world safe for democracy in which peace, improved standards of living, equality of opportunity and the assurance that men and women all over the world would be granted the basic human right of equality before the law, health, work and education. Debates which preceded the creation of Unesco in 1946 suggested that some optimists were convinced that the provision of education at all levels would ensure that these hopes were fulfilled.

They have not been realized. Widespread poverty, revolution, discrimination on the bases of sex, race and religion, intolerance and international wars have disillusioned a generation who fought in the second world war and their sons and daughters. Progress in science, technology and medicine has to be compared with the degradation of life in industrial slums and deprivations in rural areas. The social revolution, far from equalizing provisions, has widened the gap between the 'haves' and the 'have-nots' in all fields of life. Education has created new, socially privileged, elites. Economists and sociologists have claimed great social benefits for education so it is hardly surprising that some radical thinkers ascribe the ills of society to education – and in particular to the failure of the universities.

In questioning the quality of modern life some students and faculty members are critical of post-war conceptions of society and suspicious of the cynicism of those in power. No social-political system has escaped their criticism – neither traditional liberal democracies, their socialist derivations, Marxist alternatives nor the new left. Colonialism is not acceptable, but neither are some of the new forms of independence.

Systems of education have not escaped criticism. Elitism based on early selection has been attacked. Yet the democratization of education in countries such as Japan, the USA and India has not settled the doubts of many students and teachers there, though only a minority of radicals everywhere have carried the conflict of ideas beyond the debating halls and provoked violence on campuses and in the streets. There is a crisis of confidence in the social validity of the theory and practice of the modern university. While the crisis may have passed its peak there is still good reason to examine and compare concepts of the 'good society' and the role higher education should play in it. The universities are so powerful that this analysis cannot be soundly based unless concepts of the university and its role in society are studied. In this volume it is against this background that present-day problems in higher education are viewed.

Concepts of Society

A satisfactory analysis of the problems facing universities today depends upon some assessment of societal changes. This could be done on the basis of statistical data or in the light of a conceptual analysis which would reveal the social relationships in contemporary situations between the universities and the societies they serve. Few comparative studies of this kind are available. Frequently references are made to the Western, Eastern and third worlds without a philosophical analysis of these terms. Technological societies are often mentioned; right and left wing governments are compared; and terms such as 'freedom', 'authority', 'equality' and 'democracy' used. Rarely are these terms placed in a context that makes meaningful comparisons of national concepts of society possible. This shortage of careful comparative studies has made it difficult to achieve the aims of this volume.

Societal 'models' help to make sense of debates about the constituents of the good and just society. In Europe, even now, the elitism of Plato and Aristotle is debated. The broader encyclopedist view of a society in which the masses participate and are led by aristocracy of talent underlies many discussions about the bases of modern democracy. Nineteenth-century socialism offers an alternative to *laissez-faire* liberalism. Marxist theories of society as part of communist ideology are debated. Finally as a social theory pragmatism is used to justify a belief in man's ability to solve problems by the collective application of his intelligence. Frequently in national and international debates it is not easy to see from which set of assumptions protagonists argue.

In simplistic terms, men are faced today with a choice between clusters of socio-political theories which may be labelled right wing elitism, *laissez-faire* liberalism, socialism and communism. Many students do not think they are realistic alternatives. They reject them all – liberalism, socialism, communism – totally. Less radical critics of society reject some but accept other aspects of these models. It is evident that until some kind of consensus is reached on the kind of society desired it will not be easy to say what kind of role the universities ought to play and how they should perform it.

A broad distinction can be drawn between elitist and egalitarian social theories. Logically the former imply that the abilities of individuals differ, and in some theories that these differences are innate. On the other hand egalitarian social theories are founded on the belief that all men are created equal. Associated with both elitist and egalitarian theories of society is the view that the good and just society is informed by knowledge and its affairs are conducted by knowledgeable men who are wise, reasonable and rational. The epistemological assumptions which inform different political theories vary but in all of them importance is attached to the intellectual's role. Consequently in most theories institutions are proposed which should be devoted to a search for knowledge and the training of an intelligentsia for cultural and social leadership. In this analysis it is assumed that the universities have traditionally undertaken these roles. Today in the face of competing concepts of society it is no longer certain whether universities should continue to play this task, or, if they should, how they should perform it.

Man's crisis of confidence in himself may be due to the fact that no attractive alternative to liberalism, socialism or communism has been created by a philosopher of the stature of Locke, Comte or Marx. Marcuse destroys without creating. Unless the thoughtful younger generation can accept a traditional theory of society or create a new one, appropriate and agreed concepts of the university and its social purpose will be difficult to formulate. Behind student unrest is the fact that this search for new theories of society which will satisfy heart and mind has not been successful.

Concepts of the University

Thus far traditional notions have served as guidelines to university practice, which over the centuries has been modified so that it differs from one country to another. These national differences may be compared in the light of a 'model' of the traditional European university. Rashdall's analysis and his historical illustrations serve as a useful source of one such model. It should be viewed against the prevailing Platonic-Aristotelian and Christian traditions. The former suggested that men were innately unequal – in ability, in potential and before the law. The Christian belief in equality in the eyes of God introduced a novel element. Innate inequalities justified a society based on privileges accorded on the criteria of birth, wealth, and outstanding ability. Inherited secular power was most important. The authority of the church was based upon revealed knowledge. When the first universities were founded a commercial elite of wealthy men was challenging the landed aristocracy and the churchmen for power. Each of the elites attempted to control the new institutions of learning.

For this, if anything, is what the universities strove to be – communities of scholars committed to the search for and dissemination of knowledge. Research to advance the frontiers of knowledge and teaching to spread it should go hand in hand. To be sure theories of knowledge and how it can be acquired have taken on national flavours. So a comparison of the epistemologies of Aristotle, Descartes, Locke, Hegel, Marx and Peirce would throw light on some differences between Italian, French, English, German, Soviet and American universities, if it is the case that each nation pursues the search for knowledge in the light of its own theoretical assumptions.

Common to most national assumptions about the university is the notion that if it is to perform this task its members ought to be free to engage in disputations and to express radical opinions inside and outside their field of expertise. They ought not to be prevented from opening up new forms of knowledge or from pursuing fundamental research of their own choice. In short scholars ought to play critical and innovatory roles in the pursuit of knowledge.

The medieval university also prepared its scholars for the professions of medicine, law, the church and teaching and as leaders of society. Their professional authority derived from their knowledge, and, on the basis of assumptions about society and who should be its leaders, this authority was generalized. Their education was thus designed to prepare them, not as narrow specialists, but as all-round men who could competently perform the offices both public and private of peace and war. Once they left the community of scholars they served kings and princes and the church authorities.

To protect scholars and enable them to perform these critical social tasks two concepts developed. One was the idea of university autonomy. The other was the notion of academic freedom. The institutional forms given to them over the years have had to be maintained against attacks by church and state and the more insidious influences of commerce and industry.

The autonomy of the university implied that the community of scholars ought to run its own affairs. Neither state nor clerical authorities nor commercial interests should help to formulate academic policy. Autonomy has also implied that professors should appoint and promote their colleagues. Neither view has been seriously challenged. Other aspects of autonomy have been more fiercely debated. One concerns the autonomy of universities to manage their finances. Should the way universities spend public money be controlled? Another concerns the privileges universities have traditionally enjoyed, *vis-à-vis* the law. Should discipline within the community be the responsibility of its members? Ought the civil authorities to enter the university precincts? And if so under what conditions? Should civil law apply as strictly to members of the university as to ordinary citizens? Rashdall quotes many instances showing how a tradition grew up which suggested that discipline ought to be maintained by the university community itself with little or no interference from the civic authorities. The Proctors at Oxford represent this tradition. The special campus police in the USA are another example. The reluctance of the authorities to call in the police, and the police to enter the precincts of a university goes beyond the civil laws regulating the entry of police on to private property, as was shown at Nanterre.

Traditionally it has been accepted that the university community ought to be privileged in order to enable them to perform its role as a critic of society. At the same time the price of autonomy was a willingness on the part of university members *per se* voluntarily to choose not to engage in party political action. It should be stressed that distinctions are here drawn between politics and *party* politics and between *debates* and *actions*. The lines drawn are not fixed. As civil servants German professors were forbidden to enter politics. The abdication of responsibility by some of them during the Nazi period shows that members should judge issues of non-participation on their merits. Nevertheless in many situations the words of members of the university may well more effectively influence public opinion than political action.

The autonomy of the university protects the individual within its walls. It safeguards academic freedom which implies that individual professors ought to be free to accept or reject students, to teach whatever they like in a manner they think fit and through examination to admit students or deny them entry to full membership of the community. By the same token academic freedom implies that students should be free to come and go as they please and to choose freely from a wide range of subjects. The idea that all members should be able to move from one to any other university implied that these were international institutions and that the community of scholars was on a world-wide basis. Scholarship is universal and scholars everywhere should share their knowledge among colleagues.

A thorough comparative study would trace in various countries the development of institutional arrangements which reflect these concepts of autonomy and freedom. It would be desirable to trace the growth of the German universities and to see how in the nineteenth century practical meaning was given to von Humboldt's notion of academic freedom – *lern- und lehrfreiheit*. Again in Napoleon's university which was to embrace the educational system of France the corps of educationists who were to run it was to be protected from political interference. The University Grants Committee in Britain illustrates how public money is provided for universities without overt public control. In the USA the State universities too enjoy a large measure of autonomy in spite of massive public financial support.

It would also have been desirable to review in comparative perspective how academic freedom has been fought for and maintained against external and internal pressures. To mention the McCarthy investigations in the USA during the fifties draws attention to the need for vigilance even in an open and democratic society. There are, however, less obvious but nevertheless serious threats to academic freedom which are not directly related to a wish on the part of politicians to restrict within the universities the free expression of opinion and the freedom to debate controversial issues in lectures and seminars.

Such detailed studies could not be commissioned for this volume but the main assumption round which it is organized is that a number of forces are now operating on the universities forcing them to reconsider basic concepts and practices. There pressures have called into question notions of autonomy, freedom and privilege. Undoubtedly they are sufficiently strong to modify systems of higher education. Will they be powerful enough to transform universities? And if this happens will it be possible for the universities to perform their traditional function? Moreover, if in future the universities cannot perform these tasks will new institutions be able to do so?

Pressures to Change

Historical patterns of higher education have been and are being changed by many forces some of which are common while others have a national flavour. New patterns can be viewed against models derived from European prototypes which have been transplanted in Latin America, Africa, Asia, and at an earlier stage, North America. Modified to suit local conditions, universities outside Europe are reacting to forces of change by looking principally either to the USA or to Europe for inspiration. Many reformers are studying American policies and practice, while some Americans are attracted by European traditions. There is little consensus on how present pressures should be absorbed but again national patterns offer a choice of solutions.

Consider for example how universities in the nineteenth century responded to the economic factor. The universities have always provided high-level manpower but commercial and industrial development changed the nature of the demand. Historical solutions are instructive. In France during the revolutionary period the *Ecole Polytechnique* was established to prepare military leaders. It and the other *grandes écoles* trained national leaders outside medicine, law, the church and teaching and acquired a reputation and status superior to the universities. Entrance through competitive examinations (*concours*) is more difficult than to the universities and success in a *grande école* virtually ensures access to the highest positions in France. The German solution was to create technical institutions which developed into *Technische Hochschulen* or on most criteria, technological universities. Among their faculty members have been some of the most distinguished German engineers and scientists. One consequence of this development was that the older universities did not bring the applied sciences into their structure and the technological universities do not possess the full range of faculties. This binary system has been followed in many countries including Russia and later the USSR. Today faced with new manpower demands, governments are tempted to accept it as a solution.

In nineteenth-century England, engineering studies became part of the university when technical institutions grew into the new civic universities. While the status of the civic universities has never quite matched that of Oxford and Cambridge or London, the inclusion of technological and applied studies has had important consequences for English higher education. Until recently it was possible to maintain some unity in higher education but at the same time these nineteenth-century developments may well have inhibited growth in higher education then and during the first half of the twentieth century.

In the USA the land grant colleges set up under the Morrell Act of 1862 helped to preserve unity without preventing expansion. Federal grants were to ensure the economic welfare of the country and the land grant colleges had to provide courses in and disseminate knowledge about the industrial-mechanic arts and agriculture. They have grown enormously since then by incorporating the older pure disciplines and by developing technological and new professional studies. Since 1900 the growth of the latter, even at the undergraduate level, has involved an extension of the range of subjects and a shift in the proportion of students majoring in the 'new' professional courses. Some observers would say that far from following older patterns of university education in the USA the large State universities have increasingly been the trend-setters.

In their various ways nineteenth-century universities and higher education met new economic demands. Today these pressures are again creating issues of policy in most countries. How should the universities react? Should they accept as legitimate all or some of the 'new professions', such as journalism, business management, brewing and so on, and train students for them? Should they carry out research in fields which are necessary for defence, for example in applied nuclear physics and biochemistry? Massive federal funds are available in the USA for projects which promote the common welfare and defence of the country. In few countries can top-flight scientists and technologists resist demands to conduct research into the application of fundamental knowledge in ways of interest to governments.

Can the universities meet these economic and military needs without seriously modifying or abandoning their traditions? It is difficult to maintain that research carried out at the behest of a national government constitutes a search for knowledge for its own sake. Frequently the results of such work are so secret that researchers cannot make it available to their students much less to the international community of scholars to which they belong. The choice between being a traitor to one's country and a traitor to university traditions places academics on the horns of an acute dilemma. The acceptance of defence contracts in the USA has rightly troubled students and faculty, but they throw into sharp relief the question of how far universities can respond to manpower demands without infringing their autonomy and freedom.

One solution is to provide alternative institutions where the work can be done. Government research departments may well meet some research needs. New manpower needs may well be met by the expansion of separate technological institutions. This particular solution is gaining support in England and France. Where it is adopted it may well restructure higher education and have unfortunate divisive social and political consequences.

Economic arguments have strongly favoured the expansion of higher education in recent years on the grounds that individuals and society will benefit. Cost-benefit studies may well have been given a spurious precision, nevertheless they have helped to persuade more people to seek higher education and decision makers to believe that an increased investment in it would pay off. The short-term outcomes of uncontrolled expansion may have shocked many optimists. Student unrest and a flood of candidates to the social sciences could hardly have been anticipated. In Britain some observers now claim that the universities are training more pure scientists than the country needs. It may be that the balance of training at a high level should shift to the applied sciences, or that more training of top-flight scientists and engineers should be carried out in the polytechnics. The picture is obscure. The fact is that economic arguments for or against expansion generally or in favour of this or that cluster of subjects are of doubtful validity while so many graduates move into occupations, e.g. teaching, general administration, the civil service, which respond less than most to simple market pressures and for which measures of efficiency and productivity are difficult to devise. If this is so, policies of expansion or retrenchment based on such studies should be regarded with a healthy scepticism.

Other social forces are working in favour of expansion. The human rights case is one in point. Since 1945 it has operated strongly through successive stages of education. The achievement of universal primary education has been followed in most countries by a slow or rapid expansion and democratization of secondary education. Entry qualifications to universities and higher education generally have changed and many more pupils now possess them. The numbers of secondary school leavers in Germany possessing the *Abitur* and in France the *baccalauréat* exceed the ability of some faculties to accept them all. Consequently faculty and departmental tests have been introduced, for example, in France. Even in countries with less well-developed stages of primary and secondary education, such as India, the demand for more higher education has been irresistible. A major question is: ought the universities to absorb all the qualified applicants or should many of them be directed into other institutions of higher education?

Details of the human rights case make simple answers unrealistic. In general the claim is that disadvantaged groups should receive special encouragement and help. Comparative studies in the fifties and early sixties showed that the children of working-class parents were under-represented in universities everywhere. Caste and racial origins place individuals at a similar disadvantage. Also the proportion of youngsters entering higher education is frequently lower from rural than from urban areas. Policies to improve social representation call into question a host of assumptions about the distribution of ability throughout a population, the influence of environment on performance and the validity of selection tests on which access to higher education is gained. Furthermore, if proposals to introduce 'Black' or other new studies are intended to meet special social class requirements the criteria on which the content of higher education is selected have to be reconsidered.

Constraints on Expansion

Expansionist policies have been challenged. In the past the elitist character of the universities has been justified by a succession of theories which claim that only a minority is capable of acquiring the highest form of knowledge. Consequently in the medieval universities only Plato's philosopher kings ought to be educated to this level. In the systems of education proposed by Condorcet in France and Jefferson in the USA, a small aristocracy of talent ought to be selected for an education at the tertiary level. One main difference between these positions is that for Plato intellectual ability is, with few exceptions, inherited, while the encyclopedists did not emphasize this view. In both theories, individuals of outstanding intellectual worth ought to be encouraged and helped to attend the university.

Present-day objections to elitism rest on several assumptions. The notion that ability is largely inherited is unacceptable. Secondly the validity of selection procedures is doubtful. A more radical assumption is that a far greater proportion of the population than ever before is capable of benefiting from university education. A somewhat different argument is that the university should adapt itself to the needs of all young people, in other words it should become student-centred. But against all these critics of elitism the defenders of academic standards bring together in a new guise traditional social, psychological and epistemological theories.

The expansion of universities has indeed created problems. The research orientation of some academics has, for example, been questioned. Students resent professors who pursue research at the expense of teaching and this issue gets mixed up with the type of research they do. Government research projects are frequently directed to the solution of immediate pressing problems. Such contracts build up research departments but can the work done be termed fundamental research? At the same time how many of the increased number of students can engage in fundamental research or are motivated to do so? In short it seems unlikely that the older notions of university research can be maintained if radical expansion occurs. Already the research orientation of science students must be changed if they are to become satisfactory and satisfied industrial research workers.

Reference has already been made to the problems of incorporating new professional courses in the university. On what criteria should such courses be included? One criterion is that the profession's esoteric knowledge is 'pure' and is capable of application beyond the immediate skills of the profession. Another criterion is that it should be of such a level that lengthy periods of training are required. Law, the church and teaching, of course, depend upon verbal skills. Medicine already demands manipulative skills and so do the other new professions. Are they the type which can be acquired only in a university atmosphere?

University expansion raises teaching problems. Methods which served carefully selected students and faculty members may not be appropriate where students and staff are less carefully selected. For extremely able students tutorials with mediocre tutors must be painful. By the same token moderate students may well have brilliant tutors. Lectures to large audiences are frowned upon, but what takes their place? Seminars conducted by non-specialists over a wide range of specialist subjects are clearly not practical. The expense of maintaining traditional staff/student ratios is enormous, but there are also problems of finding sufficiently well-qualified staff to justify the retention of traditional teaching methods. No doubt resource centres and technological learning aids will help to meet the situation.

Finally there is the issue of content. Under conditions of expansion should the university's functions be to train future research and professional workers? Is there need for an extension, beyond the secondary level, of a general education for all young people? And should the content of such courses be geared to the educational requirements of students of widely ranging abilities? USA undergraduate courses include a general education component. In England the belief dies hard that a specialized curriculum offers the best basis of a sound general education. Less specialized courses in the Continental tradition are possible in other European countries. Courses are loosely organized and it is doubtful whether less carefully selected students will be able to profit from freedom to choose from a wide range of courses. Students in Germany, in particular, want lecture courses to be more structured.

National Policies

It is, however, with systems of higher education rather than the internal organization of studies that this volume is concerned. There can be no doubt that everywhere policies to expand higher education have been adopted. It is instructive to compare how different nations have attempted under these conditions to meet research, professional training and general education functions. There are two obvious models from which to choose. The unified or comprehensive system is favoured by the USA and Japan under conditions of rapid and massive expansion. A differentiated system of research institutes linked with academies of science, universities, and specialized institutes is favoured by the USSR. Naturally the prestige and quality of the universities of the USA vary greatly but they include some of the best in the world. It is claimed in the USSR that the differences between the universities and the specialized institutes are small but the latter do emphasize the applied, professional aspects of the subjects they teach rather more than the universities.

It seems likely that higher education will go through the same stages of development as the secondary schools. Vertical differentiation on the basis of function will be followed in many countries by the creation later of a more unified comprehensive system. In the differentiated pattern the position of professional schools and particularly teacher education institutes is of interest. In the USA they grew through teachers colleges, then liberal arts colleges into universities. In the USSR the pedagogical institutes have grown up outside the universities and alongside the polytechnics. Several choices are open to colleges of education in England. It is to be hoped that they will follow, with modifications, the USA model of development and become multi-purpose institutions in the foreseeable future.

It is evident that in the foreseeable future the expansion issue is going to dominate debates about the future of universities and higher education. Growth is bound to continue, but at what rate and in which institutions is uncertain. In some countries the universities may be kept for a carefully selected elite and the excessive demand siphoned off into other institutions of higher education. Or the universities may simply expand. A third possibility is that another stage or level of education might be introduced between the present upper secondary schools and present university undergraduate courses thus placing the latter effectively in fourth-stage institutions. The first of these solutions is favoured in Western Europe and elsewhere, the second solution has been adopted in the USA where there are already signs that the third solution, namely increased horizontal differentiation, is emerging. The second of the solutions – expansion within the framework of the university – will undoubtedly force university authorities to face painful decisions and to reconsider their role in society. The acceptance of a binary system may in the short term alleviate some of the major problems universities face but it may well postpone a radical new look at concepts of the university. Without such a reappraisal the crisis in higher education may be unduly prolonged. It is hoped that this volume of the *World Year Book* will throw some light on the reappraisals of policy which are at present taking place.

Higher Education and Society

Brian Holmes

While it is not easy to identify models of society in which the first universities were born it is less difficult to describe, as Hastings Rashdall has done, some of the main features of the latter. It was hoped that in this section some analysis would be made of the relationships which philosophers have thought ought to exist between institutions of higher education and the rest of society. Contributors have not speculated on what kind of society we are today looking for except incidentally. In this section the attention of contributors was drawn to a model of the university based upon traditional concepts. These were that the university ought to be a community of scholars dedicated to a search for knowledge for its own sake. Another concept is that the university community, because of the functions it serves, ought to be free to express radical opinions and yet be protected. It ought also to be free to formulate academic policy without interference from church or secular authorities who should recognize the privileged position of the university community. Again within the community of scholars, academic freedom has been taken to mean that individual professors ought to be free to accept or reject students as they think fit, to discourse on subjects of their choice in a way they think best and pass or fail students on the basis of their own criteria of scholarship. By the same token the tradition has granted to students freedom to come and go as they please, to attend from a wide range of subjects and to express their displeasure in a variety of ways.

Against the backcloth of modern society will these concepts of the university any longer suffice?

A nostalgia for the past (Montague, pp. 15–26) continues to inform the more conservative elements among senior members of the university. The constant threat to university autonomy and academic freedom (Limiti, pp. 27–35) is a reality in many countries today, as was evident during the nineteen-fifties when the search for subversive elements was carried into universities in the USA. The evolution of a national style in this country (Brick, pp. 36–61) and some present dilemmas facing the universities serve to illustrate in what ways some of the medieval concepts of the university have been and are now being challenged. The English tradition has also deviated from the original model in some respects. The inclusion during the nineteenth century of technological studies within the university framework (Armytage, pp. 62–74) has given to present discussions (Burgess, pp. 75–89) a particular English flavour. Everywhere there is a search for solutions which will do violence neither to common traditions nor to unique national practices.

Some of these national differences can be understood more readily against the theoretical models based on concepts of society, man and knowledge (Cowen, pp. 90–107). Comparative articles (Cerych and Furth pp. 108–119, Suchodolski, pp. 120–134, and Froese, pp. 135–146) illustrate how in their own ways academics and philosophers are trying to formulate effective new policies for the universities and with statesmen are striving to give to these proposals practical expression.

One thing is certain; until some of the present issues regarding the societal role of the university have been resolved the development of higher education is bound to show paradoxes.

1

The Historic Function of the University

H. Patrick Montague

There has never been, in the long history of the university, so much dissent, so much discussion, so much pessimism regarding its future, as there is today. Current events tend to overshadow its past, and sooner or later, those who express most concern about its present situation, and are least optimistic about its future, may find it rewarding to examine more closely what there is in its past which we are lacking today. Like so many other great institutions, the university evolved as a mighty instrument designed, by its very nature, not only to shape itself to the requirements of contemporary society, but to act as the corrective for a society which may be in process of losing its way.

If the university has a function, it must be stated, and if its function is to be stated, then it can only be against the background of its history. This, it will be said, has been done many times, but there are two important factors to be borne in mind in expressing reserves as to the merits of a further inquiry. One is that even such illustrious university historians as Hastings Rashdall[1] clearly identify the beginnings of the modern university with the recognition of the *Studium Generale* in Bologna and Paris in the twelfth century, whereas, in fact, the traditions which lay deep in the thoughts of the students of Bologna who launched the *Universitas*, had more than seven centuries of life before that event.[1]

The second factor is that the universities of today clearly reveal a variety of functions. By contrast, the dissent within the universities shows a homogeneous pattern, a fact which makes it seem constructive to return once again to its origins, not, in this case, of the student University of Bologna, nor of the Masters' University of Paris, but of the schools from which they sprang. Only in this way is it possible to see exactly what the founders of the *Universitas* were so eager to preserve, and what it was that they wanted to hand on to posterity.

Clearly, in their day, they were interested in preserving the function of the *Studium* as it had been understood for seven centuries. Equally, eight centuries later, mankind may reasonably want to know what this function was, and how, and where, it still operates. One thing is certain, that it is not universally accepted. Until we decide what it was, we cannot hope to decide what it is, and until we decide what it is, we cannot hope to reach a solution to the problems of the modern university.

The Studium

It is specially important to record the fact that when the students of Bologna formed their *Universitas*, they did not initiate a school of higher scholarship in Europe. That was already there, in the *Studium* of Bologna, one of a number of centres of learning. What these students did was to form a guild of students to safeguard their privileges and rights, a historic decision which undoubtedly led to a series of events which created the university and put the *Studium* for ever after into the class of those institutions which Hastings Rashdall tells us were the particular genius of the Middle Ages.

The records of Bologna University[2] show that there were about 10,000 students in their *Studium* when they formed the *Universitas* late in the twelfth century, a fact which gave the *Studium* the promise of continuity. When one considers that in Italy alone, there was another *Studium*, of great renown and greater antiquity than Bologna, at Salerno, and many others, it is easy to accept the fact that the actual launching of the *Universitas* was not the beginning of higher scholarship in Europe. It is also a fact that the schools of Paris and Oxford had a vigorous existence and were moving towards a solution to similar problems as those of the *Studium* of Bologna when the students there made their move. The schools of Paris were not the only schools, nor the oldest, in France. The schools of Oxford were not the only schools, nor the oldest, and possibly not even the greatest in England.

The antiquity of the *Studium*, the collection of schools each under a teacher, is a matter of precise record. A series of eminent scholars, notably the Germans, Kuno Meyer, Strabo, Wattenbach and Zimmer, and French medievalists, such as De Jubainville and Darmesteter, have stated that the scholarship represented by the *Studium*, not only began, but was sustained for centuries, by the schools of Ireland, a fact which gives the *Studium* a continuous history back to the fifth century, and possibly even earlier. Moreover, these schools sent their scholars to found and sustain many others throughout Western Europe.

Seamus McManus, in *The Story of the Irish Race*, quotes one European authority after another in this account of the debt that European scholarship owes to those Irish schools, two of which had even in the early centuries as many as 7,000 students each. One of the most generous tributes ever paid by the scholars of one country to those of another was when, in 1844, the heads of the German Colleges presented an address to Daniel O'Connell in which they expressed the debt of gratitude of the German people to the Irish scholars who rescued Germany from barbarism and ignorance. A still more striking tribute came from a French medievalist who declared that the Renaissance began, not in Italy in the twelfth century, but in Ireland in the fifth. The city of Armagh, he says, was by virtue of its schools the metropolis of civilization.[3]

It is, obviously, a profitable exercise to examine briefly the function of these schools and what traditions they embodied which the scholars of the twelfth century were intent on preserving. There is, fortunately, a source of information which makes it possible to define the role of the teachers and students in these ancient schools more so, perhaps, than it has been later. For the Brehon Laws of Ireland contain specific references to the system, which indicate that the privileges of the scholars were guaranteed. Such were the freedom to study, and the autonomy of the schools. The relationship of teacher and student was protected and, by law, the student was obliged to support his teacher even in sickness and in his old age.

There can be no question that, even in those days, society had a positive role for the scholar. He was not only allowed to travel, but he was encouraged, and trained for that purpose. The universality of the *Studium* was written into its very origins.

Consistent with this purpose, not only did the students move freely from teacher to teacher, a process which indicates the origin of our modern courses of study, but also from school to school. It was also consistent with the universal purpose of the schools that students came from many lands. Perhaps the most significant feature of these early centres of scholarship, in the context of our modern concept, was that professional training was a declared purpose from the beginning. For these schools were both lay and religious. They had both lay and religious teachers and students. They taught both rich and poor, and the Brehon Laws made provision for the latter. They attracted students from virtually the entire known world. Their purpose was to produce what we would now call graduates, but it was also their purpose to encourage their scholars to attack the frontiers of knowledge.

It is not relevant in this study to pursue the story of these prototypes of the *Studium*. By the time the *Universitas* was formed in Bologna, there were such schools all over Western Europe, not only of Irish origins, notably in France, Northern Italy and Western and Southern Germany. The traditions were firmly established, and it was these traditions that the students of Bologna and the masters of Paris sought to perpetuate in the universities which arose after the launching of the *Universitas*.

The Student and the Masters' Universities

The *Studium* of Bologna, a group of schools, known as *Societates*, was internationally famous for studies in civil and canon law and attracted to the city students from as many as sixteen recognized nations. It was, indeed, the prestige of the *Studium* and its importance to the city, which sparked off the dispute which led to the momentous events of that period. For the Commune of Bologna represented a new element in European affairs, and certainly a new element in the long history of the *Studium*. The citizens of Bologna regarded the *Studium* as a major asset to their city, and they intended to curb the privileges of the scholars as a preliminary to bringing the *Studium* under the control of the Commune.

They were obviously unaware of the strength of the traditions of the *Studium*. The freedom of movement was written into its very origins, and the citizens of Bologna were dealing with something quite different from civic affairs when they attempted to impose restrictions on movement out of the city to prevent what was called the *migratio*, especially of teachers, since this would undoubtedly mean the loss of students as well. The foreign students were the first to react, by forming the associations known as *nationes*, out of which, incidentally, arose the Rector, elected by the students, and destined to become the first head of the university. The second move was the formation of the *Universitas*, the guild of students. Thus the Commune of Bologna was presented with two problems both serious in those times. One was the determined attitude of the foreigners, many of them rich and of noble families. What happened to them was quite likely to attract to Bologna the attention of one or other of the universal authorities, the Pope or the Emperor, both of whom were beginning to view with some concern the ambitions of such as the citizens of Bologna.

It was the second problem, the *Universitas*, which brought about exactly what the Commune wanted to avoid, a more or less open confrontation with universal authority, in fact, the Pope, who was already aware of something very similar elsewhere. He was interested in the schools of Paris where the Cathedral and its Chancellor had a direct interest. He was interested in Oxford for another reason. It had recently happened that Henry II of England had put pressure on English students abroad, mainly in France, to return to England, as part of his feud with Becket, who, it is recalled, put himself under the Pope's protection. All these events were going on at about the same time, so that the dispute in Bologna gave the Pope an opportunity which was welcome at the time, to settle a universal problem, to curb the growing ambitions of civil authority and to forestall the Emperor.

There is, within the Church, an ancient principle described by the phrase *Lex Credendi*, according to which the Church confirms those beliefs, otherwise acceptable, which already appear to be widely held. Notable examples have been the doctrine of the Immaculate Conception, and the canonization of saints who have in many cases been venerated for a long time before the Church proclaims their sanctity. Such a practice has the merit of giving from the beginning a promise of permanency. In the case of the first university, the authority of the Pope added to the status of universality, the promise of long-continuing prestige.

When, therefore, the Pope confirmed the privileges of the *Studium* of Bologna, he did not set up anything new. He lent universal authority to the concept of the *Studium Generale*, the correct description of a university, and, perhaps most important of all, he created the university degree. This he did when he gave official recognition to the phrase *Ius Ubique Docendi*, the right of its graduates to teach everywhere. It is by this authority that universities have ever since bestowed degrees. The actual parent of the degree is the *Licentia Ubique Docendi*. The modern nomenclature of degrees, and their equivalent values, is chaotic, and it is therefore worth a comment that only one major country reflects in its degree system the original authority. This is in France where the universities still use the *Licence*.

The masters of Paris have had, historically, a greater impact than the students of Bologna. A universal system of higher scholarships controlled by students was never likely to succeed although interesting features of this system are strongly evident in the ancient Scottish group, the only one which could reasonably be called today Student Universities. Elsewhere, the masters' solution has on the whole prevailed. Beyond that, the story of the origins of the Masters' University of Paris is not relevant to these notes.

It is, however, relevant to examine the points in dispute between the scholars and those who sought to curb them and the clear impression emerges that what the scholars wanted was the status awarded to them by seven centuries of tradition. The problem at the time of the formation of the *Universitas* was that society was changing in a way which posed an immediate threat to this tradition. This brought up, as the first issue, the need to state in the most permanent manner possible the basic fact that the *Studium* was a world institution, and that its location was unimportant. Indeed, the famous *cessatio*, the stoppage of all activities in the earliest days of the University of Paris, was coupled with the declared intention, if the demands were not met, of setting up the University elsewhere.

Freedom to move was essential, so was a measure of immunity for the scholars. The *Studium* was not to be entered by any form of police. The community was to be autonomous, and internal control guaranteed. Academic freedom was an essential condition. These and other privileges, long accepted in the historic *Studium*, were now written into the very fabric of the *Studium Generale*, which in due course came to be called the university.

The Function of the University

In discussing the nature of the university, Hastings Rashdall quotes a medieval scholar not long after the events of Bologna and Paris as stating that the three powers essential to the well-being of mankind were the *Sacerdotium* (spiritual power), the *Imperium* (temporal power), and the *Studium* (the power of scholarship). Nothing could more clearly illustrate the fact that universality was basic, in the thinking of the scholars, to the whole idea of the *Studium*. If a university is not universal, it is not a university.

It is easier, at times, to say what is not than what is the function of the university. Surveying, however, the long history of the institution, not, as we have seen, over eight centuries, but over fifteen, it becomes clearer what its traditions were and what the scholars were so determined to preserve. At this point, if a brief reference to modern conditions may be permitted, it may well be commented that their academic descendants seem equally anxious to preserve or to revive these same traditions. Clearly, the *Studium* was essentially a community of scholars accustomed to all that was implicit in such a concept. The young and the older scholar were linked by ties of respect and loyalty, reminiscent of the ancient model of the Greek academy. If names like Irnerio inspired the scholars of Bologna, and Abelard the scholars of Paris, then Plato and Aristotle were equally the models for the early scholars. So, indeed, was Socrates the embodiment of academic freedom. Such was the material of the traditions of the community of scholars bound by human values and not by human laws.

The commitment of the university to professional training is part of its earliest origins. Bologna was famous as a centre of studies in law, Paris for theology, Salerno for medicine. Nor does this mean that the *Studium* offered training in only one profession. All the liberal arts were taught, and this was true even in the earliest days. The literature in the early schools is abundant and leaves no doubt that professional and general training was a function of the *Studium* from the beginning.

From the beginning also, society recognized the role of its scholars and accepted the fact that certain privileges must be allowed in order to carry out this role. The search for truth required the right to discuss many topics and proclaim a variety of conclusions. This was especially so within the confines of the *Studium*. Even before universal authority confirmed the status of the scholars, radical opinions were freely discussed within the community, even in the fields of philosophy and theology. The tempestuous career of Peter Abelard of Paris is an outstanding illustration of this tradition.

The basic function of teaching the students is clearly illustrated throughout history. Equally, the role of the scholar in attacking the frontiers of knowledge has been clearly accepted from the beginning. It is worth a comment that higher scholarship has often, in modern times, overshadowed the function of teaching the student body. A community of scholars will quickly disintegrate if one function takes undue precedence over another.

The community was always intended to be autonomous, and control belongs, by long-established tradition, within the community. With this has always gone the sanctity of the institution from police forces. It remains, however, to define a little more clearly what the community really means because to this day there are relics of the one major divergence between the Bologna and the Paris concepts of a university. It was implicitly the idea in Bologna that all students were full members of the community and indeed the dominant element. It was the idea in Paris that full membership was obtained only after examination, and this is really the significance, in this context, of the Master's degree. The Bologna concept had the inherent weakness that the teachers would ultimately examine the students, and could, therefore, exclude them from the community.

The freedom of the student to go to any teacher he chose was fully accepted, no matter where he was. He was free to choose his own courses. It was quite contrary to the whole tradition of the *Studium* that attendance at lectures would be taken on the modern model. The prestige of the teacher, so important to the whole system, could never survive such a process. Those modern universities, or teachers, who make attendance compulsory, expose themselves to the suggestion that the quality of the scholarship they offer is not sufficient of itself to attract those to whom they offer it.

There was, of course, a good deal in return for all this. Those outside the university were asked to accept from scholars what would not be accepted from others. It was expected that any privileges would be exercised in a mature manner, and that the community would take any necessary action in the case of obvious abuse of privilege. Indeed, this whole question was a major issue between the scholars of Paris and the citizens, as indeed it was in Oxford, during the early days. Over the centuries, student festivities have become a tradition in many universities. Notable examples are the Oxford and Cambridge Boat Race, the Charities Day Collections in Scotland, the *Festa della Matricola* in Padua and many others. On such occasions it is customary to accept as exuberance what might pass under another heading with other people than students. When the limits of exuberance are exceeded it is expected that the community will act.

Such was, and such should be, the function of this international institution, which is now called the university. In the modern age, there are two features which were not so clear, or perhaps so important in earlier days. One is the role of the graduate or alumnus, the other is involvement in politics. It cannot be said that the alumnus regards himself, universally, as having been what history declares him to be, a member of the community of scholars of his university. Too often, indeed, he is critical and sometimes hostile. In the political field, the community is such that its members do not traditionally engage in party politics until they leave the community. It is equally true, however, that politics do not enter the university, a possibility which inevitably arises when control becomes external.

The Modern University

The most significant feature in any comparison at this stage is the present situation of the modern equivalents of the parties in the disputes of the twelfth century. The university is still with us. The power of the civil authorities is now the dominant factor. The universal power of Pope or Emperor is no more. The early fears were real, and the steps taken were enlightened. The universality of the institution has largely gone. It is not a question of surveying the function of a world institution. It is a question of reviving it, and in many cases this would involve going back to the origins.

In the United States, that great and exciting centre of experimentation, a system was set up which was almost everything which the ancient model was not. Sixteen years after the arrival of the Pilgrim Fathers, they set up Harvard, on the model of Emmanuel College, Cambridge, without an existing *Studium*, not even a high school system. They established it on the basis of external control which has remained the system ever since in the United States. Harvard, then, for many years resisted the idea of a Royal Charter, since this might open the way to official Visitors. The failure, however, to accept this symbol of universal authority recognized since the Reformation might at that time have prevented Harvard from becoming the world university it now is, faced as it was with others which were so chartered after the foundation of Harvard, notably the College of William and Mary.

After the colonial period, when such establishments were springing up on the scale they did, it was left to each of the states to found universities. So, in considering the existence of the university as a world institution, we have to face the fact that excluding the old pre-Revolution group with its Royal authority not one single American university has been chartered by the President, a situation probably unique in a world in which even today it is normal for a university to carry the authority of the Head of State.[4]

With this massive example in mind, a comparison of the modern university and the traditional model is far from easy. Its population is the largest in history and it is drawn from educational systems some of which have rejected much of what was essential in the older system. Throughout the world there are varying philosophies and varying ideas on selection, examinations, and examiners. Their teachers may or may not be primarily teachers. Their universities may or may not be autonomous.

Against this unpromising background, and perhaps indeed, because of it, the university population has clearly asked for those very things which concerned the scholars when they confronted the Commune of Bologna, or when the scholars of Paris confronted the citizens of Paris and the King of France, and the scholars of Oxford confronted the citizens of Oxford and King John of England. The students of today have in fact declared that the university is a world institution and not subject to local or external control.

So the students of Columbia, who did not support the radical activists in 1968, opposed still more the decision to bring in police to remove them and they brought about the closure of the University. Some months before the students of Brooklyn College who would not support a group of activists closed their College when the police arrived to remove the group. The most spectacular episode in 1968 was where it might have been expected, in Paris, the real parent of the sanctity of the modern university, when the Rector called in the police. It is a sad commentary on the status of the university population in the western countries that the protests of the students of Prague and Warsaw stirred general admiration for reasons remote from the real cause of protest. In fact, these students were inspired at the same time as those of Columbia, Paris and others, by the same motives, which were to assert the ancient rights of the community of scholars.

External control is the accepted system in American universities, and unrest is of long standing within that system.[5] In other countries the signs of external control have become increasingly obvious and have had a profound effect on the tranquillity of the system, because the demands of external authorities have convinced the community that teaching, and by consequence the status of the student, has lost its historic place in the priorities of the university.

Academic freedom, that precious gift to society, has long been in peril. University populations have repeatedly shown that radicalism is a minority movement, yet whole universities are accused of being in its grip. For centuries the community has accepted radical thought and for centuries it has contained it. In the modern age society has divided the community. University unrest means that the university population would like to revive a united community.

The community of scholars does not, traditionally, enter into party politics, because historically politics did not enter into the running of a university. When the control of the university returns to those who compose it, the statesmen, the sociologists and the public will see the community, and with it the historic mission of the university, once more in operation. Those who flocked to Armagh or Clonmacnoise in the earliest centuries, or to Bologna, Paris, Oxford and Salerno in the twelfth century, did not complain, as the students do today, of impersonality in their relations with the university, or of irrelevance in the material of their studies. This was brought into the *Studium* by the new element which the *Universitas* of Bologna was set up to oppose.

Conclusion

While it is true that many universities of today have the outward appearance of the traditional model, it is hard to find examples which fully reproduce the structure or function. It is hard to escape the conclusion that what the scholars feared in the twelfth century has undoubtedly come to pass. The autonomy which was so essential to the life of the community is actually written into law in some countries. This is the case in Britain, yet, somehow, there have developed several distinct groups. One is Oxford and Cambridge, the other universities of England are another. London has unique features, notably in its vast examining and external degree system. Yet a fourth is, in many ways, the most interesting.

This is the ancient Scottish group which has managed to preserve important features of the original Student University of Bologna. Alone in all Europe, this group retains the student right to elect the ancient head of the university, the Rector. Here alone the Chancellor and the Rector exist side by side in the same university. Here alone does the system of *nationes* still exist. Here alone are the most senior professors expected to take charge of freshmen classes. Finally, the historic role of the graduate has been better preserved in this system than in any other, since the graduates share with the faculty the effective control of the University Court, which governs the University from within. Those who plan the future of the modern universities might reflect on the fact that this group managed to escape the widespread disturbances of 1968.[6]

The structure of a university cannot be divorced from its function. For that reason, it seems appropriate to list here under one heading the main features, which seem to be the basis of the university as revealed by fifteen centuries of life:

(1) It is by its nature universal.

(2) It must be a community of scholars, with internal autonomy vested in the community.

(3) It should offer both scholarship and professional training to its students.

(4) It should attack the frontiers of knowledge.

(5) It should allow and be allowed academic freedom.

(6) It should have certain privileges in order to carry out its mission.

(7) It should be allowed a measure of immunity under the law for its members.

(8) The institution should not be entered by police forces.

(9) The masters ultimately decide by examination who is admitted to the community.

(10) Students should be free to choose their own courses of study.

(11) The prestige of the teacher is vital to the system and cannot be maintained if compulsory attendance by students is enforced.

(12) The prestige of the teacher should be sustained primarily by the support of his students.

(13) The community must ensure that its members do not abuse any privileges they are granted.

(14) Members of the community should not engage directly in politics until they leave the community.

These are what the scholars sought to preserve in the first *Universitas*. History might escape a student. It should not escape those who found a university, or it may not be a university. It should not escape those who seek to control it, or they may have the same experiences as the citizens of medieval Bologna, Paris and Oxford. The universality of the university has been brought to the attention of the whole world by the students of Berkeley, Columbia, Paris, Prague and others. It is they who have demanded the restoration of the model. It is they who demand the restoration of the free community of scholars, not, indeed, the students who seized buildings and destroyed research material, but such as those who opposed activism and then closed their universities when the successors of the Commune of Bologna assumed the right to enter the *Studium Generale*, the ancestral home of the community of scholars. In such a home the authentic voice is the voice of the scholar. In all too many of them the face is the face of Jacob, but the voice is the voice of Esau.

NOTES

1. Hastings Rashdall, *The Universities of the Middle Ages*, (ed.) F. H. Powicke and A. B. Emden (London: OUP, 1936) for the beginnings of the University, and all the medieval institutions, including the Universities of St. Andrews, Glasgow and Aberdeen.
2. *Alma Mater Studiorum* (Bologna: University of Bologna, n.d.).
3. Seamus McManus, *The Story of the Irish Race*, for the main facts relative to the Irish schools, including the leading authorities; see also Ludwig Bieler, *Ireland – Harbinger of the Middle Ages*, English edition (London: OUP, 1966), which clearly accepts the prior claims of Irish schools over the monastic Schools of Benedict on grounds of age, professional training, and skill in Greek.

4. George Washington, alone among the Presidents, wanted to set up such a national university, and referred to this in his Will (author's note).

5. Frederic Rudolph, *The American College and University* (New York: Alfred A. Knopf, 1965), and John S. Brubacher and Willis Rudy, *Higher Education in Transition* (New York: Harper and Bros., 1958), for the history of disturbances on the campus.

6. H. Patrick Montague, 'The Scottish Solution to Campus Unrest' (Edinburgh: *The Scotsman*, 9 November 1968).

2

The Italian University

G. Limiti

Lotharius' Edict in the year 825 is regarded as the first legislative act in the history of higher education in Italy. This edict reaffirmed the status of public schools for the ancient urban schools, which had been established in Roman times in order to train *advocati, iurisperiti, causidici, notarii*. The kingdom of Italy was accordingly subdivided into nine districts.

These schools of rhetoric inherited what Vico later called *l'antica italica sapienza* through the study of the trivium (grammar, rhetoric, dialectics), the practice of medicine and the study of Roman law. Monastery libraries were instrumental in the development of that culture which was named after the eleventh-century Italian Renaissance and greatly influenced other European countries, notably Germany and France. The schools of Montecassino, Salerno, Pavia, Milan, Parma, Ravenna, Rome, Vercelli, Pisa and Lucca became famous.

A slow but deep process of detachment from the rigid cultural orthodoxy of the monasteries took place in Italy. Scholars emerged from their isolation, and joined their peers to meet the needs for exchange and protection. The first foundations for the *studia* – as universities were then called – were thus established. The favourable political situation offered by the autonomous towns led to a conscious acceptance of those new cultural initiatives.

The study of comparative law (Lombard, Roman and Canon law) and political science helped to overcome a rhetorical way of thinking and endowed new, more modern, disciplines with a scientific autonomy. Universities originated in these intellectual, amalgamating processes.

The effects of this relationship will be evident in the methodology which characterized it and which was, in turn, tied with the study of *Humanae litterae* and law. The political townships which greatly favoured individual initiative were of remarkable advantage to the universities. These were not creatures of the *Comuni*, but they strongly felt their influence. The *Comuni* on their part understood the dignity of these studies and protected them. Bologna was a fair example of the situation and its Statutes inspired the other universities.

Concepts of the University

Teaching would be started on the personal initiative of a teacher who wished to have an audience. There was to be no particular procedure or privilege bestowed by authority and there would be no control. The death of a teacher would not imply the disappearance of his own intellectual community; the 'school' would continue to exist. Irnerio, *Lucerna iuris*, will be famous forever. The close personal (in fact contractual) interchange of students with their professors allowed a cultural refinement and a social strengthening of the guilds. The school became a society of equals which found its full realization in this mutual protection and respect for culture.

The students' guilds were an emanation of an associational movement which characterized the period of the *Comuni* (see Solmi: *Contributi alla storia del diritto comune*, Rome, Foro Italiano, 1937) inasmuch as before being *universitas studiorum* they were *universitas*, that is corporations. From the very beginning Italian universities were the expression of a connexion that was not to be loosened by historical events, i.e. of the close relationship of freedom in studies with political freedom. Decadence in the universities is bound to follow the withdrawal of civil liberties. This is what happened in Bologna, along with the universities which had been created on its model; the same was true for Naples (1224), the only one of our universities to be established by a king (Frederick II, whose chancellor was Pier delle Vigne) and financed by the government.

The 'royal' origin of the University of Naples caused suspicion on the part of the other universities which were jealous of their autonomy. As a matter of fact they had little intercourse with Naples and did not recognize the value of its degrees for their teaching posts. But at Naples chairs were held, at different times, by Thomas Aquinas, Cino da Pistoia, Giovan Battista Vico and where, in 1754, Antonio Genovesi first taught economic philosophy and civil economy – later to be called political economy – after the Scottish example of Hutcheson and Smith. The organization of the university was influenced by political authority which elected the great chancellor and the *Iustiarius*, and they, in turn, chose teachers, watched over church discipline, and conferred degrees. A political class in Naples was formed in the university; this fact, of course, did not prevent the University of Naples from enjoying its moments of tension, freedom and autonomy: above all it defended the objective character of science against the character of a professional training which more and more the government tended to assign to it. Subsequently it became a stronghold of liberalism, and it could claim among its teachers such names as Francesco De Sanctis, Bertrando Spaventa, Pasquale Stanislao Mancini, Antonio Scialoja, Giuseppe Pisanelli, Angelo Camillo De Meis and Luigi Zuppetta.

As we said, Naples was an isolated case. The other universities were created after the famous Bologna, which attracted scholars from all European countries. The oldest legislative bill is the *autentica* of Frederick I (1158 *Dieta di Roncaglia*) by which he recognized the legal existence of the school as a corporation. From then on in its statutes the township of Bologna ratified privileges on behalf of the university, and imposed on students and professors an oath to prevent them from moving elsewhere. The penalty was severe. Such an imposition was not welcomed by the corporation, which referred to Pope Honorious III in order to have it repealed. However, this act was ominous. In fact, another *Bulla* of 28 June 1219 forbade public teaching by lecturers who had not obtained the necessary authorization. This was given only to teachers who professed to holding strictly orthodox views.

But the sense of freedom was strong, and defeated the threat.

National Groups

The guilds strengthened their unity further by organizing themselves into national groups (according to the student's birthplace), which elected in turn the Rector, thus providing the university with a more solid basis. Among these groups the Italians, Provençals, French and Germans were the most prominent. All the Italian provinces were represented and up to thirteen nations among the Ultramontanes could be counted.

Students elected the Rector (who has been called *Magnifico* since the fifteenth century). The Rector had full legal academic authority, and was in office for one year. However, his position was *rector scholarium*, not *studii*, and he had to have been a student of law for at least the last five years, unmarried, a layman and with independent means. The professors were *rectores studii*. Professors and students gave an oath of allegiance to the Rector and the Statutes. Assemblies, called by the Rector, were identified with the university. Their constitutions rested upon Statutes, renewable every twenty years on the initiative of eight specifically designated students. University guilds were also privileged in that they had legal authority. Courts of justice (both civil and criminal) were held by the Rector, the professors, and the Bishop.

Teachers were divided into *lettori* and *dottori*. The first-named might be fifth- and sixth year students, who were authorized by the Rector to read a particular chapter or a whole book. In this last case, they assumed the title of bachelors. In order to become *dottori*, students had to have studied civil law for eight years, taken public and private examinations, and discussed a proposition, during which students had a right to debate. The presence of antagonists was regarded as an excellent didactic method, in so far as it ensured the necessary dialectics of free research.

The conferring of a doctorate was a solemn event. The ritual took place in the Dome, and consisted in offering the book, ring and cap. A selected town dignity was connected with this ceremony, which was enlivened by academic robes, students' singing and folklore activities. The *dottore* agreed not to move away from the city; often, particular benefits were given to him. Some towns ruled that doctorates could be conferred only on citizens and the relatives of professors. Only the *dottori* could 'read' and prepare others for a doctorate. Only toward the end of the thirteenth century did they begin to hold public positions and their salaries often reached as much as twenty–thirty thousand *lire* a year, plus students' *honoraria*.

The *dottori* were supposed to give ordinary lectures (*lecturae*) on the Digest and Code, and extraordinary lectures on other books in the evening. They were also expected to tutor students and engage in debates. If they did not perform their duties punctually, they were fined.

Teaching was held in high regard: commentators frequently employed the expression *Legere in scholis* as a synonym for teaching. As a typical intellectual understatement, the teacher would 'read', i.e. would set himself to compare, comment on, and study famous authors of abstruse texts. The diversity of interests and specialization of subjects later caused a distinction to be drawn between the universities of Law and the Arts. Physicians, philosophers, grammarians and the like, were 'arts' men. This distinction led to the formation of two separate universities, with their own statutes and rules. Scholars of law enjoyed, though, precedence in honours and prerogatives, so that jealousy and strife began to emerge. The situation changed, when each discipline had a scholarly prestige of its own.

University Autonomy – Church and State

Oaths and anathemata did not prevent masters and students from migrating. Other universities were born out of these migrations. The *Comuni* vied in luring scholars to them. Scholars were exempt from taxes and from military service, they were given money for books, wines, food, clothes and substantial homes; they could borrow money at a low rate of interest. Titles of nobility and citizenship for their descendants were also granted. It is obvious that all this could not take place without some corrupt practices: the reasons for privilege were nevertheless more important. For in addition to the obvious economic and prestige considerations, the universities were expected to provide skilful scholars who would carry on the disputes with the popes and the emperors. They became thus centres of political power. Universities – born of private initiative, with the exception of Naples – maintained their autonomy in the face of popes and emperors, who wanted to ratify their existence or legalize academic titles. Some universities had a short, tormented, but glorious life; the most famous and durable ones accepted the legacy, by maintaining a position in civic life that neither church nor state pressures, foreign invasions and other factors succeeded in suffocating.

In the sixteenth century, the encroachment of the princes on the prerogative of doctoral nomination gradually took this function away from the universities: this did not occur without strife. Professors received a stable and safe state salary, which freed them from the risk of inconsistent student contributions or from the *unatantum* contributions of the *Comuni*; however, this implied an encroachment by public authorities which could jeopardize freedom of research. We may say that the universities represented the last bastion of civic liberties and that they were the sources of freedom and of *Risorgimento*.

During this period of decadence, culture often found expression outside the university which once more became isolated or at least confined to small groups and academies. Nevertheless the universities were never altogether shut off from the current of European thought. Philosophy in particular found new possibilities of development: Padua, Bologna, Pisa, Rome and Pavia were the hotbeds of a critical revival of Averrhoism, Alexandrinism, Scotism, Thomism and Aristotelianism. Pietro Pomponazzi, Giulio Cesare Scaligero and Lorenzo Valla paved the way to that *Filosofia nuova* which provided a secular solution in the conflict between state and church, of which the university, as organized culture, was an expression and which was to lead to a separation of the two powers. The provision of a political definition of the state, that is that of *regnum* during a period of major institutional crisis, is unquestionably a contribution made by the Italian universities. Later on, in the face of the Church's claims, such a conception was further clarified until it reached a kind of revival in the eighteenth century, after a slow maturation during the period of Spanish domination. In order to protect the autonomy of political thought, Vittorio Amedeo II, Carlo III, Leopoldo I and Giuseppe II, endorsed the authority and the university doctrine of Ormea, Giannone, Tanucci, Tamburini, Bandini, Beccaria against the growing ecclesiastical influence. In fact, the Faculties of Theology helped to protect the government from an excessive encroachment by the Church, and meanwhile provided a favourable environment for the formation of a learned, critically-minded clergy, free from corrupting temporal influences.

In the Faculty of Theology at Turin University, Vincenzo Gioberti received his education: we may regard him as providing an ideology of spiritual anti-temporal autonomy, the greatest Catholic representative of anti-Jesuitism and a major Catholic figure of the *Risorgimento*.

On the pretext of public order and the protection of science and scholars, absolute governments and principalities denied academic autonomy. Only the most subservient academies could thrive in the shade of such Courts.

Many scholars resigned; servility softened academic rigour. Very few scholars found refuge in thoughtful solitude.

The Decline of Scholarship

Ecclesiastical influence, diffidence toward science and the political sciences in particular, grew in the universities. Bishops were given the highest academic positions and chose those teachers who were obedient to the prince and the Church's will. The natural consequence of this was that the quality of work deteriorated. Foreign domination perpetuated this situation. Only toward the end of the eighteenth century did the influence of French Revolutionary ideals revive the ancient flame of political study and of academic freedom (*Foscolo*). But it was a weak and isolated flame, soon extinguished by the Establishment.

Political subjection coincided with progressively closer connexions between State and Church in the universities, which had as their purpose – 'uniformly regulating the development of the subjects' minds and souls' (*Bollettino delle leggi delle due Sicilie*, 2 September 1815).

During the process of unification and the *Risorgimento*, in the Piedmontese provinces (the first nucleus of a unitary State), after the promulgation of King Carlo Alberto's Statute in 1848, the universities emancipated themselves from the Archbishops' authority, thanks to the Boncompagni Act. Formerly, the Bishops were Grand Chancellors of the universities. Jewish and Protestant citizens were allowed to register in academic institutes. The Italian State defended the autonomy – although limited – of studies from the accusation of heresy and fostered its consolidation.

The formation of a liberal state is usually followed by a process of cultural autonomy. This process was met by the hostility of the Church which had so long enjoyed the privilege of supremacy over the State (Bonifacio VIII, *Unam Sanctam*, 1302). In Italy, the reaffirmed principle of Church supremacy was accompanied by a clearly defined temporal power.

The Casati Act of 13 November 1859 established the role of the Italian State with regard to the university by granting freedom of teaching. Theological faculties were maintained within the framework of subjects taught at the universities, but because of the friction between Church and State, related rules were never promulgated. It was in fact difficult for the civil authorities to regulate theological studies, in view of their open clash with the temporal power of the Church. Theological faculties assumed therefore a 'presence' role of the Church in state universities. This function can be seen by looking at the controversies these faculties caused. Proposals to suppress them were made (Correnti, Bonghi); others asked for the establishment of polemical Dantean chairs (regarded as an expression of lay thought: Bovio). The *Accademia dei Lincei*, on the other hand, was fostered in the name of modern, empirical thought (Sella).

The Casati Act stated that 'opposing the truths upon which the religious or moral order of the State rests, either through teaching or publishing' was sufficient cause to suspend or dismiss a university professor. King Carlo Alberto's Statute stated in its first article that the Catholic religion was the State religion. Nevertheless, the Liberal State did not enforce these laws. Universities enjoyed ample autonomy and freedom, which the law of 2 October 1924 – drafted by the philosopher Giovanni Gentile – recognized and extended. Although this law came to be regarded as the most fascist of reforms it was Mussolini's personal definition, given in a period in which he was still sensitive to the influence of a liberal tradition, which he was later to deny and repress.

In order to permit a higher education based on Catholic principles the Gentile Act tolerated the establishment of the Catholic University of the Sacred Heart in Milan and gave also the same legal validity to its degrees as to state university degrees, in spite of the fact that the Catholic university required its students to affirm the Tridentine profession of faith and the anti-modernist oath.

This recognition opened a new chapter in the influence of the Church on the university, which was concluded and ratified in the Lateran Concordat of February 1929. Article 5 of the Concordat provided that the State would dismiss from public office and forbid him contact with the public any priest deprived of the *nihil obstat* of the Diocesan. Under this clause Professor Ernesto Buonaiuti, an ordained priest and professor of the History of Christianity at the University of Rome, was forced – as a result of ecclesiastical censure – to resign from his position, which he had obtained in the usual way by examination and which it was unanimously recognized he had filled with scholarly and personal integrity. Article 38 of the Concordat provided that the appointment of professors at the Catholic university and the depending *Magistero di Maria Immaculata* were subject to the *nihil obstat* of the Holy See (as the State of the Vatican City was called in the treaty that accompanied the Concordat). According to Article 39 of the Concordat, all Catholic universities and institutes for the education of clergymen were dependent on the Holy See, without interference from the State educational authorities. Article 40 provided that degrees in theology granted by institutes and approved by the Holy See were to be recognized by the Italian Government.

The principles of the Concordat are still in force, in spite of the spirit of the present and of the norms in the republican Constitution of 1948. Bilateral discussions between Italy and the Holy See are now taking place, in order to resolve the dispute – possibly through mutual agreement.

The Lateran Pacts were influenced by the illiberal climate of opinion in which they were signed. They represent a turning point in fascist policies toward school and university by modifying the liberal norms of the

Gentile Act. Already, the law of 9 June 1927 had obliged university professors to give a loyalty oath 'in conformity with the moral ends of the State' (that is, with the ends of the dictatorship). Rectors and faculty deans were appointed by the political authority, the opportunity to take university appointment examinations was denied to all who would not meet the required absolute moral and political standards established by the (politicized) administration, dismissals followed when a professor found himself 'in a state of incompatibility with the general political attitude of the Government', and the function of the *Privatdozent* was abolished. In vain, Albert Einstein exhorted Italians not to prostitute their universities, whose traditions of freedom were part of a common European heritage.

In 1934, the professors' oath assumed – even formally – the character of loyalty to the fascist regime. Only eleven full professors refused to take the oath: Gaetano Salvemini, Vito Volterra, Gaetano De Sanctis were among these. The majority took the oath (this was also Benedetto Croce's suggestion), because this compromise enabled them to continue their activities and because they did not wish to facilitate the progressive acceptance of fascist policies in the university. For most professors, however, it was a purely formal oath. The fire of revolt was kindled in the universities, and the forces of patriotism originated there. The call to arms made by the Rector of the University of Padua, the Latinist Concetto Marchesi, to students and teachers inciting them to revolt against the Nazifascists, and the popular revolt in Naples that started from the university were representative of a past that Fascism had tried to suppress.

Immediately after the second world war, the loyalty oath and racial and political discrimination were erased from university legislation. Many illustrious teachers came back from exile, from jail, from seclusion, to reassume their positions.

The Constitution of the Republic of 1948 stated that 'art and science are free, and free is the teaching thereof', and guaranteed that 'institutions of higher learning, Universities and Academies, have the right to establish for themselves autonomous rules within the law of the State'.

The Italian State is young: it is only a hundred years old. In 1970 the centennial of the breach of the Porta Pia was celebrated which gave Rome back to Italy. Our Republic still has to pass legislation which will adequately meet constitutional principles. Social reality imposes new problems of correlating democratic principles and research needs. The Italian political situation has not made it possible for decisions to be taken which will actually solve these problems. Universities await new legislation, which at the date of writing was still under discussion in the Senate.

The university in Italy lives in a state of expectation and transition. It looks forward to overcoming the conflict in the norms which rule it and to finding the best solution to problems that connect it with other European universities. Meanwhile the inflation of degrees, the excessive over-crowding of universities, the prevailing professional demands imposed on the curriculum, seem to favour conditions which are in ominous contrast with its glorious past.

3

The University in the U.S.A.

Michael Brick

The modern American university is *sui generis*; it is an institution characterized by its own forces. That it can be epitomized in this way is a tribute to the evolutionary process by which the university developed and acquired its distinctive flavour. 'Evolution' is a key word. What we understand to be a university is the product of several historical transformations and mutations, each of which – accompanied by a specific educational philosophy – emerged in response to particular social needs.

As the college and university matured one of its most notable characteristics was a difference in perception between those who functioned within institutions of higher education and the people and agencies they served. The focus of this divergence concerned the role of education in society and the essence of scholarship and the educational process. This chapter proposes to discern the historical relationship between higher education and American society – broadly defined – in order to illuminate some of the convergences and dichotomies. The thesis herein advanced is that the college or university is a social institution created and altered by the state to meet felt needs. As such, higher education may be thought of as an instrument of social policy, with the result that higher education has reflected but never directed society or social issues.

Colonial Higher Education

American higher education originated not with the university, but with the college. On the eve of the Revolution there were nine collegiate foundations in existence, 'nine home-grown variations on a theme known in the mother country . . .'.[1] In each part of the New World settled by the European immigrants one of their first endeavours was to attempt the transplantation of the culture with which they were familiar at home. We may distinguish three characteristics of early colonial America and its system of higher education. Colonial culture was not indigenous. In its early stages it reflected the institutions of Europe. Thus the colonial colleges resembled the structures and aims of their European counterparts.

---

[1] Frederick Rudolph, *The American College and University: A History* (New York: Alfred A. Knopf, 1962), 1.

Second, the proliferation of higher education was purposive; it represented a desire to perpetuate a distinct type of society. Finally, while the Old World traditions were pervasive we find, on the other hand, that native American conditions interacted with these transplanted institutions and modified their development.

Influences of European Higher Education

Harvard, the first colonial college, was founded by men who attended the two great English universities, Oxford and Cambridge, and it is these institutions – particularly the latter – that furnished part of the academic model employed by the colonists. Samuel Eliot Morison has noted the following similarities between Cambridge and early Harvard: Harvard's first statutes were modelled after the Elizabethan statutes at Cambridge; the first degree formula included the phrase *pro modo Academiorum in Anglia* (According to the manner of universities in England); both institutions admitted part-time students called fellow-commoners as well as regular degree students; and the names of the four college classes – freshmen, sophomore, junior sophister, and senior sophister – were the same.[2] William and Mary, and Yale, the second and third colleges established, were not without English influence. We find that the college in Williamsburg, Virginia, recruited eight of its thirteen faculty members between 1729 and 1757 from Oxford University. At Yale, Thomas Clap prepared himself for the College presidency by studying the histories of Oxford and Cambridge, and when he secured a new charter in 1745 it was formulated upon the administrative practices at the two English universities.[3]

Also borrowed from England was the notion of a residential campus life, an ideal which defined the college much like a family relationship. Frederick Rudolph has called this the 'collegiate way', a term borrowed from Cotton Mather, and described by Rudolph as

> . . . the notion that a curriculum, a library, a faculty, and students are not enough to make a college. It is an adherence to the residential scheme of things. It is respectful of quiet rural settings, dependent on dormitories, committed to dining halls, permeated by paternalism.[4]

Unlike the great medieval seats of learning at Paris and Bologna, the English universities were located in rural settings. In order to provide suitable living accommodations for faculty and students, and particularly

---

[2] Samuel Eliot Morison, *The Founding of Harvard College* (Cambridge, Massachusetts: Harvard University Press, 1935), 5, 25–6, 40, 127, 337.

[3] John S. Brubacher and Willis Rudy, *Higher Education in Transition: A History of American Colleges and Universities* (Revised and enlarged edition; New York: Harper and Row, 1968), 3; The Yale Charter of 1745 is reprinted in Richard Hofstadter and Wilson Smith, eds., *American Higher Education: A Documentary History* (Chicago: University of Chicago Press, 1961), 1, 49–53.

[4] Rudolph, op. cit., 87.

for those of humble background, privately endowed living units known as colleges were created by wealthy benefactors. By the sixteenth century Oxford and Cambridge had evolved into federations of largely autonomous colleges. The university had its own officers and by royal decree issued all degrees, but in other areas the colleges were self-governing. They had their own statutes, administrators, and trustees (all of whom were drawn from the faculty), professors, students, courses, endowments, and property.

It is probable that the founders of Harvard and Henry Dunster, its first president, wanted to reproduce this federal system but there was no university with which to affiliate and it is doubtful if the Crown would have granted a university charter to the colonists. Thus the first American institution of higher learning became a self-contained unit – the college. The development of the residential, rural character of Harvard was also influenced by the absence of concentrated population centres and the frontier-like nature of the New England landscape.

To the English influence on colonial higher education was added that of Scotland. The Scottish institutions reconstituted or newly-created as a result of the Reformation were, unlike Oxford and Cambridge, nonresidential, professionally oriented, and under the control of laymen chosen from community governing councils. During the seventeenth and eighteenth centuries these institutions were neither colleges nor universities; rather they combined features of both; they merged a university superstructure and a degree-granting college in the same letters patent. The Scottish influence was most apparent at William and Mary where James Blair, a graduate of Marischal College, Aberdeen, and the College of Edinburgh, became its first president.

The College of Edinburgh apparently had direct bearing on one practice at early Harvard – the publication of commencement theses. As in the medieval universities, the Commencement Act, as it was called, consisted of a series of disputation on theses which were posted in advance. The English universities did not post the theses or even the names of the degree candidates, but at Aberdeen and Edinburgh, MA candidates as early as 1596 published their theses in a quarto pamphlet which contained a dedication to the authorities by the graduating class, the Latinized names of these students, and brief synopses of their arguments. This practice was abridged in 1641 and omitted the précis. A comparison with a Harvard thesis sheet of 1643 reveals 'such striking resemblances in arrangement and typography as to leave no doubt that whoever arranged the first Harvard Commencement had seen a copy of the Edinburgh thesis sheet'.[5]

A later Scottish influence on colonial colleges was introduced through

---

[5] Morison, *Founding*, 136.

the work of Rev. William Smith, an Aberdeen graduate who effected curricular change at King's College, and John Witherspoon who came to the New World in 1768 to become the sixth president of the College of New Jersey (Princeton). Briefly, the colonial curriculum was transplanted from England where it had been based on medieval scholasticism and Aristotelian philosophy. It was not until the early 1700s that Newtonian science and Cartesian and Platonic philosophy took root in Harvard. These 'new sciences' were introduced to the colonies by Smith and Witherspoon.

Unlike the English universities, Aberdeen and Edinburgh were receptive to the new tendencies in science and philosophy that came out of the Enlightenment. As popularized by Witherspoon, the Scottish 'common sense' version of the Enlightenment sought to harmonize a Newtonian universe based on empirical method with Christian religion. Dominating the moral philosophy courses which capped the student's college career, common sense philosophy remained a powerful force until 1890 when it was undermined by the Darwinian revolution.[6]

One of the most pervasive and significant European influences derives from the tradition of English college government and the Protestant Reformation and concerns the pattern of governance devised to direct collegiate institutions. The presidency is an office that stems from the English college.[7] As for the governing board, its roots are found in the medieval universities and the Reformation.

The Purposes of Colonial Higher Education

The primary reason for the Puritan migration was religious – in a broad rather than sectarian sense – and this had two sides. First, they found English culture becoming increasingly decadent to the point where devout men could not raise children morally or earn an honest living. Moreover, the living conditions for a Puritan were steadily growing worse since Archbishop Laud, a High Churchman and righthand of King James I, was closing every avenue of Puritan self-expression. The Puritan colleges of Oxford and Cambridge were being purged. As early as 1570 Thomas Cartwright, the champion of Puritanism, had been removed from his divinity chair at Cambridge and this policy was being extended to government posts. Puritan theology as stated in the Thirty-nine Articles was interpreted in a reactionary way and churches were being forced to conform to ritualist observances.

The other side of the Puritan migration was utopian. They pictured a

---

[6] Brubacher and Rudy, op. cit., 15.

[7] W. H. Cowley, *Professors, President, and Trustees: An Assessment of the Conceptual Roots of American Academic Government* (unpublished manuscript, duplicated, Stanford, California, 1961).

Christian Commonwealth of the elect, dedicated to God's glory; a place where men could worship according to Scripture (as they interpreted it) and follow an honest calling. The Puritans did not reject English society, instead they sought to re-create in New England what they felt to be good in Old England, while at the same time exclude evil. To this end they aimed to reproduce a material and intellectual cross-section of their native country.

The church was closely interwoven with the fabric of colonial life. Most of the emigrating clergy belonged to the William Ames school of Protestantism which argued that church polity was Congregational rather than Presbyterian. Thus there was no Church, no central organization, only a series of locally controlled churches. The state was not superior to the church, nor did the reverse obtain. They were both parallel aspects of the same divine sovereignty. The elect organized their own churches and chose their ruling elders (pastors and teachers); they similarly held town meetings, formed courts of election, and chose magistrates among themselves to conduct their civil affairs.

The success of this special social experiment was strongly dependent upon education. Morison explains the relationship:

> . . . the puritans were wise enough to know that however difficult it might be to establish this society of their dreams, the task of keeping it going would be far more severe, and only possible with education. Children must learn to read the Bible, that they might know God's truth, and to write and cipher, as an aid to honest living; chosen boys must be taught the learned language in which the world's best thought and literature were still to be found; and a smaller selection of youths must be given university training, in order to furnish the State with competent rulers, the Church with a learned clergy, and society with cultured men.[8]

Here then was the three-sided mission of higher education stated and implied in *New England's First Fruits*: the training of clergy and civil leaders and the preservation and transmission of the cultural heritage. This broad purpose should come as no surprise, since this was the *raison d'être* of university training in England and it was middle classs England that sailed across the Atlantic.

Harvard and her colonial contemporaries were not mere theological seminaries with a narrow purpose of training sectarian clergy. To be sure, an educated ministry and a religious outlook was the dynamic motive for its establishment. New England was founded for religious purposes and all colonial society was one of Protestant sects in need of clergy and a body of churchmen who knew the doctrines of their denomination. But the Puritans also wished to produce Christian gentlemen and transmit a

---

[8] Morison, *Founding*, 150.

culture. The identification of Protestantism with broad educational purposes and liberal education goes back to Calvin who was profoundly affected by Renaissance humanism and instituted a curriculum reflecting the humanistic influence.[9]

The goal of the perpetuation of learning and the education of a societal elite is echoed in the writings of Cotton Mather[10] and in the charter granted to Harvard in 1650.[11] That Harvard took its societal function seriously is confirmed by the fact that less than half of its seventeenth-century graduates entered the ministry; that President Dunster asked the General Court for funds to purchase books in law, physics, philosophy, and mathematics so that students 'whose various inclinations to all professions might thereby be encouraged and furthered'; and that Jonathan Mitchell, the senior fellow of Harvard, requested the General Court to establish chairs in history, languages, law, mathematics, and medicine to train 'choice and able schoolmasters, able eminent and approved physicians, and education to accomplish persons for the magistracy and other civill offices'.[12] That these chairs were not initiated is more a matter of finance than disagreement over purpose.

The curriculum established at Harvard and subsequently elsewhere was not a divinity programme. All students, whether or not candidates for a pulpit, undertook a prescribed course of studies, in six of the seven medieval liberal arts (grammar, logic, rhetoric, arithmetic, geometry, and astronomy), the three philosophies of Aristotle (metaphysics, ethics, and natural science), and Greek, Hebrew, and ancient history. The language of instruction was Latin and most of the books used were written in that tongue.

The professional study of theology began only after the baccalaureate had been taken. Undergraduates had only enough work in divinity to make them educated Christian laymen. This included study and analysis of the Bible in original tongues, some Protestant theology – which was usually Ames' *Medulla Theologica* – note-taking on the two sermons delivered every Lord's Day, and frequent quizzes on these sermons.[13]

The bachelor's degree then, was intended to provide a liberal education, having no practical value, being equally suited to a future minister,

---

9 For an extended study of Calvin's educational programme and governing arrangements see Alan Karp, 'Calvinism and Higher Education in Geneva: 1536–1700', (an unpublished paper submitted to the 'Seminar in Higher Learning' at Teachers College, Columbia University, Spring, 1970).

10 Cotton Mather, *Magnalia Christi Americana*, II, 6–10 in Hofstadter and Smith, op. cit., I, 13.

11 Harvard College Charter of 1650, in Samuel Eliot Morison, *Harvard College in the Seventeenth Century* (Cambridge, Mass.: Harvard University Press, 1936), I, 5–6.

12 Cited by Samuel Eliot Morison, *The Intellectual Life of Colonial New England* (Ithaca: Cornell University Press, Cornell Paperbacks, 1965), 32, 42.

13 Morison, *Intellectual Life*, 42–3.

physician, or magistrate. What was stressed was character-building and discipline for a broadly educated societal elite. This programme of liberal arts, sacred languages, and belles-lettres was similar to that studied by those founders of New England who attended the Puritan colleges in Oxford and Cambridge. At least 130 English university graduates had emigrated to the New World by 1646 – 100 from Cambridge, thirty from Oxford, and three had attended both. In a colony of less than 25,000 there was about one university-trained man for every forty or fifty families. And these men exerted an influence that was disproportionate to their small numbers. This was the Puritan 'Establishment', an elite which imparted its standards – religious, social, and intellectual – to the community.[14] From the very beginning, colonial higher education became associated with class interests.

As is to be expected, the same broad purposes found expression in the eight subsequent colleges that followed Harvard by 1769. William and Mary was expected to provide Virginia with its public servants. When Yale's Charter of 1701 was replaced in 1745, the new Charter stipulated that the College would train 'many liberal and piously disposed persons . . . for the service of God in the state as well as in church. . . .'[15]

The Influence of American Conditions

Social conditions in America brought changes in the academic system and divergence from the Old World models. Perhaps the initial deviation from accepted norms occurred with the first Harvard Commencement in 1642 when nine bachelor's degrees were awarded. This was bold action since Harvard had neither university status nor a royal charter. Harvard was not unique in establishing an independent degree-granting college; the Scottish foundations had done so for many years before Harvard's founding. What made Harvard really distinct was that it was founded not by a *de jure* sovereign power, but by a proprietary corporation that had used its charter to govern a royal colony.

A second American divergence was the appearance of a sectarian purpose in college founding – a mixture of denominational rivalry and the necessity of survival in an environment of religious diversity. The denominational era was ushered in with the establishment of Yale College in Connecticut in 1701 by a group of orthodox Congregational ministers, of whom the most notable was Cotton Mather, the Puritan divine. Mather was then a member of the Harvard Corporation, but his flirtation with Elihu Yale is not surprising since Puritan orthodoxy at Cambridge was declining in the face of unitarianism and the growing spirit of religious

---

[14] Morison, *Founding*, Appendix B.
[15] Charters of the College of William and Mary, 1693, and of Yale College, 1745, in Hofstadter and Smith, op. cit., I, 33, 49.

toleration. Yale was not a Harvard spin-off, but it did promise to provide what its predecessor did not – an education in which the faith of the original New Englanders would be preserved.

The next college was founded in 1746 in the fervour of the Great Awakening. This was the College of New Jersey (Princeton). The Great Awakening was a movement within the Presbyterian branch of Calvinism that stood in opposition to the older faiths and forms which now characterized the established churches and colonies. Based on a religion of conversion and revivalism, the Great Awakening spoke not for an educated clergy or even learning in general. Instead it emphasized an individually felt religious experience achieved through revivals. One consequence of this movement was the division of Presbyterians into conservatives and liberals, into Old Lights who adhered to the more austere forms of the past and New Lights who expressed the enthusiasm of the present. The College of New Jersey was initiated by New Light Presbyterians in an effort to achieve respectability and refute the charges that they were hostile to higher education and that their clergy was illiterate.[16]

King's College (Columbia) received a royal charter in 1754 after a bitter fight between Anglicans and Presbyterians. Similarly, the College of Rhode Island (Brown) was chartered in Providence in 1764 to train Baptist ministers; Queen's College (Rutgers) was founded by the Crown in 1766 for the propagation of the Dutch Reformed Church; Dartmouth College was chartered by George III in 1769 on the request of Congregationalists who were dissatisfied with both Harvard and Yale. In epitomizing this period one is reminded of the Reformation formula of *cuius regio eius religio*. It might very well have been amended during the American sectarian era to read *cuius religio eius collegio*.

Denominational rivalry was not a boon. Yale was surely weakened by the founding of Dartmouth, and it cannot be seriously maintained that New Jersey could support a college in Princeton and another at New Brunswick. On the other hand, the growth of religious diversity in the colonies, and later in the United States, made some form of denominational coexistence a necessity if the colleges were to succeed. The hostility of competing sects was allayed by granting them at least token representation on collegiate governing boards. And in order to attract more students and to enlarge their bases of financial support, the colleges stressed interdenominational policies and practices. This too was a new American direction. Some of the colleges exempted Quakers and Jews from religious requirements; the College of Rhode Island prohibited the establishment of religious tests as well as disallowing the interjection of religious bias into teaching; and the charters of King's College and the

---

16 Thomas Jefferson Wertenbaker, *Princeton 1746–1896* (Princeton: Princeton University Press, 1946), *passim*.

College of New Jersey stipulated that no student could be denied admission on the basis of their religion.

Ironically, one of the results of denominationalism was a trend towards secularism. Not only do we find an increasing number of laymen associated with the founding of colleges after 1750, but they begin to assume an active and in some instances a predominant role on the collegiate governing structures. The trend is further indicated by the increasing number of students coming from the homes of merchants and magistrates and the decreasing proportion of students studying for careers in the ministry.

Still another American characteristic of the college was its relationship with the state – first with the Crown, then the colonial legislatures, and finally, with the state governments. Generally, problems centred about the question of how the college could incorporate without surrendering its autonomy to a public governmental agency.

English law during the 1600s and 1700s required that no corporation could be chartered without royal consent. The founders of Harvard tried as long as possible to avoid a royal charter because of the corresponding necessity of royal visitation and the probable loss of religious freedom such an external power would have meant. Yale too operated without a sovereign charter for four decades due to similar reasons. Harvard retained the charter issued by the General Court until 1684 when it was cancelled with the revocation of the colonial charter of Massachusetts.

During the pre-Revolutionary period the relationship between Harvard and the Massachusetts Bay Colony was close. Support came in the form of financial aid (tax levies, land and corn revenues, and ferry rents) and administrative support (for example, the General Court dismissed Nathaniel Eaton for malfeasance).[17] William and Mary enjoyed a similarly cordial relationship with the Virginia House of Burgesses and the king. The fear of royal visitation did not exist in this college as it was a staunch supporter of the Church of England and the king generously repaid such loyalty. The charter exempted the college from the payment of taxes (Harvard and Brown were also given this medieval privilege by their legislatures); allowed the faculty to elect two of its members to the House of Burgesses; gave the collegiate authorities the revenues from a tobacco tax, and placed the entire land system of the colony into the hands of the school's land office.[18]

Colleges created during the Great Awakening were not as regularly or as generously supported as their counterparts in Massachusetts and Vir-

---

[17] Morison, *Harvard College in the Seventeenth Century*, I, 30–1; and *Founding*, 228.
[18] Hofstadter and Smith, op. cit., I, 33–9; Herbert Baxter Adams, *The College of William and Mary*, Circular of Information No. 1 (Washington, D.C.: U.S. Bureau of Education, 1887), 15.

ginia. Later colleges did not have the same success with colonial govern-ments 'largely because of sectarian hostilities and inhibitions'.[19] One of the effects of the Great Awakening was to end the pattern of what in effect were colleges of the state and the church.

The most far-reaching altercation between a college and the state occurred in New Hampshire where Dartmouth had been operating under a royal charter since 1769. About the time of the Revolution there began to appear a growing mistrust of the colleges as they were then organized and conducted. None fully answered the public need – each was the college of a sect or a faction, and thus not a college of the whole commonwealth. As the democratic spirit began to pervade American society there were those who came to believe that higher education should be a state function.

At Dartmouth, President John Wheelock, a Presbyterian and a Jeffer-sonian, broke with his trustees, the majority of whom were Congrega-tionalists and Federalists, over politico-sectarian issues and was consequently dismissed from office. Wheelock appealed to the state legislature, which generally held religious and political views akin to his own. The college charter was revised and a new state institution – Dartmouth University – was established with Wheelock as president under the direction of a reconstituted Board af Trustees supplemented by an external Board of Visitors modelled after Harvard's Overseers.

An unsuccessful suit in the New Hampshire courts brought the original trustees, represented by Daniel Webster, to appeal to the United States Supreme Court which heard the case in 1819. Under the leadership of Chief Justice John Marshall the Court, on February 2, declared by a five-to-one margin that Dartmouth was a private eleemosynary institution with the purpose of benefiting the public, and was not a public corpora-tion under public supervision. Therefore the original charter was a contract that could not be amended by the state against the wishes of the trustees.[20]

The Dartmouth College Case asserted the rights of private higher education. Five days after the decision was rendered, the General Assembly of Virginia chartered the University of Virginia, Thomas Jefferson's project and the symbol for several decades of what came to be called the 'state university idea'. Within one week the foundations of American academic diversity of control and performance were solidly laid.[21]

---

[19] Richard Hofstadter and Walter P. Metzger, *The Development of Academic Freedom in the United States* (New York: Columbia University Press, 1955), 145.

[20] For a more detailed description and analysis of the Dartmouth College Case see Leon Burr Richardson, *History of Dartmouth College* (Hanover, New Hampshire: Dartmouth College Publications, 1932, 2 vols.), I, ch. 6; Donald G. Tewksbury, *The Founding of American Colleges and Universities Before the Civil War: With Particular Reference to the Religious Influences Bearing Upon the College Movement* (New York: Bureau of Publications, Teachers College, Columbia University, 1932), 151–4.

[21] Cowley, op. cit., ch. 4, 15.

The Importance of the College to American Society

Nothing about America before the Civil War suggested that the college would become a representative institution. Shaped at first by an aristocratic establishment to meet its own ends, and later by competing denominations for whom piety and intellect were one and the same, the college was not a popular institution and had very little effect on the majority of Americans. At the time of the American Revolution there were only 3,000 living college graduates. Harvard graduated its largest class prior to the War of 1812 in 1771 when 63 men received degrees. The entire student body at Harvard in 1770 was 413 while Yale enrolled 338. Harvard, as a matter of fact, would not graduate its first class of 100 until 1860.[22] The college may have aspired to train leaders, but most people apparently lacked the desire to lead or else found other avenues of social and economic mobility open to them.

One reason for the lack of popularity of the college was the nature of its curriculum. With its emphasis on the classical liberal arts there was very little to commend it to men of practical affairs, and the influence of the Yale Report of 1828 kept the curriculum in conservative clothes until almost 1900, despite the efforts of men like Francis Wayland and Thomas Jefferson. Also working against the growth of the college were their high costs and geographic inaccessibility. As the colonies matured and as the nation was built the Puritan aristocracy devolved into merchants, labourers, and farmers. Such men did not send their sons to college; they were needed at home. Moreover, as the American frontier began to open up, the prospect of unparalleled material rewards and the frontier spirit of individualism began to engender an attitude that stressed a fundamental hostility to privileges.

Nevertheless the new nation became a land of colleges. America entered the Revolution with nine colleges but by the outbreak of the Civil War over 800 had been founded, of which 250 survived the hostilities; and 182 still endure today.[23] Whereas the colonial college was intended to serve a particular class of people, the college of the nineteenth century was characterized by its diversity of proposed clientele. Americans grouped themselves by social class, religion, occupation, sex, geographic location, and ethnicity; and the college reflected this ordering. As Jencks and Riesman point out, there were colleges 'for Baptists and Catholics, for men and women, for whites and blacks, for rich and not-so-rich, for North and South, for small town and big city; for engineers and teachers, . . .' in other words, 'special interest colleges'.[24]

---

[22] Brubacher and Rudy, op. cit., 23.   [23] Tewksbury, op. cit., 1.
[24] Christopher Jencks and David Riesman, *The Academic Revolution* (New York: Doubleday and Company, Inc., 1968), 3.

One reason for the second era of college-founding was the rivalry and provincialism of the newly created federation of states. Colleges were founded so that the revenues accruing from student and institutional expenditures would fall to local merchants rather than to those in a neighbouring state. Localism was also encouraged by the vastness of the country and the inadequate system of transportation which made it difficult for colleges to meet the needs of even those few who wished to attend.

Another reason for the proliferation of colleges was the home mission-ary movement which after 1800 concentrated its attention in the American West. Chief among the missionaries were the sons of Congregational Yale and Presbyterian Princeton. The westward movement and the attempt by settlers to re-create in their new environment the civilization of the East, particularly New England, also accounted for the growth of institutions. Oberlin, Carleton, Grinnell, Colorado, Whitman, and Pomona Colleges, among many others, owe their existence to American expansion west-wards.

As in colonial times, evangelical zeal gave way to denominational rivalry as a motive for establishing colleges. As the nation moved west so did Protestantism and virtually every sect established affiliated colleges. Even those not traditionally dedicated to a learned clergy, such as the Baptists and the Methodists, could not withstand the urge of self-propaga-tion and the need to provide adherents with a 'proper' education.

Contributing to the growth of colleges was also the notion held by educators that higher education was a social investment, that the college served society by producing graduates dedicated to the nation's continued progress and its democratic ideals. Yet this cant was more in tune with an aristocratic noblesse oblige and to the ideal of cultural preservation and transmission, than it was to a genuine effort to extend social democracy or to shape society in any new directions. Social purpose had always been one of the functions of the college, but by the end of the nineteenth century this goal was becoming increasingly diluted as colleges became more con-cerned with the expectations of their students rather than those of society.

At the core of this attenuation of purpose was the American democratic spirit and its accompanying distaste for privilege, and the belief in the self-made man who could achieve success without the benefit of a formal education. The same year in which the Yale Report was issued, Andrew Jackson was elected to the presidency. Jacksonianism promoted the cause of the common man and expressed optimism in his ability to recast society. The colleges, however, were anything but organisms of equality. The special interest colleges were bastions of separation rather than social integration. Each college represented a particular subculture from which it drew its financial support, trustees, president, and students.

There were other points of tension between the colleges and Jacksonian spirit. It is not so much that the colleges were totally insensitive to Jacksonian democracy; instead, they found it difficult to accommodate it to their more traditional functions of piety and character-building. The democrats were concerned with man and his material needs and fundamental equality. The colleges on the other hand were not advocates of human equality – intellectual or material.

In part, the control exercised by the various subcultures over their special interest colleges was in no small measure due to the unprofessional quality of the faculty. The old time professor, as the president, was often a clergyman or at least had received some theological training. His religious views were merely a reflection of the interest group from which he was drawn. Most professors had only a BA and the concept of an independent scholar with a dedication to knowledge was as yet unknown. The 'professor' was not a numerous species; there were only a few in each college and most of the teaching was left to tutors. Whereas a professor taught a subject, a tutor instructed a class throughout their entire baccalaureate programme. They were regarded more as cheap labour than apprentice scholars and were highly transient.

In summarizing the influence and effects of the college from colonial to pre-Civil War America, two observers of higher education state

> ... it is tempting to conclude that these colleges influenced neither the intellectual nor the social history of their era. Instead, it could be argued that America overinvested in higher education ... Perhaps the resources devoted to colleges might have been better allocated to libraries, scientific societies, or primary schooling.[25]

In terms of the college's effect on all aspects of society it is hard to disagree.

The American University

The university in the United States is an amalgam of several historical, yet ongoing forces which have determined its spirit and functions. First, there was the rise of German intellectualism and the attempt, in the late nineteenth century, to transplant the academic system developed in Germany. The second force is indigenous – the emergence of publicly supported higher education. The former was concerned with the unending search for truth and the German intellectual's approach with its antiseptic exactitudes necessitated an aloofness from societal events. The state university and land grant movement was people-centred and action-oriented, and asked how it could best serve the needs of America. One developed its own conceptions of a university, while the other was content to have its functions determined by the needs of others. Yet these seemingly opposite ideals merged by the beginning of the twentieth century to create a new University Idea – one that combined through a division of labour, the discovery and application of knowledge. The advent of the third historical impact – the beginning of large-scale federal support of scientific research to advance national goals during World War II – occasioned this coalescence.

The university is one of America's greatest successes and today occupies a position at the very centre of society. Still, as it ploddingly stumbles and gropes towards a new century, it is being attacked because of its success. Higher education has always been an object of criticism; what distinguishes this new indictment is that for the first time it is coming from the left and constitutes a desire to force the university to direct rather than reflect society. It is necessary to review the nature of the forces which shaped the university in order to comprehend the basis of the new demands.

German Intellectualism

The pre-eminence of the German university system as it emerged from the Reformation ideals of Martin Luther and Philip Melanchton had two causes. German philosophy produced an imposing succession of thinkers – Leibnitz, Wolff, Kant, Fichte, Hegel, Schopenhauer, and Nietzsche – most of whom taught in universities. Moreover, the universities embraced science a full two hundred years before their counterparts in other European nations. These two strands were pulled together in the early nineteenth century by Johann Gottlieb Fichte, the philosophical heir of Kant and Wolff. Wishing to make the university the crown of a great and revitalized German civilization, Fichte argued for two principal reforms: rationalistic science should be a concern in every field of thought, and every university teacher should devote himself to scientific investigation.

The essence of the German system implied a special theory of the nature of knowledge and the university. An American observer explained it as follows: 'the collective idea of a university implies a *Zweck*, an object of study, and two *Bedingungen*, or conditions. The object is *Wissenschaft*; the conditions are *Lehrfreiheit* and *Lernfreiheit*.'[26] To the German, *Wissenschaft* – the ardent, independent, and methodological search for the truth – was multi-dimensional. First there was a commitment to a theory of research carried out in the spirit of what Max Weber has called *Wertfreiheit*, the belief that research is valid only if conducted free from the bias of value judgment and social or political commitment. There also existed a faith in the eventual ability to unify truth.

Closely associated with the German theory of knowledge was the

---

[26] James Morgan Hart, *German Universities: A Narrative of Personal Experiences*, reprinted in Hofstadter and Smith, op. cit., II, 571.

notion of *academische Freiheit*, or academic freedom, itself a bifurcated concept. The first part was concerned with freedom for the scholar, *Lehrfreiheit* and was described by George Ticknor, one of the first Americans to study in Germany and a major figure in the effort to create an American university, as follows: 'No matter what a man thinks, he may teach it and print it, not only without molestation from the government but also without molestation from publick opinion, which is so often more oppressive than the aim of authority.' There was also *Lernfreiheit*, 'the freedom of learning . . . the emancipation of the student from *Schulzwang*, compulsory drill by recitation'.[27] A student, under this policy, was freed from a prescribed course of study. He could elect any course he wished and had neither a formal attendance nor examination requirement until the final examination for a degree.

Two other concepts are related to the German theory of knowledge – autonomy and professional ethics. Since the basis for the university was knowledge, it followed that only those who possessed that knowledge could properly evaluate it. Thus the idea of a free republic of scholars sitting in judgment of their peers arose. But the scholar had a special task: because only he had the ability to understand and assay his own expertise, the professional was ethically responsible to the layman to see that the integrity of his content and methodology was maintained and that his discoveries were not misused.

The German theory of a university was one of aloofness and independence from society. The university could maintain its integrity only if it existed in isolation from the corrupting forces that surround it. The German view did not preclude the study of social or political problems; it meant simply that a disinterested attitude, free from bias and vested interests, and a pure environment were necessary if these matters were to be studied and the truth discovered.[28]

As the reputation of German scholarship spread, more and more Americans crossed the Atlantic to take advanced degrees. In addition to the German eminence in university studies, the primary motivation behind the exodus was the paucity of opportunities for learning in America. The special interest college had no place for pure science, theory, research; or a free, professional, and secular faculty. Those who wanted advanced training – and there were only several hundred before the 1880s – had to travel abroad, and among those Americans who did we find some of the best minds of the nineteenth century.

[27] George Ticknor to Thomas Jefferson, Göttingen, October 14, 1815, in Hofstadter and Smith, op. cit., I, 258; James Morgan Hart, in Hofstadter and Smith, op. cit., II, 572.
[28] James Morgan Hart, in Hofstadter and Smith, op. cit., II, 573, 577; John S. Brubacher, 'The Theory of Higher Education', *Journal of Higher Education*, XLI (February, 1970), 99–103.

Transplanting the German University Model

A new American society began to form after the Civil War. Sectarian and religious fervour were declining and were being replaced by secular concerns. The frontier was beginning to disappear and with it, migration to the West. The advent of transcontinental railroads opened new national markets for goods and jobs. National magazines were starting to shape a new culture. The federal government was slowly becoming a force influencing people's lives. The cumulative effect of these trends was to overshadow, if not destroy, the Jacksonian ideal of the rugged individualist. The nation was becoming industrial, urban, specialized, and meritocratic. New types of skills would be needed as new scientific and professional areas opened. It is in this context that the American university was born.

There were several ways in which Americans who had been influenced by German ideals sought to transform established educational patterns. The first was the creation of completely independent graduate schools. These institutions were dedicated to advanced studies only and sought no connection with undergraduate education. Johns Hopkins was opened in 1876. Daniel Coit Gilman proposed a replica of the German faculty of philosophy with no undergraduate college attached. Gilman's ideal was never attained.

A second university plan was the 'bisected-college university', in which the first two years of college are left to the secondary schools and university training extends from the junior year through the PhD. Both Henry P. Tappan at the University of Michigan and William Watts Folwell at the University of Minnesota attempted such plans but they did not succeed. The first successful bisected-college university was the University of Chicago, where William Rainey Harper established an ostensible success in 1889 backed by the largesse of John D. Rockefeller, Sr. He and other members of the board of trustees wanted a college, but Harper argued for an institution concerned with research and graduate and professional studies. In the ensuing compromise the four undergraduate years were divided in half – into an 'academical college' and a 'university college'. In 1896 these names were changed to 'junior college' and 'senior college'.

The third plan became the prototypical structure for the American system. This was the 'comprehensive university' or an educational institution made up of several substructures which included the four-year undergraduate college, a graduate school of arts and sciences, and one or more professional schools. Graduate and professional structures were superimposed on the English-type college and the teaching and research functions were conjoined. Harvard under Charles Eliot, Yale under Timothy Dwight the younger, Columbia under F. A. P. Barnard and Dean W. Burgess, and Princeton under James McCosh and Dean Andrew

F. West had all taken steps beginning in the 1870s and 1880s, to achieve the status of comprehensive universities.

The German university was never entirely reproduced for two reasons. First, the American university had to come to terms with the college, so general education and research coalesced. Second, the university had to develop its pure research in conjunction with the technical and utilitarian interests of the country. This modification was the contribution of publicly supported higher education, to which we now turn.

The State University and Land-Grant Movement

The idea of public higher education has come to mean, in its broadest sense, that society must assume responsibility for providing educational opportunities; that state and federal governments, independent of religious or private corporations, are the most suitable agencies to achieve this; that the curriculum should reflect the practical and professional needs of the citizen; and that teaching and research – both pure and applied – should serve society. These are functions that have been accepted only within recent decades. The idea of public universities, however, was a long time in the making.

Public involvement in higher education, as we have seen, dates from the colonial period. However, the university movement did not begin in America until after the Civil War. One factor leading to the acceptance of the idea, if not the institutions, of public higher education, was its emphasis on agriculture and the mechanic arts. Several states specified that colleges and universities would offer courses in agriculture, household and industrial management, and admit women on an equal basis with men. In 1855 the Michigan Agricultural College was opened. This precedent was followed by Pennsylvania and Maryland while Massachusetts (1856) and Iowa (1858) created governing boards for state agricultural and mechanic arts colleges that opened after receiving funds provided by the Morrill Act.

While Jonathan Baldwin Turner in 1851 was asking the Illinois legislature to create a 'university for the industrial classes', the ideas of Justin Morrill were taking shape. Twice rebuffed – once by the Southern bloc in Congress and again by veto of President Buchanan – the Land-Grant College Bill or Morrill Act was signed into law by Abraham Lincoln on July 2, 1862.[29] The Act provided that each state, through the sale of public land scrip, could elect to endow and maintain at least one institution where 'without excluding other scientific and classical studies', the leading purpose would be to 'teach such branches of learning as are related to

---

[29] For details see Earle D. Ross, *Democracy's Colleges: The Land-Grant Movement in the Formative State* (Ames: The Iowa State College Press, 1942); and Edward Danforth Eddy, *Colleges for Our Land and Time* (New York: Harper and Brothers, 1956).

agriculture and the mechanic arts . . . in order to promote the liberal and practical education of the industrial classes . . . '.[30]

The Morrill Act was probably one of the most important single pieces of educational legislation through the nineteenth century. By 1870 thirty-seven states had agreed to sustain public universities in one of three ways: use the revenue realized through the sale of land scrip to found a new institution, subsidize an existing state university, or convert a private college or university to public control. In most instances new institutions were built.

The university that achieved academic and popular respectability for the land grant movement was Cornell which opened in 1869 under the presidency of Andrew D. White. The spirit of innovation at Cornell included the following concepts, all of which became characteristic of public higher education: the union of liberal and utilitarian education; the admission of women; non-sectarian governance and instruction; the granting of state scholarships to the best-qualified students; the encouragement of scientific study and research; and the co-ordination of public education with the university at its summit. Cornell was an immediate success. In 1871 it enrolled a freshman class of over 250 – the largest entering class in the history of American higher education.[31]

The public universities gradually strengthened their liberal arts programmes and also did research that in many cases developed applied sciences such as engineering and its various specialties. What made them the potent force they have now become was the so-called 'Wisconsin Idea', the identification of the university as an organism of social democracy and public service, as well as a centre for research and teaching. The idea was not original – certain aspects are seen in the work of Jefferson, Folwell, Charles K. Adams, Andrew White and James B. Angell – but no university enunciated the idea as successfully or completely as the University of Wisconsin under its president for fourteen years, Charles Van Hise.

The essence of the Wisconsin Idea amounted to broad use of the state university for democratic goals, political reform, economic and social improvement, and human welfare. During the Van Hise administration the 'watchtower' or service function was finely honed and became a characteristic of progressive education. The Wisconsin Idea was emulated by most public universities and its success was even felt by the research-oriented private sector of higher education. In 1902 the University of Chicago was preparing students for careers in public administration and government. Woodrow Wilson delivered his inaugural address as president of Princeton on 'Princeton in the Nation's Service'.

---

[30] Theodore Rawson Crane, ed., *The Colleges and the Public 1787–1862* (New York: Bureau of Publications, Teachers College, Columbia University, 1963), 192.

[31] Rudolph, op. cit., 267–8.

Public universities offered a new theory of higher education. Whereas the university movement stimulated by German thought called for institutional and professional neutrality in order to discover the truth as it pertained to current events, the state and land grant universities advocated that the university and its faculty be socially committed and that knowledge be used to reform and advance society.

Towards a Social Service University

The proper position of the academic community in American society has never been fully established. Societies change, however slowly, and social institutions engage in new functions and seek alliances with new constituencies. America and her academic institutions are today undergoing a period of transition which is everywhere marked by instability and chaos. The university is asked to be all things to all people. It is attacked and cajoled from all sides, from within its walls, and by external forces. It is harassed by students and young faculty liberals who want it to become more directly involved in social change, and by older more conservative faculty and politicians who want it to attend to its more traditional role of teaching, research, and service. The university's ethos has been temporarily lost and with it its internal coherence. The university today is little more than 'a series of individual faculty entrepreneurs held together by a common grievance over parking'.[32] How did this happen and what will result? It is to these questions that we now turn.

Growth of Federal Influence

Wars have always affected the development of higher education. During the Revolutionary and Civil Wars colleges provided manpower and even served as battle sites. During the first World War higher education again provided mainly recruits. It could do little else. Colleges were literary institutions that provided culture and character training and universities had only recently embraced the research function.

All of this changed with the advent of World War II. By the 1940s the universities were instrumental in the advance of science and their prowess led to their enlistment in national defence and scientific and technological development. As the Vannevar Bushes, Edward Tellers, James B. Conants, and Karl Comptons shuttled back and forth between Washington and their universities, the government-commissioned research grants and contracts they received heralded a new relationship between education and the federal government. At the conclusion of the war, the university had entered the first stage of what Clark Kerr has called the 'Federal Grant University'.

---

[32] Clark Kerr, *The Uses of the University* (New York: Harper and Row, 1966), 20.

The Successful Institution: The University at the Centre of Society

The American college and university achieved a central place in society by the willingness to perform services for business and government. The university accepted federal grants and contracts geared to national needs. Moreover, the knowledge explosion, itself a university product, and the resultant knowledge industry has permeated both government and business and has created a need for more people with higher levels of technical skills. The university is expected to train them.

The university has been asked to do even more. The professionally oriented academic institution was given the job of serving as a national certification agency and screening mechanism through which people would be placed in a productive relationship to the national purpose of power and prosperity. This 'sifting and mobility' function was described by Pitirim Sorokin as early as 1927. The purpose of education, he said, is not to provide knowledge and educate, but to

... discover in the first place, which of the pupils are talented and which are not; what ability every pupil has and in what degree; . . . in the second place, to eliminate those who do not have the desirable mental and moral qualities; in the third place, through an elimination of the failures, to close the doors for their social promotion, at least within certain definite social fields, and to promote those who happen to be the brightest students in the direction of those social positions which correspond to their general and specific abilities.[33]

Trow has arranged the functions of higher education into two categories, the 'autonomous' and the 'popular'. The autonomous functions are those which are intrinsic to the role of higher education: the socialization of young people and the creation of knowledge through pure research. The popular functions are those which have been taken on in response to external needs and requests. Colleges and universities provide education for all those who seek it. In a society based on the possession of credentials, higher education has for the first time come to be regarded as a right rather than a privilege. Higher education also supplies practical knowledge and service: elite groups are selected and certified, manpower is developed for the specialized agencies of society, and knowledge is increasingly applied to help understand and solve social and urban problems. Whether or not it is justified the typical educational response to any problem is to create another programme for its solution.[34]

Higher education has been a success. But it is this very success that has

[33] Pitirim A. Sorokin, *Social Mobility*, 1927, 188–9. Cited by Walter A. Lunden, *The Dynamics of Higher Education* (Pittsburgh: The Pittsburgh Printing Co., 1939), 12.

[34] Martin Trow, 'Reflections on the Transition from Mass to Universal Higher Education', *Daedalus* (Winter, 1970), 2–4.

created a great strain between the 'autonomous' and 'popular' functions, or more precisely between the uses to which these functions have been put.

There are many people both within and outside of academe who view the university as a free republic of scholars, a company of independent professionals where a man can study any subject. To a considerable extent this is imagery; evidence as well as argumentation is beginning to show two things. First, that as a social institution with its own interests, and existing in a society that values power, the university and people who function in it are seeking power for themselves. Second, the dependence of the university on government and corporate contracts has co-opted faculty members. Rather than forming a counterweight to the military–industrial complex the university has instead joined that monolith and has itself become part of the Establishment.

Higher education plays a crucial role in the relationship between the military and the business corporation. Both agencies depend on knowledge for their operation and the university provides it through educational programmes and acceptance of research contracts. 'A troika has developed', notes Ridgeway, 'between the university, where products or processes are conceived, the government, which finances the development, and private business, which makes and sells the finished item.'[35] Because of its trained talent the university has been nurtured by the government and large corporations. But this rapprochement has not been without its negative effects.

The most obvious effect is that the university no longer has complete control of its internal management. Federal research funds are negotiated by the individual professor with one of the forty-seven government contract research agencies; yet, the scholar's contract commits university resources and determines the time the professor will spend on teaching and research. While the government gets the best scientific advice and research personnel available, the major universities become captive to national priorities. In 1960 higher education received 75 per cent of its total research expenditures from the federal government and over 15 per cent of its total operating budget. More than two-thirds of these research funds came from the Department of Defense, the Atomic Energy Commission, and the National Aeronautics Space Administration. Not only does most of this support go to the sciences, but it is also concentrated in a very small number of schools and constitutes a major portion of their budgets. The net effect is to create a system-wide imbalance whereby the government determines which universities will expand and in what areas. In 1968, for example, eighty per cent of the operating funds of the Massachusetts Institute of Technology came from government sources; and half of

---

[35] James Ridgeway, The Closed Corporation: *American Universities in Crisis* (New York: Random House, 1968), 10.

Columbia's and Princeton's budgets were federally financed. This is only overt funding and makes no mention of the secret subsidies for classified research.[36] A further diminution of institutional control is occasioned by the fact that faculty salaries are paid by these research funds, thereby decreasing faculty loyalty which is already weakened by his allegiance to his discipline.

Additional negative effects are the imbalances created between the sciences and humanities, and the appearance of new types of personnel who, while not faculty members, conduct much of the teaching and research. Another effect that has recently become clear is the emulation of a single model of academic success. The concentration of federal money for scientific research in a few institutions has made them the most prestigious in the country. Since research and graduate education go hand-in-hand, federal monies have led to a system in which these graduate schools not only serve as models, but also impose their standards on other graduate schools and even upon undergraduate education.

There is evidence which suggests that the infusion of the values of graduate education upon the college has created a situation where schools who see the power and prestige of the federal grant university try to get a share of the glory for themselves. This is done by offering higher degrees. A recent study of change in higher education between 1941 and 1966 suggests the existence of this single status system. Each year an average of 6·5 community colleges expand to four-year institutions; 16 baccalaureate-granting colleges expand their efforts to the masters degree; and 6·4 schools begin PhD programmes.[37] As schools climb the ladder of prestige other values of graduate education are absorbed. The study cited above found that 32 per cent of the institutions in the sample reported an increase in the amount of time that faculty devote to research while 41 per cent indicated a decrease in the number of hours faculty spend teaching students. This leads to a serious questioning of the so-called pluralistic system of American higher education. Hodgkinson concludes, 'the heralded diversity in American higher education may still be a fact, but is becoming a declining force. Institutions of higher education are becoming more like each other . . .'.[38]

There is no suggestion here that only federal and corporate research funds have directly caused the emulation of the graduate school and its values. What is being said is that these monies have helped speed the process by providing resources and access to outside power and influence. Professors and institutions of higher education have their own interests to

---

[36] Figures are drawn from Kerr, op. cit., 52–4; Ridgeway, op. cit., 7.
[37] Harold L. Hodgkinson, *Institutions in Transition: A Study of Change in Higher Education* (Berkeley: The Carnegie Commission on Higher Education, 1970), 14.
[38] Hodgkinson, op. cit., 2, 56.

advance and if they can increase their own authority and influence through emulation they will, particularly where administrators have lost control over institutional management.

The Emergence of the 'Critical Function'

Universities have always been proud to be the critics of society and to be a type of social conscience that emerges to direct or redirect misguided policies of the state. The paradox is that this has never really been the case. As universities matured they themselves have been influenced by various societal agencies and have reflected rather than directed contemporary affairs. Today, however, there is hope that the function of social criticism will prevail. Criticism is coming from some of our most prestigious and influential professors and from qualified students, administrators and politicians.

Criticism is being rendered on various levels. There is an overall examination of the nature of a technologically advanced society. The society pictured by Herbert Marcuse is based on the one-dimensional domination of a technological system. In an advanced industrial system, technology determines the socially needed occupations, skills, attitudes, and aspirations, and obliterates all protest and opponents of the system. All opportunities of social change are contained. Because technology cannot be isolated from the use to which it is put, a technological universe becomes a political universe whose object is to dominate. Political power asserts itself through the technological system, which as a dominating force, controls human values through a process whereby man is preconditioned into believing that he is leading the 'good life'. Thus science is not value-free or neutral. Science, in the form of technology, enjoins theoretical and political reason and results in domination through and as technology. Marcuse's solution is to redirect technical progress so that it promotes the idea that the function of reason is to encourage the art of life. This will require 'neutral' science to become political.[39]

In questioning the supposed neutrality of knowledge and science Marcuse has opened a debate that encompasses the role of the scholar as a critic of both the university and society. There are those who argue that because the scholar is tied to a specific type of methodology he is in a poor position to serve as a critic. Tied to a predetermined technique, professors, and particularly behavioural scientists, address themselves only to those problems which can be studied and manipulated by their methodology. Other problems are ignored as unimportant. Thus scholarship, with its concern for 'hard data' subverts the role of the social critic – who is concerned with morality, conscience, and feeling – by making him 'a

---

[39] Herbert Marcuse, *One-Dimensional Man: Studies in the Ideology of Advanced Industrial Society* (Boston: Beacon Press, 1964), ix–xvi, 3–12, 157–66, 228–36.

person who constantly reiterates different aspects of the same idea in a manner determined for him by others without being critical of the conditions which have shaped his life'.[40] Another reason why the scholar is said to be a poor critic relates to the notion that specialists who get involved in government or corporate research accept American society and tend to preserve the status quo.[41]

If one agrees with the Galbraith and Marcuse analysis of society and the argument advanced that the university has actively lent its intellectual resources to a military-industrial corporate behemoth, then there is ample reason to assert that knowledge is indeed power and that it is far from neutral.

However, there is another view of research and scientific knowledge which argues that moral judgments can be made only about the uses to which knowledge is put, not about the knowledge itself. A proponent of this view is Sidney Hook who avers that it is irrelevant for a scholar to choose a research topic on the basis of its implications for humanity. The scholar's job is the free pursuit of disinterested knowledge. To hold him responsible for the application of knowledge or to take positions on current social issues is to make the university a political body, thereby destroying the basis for academic freedom.[42]

There are also advocates of a more direct societal role by the university. This means giving up the guise of neutrality and detachment by directly advocating social change. In this way, it is argued, faculty and students could design and evaluate in a real setting, the consequences of various choices and decisions.[43] Such a position, of course, calls into question the idea of institutional neutrality, the concept which declares that as a corporation, a university can take no partisan position or direct action except in defence of academic freedom. Perhaps the time is at hand to formulate a new theory of academic freedom.

Towards a Social University

The emergence of the 'critical function' has resulted in the cry for a new type of university, one that is based on the concept of social interaction, commitment, and criticism. Such a university would make knowledge moral by acting in the public interest. It would have the mission of aggressively defending the various public interests in health, ecology,

---

[40] Noam Chomsky, *American Power and the New Mandarins* (New York: Vintage Books, 1969), 25; Alan Wolfe, 'The Myth of the Free Scholar', *The Center Magazine* (July, 1969), II, 76.

[41] Chomsky, op. cit., 348.

[42] Sidney Hook, 'Barbarism, Virtue, and the University', *The Public Interest* (Spring, 1969), 29–34.

[43] Ridgeway, op. cit., 76; Edward Joseph Shoben, Jr., 'Cultural Criticism and the American College', *Daedalus* (Summer, 1970), 682 ff.

education, and social justice. It would not attempt to replace the more conventional colleges and universities, but would exist beside them. Rather than conducting abstract research it would be committed to social change.[44]

Such a university is not on the immediate horizon. Before we achieve a 'Social University' higher education will have to address itself to two immediate problems: The elimination of the scholar's contributions to a violent society, and universal higher education.

The intellectual has a special mission in the control of violence because of his dedication to a life of reason. Yet, intellectuals have in part been responsible for creating an atmosphere in which violence is tolerated. This has taken the form of a new creed which Schlesinger identifies as a cult of political existentialism and violence.[45]

There are those within the academy who no longer value reason and learning for its own sake. The university's emphasis on intellect – a product of the eighteenth-century Age of Reason – is obsolescent they say, and must accommodate itself to the Age of Feeling and Humanity. Influenced by Marx, Kierkegaard, Nietzsche, and Freud, and recent writers like Marcuse and Fanon, proponents of this view, stress existence and feeling. The aim of higher education they claim is not to prepare for life but to live it now. They are concerned not with status, but with integrity, genuineness, morality, and freedom. Politically, they refuse to state concrete goals, which they see as irrelevant.

There is danger in predicating individual action or an entire university on feeling and subjectivity. Such a position can lead to immediacy of value realization, absoluteness of conviction, and an intolerance that leads to violent confrontation. Indeed, to a certain extent, this is what has happened. Believing that the way to break the oppressive yoke of a society is through violence, the act of violence becomes a glorified means by which the oppressed individual can escape from the social and individual state of immorality and valuelessness around him.[46]

Such an ideology explains much of the violence American campuses have been undergoing in the last two years. This does not imply that violence is premeditated, only that violence and confrontation are deemed acceptable methods to apply to one's cause when that cause is 'just'. Such a position, however, can only serve the cause of the conservative right, and lead to political pressures on college administrators as well as budgetary cutbacks. If higher education is to avoid becoming a 'political football'

---

[44] William Arrowsmith, 'Idea of a New University', *The Center Magazine* (March, 1970), III, 47–60; Wolfe, op. cit., 77.

[45] Arthur Schlesinger, Jr., 'Existential Politics and the Cult of Violence', *Phi Delta Kappan* (September, 1968), XL, 9–15.

[46] See Frantz Fanon, *The Wretched of the Earth*, translated by Constance Farrington (New York: Grove Press, 1965).

controlled by reactionary legislatures it must reassert its commitment to reason.

The other immediate concern of higher education is the achievement of opportunities for universal higher education. Almost every college and university today is trying to accommodate the so-called 'social revolution'. Several trends are becoming clear concerning the enrolment boom. Most of the influx will be accommodated by public colleges and universities. Higher education, whether public or private, will be increasingly urban. Not only will students come from urban contexts, but they will be drawn essentially from the previously excluded minority groups. One way in which minority groups will be accommodated is through the policy of open admissions, such as that which is currently underway at the City University of New York. Whether or not this policy succeeds, it will undoubtedly be one of the most controversial issues of the 1970s.

Another highly controversial issue in the coming decade will be university involvement in urban affairs. The 1960s have been depicted as a decade of change in higher education. The American colleges and universities have accommodated greater numbers of students, assumed new functions, shown a greater concern for improving the quality of American life and the desire to do something about the inequalities of our culture. The question is if higher education will continue to change, will it evolve into the Social University?

It will not be an easy matter of simply drifting and waiting for this university to evolve while no one is looking, primarily because the university is a conservative institution and changes too slowly. On the other hand, there is a movement within the university for change, as attested to by such events as the Vietnam Moratorium in October, 1969, the ecology movement, the development of radical caucuses at professional association meetings, and the increasingly political positions taken by universities.

The time for change is clearly at hand. The choice is up to the educational community to either take the easy way out or move towards something purposive and necessary.

4

The Polytechnic Tradition in England

W. H. G. Armytage

Polytechnism is a word which has gone through many changes of meaning. So far we can elicit three.

(1) The Ecole Polytechnique: an institution established in 1794 to provide higher education that was selective in recruitment and confined to the physical sciences.[1] To this is contraposed another, virtually opposite type of institution.

(2) The Quintin Hogg-type society for young men of the working class.[2]

(3) A form of work-based education practised in the Soviet Union that can best be described as sandwiching theory and practice.[3]

The purpose of this chapter is to call attention to early experiments with, and rehearsals of, the idea as construed in England. It is argued round the thesis that these attempts compensate for or reflect the growing professionalization of society and are worth resurrection at a time when, as in a fair, the stalls have been set up and the cry of a 'comprehensiversity' or 'polyversity' is raised throughout the land by that most incongruous alliance of economists, students and idealists.

A patient and reflective eye reveals that it is not only the universities that possess a 'tradition' or collective super-ego with which innovation has to struggle and from which it often derives strength. For in England the polytechnic concept has already affected both the origin and the growth oι the civic universities[4] but has been ignored except in surveys of 'technical education'.[5]

Regional Polytechnic Societies

The first English society or group to use the name polytechnic had been formed in 1833 at Falmouth by two daughters of a Fellow of the Royal Society 'to elicit the inventive powers' of the community at large.[6] Like the eighty-year-old Royal Society of Arts, it worked by premiums, but unlike that Society, it aimed at developing 'capacities and talents which might otherwise be dormant'. It was not the first such society in Falmouth for twelve years earlier a 'Philosophical Society was formed in this Town, comprehending most certainly much scientific talent, but what is possibly of more value . . young and ardent minds thirsting for knowledge. These young men had sufficient experience to know that there is no "*royal* road to the mathematician" and sufficient common sense not to seek any patronage . . . according to a recent determination their transactions are to be confined to nature and Experimental Philosophy and the abstract sciences . . . lectures are delivered every fortnight.'[7]

Cornwall was the non-ferrous metallurgical larder of the early industrial revolution and its clever workmen at the Perran foundry were constantly bringing 'inventions' to Robert Were Fox, FRS. So his two daughters Anna Maria Fox and her sister Caroline secured the co-operation of seven other Cornish Fellows of the Royal Society to promote an annual exhibition of inventions. The first, held on 23 December 1833, contained a water gauge, lathes, high-pressure engines and collections of minerals. As a first patron they secured Lord de Dunstanville of Tehidy, the great magnate (to whom a monument was erected that still dominates west Cornwall), and when he died in 1835 the society sought a royal patron and became known as the Royal Cornwall Polytechnic Society.[8]

Such inventions as Loam's 'Man Engine' (for eliminating the laborious descent and ascent of ladders) were encouraged by grants, in this case of £500 for operational trials: at Tresavean mine. Similar help was given to the safety fuse which eliminated the dangerous practice of charging gunpowder-filled reeds. As its historian wrote, 'practically all the important inventions of the past century were first shown at these exhibitions, and received valuable awards and assistance from the judges':[9] by 1864 they had distributed over £4,000 in premiums exclusive of prizes.

The Royal Cornwall Polytechnic Society, with its 400 members, was typical of other centres of industrial activity which generated their own polytechnic groups.[10] The West Riding (1836),[11] Liverpool (1838) and Norwich (1840)[12] all established similar societies.[13] The first two had regular meetings at which papers were not only read on various technological topics, but subsequently published in a journal. This provided faith and momentum for the idea since the journals lasted throughout the century. Further momentum was imparted by a member of the Liverpool polytechnic society who was a civil engineer and wrote percipiently on the history of science. In 1839 he advocated a union of the mechanics' institutes. Later, also cloaked by anonymity, he published *The Polytechnic College: A Proposed institution for aiding depressed talent to complete works in progress connected with science, literature or art* (1867). However the pseudonym H.D. was soon penetrated, revealing the author as Henry Dircks, whose idea was that scientific groups like the Royal Society, the Chemical Society and the Engineers' Society should act as trustees for what would virtually be a polytechnic version of All Souls.[14]

The First London Polytechnic

Dircks' pamphlet is significant in its invocation of professional sponsorship: a social propellant of prime importance for yet another mutant of this idea. This more formal institution to bear the name of polytechnic, opened on 6 August 1838 at 309 Regent Street, London, was supported by the emergent professional groups of the capital – naval officers interested in the changeover from sail to steam, teachers interested in the sciences, polite society, and engineers on the railways. This, the first institution of that name in London, began with Sir George Cayley as the chairman and Nurse, the builder of Regent Street, as its main backer.[15] Printing presses, glass furnaces, power looms, lens-grinding wheels, a chemical laboratory, two model canals – even a diving bell, were on show at one time or another.

The aeronaut Charles Green experimented on his balloon before them in 1840. Forcault's pendulum was exhibited.

Its aim was to exhibit the process of various manufactures (hence the gallery for models, the theatre for lectures – then a chemical laboratory – and so on) and under its first manager, Charles Payne, formerly secretary of the Adelaide Gallery (an institution for teaching popular science in the Strand), this was pursued. His successor, John Henry Pepper, was a more colourful man. Author of some popular science texts and lectures to schools, he was awarded the title of 'professor'. He developed Pepper's 'ghost', a precursor of the cinema: a device whereby a transparent screen was moved between a lantern slide and a screen to produce certain effects. It was used in 1863 to illustrate Dickens' *Haunted Man*.

Nor was 'Pepper's Ghost' the only attraction for *Alice in Wonderland* was first publicly acted there. Pepper's *Playbook of Science* (1860) and *Playbook of Metals* (1861) were described by Professor C. H. Desch, FRS, as 'two excellent books which must have influenced the careers of many boys'. Certainly the great metallurgist, Sir Robert Hadfield, later gave a large number of copies to Sheffield schools 'with the object of encouraging boys to make experiments rather than to acquire knowledge merely by the reading of books'.[16] Pepper's departure to Australia (where he became public analyst at Brisbane) brought this phase of the polytechnic to a close and it languished till revived by Quintin Hogg in the 1880s.[17]

Work-based Training

Meanwhile a third mutant of the term *polytechnic* was emerging: describing a form of training that was work-based. Here the ideologue was the Glasgow chemist Andrew Ure. 'It has been the fate of this *polytechnic*, as of the best philanthropic dispensation ever made to man, to be misrepresented and reviled, not only by strangers ignorant of its intrinsic excellence, but by the very objects of its bounty, the children of its care',[18] he wrote, refuting the pastoral, anti-industrial conservatism of the then poet laureate to whom the factory system was 'a wen', 'a fungous execrescence' on the 'body politics' which 'to remove by absorption is impossible, and excision fatal'.[19]

Ure (in a disquisition that Marx was to revile but nevertheless copy) argued that 'a well regulated factory' afforded facilities 'for promoting the regeneration of human society' and cited the factory villages of Lancashire, where as a result of 'the vast circulation of the Scriptures, and the increase of Sunday Schools' religious sentiment 'lingers no more in the frigid aphelion of neologism but is advancing towards the true source of moral light and heat – the Sun of Righteousness, never again, it is hoped, to fly off in that excentric orbit'.[20]

Ure's pun on Sun/Son shows him as an unconscious energeticist!

Conversations with Dupin, coupled to his experience in trying to educate the mechanics of Glasgow, had led him to hammer out a particularly English conception of a polytechnic: not an elitist school of engineer technocrats, but a work-based school of science. Dupin was an eminent French engineer who came to Britain and was shown round Glasgow's industries by Dr Andrew Ure. He and other Frenchmen like M. Bergery cited the popularization of natural science in Glasgow and elsewhere as evidence that France should redouble its efforts.[21]

Marxian Concepts

Though he abused Ure as 'the pindar of the automatic factory' Marx accepted his vision of 'Uretopia', i.e. the trend towards inanimate energy slaves supplanting human labour. In a celebrated passage of *Das Kapital* where Marx was discoursing on the Factory Acts as a ripener of large-scale capitalism, he described mantically 'the germs of the education of the future' as 'to be found in the factory system [which] in the case of every child over a certain age, will combine productive labour with instruction and physical culture, not only as a means for increasing social production, but as the only way of producing fully developed human beings'.[22] 'There can be no doubt', Marx confidently wrote, 'that the inevitable conquest of political power by the working class will be followed by a movement in which technological instruction, both theoretical and practical, will win its place in the labour schools.' So as he argued, the old division of labour would be abolished.[23]

Adumbrated by Marx, this version of polytechnical education found congenial soil in Russia which had already acquired direct inspiration from the *école polytechnique* in the form of the Czarist polytechnics.

A further inference (as exquisite logically as any that can be drawn from that great disordered treasury of thought) would be that if machinery undermined the resistance of the workers to the despotism of capital, knowledge of the technology behind the machinery might enable the workers to plan their own supersession.[24] Thus the spiritual warrant for Soviet polytechnism was drafted from English experience.

It is worth emphasizing that the first case for a 'board of science' composed of 'all the leading men in the country, and before whom all plans should be brought that might be proposed for its advancement'[25] was drafted by the first president of the Royal Cornwall Polytechnic Society, Sir Charles Lemon, FRS, who lamented that 'the scientific character of the nation suffered' because 'the English system offers so little inducement to Mathematicians and Physicists to pursue their researches'. So yet another infrastructure of technological institutions was proposed. With a fellow West Country MP, William Tite, FRS, Sir Charles Lemon urged 'the formation of such schools of mining in such places as Cornwall &c, of schools of arts and sciences in such places as Manchester &c; of agriculture in York &c.' 'Perhaps' he wrote 'it might be found advisable to found thirty schools or colleges of this description with (it may be) an average of six professors in each. I would propose that these professors should only be appointed after a severe examination before a competent Board, the Board *not* named by the Government but by the Councils of the Universities, and of the different recognized and chartered scientific institutions.' He estimated this would cost from £18,000 to £27,000 annually in State grants.[26]

French Concepts

Admiration for a *corps d'élite* of technocrats as produced by the Ecole Polytechnique in Paris had been earlier expressed at the British Association in 1841, the writer comparing its two-year general science course with the Cambridge mathematical tripos. He confidently concluded 'that the average scientific attainments of the mass of the pupils on leaving the school are equal to those of the majority of wranglers and senior optimes at Cambridge, while there are of course among their numbers distinguished men, who would compete with those at the head of the Cambridge Mathematical Tripos'. The author trod on even more dangerous ground when he pointed out that not only were their examinations carried out efficiently but also impartially to secure rewards to merit alone. Furthermore, though no provision for religious instruction was made, yet 'cases of moral misconduct among them are exceedingly rare'.

This picture of a school for the elite of a rising generation, though allegedly anonymous, was in reality the work of an HMI, Henry Longueville Jones, whose 'Report on General Education, Superior, Secondary and Primary, in France' was the first article in the next (1842) number of the *Quarterly Journal of the Statistical Society of London* where once again he stressed the fact that in France 'the aristocratic and clerical elements of educational institutions' had 'totally disappeared'.

This article was moreover contributed by the Manchester Statistical Society, to whom Jones had six years earlier read a paper arguing that 'great encouragement should be given to the study of mathematical science, of political and social history and of the practical application of mathematics, and calculation, to the affairs of banking and commercial operations . . .'. 'What could be more suitable to the very large class of hearers whom the professors would be likely to draw around them', he asked, than 'the exemplification of mathematical knowledge to be made in the use and construction of machinery, – or on the other hand, in the calculation of mercantile and financial transactions, the principles of insurances, of public funds, and the statistical calculations, that are brought into daily use in the varied operations of commercial and manu-facturing establishments'.

Though such interest in a Manchester polytechnic was of course caught up ten years later in the Owens College, it did not prevent others from keeping the case for a polytechnic alive.[27]

Those others included many professional engineers: J. A. Lloyd,[28] John Scott Russell[29] and the Institution of Civil Engineers itself,[30] and found expression in institutions like the Royal Indian Engineering College at Coopers Hill established in 1870.[31]

Perhaps the nemesis of such private attempts and proposals was reached when William McGregor, MIEE, started his ill-fated attempt to estab-lish a polytechnic in a small room over a bonnet shop in Bournemouth. 'The term Polytechnic' he wrote grandiloquently 'is used in its fullest sense to embrace a wide field of usefulness not only in connection with Arts, Science and Languages, but answering and adapting itself to every enquiry and necessity that may open up in this age of educational advance-ment.'[32] With this conviction he launched on 24 January 1889 his poly-technic in Bournemouth. Its initial housing was modest but its aim was vast – nothing less than 'to put working men on a level with the best in Berlin, Paris or Philadelphia'.

Pump-priming in London

Indeed there is something vaguely anticipatory of the 1970 Reith lec-turer in his desire to ensure that his polytechnic would 'adapt itself for every enquiry and necessity that may open up in this age of education'.[33]

The reappropriation of the wealth of 109 minute parishes in London effected by the City Parochial Charities Act (1883) primed the pump with some £80,000 a year. City companies did the rest. The people's palace in the Mile End Road was financed by the Drapers Company with branches at Bow and Bromley. The Goldsmiths financed and maintained a polytechnic at New Cross with a branch in Deptford. Other institutions followed. The second pump-priming operation was 'whisky money', made available in the Local Taxation (Customs and Excise) Act of 1890 which gave them a third source of finance administered through the Technical Education Board of the new London County Council. By 1898 the number of polytechnics north of the Thames had risen to seven and south of the Thames to five. They catered for what the chairman of the London Technical Education Board called 'a poorer class of students than the universities' and though he acknowledged that these London polytechnics had 'no connexion with, but little resemblance to, the institutions to which a similar name is applied in France, Switzerland and Germany' he was understating the case even more than when he attributed the name polytechnic to 'a mere local accident of no significance'.[34]

Six years later Webb was boasting of the 500 polytechnic students who were working for London degrees: 'even the new provincial universities with all their dignity of charters and chancellors, diplomas and degrees, often had less work of university grade than a London polytechnic'.[35]

'Polytechnic' was for the Fabians a prestigious word. Sidney Webb's friend, ally, and indefatigable supporter, Bernard Shaw, saw it as a nursery of new men. 'We literary and cultured persons for years have been setting up a cry of the New Woman' said Tanner in Shaw's *Man and Superman*, 'never noticing the advent of the New Man.' That New Man was Henry Straker, who steps forward as Shaw's paradigm of the Polytechnician as he claims 'my business is to do away with labour. You'll get more out of me and a machine than you will out of twenty labourers.' "Enry Straker, motor engineer and New Man' said Shaw 'is an intentional dramatic sketch of the contemporary embryo of Mr H. G. Wells' anticipation of the efficient engineering class which will, he hopes, finally sweep the jabberers out of the way of civilization.'[36] Then again he referred to 'Etonian toffs and Polytechnic cads' who he said 'should contact each other only in street fights, the organization of which might be regarded as a legitimate part of their physical exercise, or in the examination halls or laboratories in which their capacities and pretensions will be tested impartially'.[37]

Yet by 1913 the polytechnics were listed by the spokesman of the Liberal Education Group in 1913 as sixth amongst eight types of 'specialized secondary institutions after the University, the Training College, Trade School, Art School and Technical Institution' and before the Agricultural School and 'specialized institutions'. Attendance at these, he suggested, should be 'accompanied with a limited amount of approved employment before reaching 18 years of age'. He argued that a Royal Commission should be appointed to accelerate the modification of university government and eliminate overlap between the various colleges at Oxford and

Cambridge, to provide for the education of women, and to ensure a greater use of buildings.[38]

Bridging Liberal and Vocational Education

Thus, in solution, awaiting the precipitant urgency of the first world war, lay polytechnism in England. One effect of that war was to energize a former member of the Liverpool Polytechnic Society, H. S. Hele-Shaw, to work for the establishment of the National Certificate System in 1919.[39] Another was to provide in Soviet Russia a macro-experiment in Marxist polytechnism. For the Soviets emphasized first, that a knowledge of the most important branches and general principles of the techniques in technology and the organization of socialized production was essential; and second that all youth should acquire habits of work and experience of being socially productive. So pupils were enabled to obtain a knowledge of the main branches of production and of the scientific principles on which these depend, whilst becoming accustomed to handling common tools: thereby bridging the gulf between a liberal and technical education. 'Polytechnism' was that bridge. Participating in, as well as studying life situations enhanced motivation. Experience of life in society made pupils aware of the fundamental processes by which society survives and prospers. Team work was encouraged.

The English roots of this concept we have explored in Marx's thesis that the labourer was alienated from the fruits of his labour by becoming a cog that could not even revolve unless placed in a machine. Monotechnic education bound workers to one skill – often a very repetitive and destructive skill. Polytechnic education unlocked many, as well as being in his phrase 'the only way of producing full developed human beings'. Marx himself acknowledged his debt to the English Quakers, to John Bellers, and the pedants can trace this back to Thomas More and Rabelais.[40]

Now, beamed back to England, this polytechnic principle was urgently commended by, amongst others, Dr B. Mouat Jones, the Principal of the Manchester College of Technology (now UMIST). Fifteen years later in 1945, he became a member of the Percy Committee on higher education which recommended the establishment of Regional Advisory Councils for Higher Education and the upgrading of technical colleges: recommendations which, like so many others, were to be virtually lost on the empty air.[41]

Embodying the Government's belief that 'the best results will be achieved by developing higher education on polytechnic lines wherever practicable'[42] polytechnics, as we know them, were designated in May 1966 as 'the main centres for the future development of full-time higher education within the Further Education System'.[43] Conceived at a time after the Government had been successfully wooed to expand higher education even more than was envisaged by the Robbins Report (a blue bird too in its day), these polytechnics were regarded as 'a distinctive sector' of higher education 'complementing the universities and colleges of education'.[44]

The logic of their parturition was, at the time, most rational. But the voice of reason was not always heard with respect then, as now, in universities, and loud cries of protest greeted the spirited and elegant presentation of the case for the polytechnic as a discrete (and that word also has a punning relevance today) institution at the Woolwich Polytechnic some months later. The mere idea was castigated by critics for instituting a 'binary' system in higher education.[45] The choice of adjective by the critics was not ill chosen. Semantically it signified rational phenomena in the natural world: astronomers use it to describe two stars or suns, one of which revolves about the other, or both revolve about a common centre; chemists, to describe a theory whereby all acids are considered as compounds of hydrogen with a radicle, and all salts as compounds with a metal replacing hydrogen; whilst mathematicians use it to describe a most modern method of computation.

Used analogically, such images from the natural world would seem an admirable endorsement of the polytechnic concept. But unlike Plato's philosopher kings, modern governments are concerned more with manpower than with metonyms and the manpower situation employed in, and produced by, the existing institutions of higher education was far from satisfactory. To begin with, as resources required for science-based higher education became increasingly expensive, the need to concentrate them at particular centres became imperative and attempts to secure that had already been made.[46] Secondly the valiant attempts made in the forties and early fifties to 'vary the mix' in higher education by new institutions whose course-patterns prescribed a sandwich involvement with, and participation in, the outside world, had been leeched off into the orthodox university circle. These new institutions, the Colleges of Advanced Technology, became Technological Universities, and, as such, took on some of the attitudes and style of their new and potent peer group.[46] In doing so they began to follow the example set by the 'civic' universities earlier in the century, jettisoning any course that was not of degree standard, converting part-time courses to full-time undergraduate ones, and, when obtaining an adequate number of doctorate students, insisting (with notable exception) that they should be full-timers too.

Modern Trends

Today new professional associations form at an annual rate of one a year. Between their professional demands and existing educational emery papers lies an abrasive interface which the CNAA is admirably designed to lubricate. For with its validating techniques, CNAA (or to give its full name the Council for National Academic Awards), personal prejudices and professional predilections can be tempered to each other. In such a tempering process, the innate and natural tendencies to narcissism or pygmalionism on the part of good teachers/lecturers can be exposed, and great change effected.

Hope that the universities would make further progress in the direction of CNAA type postgraduate courses was expressed by the Committee on Manpower Resources for Science and Technology.[47] For though CNAA has lost the now upgraded CAT's (for whom it once discharged a similar if less ambitious role confined to technological awards) it has now established a formidable catalogue of undergraduate and postgraduate awards in many fields. The twin principles of polytechnism and regular review might well be adopted by some universities or some parts of all universities in this age of rapid expansion.

The problem is a big one. As an excellent Fabian working party remarks:

> At present the polytechnics devote a lower proportion of their resources to research (the staff have a heavier teaching load), they offer few well paid senior posts, the facilities provided for their students are inferior, and so on. If these disadvantages *vis-à-vis* the universities remain, the polytechnics will, quite apart from traditional academic snobbery, be nothing more than second class institutions, rather on the lines of secondary modern schools. Equally important, the role they play will be devalued with them. What is needed is a structure for higher education that ensures responsiveness to social needs without splitting the institutions into distinct strata. In considering how this might be achieved it is necessary to examine the considerable variety of functions now performed by institutions of higher education and ask which functions most need to be carried on in conjunction with each other and which require separate as opposed to joint finance.[48]

In such consideration the distinctive tradition of the polytechnics should not be forgotten.

NOTES

1. Established in 1794 it was the first institution of a kind as characteristic of the age of the dynamo as the university was of the virgin. Its ethos, positivistic, melioristic and outward-looking, made such a deep and immediate impression that eight years later we find Thomas Bigge arguing in 1802 that 'a lectureship on subjects of natural and experimental philosophy' should be established in Newcastle with a lecture room laboratory, philosophical apparatus, models of machinery, and a mineralogical collection. The Newcastle Literary and Philosophical Society, then ten years old, appointed such a man, who was to lecture for the next thirty years, six times a week, once in the morning and once in the evening for three days a week.

Robert Spence Watson, *The History of the Literary and Philosophical Society of Newcastle-upon-Tyne (1793–1896)* (London: Walter Scott Ltd, 1897), pp. 268 ff.

Seven years later a military college on polytechnic lines was established at Addiscombe to train engineers for the Indian Service. See *Memoir of the East India Company's Military Seminary*, London 1842, and the 799-page study of H. M. Vibart (*Addiscombe*, Constable & Co., 1894).

2. F. Johnson, *The London Polytechnic Movement with Special Reference to Quintin Hogg, M.A.*, London, 1929.

Ethel M. Wood, *The Polytechnic and Quintin Hogg* (Nisbet, 1904). Rev. edn 1932.

3. Kenneth Charlton, 'Polytechnic Education: An Idea in Motion', *International Review of Education*, 14 (1968), pp. 43–61.

4. For the influence of the German, American and Russian variants of the polytechnic on English universities see W. H. G. Armytage, 'Foreign Influences on English Universities: Four Case Histories', *Comparative Education Review*, Vol. 7 (1964), pp. 246–61.

5. V. T. Crouch, *A Sociological Interpretation of the Development of Technological Education in England, France and Germany*, PhD, London, 1940.

Stephen F. Cotgrove, *A Sociological Study of Further Technical Education with Special Reference to the London Polytechnics*, PhD, London, 1957.

6. E. W. Newton, *The Royal Cornwall Polytechnic Society. A Short Summary of its Work*, Falmouth, 1932. He lists Lord de Dunstanville, MP, FRS; Sir R. R. Vyvyan, MP, FRS; E. W. Wynne Pendarves, MP, FRS; John Williams, FRS; John Taylor, FRS; G. S. Borlase, FRS. Its first president was Sir Charles Lemon, FRS, and its first secretary Richard Taylor; other members were John Buller; Charles, Joshua and R. B. Fox; L. C. Daubeny; W. Gibbins; Llewellyn Newton; J. C. Trevanion; W. Williams and Ennis Vivian.

7. *The Selector*, December, No. 12, Falmouth (1826), p. 191.

8. Newton, op. cit., p. 179. He lists in 1834 R. W. Fox's Dipping Needle Reflector (adapted by the Navy) and in 1835 William Wilton's Mining Theodolite. See also J. W. Hall, *Index to the Historical Literary Scientific and Other Essays and Papers in the Annual Reports of the Royal Cornwall Polytechnic Society*, Vol. 1 from No. 1 (1833) to No. 63 (1895), Falmouth: Typescript, 1960. Vol. 2 from No. 64 (1896) to No. 124 (1957), Falmouth: Typescript, 1959.

9. In his presidential address in 1872 Charles Fox cited a speech of Charles Gore, FRS, the one-man Birmingham research institute, that discoveries were made by men who 'were constantly making careful experiments upon the properties of matter and its forces by subjecting them to new and definite conditions'. As a 'medium of intercommunication for members of the Learned Society and Science classes throughout the county', the secretary J. H. Collins, who was also lecturer and assistant secretary of the Miners Association of Cornwall and Devon, started in 1871 *The Western Chronicle of Science*.

10. *The Polytechnic Journal: A monthly Magazine of Art, Science and General Literature*, II (1839), IV (1841), pp. 243–5.

11. The society originated, according to Henry Briggs, in a meeting of coal owners to discuss the strata of their neighbourhood. 'At first' he said it was 'merely a technical society, confining its objects to one particular branch of scientific research. Afterwards it had been thought best to extend the term and objects of the society and the name Polytechnic had therefore been added to its original designation. At present any subject may be brought forward in the Paper . . . agriculture, chemistry, and every other branch of science having in turn been discussed.' *Proceedings of the Yorkshire Geological and Polytechnic Society of the West Riding*, Vol. II (1849–59), p. 370. It held meetings in Leeds, Sheffield, Halifax, Doncaster and Barnsley each of which had a 'local secretary'.

12. *The Laws and a Report of the First Two years Proceedings of the Polytechnic Society Liverpool.* Instituted 23 October 1838, Liverpool, Smith & Gawthorp, 1841. Its *Journal* was published annually and when Hele-Shaw read his paper on friction it had 168 members. One of its members, John Grantham, a consulting engineer and naval architect, built the first tramway in Copenhagen in 1863 and patented a steam tramway car. He also helped found the institution of naval architects in 1860.

13. *The Polytechnic Journal*, III (1840), p. 426.

14. See *Notes and Queries* 6, Series XII (1885), pp. 309, 477, by H.D., E. & F. N. Spon, London, 1867. Liverpool-born Henry Dircks spent his life there as an engineer and developed an interest in the history of science a subject in which he also did pioneer work.

15. J. Lawrence Pritchard, *Sir George Cayley* (London: Max Parrish, 1961), pp. 125 ff.

16. C. H. Desch, 'Robert Abbot Hadfield 1858–1940', *Obituary Notices of Fellows of the Royal Society 1939–1941*, Vol. 3, p. 647.

17. For one who lectured there in 1869, read Henry Adams, *Some Reminiscences. Seventy Five Years Work in Civil Engineering* (London: Institute of Structural Engineers, 1925).

18. Andrew Ure, *The Philosophy of Manufactures* (1835), p. 278. H. G. Bohn continued it in 1847.

19. Robert Southey, *Colloquies on the Progress of Society* (1830), i, p. 171.

20. Ure, op. cit., p. 419.

21. Charles Dupin, *Mémoires sur la Marine et les Ponts et Chausées de France et d'Angleterre* (Paris, 1818).
    Mabel Tylecote, *The Mechanics Institutes of Lancaster and Yorkshire Before 1851* (Manchester University Press, 1957), p. 153 n. 1.

22. Karl Marx, *Capital* (Everyman edition, 1939), p. 527.

23. ibid., p. 527.

24. ibid., p. 428.

25. *Hansard*, 10 June 1856, pp. 1264–9.

26. *Report of the Parliamentary Committee to the British Association for the Advancement of Science at Glasgow on the question, Whether any Measures could be adopted by the Government or Parliament that would improve the Position of Science or its Cultivators in this country.*

27. Henry Longueville Jones, 7th wrangler in 1828 who after a period in France opened a college in Manchester which failed, later becoming an HMI inspecting schools in Wales. It is significant too that C. F. Beyer of the Beyer Peacock Engineering works at Gorton, near Manchester, himself the product of Dresden Polytechnic, left a large sum of money to Manchester University in the hope that it would turn out to be the same kind of institution. *Beyer-Peacock Quarterly Review* (1927).

28. J. A. Lloyd, *Papers Relating to Proposals for Establishing Colleges of Art and Manufactures for the Better Instruction of the Labouring Classes* (W. Clowes & Son, 1851).

29. John Scott Russell, FRS, a shipbuilder who, as secretary of the Royal Society of Arts, helped organize the 1851 Exhibition, and as builder of the *Great Eastern* had good cause to publish *Systematic Technical Training for the English People*, London, 1869.

30. *The Education and Status of Civil Engineers in the United Kingdom and in Foreign Countries. Compiled from Documents supplied to the Council of the Institution of Civil Engineers 1868–70* (London: Institution of Civil Engineers, 1820).

31. John G. P. Cameron, *A Short History of the Royal Indian Engineering College, Cooper's Hill* (Cooper's Hill Society, 1960).

32. *The Polytechnic Journal and Educational Directory*, Bournemouth, Vol. 1, No. 1 (January 1890), p. 1. This rather grandiloquently by Vol. III, No. 2 (20 February 1891) was calling itself *The National Organ of Technical and Scientific Education and Progress*.

33. ibid., Vol. III, No. 5, p. 1.

34. Sidney Webb, *Special Reports on Educational Subjects*, Vol. 2, HMSO, 1898, p. 58 and pp. 74–5.

35. Sidney Webb, *London Education* (London: Longmans, 1904).

36. Bernard Shaw, *Man and Superman* (1901–3).

37. Bernard Shaw, *Everybody's Political What's What* (London: Constable & Co., 1944), p. 61.

38. J. H. Whitehouse, *A National System of Education* (Cambridge University Press, 1913), pp. 4, 65, 67.

39. S. R. Craddock, 'The Inception of the National Certificate Scheme', *The Vocational Aspect of Secondary and Further Education*, Vol. XIII (1961), pp. 46–50.

40. Kenneth Charlton, op. cit., n. 3.

41. For earlier English endorsements of Czarist polytechnical education, see W. H. G. Armytage, *The Russian Influence on English Education* (London: Routledge & Kegan Paul, 1969), pp. 35–42.

42. *A Plan for Polytechnics and Other Colleges: Higher Education in the Further Education System*, Cmnd 3006, HMSO, May 1966, p. 9, para 28 (ii).
43. ibid., p. 9, para 28 (ii).
44. ibid., p. 3, para 1.
45. e.g. in the *Universities Quarterly*. See e.g. Circular 11/66 issued by the Department of Education and Science and the Report of the Committee on Technical College Resources appointed by the National Advisory Council on Education for Industry and Commerce issued with it.
46. For the conception behind them see the White Paper on Technical Education, HMSO, 1956, Cmnd 9703.
47. *The Flow into Employment of Scientists, Engineers and Technologists* (The Swann Report), Cmnd 3760, HMSO, 1968, p. 65.
48. *Planning for Education in 1980*. Fabian Research Series 28, Fabian Society, 11 Dartmouth Street, London, February 1970, p. 21.

5

Emerging Concepts of Universities in Britain

Johanna Burgess

The word 'university' conjures up a kaleidoscopic picture: youth, books, soaring buildings, ivy-clad towers and money. Behind this image is the reality, ranging from students shot dead on their own campus, through the anonymity of some British civic universities, to centres of genuine research and teaching which aim to conserve and extend a living tradition devoted to the activities of reason and the development of the intellect. The present picture will change, just as society will change. But in which direction and to whose benefit?

The future can only arise out of the present, and therefore to speak of emerging concepts does not require some form of crystal-gazing but rather scrutiny of the present situation for indicants of future trends. It is only in so far as it is possible to have a concept of a university that emerging concepts can be considered, in that potential models can be recognized as of this *genre* only to the extent that they conform to the existing pattern. Future universities will experiment but only within certain limits; to extend too far beyond these would be to abandon their claim to be known as universities.

In terms of individual experience it is impossible to have a single concept of a university, as its meaning is interpreted differently by teacher, student, researcher, administrator, careerist and scene-chaser each of whom regards the university as instrumental to his own needs and desires. However, it does seem possible to pose such questions as, 'What is a university?' or 'What are its defining characteristics?' Such an analysis can be begun by considering universities and related institutions along the primary dimensions of characteristic activities and quality of life, and the secondary ones of population, products, and rationale. Thus an attempt will be made to answer the questions, 'Who are there?', 'What do they do?', 'How do they do it?', 'What is the result of this activity?', 'Why do they pursue these activities?'.

The Acquisition of Knowledge

It is axiomatic to this argument that at present the defining activities of the university are the acquisition, transmission, and advancement of academic knowledge. However, not all university members will be engaged on the same task. Universities traditionally cover a wide range of topics but there is, at centre, a notion that these should be 'academic', which can result in an attempt to dress up essentially non-academic subjects in order to get them included in degree courses.

What, then, is the distinction between the academic and the non-academic? No doubt one could attempt to include tennis or institute a BA (Hons Cookery), but what would appear to rule out activities of this kind is that they do not, in themselves, represent a *general* way of codifying experience. Academic disciplines take over where particular activities leave off: they are, essentially, *meta* activities. The theoretical may need a practical illustration but if an activity virtually explains itself then it cannot, by itself, be a subject for academic study, therefore neither tennis nor cooking, alone, can qualify. Although one could study the philosophical, psychological, sociological or anthropological aspects of activities such as tennis, this would be to use tennis as a particular illustration within these academic disciplines not to justify the study of tennis in itself.

This confusion between the subject studied and this discipline used in its study has caused problems in university curriculum planning. Virtually any topic *can* be studied either if it requires a disciplined analysis for its elucidation, or if it forms a component in the learning of a discipline. If it requires no such analysis then it should be taught in a place concerned with training people to pursue particular activities – such as a ski school or typing class. For example one could learn the dynamics of riding a bike but there is no need to do so in order to ride successfully and therefore bike-riding would not be included, in its own right, in a university curriculum, but could form a component in a course in dynamics.

If, then, academic disciplines represent general ways of knowing, universities are concerned with both their acquisition and transmission. Teaching is an essential component. The absence of teaching would render it impossible to distinguish between a university and a research institute. But universities are also concerned with the advancement of knowledge – the personal or team search for that which is new. Without a commitment to this and time for faculty to pursue such an activity, universities would become middle-level institutions geared to gathering the knowledge of others. This seems self-defeating in that it would appear difficult to judge what another has done unless one is also a practitioner.

These activities are not restricted as in a college of education or academy of music, to one field or form of knowledge, although there is no need, nor is it necessarily desirable, for every university to include all subjects. Indeed, the expense of equipment and the desire of specialists to be with others of their own kind results in specific universities being noted for certain subjects. But it is necessary that they include an extensive range of studies, because cross-fertilization at all levels – but especially at the undergraduate – is essential, as only by seeing how his major subject differs from others will the student really grasp what its characteristics are. He will thus realize that his chosen method of approach is only one of many, and will be more sensitive to the type of question or problem with which he is competent to deal as contrasted with those which properly belong to another discipline.

To what extent can vocational training be considered to be a characteristic activity of a univeristy? If this is interpreted as meaning training a student for a particular job the consequent narrowing of the student's area of learning would make it inadmissible. However, if the university is concerned, even to a limited extent, with the quality of life of a community within which work forms a major component, it would follow that the university can be committed to vocational aspects without assuming an entirely instrumental view of learning.

The Life Style of a University

It is the case that universities include cultural and athletic activities in which students and faculty participate, but these are not characteristic in the same way as are intellectual ones, rather they are part of the life style which also defines a university. This cultural consciousness is as essential as the intellectual element and is exemplified in two distinct ways: firstly in the range and nature of the extra-curricula activities and secondly in the interpersonal relationship pattern existing in universities.

If the members of the university are engaged on a common pursuit it follows that personal relationships are not something external to the concept of a university but part of its core. If the common enemy is ignorance then all are engaged on a task of a similar kind, although concerned with different facets. To this extent competition is unnecessary as there is no shortage of problems. The rewards are to be gained because a particular problem is solved not because a particular person has solved it. These considerations lead to the conclusion that two of the most characteristic features of the life of a university community could be expected to be firstly, its compassion and, secondly, its honesty: compassion is appropriately expressed towards others engaged on a seemingly insuperable task, and honesty is required so that this undertaking may be efficiently discharged. The more any subject is understood the more evident become the unknown realms and the more complex even apparently simple judgements. As a result of this extension of consciousness relationships with others should take on a new quality, in that the complexity of every person becomes clear and crude stereotyping is impossible. To this extent intellectual development could be thought to affect interpersonal evaluations.

In the same way truth is what is sought in the sense that for any particular problem what is desired is to arrive at an answer which is the most accurate possible in the circumstances and uncontaminated by extraneous political or fashionable considerations. Therefore deception, bluff, and academic lifemanship can be seen to be, in the long run, self-defeating as they are inappropriate techniques. The aim in a university is to arrive at an answer which will stand for a time and to direct others towards the advancement of such knowledge: if an individual's aim has been merely to publish a book quickly or gain a promotion by bluff the result will be professional failure not because the aim was not accurate but because the nature of the target was misunderstood. It is as if a tennis player instead of attempting to hit the ball into a particular part of the court were to club his opponent with his racquet. Such a player would find it difficult to see where he had failed and would become increasingly alienated as the spectators and umpire insisted that he had not won.

It would seem that much of the present-day unrest in universities is due to a failure to understand the essentially non-competitive, non-personal nature of a university's characteristic activities. Those who wish to score personal triumphs cannot function for any length of time within a university as the rewards they seek are not available within that particular community. To solve an apparently intractable problem may lead to personal fame, but the motivation of an integrated academic is to solve the problem not to gain the fame. Excellence is its own reward since to recognize x as excellent requires a prior internalization of the criteria by means of which x is judged to exemplify excellence of its kind. This process of internalization will result in a positive attitude to the excellent so that the pursuit of academic excellence becomes intrinsically rewarding rather than instrumental to an external reward.

Thus the primary dimensions of 'characteristic activities' and 'quality of life' show the university to be concerned with academic knowledge which gives rise to a life incorporating compassion and honesty. To what extent, then, do the secondary dimensions refine this analysis?

The Characteristic Products of Universities

Our present industrial age leads to an emphasis on production and therefore it is pertinent to ask what the characteristic products of a university are, or what is characteristic of its products. A university produces people who have undergone a particular experience the result of which is the development of a critical understanding and a distinctive point of view; that is, an 'open' point of view leading to an awareness of alternatives and an acceptance of the self as an autonomous individual. Such people are characterized by a consciousness which has incorporated a critic within it so that they ask, 'Is this right?', 'Is this the best answer?', 'Is this worthwhile?'

Although they will only be experts in one or perhaps a few, related, disciplines, the method of approach, as sketched above, is what is characteristic, not the particular discipline in which it is exemplified. It is possible that many students will gain degrees who have not undergone such an experience but who have merely been adept at interpreting the cues of their tutors so that they repeat, with minor modifications, what they have been told, without ever making this knowledge part of themselves. They are the failures and their failure is due to a combination of personal inadequacy, inefficient teaching and institutional malfunctioning.

If the above qualities are characteristic of the university the final question concerns their rationale. They have been represented from the time of Newman as exemplifying the disinterested pursuit of knowledge; that is knowledge is sought 'for its own sake', not primarily for its instrumental value to the members of the academic community nor to the larger society. Thus they have been essentially theoretical and have formed one component in the complex network of institutions and organizations which forms the infrastructure of society. But their prestige and the pressure of numbers wishing to attend them have resulted in modifications some of which may be creative whereas others are essentially destructive of this traditional view. The tensions resulting from the expansion of higher education have given rise to many alternative models for universities, but whether they represent some form of organic growth or are an alteration *in kind* is the question to which we now turn.

New Concepts and Models

Although it seems that there could be a multiplicity of emerging forms which the universities could adopt, such forms can, in fact, be divided into actual and potential new concepts. The former are represented by the 'new universities'; the latter by two disparate developments. Firstly, we have five models which see the university as becoming more fully *integrated* with society, i.e. those forming units of the binary system, the 'business' university, the 'comprehensive' university, the 'open' university, and the 'continuing' university. Secondly, there are three concepts in which the universities are seen as *alienated* from society, i.e. the 'monastic', the 'independent' and the 'free' university. These alienated models imply that universities can represent an historical alternative to present-day society and promulgate a counter culture.

Integrated Institutions

(a) New Universities

The 'new universities' form a distinctive group which, although not radically different, challenge the established tradition with some interesting innovations. Here we must distinguish between the eight absolutely new institutions of which Keele was the first, the upgrading of former technical colleges such as the Heriot-Watt in Edinburgh and the establishment of the new University of Dundee which before had formed part of the University of St Andrews. Only the eight entirely new institutions can really represent 'emerging concepts', the others merely mark a further point in their development as part of the old system.

These new universities were able to start from scratch and work out both their internal pattern and external relationships with society unencumbered by past decisions and developments. Thus each forms a discrete concept which, although forming part of the present system, indicates dimensions along which change can be envisaged. For example, the University of Sussex is noted for its commitment to interdisciplinary units, resulting from a refusal to contain subject 'departments', although subject 'groups' operate within the school system. Lord (then Sir John) Fulton (1964) summarizes the thinking behind this arrangement:

> A new institution must make its own contribution in its own way if it is not to be a merely sterile replica. It was also accepted by all that it was the duty of a university to ensure that its studies involved exacting, disciplined work. Whatever varieties of courses might be introduced, they must all have in them disciplined study in depth. There was acceptance too of the view that over the next half-century change would be even more rapid than in the past fifty years; so that flexibility of mind would be a necessary condition of a fully effective intellectual contribution by the graduates-to-be. It was accepted that such flexibility would be encouraged and sustained if a main discipline studied in depth were accompanied by cognate, 'minor', 'contextual' subjects which would naturally illuminate and be illuminated by the 'major' subject and by one another. It was agreed also that there would be great educational benefit if subjects were held together (as they were in Oxford's Classical Greats) by virtue of being aspects of a single civilization. These tests were applied to all the proposals for degree courses. From the discussions there emerged projects for Schools of European Studies, English (and American) Studies, Social Studies, African and Asian Studies, Educational Studies; on the Science side Schools of Physical Science, Biological Studies, Applied Science and Engineering Science.

(b) The Business University

However, these 'actual' concepts are less relevant than the potential ones mentioned above. Of the 'integrated' group, the one that represents the most radical challenge to the traditional university is the 'business' university and already its characteristic values and methods are appearing in existing institutions. Business is primarily concerned with the transfer of commodities in such a way that the transaction is profitable for one or both parties. The idea of applying these notions to universities is apparently reasonable. Universities have something to offer – their expertise, their plant and their trained manpower; in return they need more money, more equipment and opportunities for expansion. Particularly in the sciences there is competition for scarce resources and increasingly the values of industry in terms of productivity, and cost-effectiveness become accepted and their methods incorporated. E. P. Thompson (1970) notes, perhaps exaggeratedly, the glamorization of universities:

> . . . this glamour of cash and success, this growing style of highly fee'd lecture tours to the United States, of assent to the glamour of Mediterranean conferences, television fees and industrial consultancies – is one way in which close relations with 'industry' can find expression within a university's walls.

As the universities become more like industrial plants so industry itself becomes more willing to work with them and large firms give research grants to particular academics to pursue research thought to be mutually beneficial. This results in a change in personal relationships within the universities: colleagues become competitors and productivity becomes the unit of assessment. An academic is valued if he can attract money and if he publishes regularly. There is also a prestige hierarchy relative to conferences attended or invitations to give papers received. The ordering is comparatively simple: exclusive or even distant institutions rank higher than civic or local ones, but there can be nice points as to whether speaking at Cambridge, England, is superior or inferior to speaking at Cambridge, Mass.

In such a situation the position of the students becomes unenviable since their teachers' relationships with them are viewed in terms of prestige and productivity. Research students are judged useful if they are part of a research grant package and unique, or experimental, undergraduate courses can be popular – one might get a book out of them. But once teaching becomes instrumental to the teacher's career its nature changes so that the students, recognizing that they are becoming components on a conveyer belt, naturally, if mistakenly, take industrial action and one is faced with the absurdity of student strikes.

This absurdity highlights the falsity of the whole situation. Universities cannot be totally equated with businesses, not because there is anything reprehensible about business, but because universities are not wholly profitable in the same sense, although certain departments may be. Take the (hopefully exaggerated) case of a high prestige unit with a noted professor who attracts thousands of pounds in research grants, who publishes regularly, and whose team is characterized by ceaseless activity at home interspersed with personal globe-trotting. In this situation, who profits? What is the nature of the profit? It would seem that there will only be profits where such a professor is concerned with research of obvious social utility or commercial benefit. If all this activity resulted in a cure for rheumatism or bronchitis, and the saving of working days lost in this way, or in rocket-design or man-made metals, it would be socially and industrially profitable. But, by definition, the disinterested pursuit of knowledge does not have any practical value. Is, then, the 'business' university to include only those who are socially or commercially profitable? This would be a valid conclusion for society to reach but such, no doubt valuable and necessary institutions, would not be universities as we know them as they would be deficient in many of the characteristics which have been said to be axiomatic.

This is not a question of value judgements. Although militant students may maintain that universities represent the values of the capitalist system and reject them on doctrinaire grounds, what is argued here is that there is no reason why one should not have research institutions run on business lines, pursuing profitable and socially useful research. However, such institutions would be so far removed from present-day concepts of universities that to call them by the same name couldbe misleading. Nevertheless, the decision whether to adopt this model and call it a 'university' is political not philosophical.

(c) The Binary System

The binary concept sees higher education as divided between the universities and other institutions, some of whose courses lead to a degree, although they cannot, themselves, award degrees. It is hoped that by offering degree work these institutions will gain the same prestige as traditionally attaches itself to universities. This notion seems to be based on a fundamental misunderstanding of the nature of a degree. A degree is only valuable because it is meant to indicate that the holder has undergone a certain type of experience arising from taking part in the activities mentioned above and partaking of the quality of life described. The degree-holder has been, in R. S. Peters' (1966) phrase, 'initiated into a way of life'. If non-university institutions do make possible this particular type of experience how can they be said to differ from universities? If they do not, what is the justification for their degrees? Universities differ markedly amongst themselves except in their fundamental approach to intellectual excellence and the pursuit of reason. If the non-university institutions have this approach then they should be called universities, if not why pretend that they are? It may be the case that in the future it would be politically expedient for all forms of higher education to terminate with the award of a degree as this would appear less elitist. There seems no reason for objecting to this, in that just as A-level needlework would be seen to differ from A-level chemistry so BSc (Hons Athletics) would differ from a BSc (Hons Physics) as one represents the completion of an academic study, as defined above, while the other does not.

(d) The 'Comprehensive' University

Once one has made the above concession it seems that the 'comprehensive' university must inevitably follow. By this is meant that all post-school education – up to first degree level – should be in one institution.

Clearly such institutions would include the present universities but would not be identical with them. An argument often used against comprehensive universities, or indeed enlarged universities, is that they would result in a lowering of standards. F. R. Leavis (1970) writes '. . . the more you extend higher education – and especially in an age of technological aids and open universities . . . the more insidious becomes the menace to standards and the more potent and unashamed the animus against them.' This seems to be based on a misunderstanding of the nature of a 'standard'. Standards are different in the sciences and non-sciences, but the recognition of excellence in both relies on the existence of criteria which define the nature of the disciplines concerned, and in terms of which particular instances of disciplinary study can be judged as satisfactory or not. To be able to recognize a piece of work as of a certain kind, e.g. scientific, historical or musical, is to be able to point to certain defining characteristics. Thus one is already in possession of the knowledge which would enable one to assess this particular piece of work as an excellent or poor specimen of its class. Therefore, standards cannot decline: to have recognized the subject as of a certain kind and to have initiated the enquiry is to have already accepted the standard inherent within it. However it would seem that if the universities attempt to provide something for everyone it would be difficult to get started on the type of disinterested enquiry required.

Sir Sydney Caine (1969) argues persuasively that, although the universities should not become comprehensive, the whole shape of educational provision should change so that we would get the benefits of both the extension of post-school education and the excellence characteristic of universities:

> If therefore we were now starting from scratch and designing an educational structure related to the present range of knowledge and the present scale of available resources the best structure might well be seen to be secondary schools ending normally with one year of Sixth Form work, i.e., at about age 17; colleges offering two and three year courses which would take over the top layer of current Sixth Form work but extend into what is now done in the first year or two of undergraduate work; and universities which would admit students at about the level normally now attained at the commencement of the final undergraduate year and take them up to and beyond the level now aimed at in the 'taught' master's degrees. This would largely be a systematisation of the situation which effectively prevails in the U.S.A., where children leave the High Schools with a standard of attainment probably a year behind that of good

English secondary schools, where the Junior Colleges or Liberal Arts Colleges and many indeed of the lesser-known universities perform the function envisaged for the second stage without aspiring to post-graduate and research activity, and where that activity is in the main concentrated in a minority of universities, including of course those with international reputations, which normally have highly organised separate Graduate Schools and in some cases undertake only graduate activity. Many of the colleges at the second level maintain, at their appropriate level, a very high standard.

He suggests that:

'Liberal Arts Colleges' overlapping both the most advanced work of secondary schools and the earlier years of undergraduate work as now conceived at the universities could emerge from the growth of Sixth Form Colleges and County Colleges and from the development of work in the humanities and pure science at Colleges of Technology. Bases already exist for such developments and the more deliberate creation of 'Liberal Arts Colleges' could follow experiments in such existing institutions. Secondly existing university institutions might initiate new kinds of degrees designed deliberately for the age-group 20 to 23 rather than the age-group 18 to 21.

This notion of extending higher education would appeal to a society which values individual development and is prepared to spend considerable resources on middle level work, whereas the 'business' university is attractive as a conserver of resources which could then be channelled to exactly where they are most needed. A particular society must decide whether it wishes to spend its money allowing all eighteen-year-olds to have some acquaintance with science and the arts or to allow a few twenty-three-year-olds to pursue research of such a nature that its profits would be to the material benefit of the whole nation. One could say that if all are educated to a higher level then there is the chance of fostering more intellectual giants. Alternatively, it could be that to concentrate on the few would be to give the many even greater benefits than they could have gained for themselves. Here, again, is a decision for the politicians.

(e) *The 'Open' University*

The 'continuing' and the 'open' university are the least radical of all the emerging concepts which still see the university as forming part of society. They aim to make a university experience more widely available to people at different stages of their lives. The argument for the 'continuing' university is that the increasing rate at which knowledge is growing means that people will need to return to the university at intervals throughout their lives as the knowledge they have becomes obsolete. This notion is obviously valid but it would seem that if what is required is an updating of information within a particular field it might well be done better in a specialist institution. One assumes that the open orientation characteristic of a university, will not necessarily be what is lacking, although it is true that with age, patterns of thought become set so that middle-aged conservatism is nothing more than unchanged youthful radicalism. However, we can distinguish between intellectual reorientation and a professional refresher course, although the two can go together as in T. S. Kuhn's paradigmatic change where a new piece of information means that one sees with a different view. However, in-service courses can often be restricted to new techniques and technical advances and need not, necessarily, take place within a university. Linked to the continuing concept is the notion of a vast expansion of extra-mural departments so that the universities become more clearly the cultural centre of the local community.

The Open University called explicitly by that name aims, by the use of TV, radio, and local tutorial groups to greatly extend the opportunity of taking a degree, to 25,000 students in the first instance. The suggested patterns of its foundation courses would indicate that it should be regarded as a 'new university' rather than an inflated version of a traditional one. However, the revolutionary nature of the Open University may be in its effect on the existing universities rather than as an entirely new concept. As has been shown, universities differ markedly amongst themselves, but the students have had to accept their present experience as characteristic of a university as they have had nothing with which to compare it. At least the lectures of the Open University will provide a standard against which students can measure their own teachers. It would also seem reasonable for other universities to take the Open University courses into account when planning their own curricula.

A vital question is how far the experience of a student at the Open University will be comparable with that of a full-time student in a more conventional institution. There is no doubt that it will be different, but may not differ any more than the experience of students attending the local redbrick differs from that of those at Oxbridge or a new university. What typifies all universities are the characteristics of disinterest, excellence and compassion sketched above. If these are developed by the Open University it will represent a unique conception of potential 'mass' higher education based on a new medium and obtainable within the home.

Alienated Institutions

(a) The Monastic Concept

In contrast to the above 'integrated' patterns are the group of concepts relative to an 'alienated' conception of the university. Although often associated with contemporary protest movements and the writings of Marcuse, such a notion has also been implicit in the 'monastic' concept, which saw universities as apart from, and critical of, contemporary society. This first concept regards universities as conservers of a tradition, as Christianity was conserved in the monasteries during the dark ages. Such a concept owes much to F. R. Leavis's indefatigable championship of universities as centres of consciousness for the community, where our cultural heritage could be maintained by a continuity of profoundly creative human life. To a considerable degree such views are not so much an emerging concept as a statement of what is already thought to be a defining characteristic. Nevertheless, they do differ in that they assume a non-initiated community and are more directly normative and prescriptive. The pursuit of perfection has always been a necessary condition for academic endeavour, but this desire to make it prevail represents a stronger emphasis on the second half of Arnold's recommendation. This monastic concept is totally unlike the business university, discussed above, although it does have some contact with society as it has the missionary aim of improving taste. Its relations with society will necessarily be complex as a society which welcomes such a critical creative centre within it is unlikely to require it. In other words, the more likely the monastic university is to exist, the less likely is its existence able to be justified.

(b) *The Independent University*

The 'independent' university seeks to be free from governmental control over finance to enable it to pursue an independent policy outside the national system of education, but it does not reject society as such. Students at this university would pay relatively heavy fees and it aims to be recognized as a centre of academic excellence. Considerable confusion can be generated here as its opponents fasten on to the notion of fees and represent it as a super Public school or an elitist institution for the sons of the rich. The fact that local authorities may not give grants to this institution makes it possible that this would be the result, but there is not, necessarily, any reason why this should be the case as the expressed aim of freedom from governmental interference implies no more than a desire to further the disinterested pursuit of knowledge and the activities of reason. It might be undesirable if the growth of private universities were to perpetuate the educational divisions characteristic of our school system, in so far as it can be shown that the existence of privileged institutions necessarily depresses the performance of others. However, the existence of State censorship, in some countries, of findings which are politically or ideologically deviant would suggest that the less governmental pressure a university is subjected to the better. Edward H. Levi, President of the University of Chicago, crystallizes this argument for freedom when he wrote in 1969:

The universities see themselves viewed as necessities, if not for the education of all youth, then at least as channels and screens through which all must pass. They hear themselves described as 'the central institution of the next hundred years' because of their role 'as the source of innovation and knowledge'. It is doubtful if institutions so regarded will be able to retain their freedom. The current controversy over the governance of universities is probably only a pale image, if not already the doorway, for what is likely to come. If the universities are to become a kind of mirror image of the political order, then we will have to develop new institutions weak enough to be free, but in which ideas can be developed which are strong enough to change the world.

(c) *The Free University*

A particularly powerful and radical contemporary notion is that of the 'free' university; not in the sense of freedom from pressure, but of freedom arising from a refusal to submit to the dictates of society or conventional thinking. This is to see their role as directed towards the overthrow of contemporary society. They are not content merely to be critical but wish to instigate direct political action.

H. Marcuse (1964) argues that today the quality of life is such that protest is stifled by the omnipresent comfort of life and the persuasive powers of the language we use, which make it impossible to analyse our concepts with any degree of objectivity:

> No matter how obvious the irrational character of the whole may manifest itself and, with it, the necessity of change, insight into necessity has never sufficed for seizing the possible alternatives. Confronted with the omnipresent efficiency of the given system of life, its alternatives have always appeared utopian. And insight into necessity, the consciousness of the evil state, will not suffice even at the stage where the accomplishments of science and the level of productivity have eliminated the utopian features of the alternatives – where the established reality rather than its opposite is utopian.

The only reply to this is to refuse to play the game, to reject the corruption of consciousness which spells security:

> The totalitarian tendencies of the one-dimensional society render the traditional ways and means of protest ineffective – perhaps even dangerous because they preserve the illusion of popular sovereignty. This illusion contains some truth: 'the people', previously the ferment of social change, have 'moved up' to become the ferment of social cohesion. Here rather than in the redistribution of wealth and equalization of classes is the new stratification characteristic of advanced industrial society.

In his 1969 *Essay on Liberation* Marcuse looks to the students to provide this protest. The acquisition, transmission and advancement of knowledge are to give way to direct social action aimed at changing the life style of every member of the society. A paradoxical note is struck when one remembers that these students were nurtured in the conventional institutions they now reject – have they really achieved such a refined sensibility despite their parents, homes, schools and society? To assent to this would be to deny a considerable body of evidence relative to environmental effects on intelligence and personality, leaving one with a choice between a genetic hypothesis or one based on some form of revelation.

In addition to direct political action the university is urged to provide the basis for an academic revolution against the positivist, rational, approach which at present typifies many forms of academic enquiry. Such a concept positively advocates a 'feast of unreason' so that new forms of experience are sought and the sovereign power of reason is challenged, leading to an anti-intellectualism and the rejection of traditional disciplines. Marcuse argues for such a view as follows:

> The advancing one-dimensional society alters the relation between the rational and the irrational. Contrasted with the fantastic and insane aspects of its rationality, the realm of the irrational becomes the home of the really rational – of the ideas which may promote 'the art of life'. If the established society manages all normal communication, validating or invalidating it in accordance with social requirements, then the values alien to these requirements may perhaps have no other medium of communication than the abnormal one of fiction. The aesthetic dimension still retains a freedom of expression which enables the writer and artist to call men and things by their name – to name the otherwise unnameable.

If universities are concerned with knowledge for its own sake it seems axiomatic that all ways should be explored and none ignored because they are not in accordance with current academic fashion. It is sometimes necessary to willingly suspend one's disbelief, as Freud did in the fantasies of his patients, in order to advance present knowledge. Thus esoteric areas from extra-sensory perception, through notions of the validity of schizophrenic experience, to the knowledge and awareness arrived at through drugs would all appear to be valid areas for enquiry. Yet it is difficult to see how one could be said to know anything at all independent of reason. To know something means to view it under a certain aspect, to recognize it as being of a certain kind: this viewing, or recognition, requires the activity of reason.

Therefore a refusal to be confined within a closed intellectual system is essential for academic enquiry, but any such enquiry can only be understood within a rational framework which is a precondition for their being any enquiry at all.

The 'alienated' university would seem to lead to an isolated university viewed with hostility or indifference by a society which, as a whole, would be excluded. The 'integrated' university would not necessarily result in an institution wholly identified with the values of society unless, by mass involvement in education, the two drew together.

There is no reason to believe that evolution, in any of its manifestations, will come to a stop in the 1970s. Therefore the reciprocal influences affecting universities and society will result in changes, possibly in the directions indicated above, but more probably in unexpected ways as practical activity seems to move at a tangent to theoretical predictions. However, there are some aspects which cannot change without the nature of universities being modified to such an extent that they could no longer be considered as phenomena of the same kind. It has been argued that if it is axiomatic that the function of universities is the acquisition, transmission and advancement of academic knowledge, and if their concern is disinterested, then they will continue to be characterized by a quality of life which, integrally, includes tolerance, honesty, and compassion.

BIBLIOGRAPHY

M. Arnold, *Culture and Anarchy*, J. D. Wilson (ed.) (Cambridge, 1932).

Sydney Caine, *British Universities: Purpose and Prospects* (London: The Bodley Head, 1969).

J. Fulton, *New Universities in Perspective*, in D. Daiches (ed.), *The Idea of a New University* (London: Deutsch, 1964).

T. S. Kuhn, *The Structure of Scientific Revolutions. International Encyclopedia of Unified Science*. Vol. 11 No. 2 (Chicago: University of Chicago Press, 1962).

F. R. Leavis, ' "Literarism" versus "Scientism". The misconception and the menace', *The Times Literary Supplement*, Thursday, 23rd April 1970, No. 3,556.

Edward H. Levi, *Point of View* (Chicago: University of Chicago, 1969).

H. Marcuse, *One Dimensional Man* (Boston: 1964). Quotations from Sphere Books edn. London, 1969.

H. Marcuse, *An Essay on Liberation* (Boston: 1969).

J. H. Newman, *The Idea of a University* (London: Longmans, 1910).

R. S. Peters, *Ethics and Education* (London: George Allen and Unwin Ltd., 1966).

E. P. Thompson (ed.), *Warwick University Ltd.* (England: Penguin Books Ltd., 1970).

6

The Utilitarian University

Robert Cowen

The problem to which this chapter addresses itself generally is the nature of the linkages between universities and their host societies in England, France, the USA and the USSR. In particular it will concern itself with the analysis of one hypothesized factor in this linkage: nationally based theories of knowledge and models of man as constraining devices or as indices of constraints on universities. What happens, or might happen, if different national university systems are confronted with the demand that the education they provide should be more utilitarian; utilitarian in the sense that university education should contribute directly, intentionally and immediately to the pressing economic and social purposes of society?[1]

The analysis proceeds through a number of stages: firstly, it is suggested that education systems reflect or embody models of man and theories of what knowledge is of most worth; secondly, the methodological possibilities for outlining these models and theories are briefly examined; thirdly, a number of deductions are made, from certain nationally-based models and theories, about likely university responses to utilitarian demands; and fourthly, differing national institutional adaptations are examined.

Models of Man and Priorities in Knowledge

As people lead colts up to alarming noises to see whether they are timid, so these young men must be brought into terrifying situations and then into scenes of pleasure, which will put them to severer proof than gold tried in the furnace. If we find one bearing himself well in all these trials and resisting every enchantment, a true guardian of himself, preserving always that perfect rhythm and harmony of being which he has acquired from his training in music and poetry, such a one will be of the greatest service to the commonwealth as well as to himself . . . we shall set him as a Ruler to watch over the commonwealth . . .[2]

Thus Plato would select his Rulers. The other institutional arrangements – lack of private property, of tangible gold and silver, the systematic education designed to build upon hereditary gifts – combine to produce both philosophers and kings. The philosopher is worthy of being a king because his selection and training have made him passionate for knowledge, truthful, temperate, free from the love of money, meanness, pretentiousness and cowardice, and fairminded, gentle, sociable, quick to learn and remember, as well as magnanimous and gracious.[3] The guardians of Plato's utopian republic are also possessed of (true) knowledge, knowledge of Forms,[4] approachable for selected persons through mathematics and the Dialectic.[5] So what, among other things, Plato offers in the *Republic* is a model of the ideal, just man, a theory of how he is to gain knowledge, of what sort this knowledge is to be, and a suggestion about how such a man should be used by society after his training. The four ingredients are all stated at length, and are unusually tightly combined. This is because they are, in Plato's view, logically related and seen as part of a single theoretical scheme.

Less prescriptively, Max Weber has considered the education of the Chinese literati.[6] Concerned centrally though he was with the nature of authority and the relationship of the literati to political power, he also delineated a model of man towards which the education of the literati was biased. Weber's analysis, in terms of the typologies of education[7] he posited, placed the literati in the 'cultivated' rather than the 'expert' category. The cultivation was brought about by a '. . . highly exclusive and bookish literary education'.[8] The examinations through which the progress of the literati were marked '. . . tested whether or not the candidate's mind was thoroughly steeped in literature and whether or not he possessed the *ways of thought*[9] suitable to a cultured man and resulting from cultivation in literature'.[10]

The 'ways of thought' were designed to enable the literati to attain the ultimate end of education, order, beauty and harmony within the self, a release of '. . . the *yang* substance in the soul of man'.[11] Such a man would possess charisma (not expertise), an index of which was his ability to write in the correct forms, and to converse suitably, using puns, euphemisms and classical allusions.[12] It was this cultivated gentleman-mandarin who was the product of the education and examination system and who 'in the eyes of the Chinese masses . . . was a proved holder of magical qualities'.[13] Here again, as with Plato, a model of man and a theory of what knowledge is most worth possessing are closely interlocked. One difference is that, whereas Plato's suggestions were visionary and prescriptive, Weber's were a result of an analysis of an historical and actual situation, and a working educational system.

Similarly, within the literature of comparative education, it has been suggested that different national systems of education may implicitly operate towards differing conceptions of the ideal man, and how he should be trained. Joseph A. Lauwerys has argued that '. . . the approach to general education differs from country to country because those who guide the schools and those who teach in them make proposals which are, more or less unconsciously, affected by the history of thought and by the philosophy current in their own cultural environment'.[14] Drawing out the consequences of this idea, he goes on to suggest that 'traditional concepts of general education' show variation in England, France, Germany, the USA and the USSR. Lauwerys' detailed and sensitive argument is too long to be summarized properly here,[15] but as examples consider the general lines of his analysis for England, France and the USA. For England, Lauwerys argues that Arnold's dictum that the school should provide 'first religious and moral principle; secondly, gentlemanly conduct; thirdly, intellectual ability' is still, though modified, not without force. The main mechanism by which this training was and is to be achieved is specialization, 'some one principal branch of study'. In France, truth must be pursued through reason; the critical mind, perceiving truth through rigorous rationality, also perceives the good. The traditional means to this end was training in mathematics, Latin and French. In America, knowledge useful for production and for social living, approachable through the processes of problem solving, defines the core of general education.

In the suggestions and analyses of Plato, Weber and Lauwerys, both a number of common themes and a number of differences are discernible. All proffer conceptions of the ideal man; interestingly, all link the concept of the ideal man to a moral theory of the nature of truth and goodness; and all underpin their outlines of the ideal man with a theory of what knowledge is of most worth and how it is to be gained. There are differences, too, between the approaches. Plato provides a single theoretical scheme; Weber and Lauwerys analyse actual historical situations. Weber's analysis is a case study; Lauwerys' approach is explicitly comparative.

Nevertheless what may perhaps be reasonably concluded from the preceding review is that education systems in intention and in practice may reflect both a model of man and preferences for certain sorts of knowledge. In certain cases this may be because a writer has been taken explicitly as a theoretical base for an education system,[16] or because a school of philosophy has summarized either coincidentally or with causal effect many significant features of a nation's history.[17]

The Utility and Application of Models of Man and Knowledge

One problem in comparative education generally is to establish useful indices – specifically here models of man and theories of priority in knowledge; a second problem is how to operate with them.

Clearly it would be possible for certain purposes to take Plato's schemata or Weber's typology of the expert and cultivated man and use one or both of them as a *tertium comparationis* against various education systems. The conclusions would then stand as hypotheses about the gap, firstly, between the model chosen and different national realities, and, secondly, between the different national realities. These realities would have been measured along the axes suggested by the model, the model deciding what were relevant data. For the particular purposes in hand it is held that neither Plato's nor Weber's model is sufficiently sensitive to illuminate national differences in adequate detail.

The methods used for selecting relevant data in the philosophic models devised by Lauwerys are indicated elsewhere[18] than in the article quoted. Brian Holmes has improved on these methodological suggestions in his succinct discussion of 'rational constructs'.[19] Concerned to measure, in a value-neutral way, theories of the individual, society and knowledge as normative patterns which '. . . give coherence to the multiplicity of beliefs held by members of any society',[20] Holmes suggests selecting representative thinkers who have provided 'regulating theories',[21] and tracing through the divergencies and similarities between them. It would not, perhaps, do violence to Holmes' general methodological position[22] to suggest that the selection of representative thinkers might vary with the 'problem'[23] being investigated.

The issue under investigation here is to what extent national university systems might differ in the degree or kind of response which they make to general societal demands for an increased contribution to utilitarian education. To explore these reactions it is proposed to utilize part of the methodological suggestions of Holmes and Lauwerys. Four thinkers will be taken, rather arbitrarily, as potentially providing regulatory theories for the four national systems in question. Their views on what knowledge is most worth possessing and their implicit or explicit models of man will be briefly summarized. From these summaries will be deduced the logical reactions of a university system purportedly based on their theories. These deductions will thus provide a set of hypothesized 'predictions'.[24] These predictions will then be assessed in contrast with relevant institutional arrangements in the university (and higher education) sectors of the four countries.

Thus what is being suggested is not that the four thinkers chosen are the only possible ones.[25] Nor is it being suggested that they accurately reflect or produce a determinist set of events. The four thinkers are being used as methodological yardsticks; their usefulness, not their 'truth', is the issue. To the extent that the models provide a set of 'predictions' which are not refuted in major features by an examination of the various national institutional patterns, they may point to interesting correlations and/or act as shorthand summaries of relations between universities and their host societies; to that extent they may suggest future and likely patterns of university response to utilitarian demands.

Locke, Descartes, Marx, Dewey and National Institutional Patterns[26]

The model of man outlined by Locke in 'Some Thoughts concerning Education'[27] displays two major characteristics. It is class-specific and it prizes moral, non-cognitive qualities highly. The education which is of major concern to Locke in his 'Thoughts' is that of the gentleman: '. . . that most to be taken Care of, is the Gentleman's calling. For if those of that Rank are by their education once set right, they will quickly bring all the rest into Order.'[28] The ends to be attained in the gentleman's education are moral and social qualities primarily: 'That which every Gentleman . . . desires for his Son . . . is contain'd (I suppose) in these four Things, *Virtue, Wisdom, Breeding* and *Learning*.'[29] Virtue is a mixture of belief in God, good nature and truthfulness, whilst wisdom and good breeding are essentially social virtues ensuring that the gentleman may maintain his social and economic position with skilful ease. Learning is not merely listed last, it is held in least esteem: 'Reading, and Writing and *Learning*, I allow to be necessary, but yet not the chief Business. I imagine you would think him a very foolish Fellow, that should not value a Vertuous, or a Wise Man, infinitely before a great Scholar.'[30]

The qualities which Locke prizes are cultivable in the tutor-tutee relationship – i.e. a properly structured environment – which enables correct habits to be developed. 'Company', the exposure to corrupting servants or peers, needs careful control: 'Having named *Company*, I am almost ready to throw away my Pen. . . .'[31]

The picture which Locke provides of the gentleman's education in his 'Thoughts' is modified to some extent by his essay 'Conduct of the Understanding', which stresses to a greater degree the development of reason as a means for understanding the world and controlling one's actions within it. The main mechanism of this training in reasoning is to be mathematics '. . . not that I think it necessary that all men should be deep mathematicians, but that having got the way of reasoning, which that study necessarily brings the mind to, they might be able to transfer it to other parts of knowledge as they shall have occasion.'[32] What is noticeable about the argument – apart from a transfer of training argument – is that it merely converts the gentleman into an enlightened or educated gentleman. There is no suggestion that rationality or 'learning' becomes the first priority. The gentleman remains, first, a gentleman.

Contrast this with the position and significance which Descartes accords to mathematics:

> Those long chains of reasoning, simple and easy as they are, of which geometricians make use in order to arrive at the most difficult demonstrations, had caused me to imagine that all those things which fall under the cognizance of man might very likely be mutually related in the same fashion; and that, provided only

that we abstain from receiving anything as true which is not so, and always retain the order which is necessary in order to deduce the one conclusion from the other, there can be nothing so remote that we cannot reach to it, nor so recondite that we cannot discover it. And I had not much trouble in discovering which objects it was necessary to begin with, for I already knew that it was with the most simple and those most easy to apprehend. Considering also that of all those who have hitherto sought for the truth in the Sciences, it has been the mathematicians alone who have been able to succeed in making any demonstrations, that is to say producing reasons which are evident and certain, I did not doubt that it had been by means of a similar kind that they carried on their investigations. I did not at the same time hope for any practical result in so doing, except that my mind would become accustomed to the nourishment of truth and would not content itself with false reasoning.[33]

Mathematics here is accorded a central position both in priorities in knowledge and in a model of man. The virtues which it inculcates are intellectual. There is a central emphasis on cognitive qualities and rationality, on step-by-step deduction from examined and then axiomatic premises, as suggested by the 'four rules of method' – 'the first of these was to accept nothing as true which I did not clearly recognize to be so . . .'.[34] The emphasis on analysis '. . . to divide up each of the difficulties which I examined into as many parts as possible',[35] logical order,[36] and deduction '. . . in all cases to make enumerations so complete and reviews so general that I should be certain of having omitted nothing',[37] the general celebration of cognitive qualities contrasts with 'virtue, wisdom and breeding'. Man, the thinker, is the focus and any necessary practical utility is dismissed as an irrelevance.

The mode of man outlined is, in one sense, culturally free:[38] it suggests neither a social structure for which the thinker is to be fitted nor a class bias in his selection: '. . . the power of forming a good judgement and of distinguishing the true from the false, which is properly speaking what is called Good sense or Reason, is by nature equal in all men'.[39] The purpose of education is to develop that humanity – i.e. rationality – which is common to all men; and the development of rationality is justifiable intrinsically.

It seems possible to suggest in outline, from the models of man and priorities in knowledge delineated by Locke and Descartes, prescriptions for ideal-typical universities. Both universities would tend to stress the individual and his development, rather than society and its problems. This would be truer of Descartes than Locke, for Locke's model of education does pay some attention to the education of a class which is to give leadership in society, but, even here, Locke's model is primarily aimed at ensuring that the private existence of the gentleman is secure; from this personal security accrues any benefit which society may gain.

Again both universities would allow of study in depth. Here, however, serious divergences emerge. Whereas Locke's university would subordinate study (of, say, mathematics) to the cultivation of more important virtues, which in some degree are both moral and social, Descartes' university would hold these depth studies as the central purpose of the university. The gains in intention would be individual or, at best, for the intellectual community. At the cognitive level Locke's university would produce, through an essentialist curriculum, an ability to look at both intellectual and societal problems with some degree of enlightened rationality, illuminated by commonsense; whereas Descartes' university, through an encyclopaedist curriculum, would cultivate a thorough-going intellectual, analytical and deductive rationality, through which all problems would be viewed.

To ensure 'virtue, wisdom and good breeding', which are qualities of character particularly susceptible to the environment ('company'), the internal (and external) environment of the university would be controlled. Presumably every effort would be made to ensure that, internally, the tutor-tutee ratio was such as to allow adult domination of the university. No such social arrangements are visible in the Descartes' model.

Both universities endorse non-utilitarian learning in slightly different ways: the Cartesian model because of its emphasis on the clear, the analytical, the deduced and the theoretical; the Lockean model because of its emphasis on character training and its class bias. Trade, for example, is not a fit activity for a gentleman. To reverse the point, utilitarian education would be rejected as a pollution of purity, a disturbance on the one hand of intellectual pursuits and on the other of a socially based gentlemanly ethos, which eschews vocational concerns.

The protection of 'purity' in the English university is well attested by the following statement:

> But it is a great mistake . . . to blur the distinction between the university and the technical college. It is here that Oxford and Cambridge can be of peculiar service, because they have a peculiar power, from their very position, of keeping the true and pure 'idea of a University' . . . the old universities . . . have a great and bounden duty of defending, for the sake of the rest, the stronghold of pure learning and long-time values against the demands of material progress and the zest for immediate values and quick returns.[40]

This defence of purity by Oxbridge on behalf of all English universities was manifested in the last century by allowing the (newly created) provincial universities to educate the middle classes,[41] and in this century by their reluctance to make provision for the social sciences.[42]

The process, *mutatis mutandis*, seems to be continuing. In the United Kingdom in the 1960s there was a considerable expansion[43] of the number of university institutions. Most of these universities devised new curricula[44] which placed greater stress on inter-disciplinary study, the single honours degree being seen increasingly as an anachronism. Vocational subjects seemed still, however, to be suspect in the new universities: 'All of them without exception have established schools, faculties or departments in the traditional fields of arts, social sciences and pure science. . . . Technology, on the other hand, has been avoided by most, not as a permanent policy but as a lower priority to be developed organically out of the pure sciences when they [sic] are firmly established. . . .'[45] Similarly medical and dental schools, agriculture, forestry and veterinary science courses have not, with one exception, been established in the new universities.

Notice also that the proposal of the Robbins Report to establish five 'Special Institutions for Scientific and Technological Education and Research' was opposed by the other universities and the Association of University Teachers.[46] All this, together with the rapid expansion of the non-university sector of higher education which, in general, provides a strongly vocational education biased towards the needs of industry, makes it difficult to avoid drawing the conclusion that the liberal education of the gentleman, in new guise, is still – when seen comparatively – the primary[47] function of the English university.

That purity, of which the *Grandes Ecoles* and the *Facultés* are the French institutional symbols, is a purity of rationalism. Marcel Hignette[48] has described graphically the influence of the Cartesian tradition on curriculum and pedagogy. Indeed even the phrasing of a Ministerial directive which he quotes is reminiscent of Descartes: pupils '. . . will need to be able to examine every matter . . . taking into account only facts that have been well and duly established; they will have to be trained to observe, to measure and to criticize their own observations by submitting them to strict scrutiny, exhaustive analysis, and conclusive proof . . .'.[49] It is from higher education that secondary education takes its biases in content and pedagogy and even examinations. The *explication de textes*, the *dissertation* in the baccalaureate, and the thesis at university level, all on French evidence,[50] are seen as stressing logicality, exact verbal skills, intellectual 'penetration' and rhetorical, speculative ability.

Certain tendencies, which affect the degree to which the university may involve itself in utilitarian education, can emerge from such a Cartesian tradition in education. Hignette argues that a cult of intellect '. . . readily gives rise to a scorn for *the application of knowledge* to reality, that is to say, for technology and, more generally, for action'.[51] In addition when such a Cartesian tradition, allied with certain institutional arrangements, becomes pervasive, institutions originally established for one purpose may come to serve others. Thus the *Ecole Polytechnique*, established to give a modern scientific training to engineers, provided France with superb engineers in the nineteenth century. However 'the student at the *grandes écoles* learned the content of science but not the methods of science'.[52] The Napoleonic institutional arrangements and their heritage – the fragmentation of the university *facultés* and the *grandes écoles*, and the growth of specialized research institutes – prevented a unity of theory and practice, as well as – in general – of research and teaching. As a consequence, the two main *grandes écoles*, for example, both founded for quite specific purposes, suffered a diffusion of function[53] – which whilst making them no less useful, certainly made them less utilitarian. As a further consequence of this institutional pattern, it has been strongly questioned by French writers[54] whether recent reforms in French education, especially the *Instituts Universitaires de Technologie*, do in fact constitute a change in the structure of higher education. Similarly the degree of centralization which is a feature of the French higher education system (and which helps prevent it making a utilitarian response to local or regional needs) is an object of reform.[55] It remains an open question whether it will succeed.

Briefly one may point to other major features in the Locke and Descartes models of universities which show institutional provision. The tension between the individual and the social, the demand for equality and the need to select are visible in the *grandes écoles*,[56] and the educational system in general. Similarly, it is noticeable that the French university, with the exception of certain of the *grandes écoles*, places less emphasis on the social arrangements of interaction between staff and students[57] than the English. English universities tend to be small and in general[58] to be located in relatively small towns. This coupled with the English emphasis on the tutorial system presumably allows them to diminish the malevolent impact of 'company'.

Thus in the two (social and academic) areas posited in the Locke and Descartes models of the university there does seem to be some correspondence between the deduced and the actual institutional patterns. Clearly counter-pressures are visible, and the current solutions or proposed reforms for the problem of utilitarian education are interesting. In general both the English and French have stayed with the view that, in practice, universities are elitist institutions, and national rather than local organizations. Both countries have tended to the view that the university is responsible for a (differentially interpreted) liberal education rather than training; and both have tended to fragment their higher education system, creating new specialist institutions when such training is seen as being directly linked with commerce, industry or economic growth.

Like Plato, Marx outlines a model of man and a theory of knowledge which is part of a complex *gestalt*. A further difficulty is that much of Marx' writings are a critique of the world as he saw it; consequently many of his points are expressed negatively. Nevertheless there seem to be two main areas which may be selected as providing the ingredients of a model. One is Marx' view of alienated labour as an aspect both of the importance of work and the formation of consciousness, and the other is his view of the role of knowledge. From these follow, in large measure, his conception of education.

> It is just in his work upon the objective world that man really proves himself as a *species-being*. This production is his active species life. By means of it nature appears as *his* work and his reality. The object of labor is therefore, the *objectification of* man's species life; for he no longer merely reproduces himself intellectually, as in consciousness, but actively and in a real sense, and he sees his own reflection in a world which he has constructed. While, therefore, alienated labor takes away the object of production from man, it also takes away his *species life*, his real objectivity as a species-being. . . .[59]

This alienation from the product of his labour that man experiences has a number of consequences. He is unable to enter into true and satisfactory relationships with other men, communal life becomes an impossibility. Man becomes dehumanized, an objectivated individual, surrounded both by persons and objects which bear no meaningful relationship to himself. Alienation is in no way removed by education for '. . . is that not also social, and determined by the social conditions under which you educate, by the intervention of society, direct or indirect, by means of schools, etc?'[60]

To remove this alienation it is necessary to alter man's consciousness, which in turn is dependent on altering the relations of production, i.e. on removing a given ruling class in favour of the proletariat. At some point in this process a true (i.e. Marxian) understanding of the nature of social reality must become available to human actors.

Thus for Marx thought, especially social thought, becomes a fulcrum for social action. ('The philosophers have only interpreted the world differently, the point is, to change it.') Intellectual analysis is rooted in life, initially providing the means to devise a realistic sociology of both power and knowledge, and ultimately an understanding of the necessities of history and the dynamics of social change. The social world has become a fit, indeed necessary, subject for knowledge. Action and thought, the individual and the social interlock. The end product of this process, communism, is '. . . the *definitive* resolution of the antagonism between man and nature, and between man and man. It is the true solution of the conflict between existence and essence, between objectivation and self-affirmation, between freedom and necessity, between individual and species.'[61] An education system can be built for this condition: 'From the factory system budded . . . the germ of the education of the future, an education that will, in the case of every child over a given age, combine productive labour with instruction and gymnastics, not only as one of the methods of adding to the efficiency of production, but as the only method of producing fully developed human beings.'[62]

So the hypothetical Marxist university deals with the problem of man in industrial society. Central to its concerns is the productive man. The nature of the work situation decides the degree to which man's humanity (seen with Rousseauist assumptions of goodness) is released, which in turn determines man's relations with his fellow men and allows individual man to be, at the same time, communal man.

The educated man is he who is of the world, participates in it and changes it. The knowledge which is of use is technical, both in the sense of technological and in the sense of access to the Marxian dialectic. Not only are technology and work relations proper objects of knowledge but societal and power relations require participation or attention, depending on the circumstances. In the new social (communist) situation, the basic ingredients for correct class consciousness are provided by the revised means of production, but the maintenance of this class consciousness is facilitated by knowledge of the Marxian dialectic.

The university is an organic part of the whole society, serving societal purposes, and the Lockean balance between individual benefit and social benefit is a non-issue. The hypothetical Marxian university serves to unite theory and practice, existence and essence; and is perhaps more oriented to the future than the past.

> . . . the educated man has a major task to perform. It is to study the changing world as he finds it and to improve it. He identifies the competing forces that are inducing change, creating problems, and tending to give social development direction; one complex of forces is operating to make change take one course, while another complex is moving it in another direction. The individual's responsibility is to decide which forces he will support.[63]

With the possible exception of the last sentence, this could be a commentary on Marx. In fact it is part of an extensive commentary on John Dewey. Like Marx, Dewey's education man is a social being, involved in society's problems and action oriented. But the 'knowledge' which he uses is a technique rather than a prescription. Between being confronted with a perplexing situation and resolving it, an educated man may move through the five stages of reflective thought, which involve thinking of solutions, intellectualizing the problem, choosing a hypothesis and testing it. The knowledge which is useful in solving the intellectualized problem is decided by the perplexing situation. The answer may lie within traditional disciplines or it may not; where it does not, information is taken pragmatically from a variety of disciplines or established independently. The educated man is not a possessor of information but the exponent of a mode of analysis, in principle applicable to any issue. His conclusions stand, not as knowledge, but as hypotheses to be refuted by 'overt or imaginative action'. Cartesian certainties are out of place here.

Many of the problems facing the educated man emerge from society: 'Our problems grow out of social conditions: they concern human relations rather than man's direct relationship to physical nature'.[64] The problems arise because society is both complex and changing. Forces of change (e.g. technology) act differentially on various parts of society. In turn, 'technology, taken in its broadest sense, offers an answer to our problem'.[65] Only when man has learnt to use reflective thinking for the creation of 'organized intelligence' are societal problems likely to be solved. This scientific mode of thinking, in itself a public and communal activity, is as applicable to human or social problems as to the traditional concerns of science.

This active role for education, social reconstructionism,[66] is not carried out by individuals who are isolated from their society. Like Marx the utopian, Dewey does not recognize the traditional dichotomy between the individual and the social; neither is meaningful without the other: '. . . I believe that the individual who is to be educated is a social individual and that society is an organic union of individuals. If we eliminate the social factor from the child we are left only with an abstraction; if we eliminate the individual factor from society, we are left only with an inert and lifeless mass.'[67]

Thus for Dewey all education is utilitarian in the sense that for the education to be meaningful it must arise from immediate and pressing puzzlements which the individual experiences. Education is utilitarian at the societal level also; it is an agent for the transformation and reconstruction of the social order. It not only attempts to solve the problems created by societal change, but it also attempts to predict and influence future changes. The knowledge which is utilized for these purposes is eclectically and pragmatically selected. Knowledge is always hypothetical and contextual, and gains its vindication in action.

The universities for which Dewey and Marx provide rationales thus seem in general to focus around a rather different set of concerns from the universities posited for Locke and Descartes. Marx and Dewey emphasize the unity of the individual and society; they stress the general societal problems created by the industrial order; they underplay both elitism and abstract reasoning; and eschew the dichotomy of essence and existence. Knowledge is necessary in and for action. It is an encyclopaedist tool, in different ways, for social reconstruction and it is the moral responsibility of an educated man to have the knowledge which allows him not merely to be involved in society but to change it.

Consider the two following quotations:

> The work of the Soviet institutions of higher or secondary education is always determined by the problems which the State places upon the agenda at any given stage of the building of communism,[68]

and

> During the past twenty years the leading universities of the country have changed markedly in form and function, carrying with them – part way or altogether – the eighteen hundred other establishments called colleges and universities. . . . The universities are expected, among other things, to turn out scientists and engineers, foster international understanding, provide a home for the arts, satisfy divergent tastes in architecture and sexual morals, cure cancer, recast the penal code, and train equally for the professions and for a life of cultured contentment in the Coming Era of Leisure.[69]

Though through a different system of linkages both quotations point to the direct involvement of the universities (of the USSR and the USA) in societal concerns. In the USSR the institutions of higher education are normally seen as being divided into two groups.[70] The universities which contain a smaller proportion of the students tend to produce research workers and teachers with high qualifications in 'traditional' major fields; the specialized institutes are intended to produce specialists for particular fields of study or positions in the national economy. 'The chief types of institutes for definite fields are pedagogical, agricultural, medical, metallurgical, mining, chemico-technological, civil engineering, and certain others.'[71] The parallel, in this apparent split of function, with the *grandes écoles* and the French university *facultés* is striking, but should not be pushed too far. The graduate of the Soviet university is expected to be trained for a specific job (e.g. school teaching) and is also the product of a system of education which is organized on the polytechnic principle.[72] But the links between the individual, the educational system and society in the USSR are not, as would be expected if only from the discussion of the hypothetical Marxian university, a one-way process aimed at the production of socially useful labour. As well as expecting a contribution to society from the individual, the education system aims at '. . . the production of well-informed, integrally developed and educated citizens capable of . . . taking an active part in the various spheres of social, governmental and cultural life of the country'.[73]

So the university and specialized institute in the USSR at the level of stated aims is concerned with the development of the rounded Marxian man. But because higher education is seen as a crucial key to the development of society and to economic growth,[74] it is also heavily involved with science and industry. Thus it is apparent in curricula[75] as well as the formal interconnexions and interpenetration of industry and education departments. On the one hand, 'an increasingly active part in the work of departments, particularly in connexion with scientific and technical problems, is also taken by highly placed officials in industry and agriculture – chief engineers and chief technologists in works, factories and mines . . .'[76] and on the other the industrial and economic VUZy (Institutes of Higher Education) help to cut production costs and apply new scientific and technical knowledge to local industry.[77]

A similar process would seem to be at work in the USA and in certain circumstances the university seems to take on some of the characteristics of an industrial institution:

> The University of California last year had operating expenditures from all sources of nearly half a billion dollars, with almost another 100 million for construction; a total employment of over 40,000 people, more than I.B.M. . . . operations in over a hundred locations, counting campuses, experiment stations, agricultural and urban extension centers, and projects abroad involving more than fifty countries; nearly 10,000 courses in its catalogues. . . . Over 4,000 babies were born in its hospitals. It is the world's largest purveyor of white mice. . . .[78]

This kind of involvement of the large State universities in local and national society is assisted by their locations (in cities) and resources, and is in no way hampered by the traditions of the land-grant movement, the 'Wisconsin idea' and, now, increasing Federal grants to universities.

These tendencies also in no way run counter to the view of knowledge-in-action as a solution to 'problems'. This theme is present both institutionally and in the Flexner-Dewey-Hutchins debates on the nature and purposes of the American university. In this debate Harry Gideonse argued strongly for the involvement of men of learning in society's problems and stressed 'the problem approach' to knowledge.[79] Inside the university, in curricular terms, this view of knowledge and more generally a move from a discipline-based curriculum is witnessed by the appearance, at different times and in different places, of 'electives', of 'survey courses' of 'functional life adjustment programmes' and the inclusion in university curricula of such courses as business administration and home economics.[80]

In the curricula of institutions of higher learning in the USSR an understanding of the nature of industrial processes is given through the polytechnical approach to knowledge. An integral part of such an understanding is a knowledge of socio-economic subjects; not simply because of the demands of industry, but because such knowledge is necessary for an educated man: 'Without an understanding of these laws . . . [of economic development] . . . no person, no matter in what sphere of activity he works, can be considered a fully trained specialist and an educated man in general.'[81] So the Marxian man gains access to that social knowledge which the hypothetical Marxian university seemed to suggest he should have.

To a large extent, then, it seems that many of the elements present in the 'predicted' universities of Marx and Dewey are present in the institutional arrangements of higher education in the USA and the USSR. The firm focus on the problems of industrial society, knowledge as necessary for action and the moral responsibilities of the educated man as an agent of change are all themes which are readily discernible.

Conclusion

What is interesting about the analysis is not simply the divergence, whether at the level of norms or institutions, of the four countries one from the other, nor the similarities between France and England on the one hand and the USSR and the USA on the other; nor is it the themes of mass and elitist education which are apparent in the analysis.

Perhaps three general themes are of greater interest. Firstly, to the extent that governments demand, as the price of increased financial support, greater 'utilitarian' returns in education, and to the extent that universities in Europe do not respond, may we expect the universities (as distinct, for example, from research institutions) to become the dodos of the educational world? Secondly, if models of man and priorities in knowledge do act as 'regulating theories', 'implicit rules of the game', then precisely by what mechanisms and on which publics do they work? And thirdly what is raised by the analysis are the general patterns made by the roles of the educated man, of education as a set of institutions and of knowledge. These three roles seem to pick out a major theme running consistently but not always explicitly through the analysis: the education system, with the university at its apex, as conserving knowledge as tradition, knowledge as social capital and knowledge as social power in tension and in contrast with an education system changing social capital and redistributing social power.

NOTES

1. Rupert Wilkinson in *The Prefects: British leadership and the public school tradition* (OUP, 1964) has indicated in a masterly comparative analysis how those educated through apparently non-functional criteria may be used to fill the highest political and administrative offices. Similarly Marjorie Reeves in her essay 'The European university from medieval times' (in *Higher Education: demand and response*, ed. W. R. Niblett) has argued that in Western civilization both institutions of higher studies and the men of learning in and from them have always been products of social needs and pressures. The general arguments of Wilkinson and Reeves are not, taken in conjunction, denied. The concept of utilitarian which is being used here focuses on the rapidity with which university institutions may be expected to react to societal demands for new types of training, and the degree to which these demanded studies are seen as the legitimate concerns of universities. The issue is not simply that certain ('professional') forms of vocational training, e.g.

medicine and theology, may not carry the term utilitarian, whilst other (non-professional) vocational trainings do. The issue also covers the extent to which the universities are responsive to regional as well as national demands, the extent to which the universities are prepared to carry out research for governments and industries. How responsive, in other words, are universities to short-term interpretations of social and economic needs from a variety of publics?

2. *The Republic of Plato*, translated with introduction and notes by Francis MacDonald Cornford (Oxford: Clarendon Press, 1941), pp. 102–3.

3. op. cit., chapter XX, 'The Philosopher's Fitness to Rule'.

4. op. cit., pp. 175 ff.

5. op. cit., pp. 216–21.

6. See *From Max Weber: essays in sociology*, translated, edited and with an introduction by H. H. Gerth and C. W. Mills (London: Routledge and Kegan Paul, 1970), paperback edition, chapter XVII, pp. 416–44.

7. op. cit., p. 426.

8. op. cit., p. 428.

9. Italics in the original unless otherwise stated.

10. op. cit., p. 428.

11. op. cit., p. 436.

12. op. cit., p. 437.

13. op. cit., p. 433.

14. Joseph A. Lauwerys, 'Opening Address', *General Education in a Changing World: Proceedings of the Comparative Education Society in Europe*, Berlin, 1965, p. 9.

15. For the full analysis, see Lauwerys, op. cit., especially pp. 10–23.

16. Perhaps Marx in the USSR.

17. Perhaps pragmatism in the USA.

18. See 'The Philosophical Approach in Comparative Education', Joseph A. Lauwerys, in 'Thoughts on Comparative Education: *Festschrift* for Pedro Rossello', *International Review of Education* ('s-Gravenhage: Martinus Nijhoff).

19. See Brian Holmes, 'Rational constructs in comparative education', *International Review of Education*, Vol. XI, No. 4, 1965.

20. op. cit., p. 469.

21. op. cit., pp. 471–2.

22. See Brian Holmes, *Problems in Education: a comparative approach* (London: Routledge and Kegan Paul, 1965).

23. The word 'problem' here is used in the technical sense in which Holmes consistently uses it. See Holmes, op. cit.

24. cf. Daniel Bell, 'Twelve Modes of Prediction' in *Penguin Survey of the Social Sciences, 1965*, ed. Julius Gould (Harmondsworth, England: Penguin Books): '. . . the function of conjecture is not prediction but explanation . . . Conjecture, in this sense, stipulates a set of future predicates whose appearance should be explainable from theory . . .' (p. 97, op. cit.). The four thinkers are being treated here as potential sources of 'operational codes': '. . . the "do's and don'ts" of conduct, the implicit rules of the game' (p. 106, op. cit.). Here the gap between the hypothesized 'operational code' or 'regulating theory' and later or future institutional provision is being examined.

25. It might be equally illuminating to take H. Spencer for the USA or T. H. Huxley for England.

26. Clearly in a study of this length descriptions of institutional arrangements can hardly be thorough – they must at best be illustrative. The illustrative material on institutional patterns is introduced after each pair of thinkers.

27. See *The Educational Writings of John Locke: a critical edition with introduction and notes*, James L. Axtell (Cambridge: CUP, 1968).

28. op. cit., pp. 112–13.

29. op. cit., p. 240.

30. op. cit., p. 255.

31. op. cit., p. 165; cf. pp. 158–72,

32. John Locke, *Conduct of the Understanding*, ed. Thomas Fowler (Oxford: Clarendon Press,

1890), quoted in Paul Nash, ed., *Models of Man: explorations in the Western educational tradition* (New York: John Wiley and Sons, Inc., 1968), p. 257.

33. Descartes, *Discourse on the method of rightly conducting the reason and seeking truth in the sciences*, quoted in *Three Thousand Years of Educational Wisdom: selections from great documents*, edited and commented on by Robert Ulich (Cambridge, Mass.: Harvard University Press, 1961), 2nd. ed., pp. 319–20.

34. op. cit., p. 319.

35. idem.

36. See op. cit., p. 319.

37. idem.

38. The model of man, of course, is not culturally free in its explicit emphasis on a certain kind of thinking, nor in its implicit valuation of leisure time for thinking.

39. op. cit., p. 312.

40. Ernest Barker, 'Universities in Great Britain', in *The University in a Changing World: a symposium*, ed. Walter M. Kotschnig and Elined Prys (London: Oxford University Press, 1932), p. 119.

41. See Joseph Ben-David and Awaraham Zloczower, 'Universities and academic systems in modern societies', in *Science and Society*, ed. Norman Kaplan (Chicago: Rand McNally and Co., 1965), pp. 76–8.

42. Joseph Ben-David and Randall Collins, 'A comparative study of academic freedom and student politics', in *Student Politics*, ed. Seymour Martin Lipset (New York: Basic Books, Inc., 1967), p. 164.

43. See *Case studies on innovation in higher education: New Universities in the United Kingdom*, H. J. Perkin (OECD, 1969).

44. op. cit., pp. 115–31.

45. op. cit., p. 134.

46. op. cit., pp. 47–8.

47. cf. the firm establishment of technological universities in Britain, which display a marked counter-tendency to the Locke model. See 'The technological universities', R. A. Buchanan, *Universities Quarterly*, Dec. 1966, Vol. 21, No. 1, pp. 71–90.

48. Marcel Hignette, 'The primacy of the rational in French secondary education', in *Year Book of Education 1958: The Secondary School Curriculum*, joint eds., George Z. F. Bereday, Joseph A. Lauwerys (London: Evans), pp. 233–41.

49. op. cit., p. 235.

50. e.g. R. Aron, 'Some aspects of the crisis in the French universities', *Minerva*, Vol. II, No. 3, Spring 1964, p. 283. e.g. *Case studies on innovation in higher education: French experience before 1968*, C. Grignon and J. C. Passeron (OECD, 1970), p. 98.

51. op. cit., p. 238. See also for the 'corruption' of Cartesian humanism, 'An enquiry into the state of university education in France, III', P. Mansell-Jones, *Universities Quarterly*, Vol. 7, 1952–3, pp. 387–93.

52. Robert Gilpin, *France in the Age of the Scientific State* (New Jersey: Princeton University Press, 1968), p. 90.

53. See 'The *Grandes Ecoles*', Michalina Vaughan, in *Governing Elites: Studies in Training and Selection*, ed. Rupert Wilkinson (New York: Oxford University Press:, 1969), p. 91.

54. Grignon and Passeron, op. cit.

55. See *Reform and expansion in higher education in Europe: national reports 1962-7*, Council for European Co-operation, Council of Europe, Strasbourg, 1967, p. 105.

56. See Vaughan, op. cit., *passim*.

57. cf. Grignon and Passeron, op. cit., p. 61; W. D. Halls, *Society, Schools and Progress in France* (Oxford: Pergamon Press, 1965), p. 152.

58. e.g. the universities of Reading, Leicester, Durham, Exeter, Hull, Keele, Sussex, York, Essex, Canterbury. There are obvious exceptions.

59. From Karl Marx, *Early Writings*, translated and edited by T. B. Bottomore (London: C. A. Watts and Co. Ltd, 1963), quoted in Paul Nash, op. cit., p. 331.

60. *Manifesto of Communist Party*, quoted in Nash, op. cit., p. 326.

61. Bottomore, op. cit., quoted in Nash, op. cit., p. 332.

62. 'Karl Marx, *Kapital*', quoted in *Polytechnical Education in the USSR*, ed. S. G. Shapovalenko (UNESCO, 1963), p. 24.
63 Brian Holmes, 'The Reflective Man: Dewey' in *The Educated Man: Studies in the History of Educational Thought*, eds. Paul Nash, Andreas M. Kazamias, Henry J. Perkinson (New York: John Wiley and Sons, Inc., 1965), p. 331.
64. John Dewey, 'Towards a new individualism', *The New Republic*, Vol. LXII, No. 794, quoted in Nash, *Models of Man*, op. cit., p. 372.
65. Dewey, op. cit., in Nash, op. cit., p. 373.
66. cf. '. . . through education society can formulate its own purposes, can organise its own means and resources and thus shape itself with definitiveness and economy in the direction in which it wishes to move'. John Dewey 'My pedagogic creed', *The School Journal*, Vol. LIV, No. 3, quoted in Nash, op. cit., p. 368.
67. Dewey, op. cit., quoted in Nash, op. cit., pp. 361–2.
68. K. Nozhko, E. Monoszon, V. Zhamin, V. Severtsev, *Education planning in the USSR*, UNESCO, International Institute for Educational Planning, 1968, p. 178.
69. Jacques Barzun, *The American University* (New York, Evanston and London: Harper Row, 1968), p. 2.
70. V. A. Kitaitzev, 'U.S.S.R.', in *Access to Higher Education, Vol. II (National Studies)*. UNESCO and International Association of Universities, 1965, p. 406.
71. idem.
72. See Shapovalenko, op. cit.,
73. Nozhko *et. al.*, op.cit., p. 21.
74. op. cit., p. 64.
75. '. . . in Leningrad Polytechnical Institute there are nine faculties: physics and metallurgy, mechanical engineering and machine construction, power machinery engineering, electrical engineering, engineering physics, hydraulic engineering, radio engineering, etc. Each faculty covers the specialised trades related to it.' op. cit., p. 65.
76. op. cit., p. 69.
77. idem.
78. Clark Kerr, *The Uses of the University* (Cambridge, Mass.: Harvard University Press, 1964), pp. 7–8.
79. 'The university must seek to train men who will use learning in the service of society about them. For such a goal the first requirement is the habit of deriving conclusions from the analysis of relevant data, and this habit is best achieved, perhaps uniquely achieved, by work on concrete problems.' Harry D. Gideonse, 'The higher learning in a democracy', quoted in *American Higher Education: A Documentary History*, ed. Richard Hofstader and Wilson Smith, Vol. II (University of Chicago Press, 1961), paperback edition, p. 943.
80. See John S. Brubacher and Willis Rudy, *Higher Education in Transition: an American History 1636–1956* (New York: Harper and Bros., 1958), especially Chapter 13, 'Innovations in curriculum and methods'.
81. N. Oparin, 'The teaching of political economy', in *The Humanities in Soviet Higher Education*, ed. Douglas Grant (University of Toronto Press, 1960), p. 47.

7

The Search for a Global System: Unity and Diversity of Post-Secondary Education

Ladislav Cerych and Dorotea Furth

Future historians might possibly view the development of higher education during the period 1950 to 1970 as having been dominated by three major preoccupations: quantitative expansion, reform of individual institutions and/or specific aspects of higher education and reform of the higher education system as a whole. To some extent, these three preoccupations can be said to have appeared consecutively during this period. The fifties and early sixties were marked mainly by the 'explosion of numbers'; the early sixties represented essentially a period when new institutions were created and when sometimes radical partial reforms took place (in teaching content and methods, in organization and governance in various institutions, etc.); in the late sixties some decisive steps were taken towards a global planning approach to the system of higher education.

There is, of course, overlapping between the three stages. Quantitative expansion is also a phenomenon of recent years, and very probably will remain so in the seventies; new universities and colleges deviating from established patterns appear throughout the sixties. But it can probably be said, with some degree of simplification, that these are the three themes which appear one after another in discussions, headlines and policy deliberations concerning post-secondary education during the period 1950 to 1970.

Parenthetically in this article the term 'post-secondary education' is intended to cover all formal education above the secondary school level, i.e. institutions in which students enter normally at the age of 17 to 19, after 11 to 13 years of previous schooling. It includes universities as well as all other establishments admitting students with secondary school qualifications. We do not make any distinction between this term and the term 'higher education'; both are comprehensive as is our understanding of the term 'tertiary education'. This terminology is now used by almost all international organizations; it differs from the one employed in certain countries where 'post-secondary education' might not cover universities and equivalent institutions. In adopting this wide coverage (including postgraduate education) we already anticipate the requirements of a trend briefly analysed in the present article, namely the need for unity of all education after secondary school. This terminology implies also a radical change with regard to some countries where higher education meant in the past simply university education.

It is the third theme – the reform of the higher education system as a whole – which will be considered here. In many ways, it constitutes a response to the challenge and failures of the previous stages.

A System Typology

When looking at higher education systems of the Western world[1] with particular regard to their main institutional components and to the type of interrelations between these components three major systems can be identified – the American, the continental European and the English.

The American model is characterized by a rather wide range of institutional types, from Junior Colleges to prestigious private universities (or even, more recently, to pure research establishments of the 'think tank' variety). The administrative and legal links between these various institutions are, in general, very loose or even non-existent. Yet the system possesses, in a certain sense, a high degree of unity. In particular, it allows, on paper at least, students to move relatively easily from one institution to another. The bottom of the institutional pyramid – the Junior or Community College – provides both terminal (vocational) and intermediate (transfer) education, and so does many another private and public college and university. In general, most of the institutions, with the exception of specialized professional schools, are multipurpose; they offer a variety of both vocationally and academically oriented courses.

The continental European model consists of two main sectors: universities (and university-status institutions) usually with open access, and other post-secondary establishments. The duration of studies in the former is considerably longer than in the latter and there is a rather significant difference between the prestige value of the degrees delivered in the two sectors. Student mobility between them is nil or negligible and curricula have a different orientation: more abstract and theoretical in the one, more practical and vocational in the other.

There are several variations to the European model, the most significant probably being the French system. This is a system which has three main components:[2] the *Grandes Ecoles*, the universities and the other post-secondary institutions of various types. The first category represents a small minority of the institutions in the system and is of an elitist nature, but there are a number of links which exist between this type of institution and the universities which, unlike the *Grandes Ecoles*, traditionally exercise no selection in admission apart from possession of the baccalaureate. Both types offer either high-level professional training (medicine, engineering) or a multipurpose education of a more academic nature. The third category, with the exception of the newly created *Instituts universitaires de technologie* (IUT), has little or no links with the previous two and provides mainly specialized and vocationally-oriented training.

The English model constitutes an extreme of separation between the university and non-university sectors of higher education. In fact, these are two independent systems where, contrary to the preceding models, studies have the same duration and can – at least theoretically if not in social prestige value – lead to identical degree levels. As in the continental European model, there is practically no student mobility between institutions or between the two sectors; and one sector is more theoretical and general, the other more practical and specialized.

This typology obviously represents an oversimplification. Overlapping has occurred and mixed models have been developed, especially during recent years. Each of the models has a number of characteristics related to variables such as the degree of institutional autonomy and system centralization, density of links with the outside world or differentiation between research and teaching functions. All three models imply a distinction between the 'noble' and 'less noble' parts of the system which is at the root of the present search for appropriate reforms.

If this distinction does not apply to some systems, it is only because the non-university sector does not exist or is negligible (e.g. Austria, Italy). These systems might have been presented as a fourth model with universities and equivalent institutions (usually technical universities) being the only, or almost only, component. This situation, however, is not the result of a deliberate policy aimed at unifying the system, but is simply a consequence of the fact that none of the teacher training institutions or those of technical secondary education have developed into post-secondary establishments which was precisely the origin of most of the institutions in the non-university sector in other countries. It is almost inevitable that such a development will take place in the future mainly because of the pressure of numbers on higher education and of manpower requirements. This group of countries will therefore face the same kinds of problems as those facing countries characterized by one of the three previous models.

Some Deficiencies of Present Systems

Two aspects of the present situation should be mentioned before the main deficiencies are analysed.

First, the majority of the systems maintain a certain stability with regard to the relative weight of their 'noble' and 'less noble' insitutional components. The growth rates of the university and non-university sectors have been, in general, similar over the last fifteen to twenty years. If, in a few countries, the latter expanded considerably faster than the former, e.g.

Junior Colleges in the United States and two-year colleges in Yugoslavia, it in no way altered the *dichotomic nature* of the system. Thus, the drawbacks which these dichotomies generated were perpetuated and even strengthened.

Secondly, most countries have witnessed what might be called an institutional upgrading trend. This is probably best illustrated by the example of various United States colleges. Two-year institutions attempted to, or did, become four-year establishments; and four-year establishments tended toward or were actually transformed into universities. Those awarding BA degrees exclusively also began to offer MA courses, and those awarding MA degrees aspired to offer PhDs. In the United Kingdom some of the colleges of further education became Colleges of Advanced Technology and subsequently acquired full university status while the new Polytechnics grew to occupy an intermediary position, some of them probably aspiring (though against declared policies) to the CAT-type promotion. Similarly in other countries, two- or three-year institutions when unable to transform their academic status try to add at least a third or fourth year to the length of their course of studies, and/or to give more emphasis to full-time as compared with part-time studies.

This 'status seeking' trend results to a greater extent from individual, local and institutional pressures than from central planning and policy measures.

These two aspects contribute considerably to the five major deficiencies of the present systems which will now be briefly analysed.

Equality of Opportunity

None of the systems really ensures or develops sufficiently equality of opportunity. This is a major objective in almost all countries and everywhere it is far from being achieved. In spite of the rapid quantitative expansion of the last fifteen years, students from lower classes continue to be heavily under-represented in total enrolments as well as students from other underprivileged groups (in particular ethnic or regional) of the population. The bi-polarization and disarticulation of the system have undoubtedly contributed to this situation. In countries where the university sector is rather selective – i.e. in the United States and United Kingdom models – the less favoured groups, to the extent they increased their participation rates, have done so mainly by entering institutions with less stringent admission requirements or created especially to cater for them. This, however, has strengthened the institutional dichotomy, producing lower-class establishments on the one side and upper-class ones on the other.

The advantage of the American model is that it allows transfers between the two sectors; but, in fact, the proportion of those who actually do transfer from two- to four-year colleges or universities is small, the former operating as a selection (or, to use Burton Clark's term, 'cooling out') mechanism for the latter, yielding heavy drop-outs of which the underprivileged classes are precisely the main victims. Thus, in the American system, the degree of equality of opportunity will be relatively high upon admission into the system and during the first one or two years of study (because of the comprehensive and generalized system of secondary education) but much lower at the level of graduation; in other words equality of opportunity in access leads only slightly to equality of achievement.

This discrepancy between equality of access and achievement is less pronounced in the British model which does not readily permit transfer from one sector to the other but where the non-university sector provides opportunity of study at higher degree levels. The drawback here, however, is that, because of different admission criteria and the differentiation already taking place at the secondary school level, the ability range (related to the social composition of the student body) is clearly higher in universities. This, as in the American model, leads to considerably larger drop-out rates in non-university than in university establishments.

In the continental European model, admission to universities is, in principle, open to all graduates of academic secondary education (although more and more exceptions to this rule have been made during recent years due to lack of space – mainly in fields requiring costly equipment). Thus, there are no *prima facie* obstacles, as in the British and American models, to the university sector's receiving as many students from lower classes as the non-university sector of higher education. In fact, the differentiation exists as a consequence of the selection process taking place in the course of secondary schooling. Those entering universities come mainly from general or academic secondary schools and those admitted to non-university institutions from other types of secondary education, students from middle and upper classes being represented more heavily in the former than in the latter. As passage from non-university to university establishments is difficult if not impossible and as the non-university sector represents for the most part short cycle higher education, the system generates blind alleys, i.e. except for the most able and highly motivated, students who enter non-university institutions are prevented from continuing their studies up to the university-degree level.

Qualified Manpower

None of the existing systems seems to respond adequately to the requirements of modern societies for a wide and sufficiently diversified range of qualified manpower.

Historically, the non-university sector grew up in order to provide qualifications and skills for which university education was at too high (and too theoretical) a level and secondary education at too low a level. This preoccupation was dominant especially in the English and the continental European models while, in America, the desire to provide post-secondary education to underprivileged groups represented the central objective of the Junior College movement (though manpower needs were also a factor). Difficulties arise from two developments. On the one hand, in most countries the non-university sector probably did not grow rapidly enough, particularly in certain new fields of study, and this resulted in a rather paradoxical situation, especially in continental Europe where non-university institutions are, in general, more selective than universities. On the other hand, however, the social prestige of the non-university institutions did not increase sufficiently (except in two or three countries) to relieve the pressure of demand on universities. This is probably due to the combined effect of large salary differentials between university and non-university graduates, status considerations which the majority of students attach to traditional university education (where, in addition, admission might be easier) and the 'blind alley' nature of many of the non-university establishments as perceived by students and their parents.

As a result, most of the higher education systems, although expanding almost twice as rapidly as the respective economic systems, were rarely able to provide the appropriate mix of qualifications either in levels or fields of study. In addition, students entering universities were increasingly attracted to fields of study in which there were not yet (or no longer) job opportunities available in sufficient numbers, while ample possibilities existed in fields for which candidates were relatively scarce.

Financial Difficulties

Almost all higher education systems are facing great financial difficulties. It may be that these are more political than technical and that the proportions of GNP and the public budget allocated to education (and within this allocation to higher education) could still be considerably increased, as they have been in the past, provided that society (through its legislative and executive machinery) decides to do so. The fact remains, however, that the two trends witnessed almost everywhere during the last fifteen to twenty years – rising enrolments and rising unit costs – leading in Europe to an average annual increase of expenditure on higher education of some 10 to 15 per cent, cannot continue indefinitely, and that better utilization of available resources is now urgently required. However, the present disarticulation which developed by historical chance, usually as an uncoordinated response to various formal and informal pressures, makes this better use of resources very difficult. The sharing of equipment, and teachers, the full utilization of buildings, three- or four-term (12-

month) academic years and similar measures can and do provide important savings, but they would have to be undertaken on a much larger scale than at present to have real impact. In particular they would have to be applied between institutions of different types and levels where pooling and co-ordination have been, up to now, almost non-existent despite complementary functions and, often, geographic proximity. In this respect the situation is probably worse in the American and British models which are characterized by a high degree of institutional autonomy and where co-ordination cannot easily be brought about (or not at all) by administrative action from above. Theoretically this might be possible in some continental European systems, but, in practice, even there the solution often seems out of reach because different administrative and budgetary procedures apply to the various components of the higher education.

Flexibility and Change

None of the existing systems seems to be able to ensure flexibility and the necessary capacity for change.

Innovations have been introduced during the last years into all systems through the creation of new universities and through the reform of specific aspects of higher education such as teaching methods, the degree structure or the decision-making procedures in one or several institutions. But almost nowhere have these partial innovations affected the system as a whole; they remain, at the best, isolated or have been somehow counterbalanced or distorted by the traditional system. This resistance to the diffusion of innovation is due to many factors, but there can be no doubt that the existing structures which limit the reallocation of finance and the mobility of students and teachers also limit receptiveness to innovation. The 'noble' institutions have an almost natural tendency to ignore or neglect innovations introduced by or through the 'less noble' establishments and the latter, even when innovating at the outset, tend because of the 'up-grading law' to imitate the prestigious (in most cases traditional) institutions, and thus discard their initial innovative character. This mechanism of resistance to innovation obviously does not apply in all instances; it has numerous exceptions, especially in the American and also in the British model. For in the case of innovation, contrary to what happens in the financing and pooling of resources, institutional autonomy plays probably a very favourable role. But it means, at the best, that the innovation process occurs as a rather isolated phenomenon, in no way organized or rationally oriented, somewhat like scientific progress as the result of separate individual efforts which are not based on any general policy for science.

Quest for Self-fulfilment

Finally, none of the present systems seems to respond to the quest of new generations for 'self-fulfilment', for 'quality of life', for 'individual development'.

These objectives are today still vague but they might be in the last analysis among the most important ones, as student unrest of the sixties has clearly shown. No doubt, much more is at stake than institutional structures and inter-institutional linkages: it is the question of pedagogical relations, the problem of relevance of studies and the whole concept of the learning situation. But it cannot be assumed that any of these fundamental issues can be solved other than in an experimental way without profound modifications in the overall institutional framework. Pilot colleges and schemes can provide an answer for the benefit of small groups of students, and they can serve as models; the diffusion process being what it is, however, pilot projects cannot solve the general social phenomenon of changing attitudes and expectations among the young. Blind alleys, degrees without appropriate job opportunities, teaching unrelated to aptitudes and interests, choices made once and for all, dropping out virtually equivalent to complete loss of time and effort (and prestige) – all these are finally some of the main, conscious or unconscious, reasons behind student dissatisfaction. And all these reasons are directly linked to the existing structures of higher education which thus reflect a framework unadapted to pursue and generalize values such as those which the new student generation advocates.

Trends and Solutions

The above analysis of the main deficiencies in the existing systems of higher education has been over-dramatized for the purpose of showing more clearly some of the important motivations behind the new trend towards the reform of the higher education system as a whole.

It is probably in the German Federal Republic that the most appropriate single term for a redefinition of the concept of higher education has been formulated: *Gesamthochschule* and *Gesamthochschulplanung*. Similar concepts, though often not quite so comprehensive, exist in other countries: state-wide planning in the United States or the University Centre idea in Denmark are two examples. And even where no words have been invented, the issue is a burning one. Hence, discussions on the binary system and 'transbinary mechanisms' in the United Kingdom as well as arguments and philosophies behind the launching of new types of post-secondary institutions – District Colleges in Norway, IUTs in France – reflect to a great extent the dominating preoccupation: the development of a multi-purpose structure, the components of which should be linked in a more organic and sensible way than hitherto.

All new solutions, whether already implemented or still in the blue-print stage, try to conciliate two seemingly contradictory requirements: integration of the system and diversification or, in other words, unity without uniformity.

The first type of measures directed towards this aim could be considered as institutional. In the most radical sense they imply the creation of a new organizational entity which would comprise all existing and, so far, independent and isolated establishments of which the new entity would in some sense be a federation or confederation, for example, the German *Gesamthochschule* (comprehensive university) and the Danish University Centres. The key word in general – and used especially in Germany – is 'permeability', meaning essentially that the new system should allow relatively easy transfers between different types and levels of study and that status differences between various institutions of higher education should be attenuated if not disappear altogether.

In most cases measures tending to reduce differences between the 'noble' and 'less noble' institutions are primarily connected with the special status given to the new non-university institutions. Thus in the French IUTs (created in 1966) the word 'university' is incorporated into the name of the new establishments (*Instituts Universitaires de Technologie*) and moreover all of them became administratively (though often from only a formal point of view) part of different universities in spite of their very different functional characteristics (much shorter duration of study, more vocationally-oriented instruction). Furthermore, their degrees are to be considered of the same level as those awarded after the first two years of university study. Transfer, thereby, became theoretically possible. However, in practice important limitations are introduced so that only a minority of IUT students effectively transfer to the long cycle of university education. The idea is to allow the IUTs to maintain and develop one of the main functions for which they were created, namely, to train students in fields of study and at levels not existing in traditional universities.

Similar objectives and characteristics are found in the Norwegian District Colleges which have been operating on a small scale since 1969 but are expected to constitute, eventually, a nation-wide network of post-secondary education. These institutions are administratively separate from universities but, more than in France, there is emphasis on transfer possibilities and their multipurpose function, that is, on provision of both academically and vocationally-oriented courses. The dichotomy between 'noble' and 'less noble' institutions, although existing in Norway, has less impact, probably because of the very small salary differential between university and non-university graduates. Moreover, university studies are very long and this directs an unusually large proportion of students away from academic secondary education to non-university institutions. This justifies the main aspiration of the District Colleges, namely, to become powerful poles and catalysers of innovation in the system as a whole, especially through the content and method of studies which they introduce and by their organizational structure and linkages in regional development.

In contrast, Sweden has started by enlarging existing universities through a network of affiliated institutions (Affiliated or Branch Universities). The main objective here is to widen the geographical distribution of higher education facilities (and thus improve equality of opportunity). This also implies a sharing of teachers and other resources between the central university and its provincial branches. Since all degrees are awarded by the former, institutional status differences are thus being avoided.

In Spain, a rather similar solution has been found through the creation, by a 1970 law, of university colleges (*Collegios Universitarios*).

Another approach is adopted by the CEGEP (*Collège d'enseignement général et professionel*) of Quebec. These institutions are, as the Norwegian District Colleges, both academically and vocationally oriented but, not as in Norway, everyone who wants to enter university must pass through the academic stream of these institutions which thus represent the first two years of university study.

Some systems apparently do not encourage unification measures of the kind mentioned so far; the two existing sectors (or one of them, generally the universities) resist any real integration. A typical example is found in Great Britain where the binary system has induced the non-university sector to develop some of the characteristics which give to universities their prestige: the award of high level degrees, similar admission requirements to those of universities, an extension in the length of studies, the inclusion of fields considered traditionally to be appropriate to the university (humanities, languages, social sciences). In addition to the United Kingdom polytechnics, recent developments in Belgian technical education are a good example of this trend. However, even in the British binary system some important steps towards linking the two sectors were undertaken. The most important of these might be the special relations established between some of the universities and Colleges of Education and also, in a sense, the creation of the Open University which cuts across the two main components of the system. Institutional solutions will be conditioned by the wide acceptance of more profound measures. The first of these is anything that makes more possible the mobility of students between various parts and levels of the system. From a formal point of view some of the examples quoted already imply such measures. In the long run, the actual student mobility will depend on finding a solution to the problem of assimilating curricula between different types of institutions: the extent to which and conditions under which courses and studies in a vocationally-oriented institution following immediately after secondary school can serve as a basis for and/or be common to courses and studies at a higher and often more theoretical level. This raises the questions of basic courses common to several fields and levels of study, of interdisciplinary courses, of desirable and appropriate sequences of courses, etc. No real solutions have yet been found and many have failed. Of these, at least conceptually the most interesting was the Yugoslav essay of 'curriculum inversion'. According to this scheme, the practically and vocationally oriented courses were to come at the beginning of post-secondary studies and the more theoretical courses afterward. This would have allowed a complete equivalence between short-cycle technical (vocational) higher education offered by the new two-year post-secondary colleges (*Visa Skola*) and of the first two years of regular long-cycle university education, students in both institutions having at the end of their first two years the choice either of continuing their studies or of entering the labour force with a recognized intermediary degree. The scheme was not successful, partly because neither its pedagogical nor its conceptual implications were really solved and partly because it resulted in an over-high transfer rate of students from the non-university vocationally-oriented to the university and theoretically-oriented sector.

The danger of excessive mobility must indeed be considered. Such mobility causes the short-cycle institutions to lose one of their main social functions, namely, to provide the economy with a sufficient number of manpower with intermediary (high but not the highest) qualifications.

Whatever the optimum of student mobility and institutional permeability is, one of the main instruments of providing it seems to be a common credit point system. Such a system is now envisaged in many countries and could be compared to a common convertible currency; it should permit validation of studies on an inter-institutional and inter-sectorial basis, across levels and types of courses. A very elaborate model in this sense is the German 'Brick-box' system (*Baukastensystem*) which is only a blue-print but shows a trend towards a solution.

More progress has already been made in the mobility of teachers and, in general, in equalizing the status of teachers in different types of institution. In some cases almost the same salary scales are applied in both the university and non-university sectors (although, usually, the highest echelon can be achieved only in the university sector); if research is not pursued in certain of the non-university establishments, some possibility for research work is nevertheless given to their teachers.

Finally, important developments are taking place with regard to the overall planning and co-ordination of higher education – across the sectors, levels and institutional types composing the system. Numerous examples can be quoted: state-wide planning boards in the United States (and even inter-state regional consortia), the Central Council for Education (and in the future probably also a National Council for Planning of Higher Education) in Japan, the Ottosen Committee in Norway, the U 68 Commission in Sweden, the Common *Bund* and *Länder* Educational Planning Commission in Germany, and special bodies created by Ministries of Education in the majority of European countries; these all represent a network of real or potential 'Robbins Committees' responsible for considering and reformulating policy regarding the overall structure of post-secondary education.

Some of the deficiencies of the existing systems and, in general, a reconciliation between the integration and diversification processes in higher education might, however, require still more profound innovations than all those mentioned in the present article. One of them would certainly be a radical reform of upper secondary education. Another might be the implement of the recurrent education concept and of a common nation-wide (and why not international?) credit point system as a framework for a real inter-institutional student mobility. These solutions should help to fulfil the main objective of the present search for unity and diversity, namely a student-oriented rather than institution-oriented system of post-secondary education.

NOTES

1. Most of the information contained in this article is based on investigations undertaken within the Higher Education programme of the Organization for Economic Cooperation and Development. They concern mainly countries of Western Europe and North America. Statistical data are derived from *Development of Higher Education, 1950–1967, Statistical Survey*, OECD, Paris 1970, and *Development of Higher Education 1950–1967, Analytical Report* (to be published).

2. This applies to the situation before 1968, but even the important reforms of that year did not profoundly change the situation in this respect.

8

The East European University

Bogdan Suchodolski

East European universities belong to the great family of European universities moulded during the Middle Ages, the Renaissance, and the Enlightment. Prague University was founded in 1348, Cracow University in 1364, Pecs University in 1367. During the sixteenth and seventeenth centuries universities were founded in Vilna (1578), Budapest (1635) and Lwow (1661). In 1755, in the cultural atmosphere of the Enlightment, Moscow University was established, and during the nineteenth century universities in Warsaw (1816), Petersburg (1819), Jassy (1860), Bucharest (1864), and Cluj (1872) emerged.

The role of these universities in the life of the Eastern European nations has been indeed great. They contributed both to the maintenance and extension of cultural links with the larger European tradition, and to the development of modern scholarship, science and technology. They have always been geared to the needs of their societies and states, they have educated managers and experts, and they have influenced policy, jurisprudence and the economy. They thus fulfilled purposes for which they were founded, and which were mentioned in the statutes which established them. According to the act establishing Cracow University, for instance, this stated that 'learning shall be the light enlightening the whole Kingdom'.

However, the organizational structure and spiritual atmosphere of these universities reflected the needs and aspirations of a society in which the ruling classes had at their disposal all the facilities and privileges in the domain of education and culture. The ideal cultivated in the universities was that of disinterested and detached learning, and their programme of education was avowedly elitist: graduation from a university meant not the bestowal of an expert's certificate, but rather a ticket to enter the intellectual elite of a nation.

Only a few individuals from the lower classes could gain access into this elite. The universities – particularly during the nineteenth and twentieth centuries – remained strongholds of elitist and detached cultural activities, while their links with the economic and social needs of the nations became looser.

New Conditions and New Tasks

During the twentieth century the East European universities have had to face new social conditions and new tasks. In 1917 the October Revolution abolished the capitalist system and the rule of the Czar in Russia, establishing a new, large and multinational, but socially uniform state organism, the USSR. In the years 1944 and 1945, as a result of World War II, revolutions were successful in most Eastern European countries. Socialist people's republics were established in Poland, Czechoslovakia, Hungary, Rumania, Bulgaria and Yugoslavia.

The abolition of the class system and traditional privileges, the introduction of nationalized and planned economies, the political and vocational awakening of the masses and extensive programmes to accelerate the processes of industrialization and modernization constituted basic elements in the new situation.

The process of democratization of higher education is characteristic of all industrial countries in the twentieth century. However, in the socialist countries it reveals special features which are worth analysis and reflection. They result from the specific social and economic conditions underlying this process, as well as from unique cultural and educational traditions.

The process of democratizing higher education which started after 1945, was intended to facilitate the access to it of students from social groups which had not had such opportunities previously, as well as to supply highly qualified staff as quickly as possible for the national economies.

The coincidence of the two tasks – of social justice and the needs of developing economies – has been a dynamic force in reshaping higher education, and bringing about a growth and rapid increase in the number of students, and more particularly in the numbers of students from worker and peasant stock.

During the twentieth century significant progress has been made in the growth of higher education, necessitated by transformations in the economy and culture, by the development of industrialization, and by the growing need for educated personnel in all walks of life.

These achievements, however important, are still by no means sufficient. The rate at which the need for educated people has grown is greater than increased rates of output of academic level schools. Hence, a significant number of those who occupy middle and even higher positions in various fields are compelled to undertake supplementary studies without quitting their jobs. This system of higher education for working people has thus been developing ever since the first years of the post-October Revolution period, and it is still an important way of turning out skilled personnel.

This type of higher schooling, however, not only increases the output of educated people, but provides more general access to higher education.

Even though the middle-level or high schools, of both the liberal and vocational type offering formal access to studies are fairly widespread, and the existing system of aid for students facilitates study, still in individual cases there may always be reasons which prevent a student studying at the proper time. This system for working people enables them to undertake higher studies, theoretically at least, at any time of their lives. Such a decision may be dictated either by the need to build up professional knowledge, or by a desire to secure promotion in their work.

However, the two-fold approach to the problem of the development of higher education from the point of view of the need for highly trained personnel, and from that of the pursuit of equal educational opportunities, is by no means sufficient. There is still another viewpoint which reveals interesting characteristics in the process in the socialist countries.

What we have in mind is the fact that the group of educated people is growing very rapidly. In comparison with similar groups in Western European countries, the group is marked by two characteristic features; firstly, its social make-up is neither closed nor fixed by any stable system of privileges allowing access only to certain individuals; secondly, the fact that there is no bourgeoisie imposes upon the group of people with academic education not only professional but also social and cultural tasks.

In this social situation the specific role of the intelligentsia and its cultural ideal is highlighted and accentuated by a belief that intellectual and artistic values are particularly valuable.

The interests typical of people with higher education in science, technology and art are reflected in many ways: in the circulation of books, in the number of literary and learned periodicals, in the development of institutions for the propagation of knowledge, in the intensity and number of courses and summer schools of all types and levels, in the growing audiences in theatres, museums, concert halls and so on.

The strength and scope of these interests are such that they become an important factor in shaping the tasks of academic schools. We are witnessing a characteristic feed-back: higher education is becoming more and more democratic and so producing a growing number of educated people who then exert pressure upon institutions of higher education to make them satisfy the need for postgraduate instruction.

A New Model of University

The new situation and new tasks, similar in all Eastern European countries, have been the starting point of policies to reshape the traditional model of the university. We shall try to point out the main directions of change.

In principle a university has retained its traditional disciplines, such as the philosophical, social and humane studies, mathematics and all the natural sciences. Theology, which used to hold an eminent position, has

:en expelled, and so have the medical sciences, which have found a place
separate academic schools.

The traditional distinction between universities and higher institutes of
chnology, called polytechnics, has been retained. Nevertheless, the line
parating the new university from a polytechnic is by no means clear, and
becoming more and more blurred. This matter has only recently become
ie subject of discussion. Doubts are expressed whether rational reasons
ın be found for the belief that the teaching of chemistry in a university
ught to be essentially different from the teaching of chemistry in a
olytechnic, or whether the teaching of biology ought to be different in
ı agricultural school from a medical school. The stress laid on a closer
onnexion between theory and practice is favoured by those who believe
iat there ought to be less difference in the teaching of the natural sciences
the two types of schools. Still dominant however is the position of those
ho defend the traditional pattern and assign more theoretical tasks to the
niversities, and more practical ones to the polytechnics. Universities are
ipposed to develop theoretical research and co-ordinate the teaching of the
called basic disciplines, as well as to train those who would be able to
ursue them, while polytechnics are expected to concentrate their efforts
n tasks somewhat connected with technological and industrial work.

While the traditional model of a university has been retained with only
ıinor changes, its character has been largely modified. The traditional
niversity used to be an exceptional institution, with a special position
ithin the educational system and enjoying particular prestige among the
ublic. While reforms have tended to bridge the gap between a university
ıd a non-university institution of academic standing the universities have
cen becoming vocational schools, even though they could still retain a
)ecial position, as we shall see later.

This move among universities towards other institutions of higher
Jucation has found expression particularly in the pattern of internal
rganization. Universities are no longer places where eminent professors
cture on what interests them, and students choose such lectures as they
refer; they no longer are intellectual centres in which the exchange of
10ught and learned discussions, rather than examinations and diplomas,
their true and essential concern.

Rather, universities have become schools with definite curricula leading
) definite professional qualifications. Thus the interference of the state in
niversity curricula tends to increase, and they are established by educa-
onal authorities in collaboration with experts. These curricula, even if
ot so flexible, do provide a limited opportunity for professors to present
ie results of their own research, while the students can choose, again
ithin limits, the most interesting lectures. The role of the state in provid-
ıg material aid for students also increases. Various facilities, like boarding

houses, canteens, scholarships, allow the less well-to-do young people to go through the university, but at the same time they are a factor in the more strict discipline of studies. Studying in a university is no longer a private affair of the wealthy who can study for as many years as they wish, but it has rather become a training with a definite programme, terminated by a diploma after a specified period of time.

Thus universities have become similar to all other 'schools', and many people still recall with regret the loss of their former character as places of free scholarship. But just because universities have become 'schools', they can be geared to the general system of education and fulfil their important role of training qualified personnel for the planned economy of the state.

These changes have also involved transformations in the internal administration of universities. They are no longer autonomous corporate bodies which they used to be. University authorities are appointed by the minister of education, and the appointment of a *dozent* or of a professor also rests with the minister, although an opinion and a proposal from the university are required.

The 'school-like' character of the new university is to some extent balanced by the fact that, compared with other educational institutions, universities have research tasks of their own. In all the Eastern European countries there are special research institutions of higher education, notably Academies of Science. The universities in particular have the important tasks of elaborating research plans which are discussed and accepted by ministerial committees on which all universities are represented. These plans have a dual aspect: part of the research problems suggested by universities is eventually included into the larger state plan of research which is of particular national importance, while other problems have inherent scientific significance though their social implications may be not immediately clear. This structure ensures that research has social values and allows freedom and initiative to scientists.

All these transformations of the traditional model of a university define its new situation and a new role in a socialist society. Universities, as a link in the chain of the educational system tightly connected with all the others, have become an important factor in the progress of research and education, a warrant of economic and social growth, and a source of the dissemination of knowledge, and thus of the development of democracy.

The new university appears as an institution of the new society which attempts to attain maximum equality in free access to education, and to open up optimal opportunities of self-realization and of involvement in the social and cultural life of the country for each of its citizens.

The process of developing the new university has been intensive during the last decades in all the East European countries. It has been helped by the mutual exchange of experience between these countries, as well as between them and the Soviet Union, which started on its road to socialism a quarter of a century earlier. However, such an exchange of experience has not meant that directives applying to all these countries have been laid down; rather, it has been a factor stimulating analysis and reflection about the ways the traditional model of a university can be adjusted to new conditions and tasks.

Problems of the New University

A general description of the new model of the university in East European countries must now be supplemented by information about the problems which are at present most vigorously discussed. The most important among them seem to concern the education of highly trained specialists, and the role of universities in disseminating liberal culture.

The growing role of science in contemporary life brings about an increasing need for highly trained specialists. This need must be met by academic institutions. This is now their most important and urgent task. The number and quality of the highest trained personnel are indices of the further development of the economy and culture of a nation.

A difficulty which is already apparent, and which may be expected to become more and more acute, arises from the fact that the need for quantity is important and cannot be reduced, but to fulfil it often means a serious threat to the quality of the mass-trained students. At one time, when the need for specialists was growing rather slowly, the problem of quality could remain the only concern of institutions of higher education, now it can be only a part of the concern. An essential new task of these institutions is to reach the highest possible standard of scientific training without at the same time failing to meet the demand for quantity. The difficulties which arise are manifest. They concern both teaching staff, and methods of teaching which need to take into account larger groups of students.

Another important problem of professional training in academic institutions concerns the character of specialization which may and should be expected. The problem is controversial, and two different solutions are suggested. Employers, as well as graduates, demand emphatically that institutions of higher education like vocational schools at the middle level, prepare young people for specific professional functions, in such a way that they do not meet immediate difficulties in their first job. Under the impact of such demands, the programmes of studies in institutions of higher education have been undergoing modification to achieve this type of preparation of graduates. Those schools which do not meet this are severely criticized.

The opposite principle, that higher studies ought to provide a scientific background for a wide range of possible jobs, involves the need to provide for specialized training outside the normal academic curriculum. Such training can be organized either by special institutions, or by companies. Both cases concern people who are already qualified and who have some practical experience.

The distinction between the two elements of professional training leads to a rather important problem namely relationships between them and timing. The long established and most common pattern, which appears sound and natural, is based upon the principle of a theoretical-scientific background prior to practical training. Even though this kind of structure of professional education seems well justified, it does not exclude other possibilities.

To start with practical experience supplemented by theoretical studies seems impossible and unreasonable. But it should be realized that in various fields there are many clever people with middle-level liberal or vocational education in some cases enriched by private study who are apt to pursue higher studies so as to gain deeper theoretical knowledge. Their practical knowledge is a valuable asset in higher studies.

Students belonging to this group are in a more difficult position than young graduates. Usually those with practical experience have families, and they can hardly ever obtain leave from their jobs for periods sufficient for study, while it is by no means easy to reconcile full-time work with academic studies, even if it is geographically possible.

To facilitate studies for this category of people is an important consideration for the future: one reason being that they can be a valuable element in the supply of academics. Professional activity in various fields has become so complex theoretically that those who work in them, gain extensive knowledge while performing their jobs. Developments of science and technology increase the demands they must meet in their everyday work; they are becoming less and less routine workers trained to perform definite manipulations without understanding. In some most modern companies the technological-scientific level is so high that the difference between laboratories in institutions of higher education and factories becomes less and less marked.

Thus 'routine workers' are particularly well qualified to follow higher studies, thereby rapidly and significantly increasing their professional efficiency.

Another reason justifying improved facilities for higher studies for employees, is the more general political concern to achieve equal access to education for all.

Postgraduate Training

The acceleration of scientific change makes postgraduate training increasingly important. Academic institutions like any other traditional institutions were shaped under the influence of relatively stable conditions. The education acquired in them was expected to be final and complete. Indeed, the student could be sure that the amount of information and skills which he had acquired would be sufficient for his whole life, without any need to supplement them, or fear that anything would become useless or wrong.

This type of belief still prevails. A diploma of graduation appears as a kind of lifelong qualification. He who has received it, believes that he can legitimately work in his profession to the end of his days, without undergoing any further courses. Such courses would seem to reflect a lack of confidence in institutions of higher education and in their graduates. Thus the years of study become the capital which need not be augmented to reap indefinitely, financial benefits.

Nevertheless, the present situation is quite different. The progress of science is so rapid that during one lifetime, fundamental changes occur in views, methods and discoveries. This fact is the most revolutionary feature of our time even though it is not appreciated sufficiently. It seems that its impact upon the tasks and organization of academic institutions will be a most significant transforming factor.

Even today, a graduate cannot remain satisfied with the knowledge he acquired during his course of studies. He cannot afford to lag behind current developments in his discipline, if he wants to remain an efficient worker. Certainly, as before, some individuals wished to add to their formal education. However, it was their private decision. Their basic knowledge was both sufficient and valid; if they extended it, it was to their credit, but it was neither a social nor a professional necessity.

Today, postgraduate training has an essentially different character. After a time, university knowledge is no longer sufficient or even valid. It must be supplemented, renewed and transformed. Otherwise work will become inefficient or even outright harmful and dangerous. This is why post-graduate training cannot be left to the goodwill of individuals. It must become obligatory.

This task must be assumed by academic-level institutions. Their duties towards those who have begun and finished their studies in them cannot be considered to be at an end as soon as a degree has been conferred. Institutions of higher education must make the effort to keep their former graduates abreast of current developments. The task is difficult and com-plex, but there is no other agency able to undertake and perform it, but only the institutions of higher education as centres of science and education at the academic level. Even if we make a radical division between teaching and research, postgraduate training would remain the duty of educators rather than researchers.

Some thought needs to be given to the organization and methods of postgraduate training. Proposals must be formulated and presented to the trade unions and the leaders of social and economic life. As yet very little has been done in these fields, but the task is becoming more and more urgent. Institutions of higher education, which have been centres of professional preparation, will become centres of training for those who are already active in their professions. New types of student will appear, with different backgrounds, different needs, who time and choose the type of their studies differently. New opportunities to contact current life and work will emerge for such institutions and new possibilities exist for gathering experience.

In connexion with these new tasks an important question arises. Should institutions of higher education operate side by side with the older ones, or in closer relation with them? Differences in age, length of study and the character and backgrounds of the two groups of students, seem to determine the need to separate work along two lines of teaching. Nevertheless it cannot be denied that contact between those who come back to the school for a short time to supplement their knowledge after years of professional work with those who are obtaining initial qualifications would be desirable and advantageous. This problem will have to be solved in future. Today it would be premature to analyse it in any more detail as we are only at the threshold of an effort to organize postgraduate training.

However, the perspective of mass postgraduate training brings another issue to light. It has been the aim of schools and of institutions of higher education in particular, to give a liberal education, that would be sufficient for a lifetime, and similarly academic-level schools have been attempting to give a complete professional training. In both cases the result of these tendencies has been an increase in the length of the courses.

Since the older ideal of an education which is sufficient to meet the needs of a lifetime is no more attainable, the question arises whether some portion of the knowledge and skills now taught during preparatory studies should not be moved to the supplementary training periods? The problem of shortening basic studies is often approached in a one-sided manner, namely how to get rid of what is unnecessary. Of course, every programme includes unnecessary material. But they are relatively few, and the time saved by this method can never be really significant.

If the problem of shortening the period of basic studies is to be approached in a socially profitable manner, it must be conceived within the perspectives sketched here. A reduction in the programmes of studies should take into account not only what is unnecessary but also and mainly what can be taught during later training periods more fruitfully than during the basic preparatory studies.

Institutions of Higher Education and Liberal Culture

Liberal Culture as a Scientific Image of Reality

What we have said above, concerns the new conception of academic institutions as centres of professional training. However, academic schools have always aspired to play a more important role, and they want to be something more than mere professional institutions. They have a cultural mission among the highest social strata. They want not only to train specialists, but to educate a spiritual and moral elite. They want to have a voice in the basic issues of culture and man. These intentions hark back to their historical traditions.

But precisely for that reason these ambitions have encountered acute contemporary criticism. It has been argued that today such ambitions are superfluous. Institutions of higher education ought to become professional schools as soon as possible, the more narrowly specialized the better; they should supply good experts, without caring about anything else. The academic schools, and universities of the past, cannot be a model for the present.

Actually, both positions, if their basic principles are considered, are not opposed to each other. The belief that institutions of higher education ought to provide liberal culture can be thoroughly modern while the claim that they ought to be mere professional schools can be as thoroughly conservative. Only by putting new content into both of these tasks can we fulfil them.

The first issue concerning the content of a modern liberal culture is a matter of what, providing a synthetic scientific image of the world, the institutions of higher education are expected to disseminate. The claim that an academic institution ought to give its graduates an education allowing them to understand reality in scientifically accepted terms seems sound and justified. However, is it at all realistic in a context of the principle of specialized training? The development of science and technology during the nineteenth century has thrown into relief the value of specialization. Sometimes it appeared as a synonym for knowledge and skill in general.

Today, we understand that the problem of specialization is much more complex, and that its growth is advantageous only up to a certain point. It is fruitful as long as it does not hinder a view of the whole. When this happens, specialization no longer leads to a better understanding of things, and it may even lead to false approaches. Since the character and role of elements making up a whole are in varying degrees determined by the whole, the limits of specialization in various fields may differ. What is always necessary is some link with a larger body of knowledge about the whole, as it is within such a system of knowledge, and not in spite of it, that frontiers between specializations have to be drawn if they are to be meaningful and fruitful.

However, the modern problem of specialization is even more complex. Any narrow focus is always an expression of concern for some fragment of a definite whole. It thus presupposes a certain concept of the whole in relation to which specialization constitutes a more detailed inquiry. Hence, the problem of specialization involves not only the pattern of co-operation of various experts within larger research tasks, but it may also involve the problem of who is supposed to investigate what, and how.

The nineteenth century was the period of emancipation for independent special disciplines from older more inclusive fields. However, it slowly became apparent that many problems, some of them of the utmost significance, were frontier territories on the map of reality divided up into narrow disciplines. Hence, a tendency to emphasize unique methods and approaches in independent disciplines has been opposed by a tendency to emphasize the import of investigations requiring interdisciplinary effort. The efficiency of such co-operation was becoming more and more apparent. The most significant and creative achievements have been emerging out of interdisciplinary enterprises on the frontiers of psychiatry and psychology, psychology and sociology, sociology and economics, biology and psychology, biology and chemistry, chemistry and physics. The bulk of the great discoveries of our time have been made by people on the frontiers.

There is still another aspect of the issue here discussed. When the frontiers of the whole change a question arises: what is basic, and what is subordinate? We are now witnessing a characteristic shift of attitudes. During the nineteenth century science tended to focus on the concrete and the detailed. But the twentieth century has discovered the import of the fundamentals and of the whole again. The new approach is of course different from its earlier counterparts, but still it is clear and distinct.

With the progress of specialization, with scholars taking up more and more detailed problems, what has been realized is the importance of investigating the ultimate origins and principles of facts, as well as of methods of building general theories. Most prominent examples of this tendency are modern mathematics and physics. What is now emerging can be paradoxically described as specialization with a framework of general knowledge, i.e. basic to many disciplines. Such specialization will be necessary and fertile. This type of 'general knowledge' has its share in the general view of reality elaborated by the particular sciences, and it makes it possible to see the outlines of an even more general synthesis.

It is at this point that we must face an important and difficult problem. Even if we assume that students should be taught in their special disciplines so as to see problems in neighbouring fields, principally concerned with ιe same object of study that they should be introduced to important ιterdisciplinary issues and that they should gain insight into the basic ɾinciples of their own discipline, philosophically reaching beyond its ɔope – even if we assumed all this, still the problem of providing an ɔcess to a most general scientific synthesis of reality would remain open.

What are the possibilities of grasping the main lines of the more remote ιisciplines? What can and ought a student of physics learn about philology ɾr economics, and conversely? Is it at all possible and how can an en- ɔunter between the remote disciplines be organized so as to gain anything ιtellectually?

In answering these questions, some distinctions must be made. Firstly, ɾom almost every discipline conclusions and some superficial knowledge ɔan be drawn which is useful in the everyday life of individuals and which ɔught to be possessed by educated people. Everyone needs in his life some ιlements of psychology and pedagogy, some knowledge about health, ɔeeding, economics, sociology, history, geography, art and nature.

However, such encyclopaedic knowledge reaching beyond one's own ιiscipline is not what is most valuable from the point of view of the role ɾf institutions of higher education in the intellectual education of people. Λuch more important is an opportunity to learn about the results of ɔcientific investigations in other fields which are at the moment most ιmportant for science as a whole and for society. We know that contribu- ιons from particular disciplines to the general progress of science vary, ιnd that at different times different disciplines can boast of very general ιgnificant achievements. Interesting information about them can be read ιn monthly and weekly reviews, and even in daily newspapers. Students ιn institutes of higher education should be able to find more sound and ɔliable information on these matters, if there are highly competent ex- ιerts among their professors.

It seems desirable that in institutes of higher education there should be stimulating intellectual atmosphere for the presentation and discussion ιf the most important and novel achievements in various disciplines. It ɹoes not seem appropriate that students should seek this kind of informa- ιon outside their institutions through media accessible to the larger public: valid opinion seems to be that it is the institutions of higher education ɯhich ought to become the radiating centres of information for both their ɔwn students and for the larger public.

There are two levels at which to solve the problem of learning about the ιewest and most significant achievements of science. One of them is ɾelated to simple intellectual curiosity which is by no means contemptible. ɹut from the point of view of our discussion, another and higher level is ιnore important. On this level a deeper understanding of scientific achieve- ιnents is involved. It seems important and useful that students learning their chosen fields should be able to glance now and again at the scientific and methodological problems of some other disciplines, either similar to, or remote from their own. A synthesis-oriented analysis of their achievements can produce important educational results.

Finally, establishing closer relationships between studies in a narrower field with a more general understanding of science as a whole is facilitated by a knowledge of the history of science. It imposes a synthetic view of the development of human knowledge, and of the ways and methods of acquiring it. The educational import of this discipline is more and more clearly and generally seen.

The growing interest in the history of science and technology has its deep social causes. It is an expression of the needs of an epoch in which the role of science and technology is particularly great and is still growing. In this epoch, when the bases of socialism are established over great areas of earth, science and technology are called to the service of human welfare, while the increasing participation of the masses in the management of the economy and social life requires that elements of the scientific outlook should be instilled in them.

When we talk about the import of learning by higher schools students of a general scientific image of the world, we do not mean any 'synthesis' of knowledge, which is unrealistic today. We believe, however, that the methods here discussed (which are: reaching beyond the chosen field towards its frontiers and fundamentals; knowledge of the history of science and of the studied discipline in particular; studying the methodological structures of other disciplines; studying some chosen achievements in as thorough manner as possible) contribute to the formation of a deeper intellectual culture of the students, and to the shaping of their outlook based upon a scientific approach.

Liberal Culture and Understanding Society

The tasks of institutions of higher education in the field of general education are not limited to the formation of an intellectual culture and a scientific outlook; they also involve an introduction to the social problems of each of the several professions taught and thus into the social problems of the nation and of an epoch, since it is only against such an extensive background that it is possible to analyse the social duties of the people who possess higher education.

These matters, though hitherto neglected, are nevertheless very important. Higher levels of the professional hierarchy require not only more knowledge, technological competence and responsibility, but also a greater sense of social responsibility for production, the atmosphere in a large team, and even for the fate of individual people. An engineer, an economist, a physician, a lawyer, an architect, a teacher usually occupy positions which make many people more or less dependent on them. Specialists are valuable not only because they know something, or how to do something, better than others, but also because they can thereby contribute to the common welfare. Two types of people are equally useless to society, namely those who cannot contribute to anything and those experts who are concerned only with the interests of their own special field and try to pursue them without taking into account the needs and values of other people.

Specialization is a good thing, but like everything else, it may outgrow itself and become distorted. It must be protected from these dangers by encouraging a feeling and understanding that it is a social function. The building of a house, the organizing of a company or a system of law, are not activities controlled by their own inherent criteria only. They must be also appreciated from the point of view of general human values.

What is involved here, is not goodwill and individual eagerness: it is rather a clear and concrete understanding of the tasks and possibilities of a definite kind of work in the life of the whole society. It requires knowledge of the structure and of tendencies of development of an epoch. Such knowledge becomes more and more difficult in proportion to the degree that lack of stability and the presence of novelty exist in the actual conditions of life. It cannot be achieved by intuition and experience alone; it requires a solid background of study.

Thus it is social training which becomes the main factor in the 'formation of man'. If we understand this fact, we also understand the general educational character of social training. It is so-called liberal culture which has been supposed to be the factor in the 'formation of man'. It retains this function even now, though its contents have been changed.

The notion of 'liberal culture' ought to be revised now, and enriched by introducing the problems of social life into it. The main end of contemporary education is to cultivate an ability to think; the most important task in this respect is to educate the people so as to make them able to think in social terms. The traditional humanistic conception of liberal culture has been a culture of words. Now it ought to include thought and social action. Even though word and thought are very strictly related, educational principles take on a different emphasis depending on whether they are based on rhetoric, logic, or praxeology.

The University as an Open Source of Culture

The role of the university in liberal culture is not limited to the dissemination of a scientific image of reality and to teaching people to define their place in society. There remains an important and extensive area, difficult to describe in any systematic manner, where manifold interests in past and present culture overlap. This area, involving philosophy and art, the natural and social and political sciences, technology and urban planning, constitutes the limits of what is culturally significant for a modern man.

It can be safely predicted that this type of interest will increase in future. People will have more leisure, and material welfare will require less effort. Cultural interests may be thus expected to flourish. However, it requires adequate patterns of stimuli, and a proper organization of life. It is probably in this field that the struggle for the way of life in future civilizations will be fought. At stake is the model of life either of passive idleness feeding on mass entertainment, or of awakened creative tendencies, of active cultural participation, of culture as the manifold kingdom of all human values.

If life in the future is to be fully human, universities cannot refuse to participate in the efforts towards a systematic arranging of the stimuli leading to this end. Universities have been traditionally centres of creative attitudes towards life and culture. The controversies about the basic human values, the ways of understanding and of continuing them are fought inside universities. It is in them that science becomes a matter of criticism and creation and the transmitting of culture is a vivid and thoughtful concern.

For these reasons universities can hardly be expected to remain closed institutions of higher education in future as they are now. Even today, objections are raised against the fact that the best intellectual manpower gathered in universities serves only the needs of their students, instead of the larger population of those interested in culture and science at the higher levels. It can be expected that to limit the role of universities to the students, whose number is determined by the needs for qualified experts, will finally be overcome and that universities will become open schools serving the diversified needs of people interested in learning and not in diplomas.

They will then become as important for the whole society as they used to be for its limited circles. The double meaning of the word *universitas* – as full knowledge and general participating in its development – will then reach its realization, in accordance with the dreams of pedagogues who, like Comenius, wanted 'everybody to know all about everything'. If we interpret this formula as Comenius understood it, as knowledge about the structure of the actual and possible world, and about man as a being who creates his own life, as a Pansophia, rather than in a narrow quantitative way, we shall understand fully the possible future of the university in a socialist society.

9

University Reform: A Comparative Analysis of the American, Russian and German Universities

Leonhard Froese

What points for discussion arise from the proposals for new university legislation and from the university models on which these proposals are based? The question, when analysed, seems to be: are the institutes of higher learning, the traditional type universities, fitted for the tasks of our time? One might also ask: are the universities still suited to perform their own duties?

Two questions are thus opened up, which cannot necessarily be brought together. The history of higher education both at home and abroad illustrates this. In the first instance the question is being raised outside the university of its relevance to our present times. The criterion being used is the concept, which may or may not be defined, of 'the task of our time'. A more precise definition establishes this as a 'social task', which, on further elaboration, becomes the vaguely described task demanded by structural changes in the modern socio-political set-up. Structural changes in contemporary society present a challenge to the universities as well, provoking them on the one hand to make a scientific study of these phenomena, to research into them and to come to terms with them, and on the other hand to ask themselves if, in fact, the university institution, its organization and *modus operandi* are up to date, i.e. whether they can be socially integrated. Any discussion of the second question, whether the university is still suited to performing its task, must also begin at the same point as the traditional style *Universitas litterarum* in asking itself: am I merely an historical fact or am I still, even as an historical institution, a factor of importance in the contemporary world? When speaking of the task of the university, whether in a general sense or within the context of its historical development, one cannot mean anything other than its original task; and then one cannot avoid discussing the idea of the university in the way that Karl Jaspers, Wolfgang Clemen, Ernst Anrich and others do. On the basis of this central idea one must then establish a relationship between the task of the university and the task of a particular age.

The difficulty begins when one tries to bring together the two concepts of 'the role of the university' and 'the needs of society'. The university never was intended to be either a Platonic Academy or a pedagogical institute, a cloister or an ivory tower, a scholars' enclave or a Castalian. Right from its origins it has never encouraged either pure research or learning for its own sake – it had no time for intellectual glass-bead games. As Herbert Grundmann recently demonstrated,[1] the university was an institution with a quite practical, even useful purpose. The concept 'university' originally meant – as defined in Paris in 1213: 'The *universitas magistrorum et scoliarum* or *studentium*, the totality, community, and association of teachers and pupils, professors and students, who organized themselves for the better pursuit of their common interest in study.' It is here that the institutional idea of the university originates. The second point arising from this is that the university was not originally intended to embrace all fields of learning. In these early days universities consisted of one, or possibly several faculties, but rarely would every faculty be represented. A third point which arises in this connexion is that from the very beginning the universities did not engage solely in the pursuit of specialized study but also offered academics a professional training. In the charters of the first universities there is nothing of *universitas litterarum*.

External and Internal Autonomy

The concept of university as *universitas*, that unique product of the European mind which circulated throughout the world, is the result of an historical development which proceeded in fits and starts. It was through their own efforts, rather than through the generosity of State and Church, that the universities won that external autonomy which is the essential institutional characteristic. Grundmann continues: 'the universities themselves rather than any secular or ecclesiastical courts, created all those forms and institutions of corporative self-government which were adopted later by royal founders of universities, and which – with many slight variations – still characterize the university in contrast to other schools and educational institutions: namely, the administration is headed by a Rector who is elected from the university's own members and has jurisdiction over these members; the division of fields of study into faculties, each of which is likewise headed by a Dean elected to office for a given period of time; their right to examine students and to confer degrees, the right to teach, and many other smaller points right down to the official designations of professors, lecturers, the traditional cap and gown, beadles, the matriculation ceremonies of the students, appellation of the lecture, lecture room, great hall, and so on'.[2]

The essential characteristic of academic freedom, the internal autonomy of the university, was likewise won by its own efforts. It is this principle of intellectual freedom – applying to lecturers as well as students – which underlies the idea of combining research and teaching. Jaspers defines it thus: 'the university has the task of seeking truth in the community of researchers and students – it has its own independent existence, free from State intervention and based on an eternal concept – a concept with the same supranational universal character as that of the church. It lays claim to and is granted the freedom to teach; that is to say, it must teach the truth regardless of any wishes or directives either from outside or from within the university. The university is a school but is unique in its kind. Here it is not intended that the pupil should merely be taught but that he should participate in research and thus receive an academic training through which he shapes his life. According to this notion pupils should be capable of an independent, critical approach to what they are taught. They have freedom in learning. Through the university, Society and State can attain the clearest awareness of their age. Here teachers and pupils may come together for the sole purpose of understanding truth.'[3]

The concept of combining research and teaching has only recently been won. It is likewise a communal European achievement although it was first given concrete form in Germany in the type of university inspired by Humboldt. The Englishman Newman, America's Abraham Flexner and the Russian N. I. Pirogow are all well-known examples testifying to the widespread effect of this idea outside Germany and to the great impetus which was given by the new type of university founded in Berlin in 1810. As the result of a century-long evolutionary development, tried out first in Göttingen and finally winning official recognition in Berlin, there came about that unique cross between school and academy which Alois Dempf has called 'the personal union of researcher and teacher'. It is concerned neither solely with the transmission of knowledge nor solely with research, but devotes equal attention to both pursuits. There has always been disagreement as to whether teaching and research should be separated and hence carried out in special colleges and research centres respectively and it is this very question which forms the background to the discussion over a new type of university in West Germany.[4]

If society and the governments which represent it agree with Schelsky in demanding that the university should provide the future leaders of society with a training geared to the needs of a scientific civilization and no more, then there remains no alternative – the university must become a college for specialized education. Other contemporary social systems are often cited as examples of this. If on the other hand society identifies its interests with the universities' scholarly task, if in its own interests it supports the principle of *libertas philosophandi*, i.e. freedom of thought and learning for lecturer and students, thus endorsing the ideals of the Enlightenment which Kant once termed *sapere aude*, then again no alternative remains: Society must allow the university to remain as it is, knowing this to be necessary for the conservation and furtherance of its own intellectual well-being.

As all the arguments concerning educational reform always come back to the fact that the FRG is one of the world's leading industrial states and should therefore have an educational system in keeping with a modern economic and social structure, a comparison with the situation in the United States and in the Soviet Union is called for.

The Russian and Soviet University

The concept and function of academic freedom and self-government in Czarist Russia and the Soviet Union, like the concept and internal structure of Russian universities overall, originate from the European, and in particular the French and German models. It was the university statute of Alexander I in 1804 which established them on this basis. The old Czarist University of Moscow (1755) now named after M. W. Lomonossov, and also the Universities of Kharkov (1805) and Kazan (1804), Dorpat (1802) and Vilna (1803) were given complete autonomy. The right of self-government was given to the universities and that of teaching freedom to the professors. The statute of Alexander II in 1863 confirmed and extended these rights. In the nineteenth century the Russian universities followed the German example of forming separate faculties, each with its own rights and duties. The extent of this freedom was restricted, however, in respect of the much greater State control exercised through the Chancellor upon the elected Rector and Council, the Deans and Professors, and thus indirectly upon the students. Particularly at the time of the reaction which had already begun under Alexander I, and which came to a head during the reigns of his successors, these rights were progressively reduced until eventually only a shadow of the university idea remained. The right to appoint professors was transferred first to the State-established University Boards of Trustees and later to Government ministries. The choice came to depend not so much on academic qualifications as on political 'reliability'. University teachers were required to give the Ministry precise details and reading lists for their courses. The Deans, to whom professors were directly answerable, had to make known to the authorities the slightest alteration in the agreed material. The professors were given a strict political brief to instruct their students in accordance with the prevailing political ideology. Lecturers and students were kept under political surveillance and a social *numerus clausus* was introduced. These historical events together with the events of October 1917 provide the background for the university reforms which took place in the Soviet Union after the Revolution. These entailed: the introduction of a social pre-university college and of a renewed social *numerus clausus* – this time for the benefit of the children of the proletariat; the centralization of university administration: the appointment of chancellors, deans and professors by the State; the idealization and politicization of every aspect of teaching: the temporary appointment of so-called red professors whose duty was to adapt the old philosophical faculties for the furtherance of Marxism-Leninism; the splitting up of faculties and re-grouping of disciplines to aid better control; the regimentation of the entire study and examination structure: the students lost their freedom of study and were directed to adhere strictly to the prescribed curriculum of their own particular subject, and in addition they had to complete a so-called course of basic social principles. The State hegemony over universities did not change under Stalin or Khrushchev. The University Statutes of 1938 and 1961 bear witness to this.

Let us consider those three aspects of the 1961 regulations governing universities in the USSR which are of most interest to us.[5] The Chancellor is responsible for 'the entire range of university activities'. No distinction is made between the functions of pure administration and academic administration. Although the Chancellor is selected from amongst 'those members of the university with the highest qualifications and the best academic background', he is none the less regarded as an authorized representative of the State. The Soviet university thus embodies the interesting concept of a single, dual-purpose administration. Neither is the entire non-academic administration merely placed under the State-appointed Chancellor but is rather entrusted to him. He is responsible for everything, from the supervision of study and research programmes to the direction of activities connected with ideological education amongst lecturers and students, clerical and non-clerical staff even down to the personnel and financial aspects of administration. The Vice-Chancellors, appointed in the same way and responsible for 'teaching and research', assist the Chancellor in these tasks. In addition there is a 'Vice-Chancellor for financial administration', and furthermore a 'University Council' exists to assist the Chancellor. The structure and function of this Council are so typical of the Soviet university, that it is highly appropriate to quote the following excerpts as they stand: 'The University Council shall consist of: the Chancellor (as Chairman), the Vice-Chancellors, the Deans of the Faculties, the Professors of Social Science and of other important subjects; representatives of the teaching body elected for a period of three years by the Councils of the individual Faculties; representatives of the social organizations of the University. The University Council is empowered to appoint on to its committee important Scientists and specialists from institutes and organizations connected with the work of the University' (para. 50).

The Councils of the individual Faculties are made up in a similar way.

The Faculty is termed both academically and administratively as a 'sub-department of the University, providing for the instruction of students and post-graduates in one or more related fields of specialized study, for the improvement of qualifications of the leading workers and engineers in the appropriate branches of economics and culture'. Then follow the words: 'and for the guidance of research work undertaken by professors' (para. 34). Departments may be set up within the Faculties. The Faculty is headed by the Dean, who is elected by secret ballot for a period of three years. This is a noteworthy divergence from the University Charter of the Stalinist era; its significance is limited however by the fact that it is not the Faculty which elects him, but the University or Faculty Council. The Dean, who may be appointed from amongst either the professors or the lecturers, heads 'teaching and research work' in the Faculty and supervises the entire organization of study, including practical examinations and the encouragement of promising students. He sees to it that the students move up, distributes grants to them, and admits them to examinations. He alone is responsible for ensuring that 'the teaching staff improve their qualifications'. The Soviet system of study and examinations can only be described as strictly orientated towards achieving the desired results. Although the Constitution gives to every Soviet citizen aged between 17 and 35 who has the necessary qualifications the right to study at a university, in practice a limit is imposed by a *numerus clausus* which operates on the *Kader Production* basis. Applicants for places as determined by the authorities have to pass through the double filter of admission regulations and entrance examination. Party, trade unions and youth organization, all play an often decisive part in this. The duration of study is estimated at around five years, follows strictly laid-down lines and concludes with a State or Degree examination. In his first years the student pursues a kind of basic study which includes the obligatory social sciences a foreign, language and courses of practical work. During the final years the entire academic work of the students is concentrated on the specialized field of study in which he is to be examined. The academic year is divided into terms each followed by a vacation. According to the 'Regulations governing annual examinations', the student must sit an exam at the end of the academic year.

The American University

American college structure was also originally influenced to a great extent by the European type of university, in particular by those in England and Germany. Initially based entirely on the English college ideal, there finally emerged during the period after the Civil War the American university structure, the result of various influencing factors. Aspects of the German university, of the German technical college and of the American college are present. Just as John Harvard, the founder of the oldest and most re-nowned university in the United States, had studied at Cambridge, so the student and later President of Harvard, Edward Everett (the first American to receive his doctorate at Göttingen), was influenced by the German conception of a university. This is the age of Bancroft, Ticknor, Cogwell, Longfellow and Motley, Bismarck's university friend. Harvard and Göttingen had close connexions at that time – and indeed all these men had studied at Göttingen, the predecessor of the type of university established by Humboldt. During his Presidency at Harvard, Everett had striven together with these men to introduce the structural features of the German university. Academic freedom, the seminar, the doctorate and the formation of faculties were adopted. Under Charles William Eliot, who had introduced freedom of choice of the subject to be studied, Harvard became a proper university. The Johns Hopkins University in Baltimore, and indeed other famous universities, such as the University of Chicago, followed this example.

This tendency in some of the great American universities in the industrial East, was accompanied and impaired by that other development associated with the settlement and emigration in the West. It was here that after 1862 the State-endowed land-grant colleges (Morrill Act) sprang up, the germ cells of the great State universities of America. Their origins are essentially older. The first State university was brought into being in 1766 in New Jersey. After the War of Independence it was followed by Georgia (1785), North Carolina (1786) and then by a succession of large and small universities under the administration of the individual States, so that by 1860 there were already seventeen, and by 1910 eighty-nine (out of a total of 581). Today more than half of all American students study at State universities. The State universities adopted the Presidential constitution which was generally characteristic of the American university. The President, occasionally also termed Rector or Chancellor, is the head of the unified academic and State administration. But it was in the State universities that right from the start he found himself to a great extent dependent on the supervisory committees who exercised control over finance. The danger of such dependence did and still does of course exist in the private mostly denominational universities, but in practice the effect is not so pronounced as in the State institutions. This tendency has increased as the Federal State has, to an ever greater degree in recent years, given more and more support to universities in need of subsidies – particularly since the National Defense Act of 1958. This is exemplified by the statement: 'the university is at the service of the State and the Nation and serves teaching and research'. The President, who is appointed by the Board of Trustees for several years, should be but does not necessarily have to be an academic. In the various administrative functions – teaching staff, student body, finances, public relations – he is assisted by the vice-presidents, directors, and deans. According to the older but frequently still valid university laws and charters the President is head of the entire administration. Correspondingly he is also superior to the professors in their capacity as teachers and researchers. The institution of presidency is in fact the executive organ of the university. He is responsible for moral well-being and order, for teaching and research programmes, just as for study schemes and the public relations of the university.

As the position of the President *vis-à-vis* the Governors became more autonomous and consolidated, an analogous development took place in the faculties, which tended towards preventing the powers of the President from becoming too extensive. The faculties of the large State universities are now, for their part, striving to extend and legalize the scope of the academic self-government awarded to them. Not only do they wish to elect their Dean themselves, but also to play an influential role in the appointment of the President. They aim to be free of the feeling of working in an undemocratic, oligarchical atmosphere governed by officials. They would like to participate in a delegated system of academic self-government which has its roots at the lowest strata.

The position of the Dean of the Faculty is, according to traditional academic custom, defined as that of a *primus inter pares*, but at the same time he is the chief administrator on the middle structural level. The Dean represents not only the interests of the Faculty and the individual members *vis-à-vis* the Directors, vice-presidents, members of the Board of Governors and the President, but also has the function of ensuring that the decisions and directives from the upper levels of administration reach the lower levels. At the same time he is a kind of personnel and financial Director of the school or college encompassing or encompassed by the Faculty. The Dean draws up the budget of the Faculty and its institutions. He is moreover the only Faculty member who is able to exercise influence on the appointments policy of the President and the Board of Governors. The Chairman or heads of departments, of institutes and seminars of the faculties, schools and colleges are answerable to him. Like the Dean himself these are not elected but are appointed by the President and the Board. The same applies in principle to the professors. Advised, supported, and to a certain extent controlled by compulsory committees in all important matters, he is also responsible for enforcing the rules regarding syllabuses and examinations.

These, like most aspects of the university, vary from State to State and even from university to university. They are, however, indicative in each case of the didactic-methodical system, which, as in the Soviet Union, produces a mode of study which has more in common with school than university. This is particularly true of the so-called undergraduate work consisting as a rule of four years of general study up to baccalaureate, with the beginnings of specialization. Following on to this is the graduate work – research and special study organized in particular 'schools' and faculties or departments and leading to a diploma, master's degree, or doctorate.

Considerably greater academic freedom prevails here, but there are limitations as well in so far as courses of study are more or less firmly laid down. The academic year, which lasts nine months, can be divided into either two or three terms. Of interest are the widespread summer courses. They offer students and professional people with a corresponding standard of education the opportunity to shorten their studies by up to one year.

West German University Reform

The model upon which rest the ideas for the new West German Colleges of Higher Education and their legal framework is moving to a certain extent closer and closer to the American and Soviet Russian system as it moves away from the traditional German form. The proposals are as follows:

(1) The Rector or President would be elected for a longer period, perhaps for six to eight years. Since re-election would be permissible and the period of office as Vice-Rector would come in addition to this, it would be conceivable that one person could preside over the university for sixteen years. Already the suggestion has repeatedly been made that a university President be appointed for life. Bearing in mind that for obvious reasons the leaders of the new universities would not be elected but would be appointed by the government, it becomes clear to just what extent the principle of university self-government would be affected by this. This tendency is underlined by a strengthening of the position of the Senate and the Convention to the detriment of the former rights and functions of the Faculty.

(2) In this connexion the question of sub-dividing or splitting the faculties and departments on Anglo-American, and for that matter Soviet-Russian lines, was initially discussed. However, the principle of division into individual subjects has been decided on instead. The Dean of the particular subject would be elected for a longer period than previously and would receive more far-reaching supervisory and administrative powers.

(3) Study would be shortened and more strictly controlled than before. Professors and students would be obliged to offer and attend lectures and classes which adhere to a clearly defined system of study. Academic freedom and freedom of movement from one university to another would therefore be restricted. Term times would be lengthened and altered; during vacations supplementary courses for students and those already in employment would be held. The parallels to the Soviet-Russian and American procedures is also evident here.

From the foregoing we may draw the following conclusions:

(a) The scholarly, academic, and educational work of the university is its sole directive and task. It is exclusively determined by that which is termed the 'Idea of the University'. This autonomous task of the university carries with it certain legal, administrative, institutional, and organizational elements. The idea and task of the university on the one hand, its form and structure on the other, are interdependent.

If the fundamental nature of the German type of university is to be retained:

1. The principle of academic freedom must be affirmed. The three Fs of the German concept of higher education are freedom of research and teaching, freedom to participate voluntarily in these and freedom of movement with regard to place of study.[6]

2. The principle of unity of research and teaching must be adopted. University teachers, students and institutions are to be equipped with a framework which provides on the one hand for sufficient personnel, finance and apparatus, and on the other for sufficient space and time.

3. The principle of self-determination and co-operative determination of the student must be adopted. As a *civis academicus* with responsibility for his own actions, the student has a part to play in the life of his university and cannot allow himself to be dictated to by it from either a political or educational point of view. Through both specialized study and general education he should acquire the powers of both scholarly judgment and political action.

4. The principle of partial joint administration by the State must be retained. As the source of revenue the State has not only a general right in matters of surveillance and appointment, but also a right, which must however be exactly defined, to encroach upon academic self-government. On the other hand, however, it follows that it has a duty to safeguard and promote this self-government.

(b) The role of the university in a social, State, and professional context is subject to a different law, a law which binds it in form and content to an order of things upon which it can exert little influence, and which is imposed on it from outside. This task is governed by what is termed the 'claims of the time'; these are of a socio-political nature and involve legal, institutional, administrative and organizational matters. They are not prejudicial to the idea and task of the university but they do affect its form and structure. The opposing demands of both worlds must be settled within this framework. If a university aims to be a socially integrated institution, it is not sufficient:

1. For it to conform to State and society and align itself with a constitution which has legitimately come about. It must assimilate itself to the State and society as an authority which has validity here and now. That means that it must acknowledge its role as a political instructor.

2. For it to comply with its task of research and teaching. It must include within its scope the task of career training, in so far as this has a

place within its scholarly confines.

3. For it to acknowledge the interest of the world outside by observing the established examination norms, subject combinations, and limits to duration of study. It must undertake the supervision and examination of occupational courses, where they cannot be more efficiently undertaken elsewhere.

4. For it to merely tolerate student self-government. The right of the student body to share in decision-making machinery must be taken seriously. The right to be heard in matters immediately affecting it is only one aspect – student self-government must be integrated with academic self-government.

Should Intellectual Activity be Subject to Controls or be Free?

Since its inception, irrespective of time, place and form, the university has been conscious of its social task. It could not however always assume that State and society were, for their part, conscious of its academic role as a university. It was, and indeed still is, very much easier for the State to demand that the university should acknowledge its social function than for the university to be able to expect that its own interests be respected by the State. Where this did not and does not happen, it has no choice, if it is to remain true to its role, but to fight for the preservation of its intellectual freedom. This may conflict with the requirements of the State at a given time; it may also, either apparently or in fact, conflict with the current needs of society – but the defence of the university's role cannot stand in contradiction to its social role as such. For if society is to mature and develop, then the university will be serving its interests by preserving and upholding its own intellectual and institutional autonomy. It was with his statesmanlike insight as a politician, and his wisdom as a scholar, that Humboldt said that intellectual freedom is in the long run politically more lucrative than intellectual subjection. This applies above all to the intellect itself. Ever since State and society have been aware of this they have embodied that great concept in their constitutions: 'art and knowledge, research and teaching, are free'. Alongside that which may be termed the European contribution to the establishment of the idea and reality of the university is the particular German contribution. This is based on the notion that the State itself declares its role as the protector and promoter of both the internal and external autonomy of the university and recognizes the usefulness of independent investigation and teaching of the truth. In doing so it would prevent that potentially dangerous situation arising in which the university takes up a position of opposition within the State instead of the healthy contradiction which should always exist between the two. In the former instance, the university becomes a State within a State and an adversary more dangerous than the most rebellious army. History affords many examples of universities that became the intellectual focal point of a revolution or counter-revolution, just as there are examples of their refusing to become involved even when called upon to do so.

Today as well, the insight and breadth of vision of a Humboldt is what is required to ensure that not only political expediency, but also scholarly wisdom prevails in the carrying out of the necessary university reforms.

NOTES

1. *Vom Ursprung der Universität im Mittelalter*, Darmstadt, 1960.
2. ibid., pp. 16 f.
3. *Die Idee der Universität*, Berlin, 1946; Introduction.
4. cf. R. Heiss, *Hochschulnot und Hochschulreform*, Merkur 1965/2, p. 137 and onwards.
5. cf. K. Meyer, *Das Wissenschaftliche Leben in der USSR*, Wiesbaden, 1963; Bibliography.
6. cf. 'Reeducatio ex post', *Deutsche Universitätszeitung*, 1963/2, by the author.

Factors Influencing Policy in Higher Education

Brian Holmes

Among the most general factors which have created problems in the universities and other institutions of higher education, changes in popular expectations, the growth of population and technological developments are the most powerful. These world-wide phenomena should be seen in context. Thus the demand for higher education as one of the human rights, though strong everywhere, could be more easily satisfied in countries where there is a substantial provision of secondary education. The impact of manpower considerations in terms of skilled personnel has been different in economically developed countries from those seeking to 'take off' economically. The post-war population explosion meant that everywhere during the sixties more and more young adults were clamouring to get into the universities or, failing these, other institutions of higher education.

In this section comparative articles and case studies are designed to reveal the extent to which political, economic, social and demographic arguments have created problems of policy in higher education and to indicate some of the proposed solutions.

Political independence has influenced policy in education generally and it is not surprising that it has been a factor in formulating policy in higher education in those colonial territories, which previously sent most of their students abroad to be trained. Again comparisons can be made between nations governed by parties informed by socialist or communist theories (Glowka, pp. 175–185) and more conservative governments. Each has to respond to some extent to similar pressures as they occur, but the emphases differ. Among those who argue for the reform of the universities in political terms, articulate students have been persuasive and prepared to take action (Williams, pp. 186–190) to have their case heard and accepted. In the USA political arguments have been closely linked with demands to improve opportunities for the disadvantaged groups (Gumbert, pp. 191–201), most important of which are the Negroes or black.

Economic arguments have reinforced demands to expand higher education as a human right. The complexity of modern industry has created problems of training at the tertiary level (King, pp. 202–215) which cannot easily be solved on the basis of projected manpower investigations (Wood-hall, pp. 216–226). Moreover whether the university can continue to fulfil for society its critical role in a pluralistic society (Scherer, pp. 227–237) remains an open question. The cost benefit arguments do not convince some people either because they suspect the validity of the techniques used or because they think that the quality of higher education ought not to be measured exclusively or even partly in these economic terms. Yet the economics of providing higher education may well be decisive particularly in light of the population explosion (Hecquet, pp. 149–160).

In some ways universities throughout the world have remained faithful to their traditions and have resisted pressures to make them the servants of politicians or of the new technology. In the next section some national responses to the influences illustrated in this section are described.

10

Demographic Change as a Factor Influencing the Development of Higher Education[1]

I. Hecquet

There is no doubt that higher education in the industrial countries has seen an unprecedented growth in the number of students during the last ten to fifteen years; in those countries which are members of the OECD nineteen out of twenty-three at least doubled the number of higher education students between 1955 and 1965[2] which is an average annual growth rate of more than 7 per cent.

Much has been said and written about the factors behind this growth. Among those usually quoted are: the general rise in the standard of living; the increased demand for qualified personnel in many areas of economic life; the effect on higher education of increased school attendance at secondary level in the 1950s; the arrival at university and at other institutions of post-secondary education of particularly numerous groups of people of eligible age for higher education, following the revival of the birth rate during the Second World War and, above all, following the baby-boom immediately after the war.

This article will deal with the effect of one factor only – demographic variation – on the growth in numbers of students in higher education observed between 1950 and 1965.

More precisely, it will deal first with the development of the age group from which students go on to higher education, then with measuring, as exactly as available statistics will allow, the effects of demographic variation and of expanding school attendance on the growing numbers of higher education students. Finally, it will try to draw certain conclusions, on the basis of available population forecasts, about the role which the development of the reference age group is likely to have on variations in the student population during the 1970s.

The Development of the Age Group from which Students went on to Higher Education between 1950 and 1965

The development of the age group from which students went on to higher education[3] was particularly erratic between 1950 and 1965 in all the OECD countries (see Table 1); although this development varied

TABLE 1

TRENDS IN THE POPULATION OF ELIGIBLE AGE FOR HIGHER EDUCATION BETWEEN 1950 AND 1965 AND FORECASTS UP TO 1980 (in thousands)

	Age groups	1950	1955	1960	1965	Forecasts 1970	Forecasts 1975	Forecasts 1980	Indices of increase in 1965 1950=100	in 1965 1955=100	in 1980 1970=100
Austria (1)	19 to 24 years	581·9	514·0	633·7	618·6	584	574	672	106	120	115
Belgium	18 to 23 years	779·1	710·8	646·7	767·0	867	...	...	98	108	...
Denmark	19 to 25 years	415·5	403·8	422·1	547·0	581	520	512	131	134	98
Finland	19 to 24 years	391·5	361 5	393·8	468·3	565	505	466	120	130	82
France	18 to 23 years	3,867·8	3,608·4	3,283·2	4,203·6	5,029	4,871	4,888	109	116	97
Germany	20 to 25 years	4,439·4	4,552·7	5,777·9	5,103·2	4,442	4,518	5,894	115	112	115
Greece	18 to 24 years	1,069·5	1,084·1	1,002·4	880·4	993	964	989	83	82	100
Ireland	18 to 22 years	215·5	200·1	122·1	215·3	249	263	276	100	108	111
Italy (2)	19 to 25 years	5,647·6	5,501·1	5,560·4	5,466·0	5,741	5,497	5,650	97	101	98
Netherlands	18 to 24 years	1,133·5	1,102·9	1,156·6	1,436·8	1,602	1,574	1,613	127	130	101
Norway	19 to 24 years	272·7	293·5	252·3	330·5	376	363	364	121	136	97
Portugal	18 to 24 years	1,086·3	1,082·4	977·8	993·3	...	...	...	91	92	...
Spain	18 to 24 years	...	3,613·0	3,085·3	3,376·6	3,513	3,604	3,822	...	93	109
Sweden	20 to 24 years	459·3	429·1	466·2	615·0	644	559	545	134	143	85
Switzerland	20 to 25 years	420·8	421·5	488·7	522·1	—	—	—	148	148	—
Turkey	18 to 23 years	2,618·8	2,911·1	2,876·7	3,050·1	...	...	...	116	105	...
United Kingdom	18 to 23 years	3,259·7	3,205·0	3,293·4	4,038·1	4,075	3,894	4,410	124	126	108
Yugoslavia	19 to 25 years	2,226·8	2,443·6	2,290·4	1,999·0	...	...	2,659	90	82	...
Canada (3)	18 to 23 years	1,289·0	1,347·3	1,479·7	1,727·8	1,870	2,210	2,381	134	128	127
United States	18 to 23 years	1,366·2	1,269·6	1,396·2	1,774·1	21,565	23,558	25,075	130	140	116
Japan	18 to 22 years	8,102·2	8,645·4	7,849·6	9,035·7	11,038	8,273	7,779	112	105	70

(1) Austrian population only   (2) 1951, 1956, 1961, 1966, 1971, 1976, and 1981   (3) 1951, 1956, 1961, 1965, 1970, 1975 and 1980

widely between countries, it could be said to fall into two main groups according to the nature of the demographic variations:

(a) The majority of OECD countries (i.e. excluding Mediterranean countries and Japan) witnessed in the early 1950s a decrease – or at best a standstill (Germany, Canada, Switzerland) – in their population of an age to enter higher education; this decrease was the direct result of the lower birth rate recorded in all these countries between the two World Wars; the revival of the birth rate during the Second World War[4] and the baby-boom[5] immediately following it spectacularly reversed this trend; in most countries within this group, these more numerous peer groups reached the threshold of higher education from the end of the 1950s onwards and their major impact on the number of students in higher education made itself felt in the first few years of the next decade, the period 1960-5. Germany and Austria were, however, two exceptions to this pattern; in these two countries the revival of the birth rate did not occur until the middle of the 1950s, that is to say 10 to 15 years later than the other countries.

In reference to the year 1955 all these countries saw an increase in the numbers of the reference age group: about a third or more in the Scandinavian countries and the United States.

(b) The Mediterranean countries and Japan have had a quite different development (if not a contrary one) for after a period of more or less noticeable growth in the early 1950s (with the exception of Italy) the numbers of an age to enter higher education showed a marked decline during the next ten years (in Greece and Yugoslavia) or showed little sign of change: Spain, Italy, Turkey and even Japan. All these countries witnessed a relative stability in their annual birth rate during the corresponding period (1930 to 1950), and this stability was hardly affected by the postwar baby-boom. It should be added that considerable emigration took place from some countries: Spain, Italy, Portugal.

This irregular development of the population of an age corresponding to higher education explains why the effect of the demographic factor on the growth of student numbers at this level of education varied according to time and place. In countries of the first group and during the first half of the 1950s, the effect was nil, for the reference age group showed a noticeable decline in numbers during that period; the same thing occurred in countries of the second group, but for the whole of the period under consideration. On the other hand, the increase in numbers of the same age group seen in countries of the first group between 1955 and 1965 was to restrain the quantitative development of higher education possibilities in those countries, particularly during the early 1960s. This period of demographic growth is likely to continue in most countries until the end of the 1960s, though probably at a gradually lessening pace.

Demographic Changes and the Expansion of Student Numbers

Firstly, to state a definitional tautology: the number of students at any one time is the product of the total number in the age group from which those students are drawn, multiplied by the percentage of that group attending institutions of higher education (i.e. the enrolment rate). From this it is possible to calculate what would have been the number of students recorded in 1965 given the hypothesis that only the size of the age group in question had varied in the intervening period 1955–65; this in fact means that one is applying to the 1965 population of this age group the percentage of enrolment recorded in 1955. According to this hypothesis the number of students would have represented only 45–70 per cent (according to country) of the figures actually achieved in 1965.[6]

Another method is to calculate the proportionate growth in numbers of students between 1955 and 1965 produced, respectively, by the variation in numbers of the relevant age group and by the increased enrolment rate. For this purpose the variation in numbers of registered students in each country has been calculated on the basis that the enrolment rate had remained the same for the ten-year period considered, but that changes in the size of the age group should be taken into account. The variation in numbers of higher education students this recorded would thus be solely the result of demographic modifications. In the same way the growth of numbers recorded in each country has been recorded on the basis that an increased enrolment rate attendance related to numbers in the age group which remained constant during the ten-year period: this gives the growth in number of higher education students resulting solely from an increased school attendance. There remains, however, a difference between the sum of these two partial assessments and the actual growth in the number of students registered (this difference is more or less evident in different countries): it is the result of the combined effect of modifications in the numbers of relevant age and of enrolment rates.

The results of these calculations are shown in Table 2: the first four columns are concerned in turn with the total growth in the number of higher education students recorded between 1955 and 1965, the variations due to the demographic factor, those due to the enrolment rate, and the variations resulting from the combined effect of the previous two factors.

Columns 5, 6 and 7 express, in percentages, the part played in the total increase by the demographic variations, the school attendance variations and the combined effect of these two factors. Finally, and this is an arbitrary arrangement, the combined effect has been divided between each of the two contributing factors proportionately to their respective weight (columns 8 and 9).

TABLE 2

INCREASE IN ENROLMENTS FROM 1955 TO 1965 DUE TO DEMOGRAPHIC CHANGES AND TO CHANGES IN THE ENROLMENT RATES

| | Increase in thousands | | | | As a percentage of the total increase | | | | |
	(1)	(2)	(3)	(4)	(5)	(6)	(7)	(8)	(9)
Austria	24·3	3·1	17·5	3·6	12·8	72·3	14·9	15·0	85·0
Belgium	45·6	3·0	39·8	3·1	6·5	85·7	6·8	7·0	93·0
Denmark	30·1	7·5	17·0	5·8	24·8	56·1	19·1	30·7	69·3
Finland	27·9	5·9	17·0	5·0	21·2	60·9	17·9	25·9	74·1
France	308·8	35·7	234·5	38·7	11·5	75·9	12·5	13·3	86·7
Germany	221·7	24·2	177·6	21·5	10·9	79·5	9·5	12·1	87·9
Greece	37·1	-3·7	49·9	-8·9	-9·9	133·8	-23·9	—	—
Ireland	8·0	0·7	6·8	0·5	8·8	85·0	6·2	19·4	90·6
Italy	251·3	-1·4	253·0	-1·6	-0·6	101·2	-0·6	—	—
Netherlands	66·5	17·4	37·5	10·3	26·3	56·6	17·1	31·7	68·3
Norway	21·4	2·7	13·6	4·9	12·7	64·2	23·1	16·5	83·5
Portugal	13·7	-1·5	20·6	-1·7	-8·6	118·4	-9·8	—	—
Spain	108·6	-6·1	122·8	-8·0	-5·6	113·0	-7·4	—	—
Sweden	50·4	11·7	27·0	11·7	23·2	53·5	23·2	30·2	69·8
Switzerland	21·8	9·0	8·9	4·2	40·7	40·3	19·0	50·2	49·8
Turkey	61·5	1·8	55·3	2·6	3·0	92·5	4·4	3·1	96·9
United Kingdom	229·3	52·5	141·0	36·7	22·8	61·3	15·9	27·1	72·9
Yugoslavia	115·2	-12·9	153·9	-28·0	-11·4	136·2	-24·8	—	—
Canada	217·7	30·8	145·5	41·1	14·2	66·9	18·9	17·5	82·5
United States	289·2	106·4	130·8	52·0	36·8	45·2	18·0	44·9	55·1
Japan	475·4	27·7	423·6	19·1	5·9	90·0	4·1	6·2	93·8

(1) Total increase
(2) Due to demographic changes
(3) Due to changes in enrolment rates
(4) Due to the combined effect of (2) and (3)

(5) Due to demographic changes
(6) Due to changes in enrolment rates
(7) Due to the combined effect of (5) and (6)
(8) and (9): =(5) and (6), after distribution of combined effect.

Progress in School Attendance

It therefore appears, contrary to the theory that has frequently been advanced, that the explosion of student numbers in higher education is not principally the result of a demographic expansion: in nine of the sixteen countries (where the age group eligible for enrolment into higher education has progressed in a positive manner) less than 20 per cent of the growth in student numbers is attributable to variations in demography; the latter would explain more than a third of the growth rate in numbers in two countries alone: the United States and Switzerland. In all these countries, the major cause of *the growth of student numbers in higher education is traceable directly to the progress in school attendance* and variations in demography have played only a secondary role.

This conclusion is however subject to certain reservations; in fact, if the period 1960–5 is considered separately, the effect of the growth of the age group in question appears more important: it is however never greater than that of school attendance with the exception of five countries. During these years, the universities and other institutions of higher education in most of the countries have therefore had to face considerable difficulties in responding to the demand for places expressed by a growing population ever desirous of a larger proportion of this level of education.

It is remarkable that the USSR at the beginning of the 1960s found itself in exactly the opposite situation: the age group eligible for higher education in fact diminished by almost half as a consequence of the marked drop in the number of births during the Second World War. In order to compensate for this reduction, the Soviet authorities were obliged to relax quite considerably for this period the standards of selection for entry into the institutions of higher education.

Finally one can ask whether this phase of demographic growth has not had as a consequence the effect of slowing down the increase in enrolment in secondary education during these years. There are in fact grounds for thinking that increases in enrolment will be more difficult to maintain if the population of the corresponding age group increases at a still higher rate: a not inconsiderable portion of the new places created in the institutions (and therefore of the assets in terms of equipment and teaching personnel) being required to meet this demographic expansion.

It would seem, however, that if it were possible to confirm the existence of an inversely porportionate ratio between the rate of growth in enrolment and the variations in the numbers of those eligible for entry into higher education, then this would nevertheless be far from absolute, both in time and space:

1. It is true that the majority of the OECD member countries saw their rate of enrolment in higher education grow less rapidly between 1960 and

1965 than between 1955 and 1960. However, the rate of progress of enrolment figures during this period (1960–5) has been higher than that which characterized the first half of the 1950s, even though all these countries recorded a levelling out or a reduction in size of the age group concerned during that period.

2. The relationship between the growth line for enrolment in higher edu-

Graph 1: Increase in enrolment rates and in the population of the corresponding age groups from 1960 to 1965

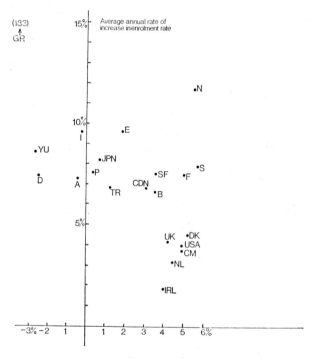

Average annual rate of increase in the age group population

	x-axis	y-axis		x-axis	y-axis
D (Germany)	−2·5	7·4	NL (Netherlands)	4·4	3·1
A (Austria)	−0·5	7·3	P (Portugal)	0·3	7·6
B (Belgium)	3·5	6·6	UK (United Kingdom)	4·2	4·2
DK (Denmark)	5·2	4·5	S (Sweden)	5·7	7·9
E (Spain)	1·8	9·6	CH (Switzerland)	4·9	3·7
SFL (Finland)	3·5	7·5	TR (Turkey)	1·2	6·8
F (France)	5·0	7·5	YU (Yugoslavia)	−2·7	8·6
Gr (Greece)	−2·3	18·3	CDN (Canada)	3·1	6·8
IRL (Ireland)	4·0	1·8	USA (United States)	4·9	3·9
I (Italy)	−0·3	9·6	JPN (Japan)	0·6	8·2
N (Norway)	5·5	11·7			

cation and that of the population of the corresponding age group, as shown on a graph, revealed just such a negative ratio for the period 1960–5:[7] it must be pointed out, however, that a rapid growth in the age group in question has not prevented countries such as France, Sweden and above all Norway, from achieving a rapid increase in terms of the participation of the population in this level of education. One obtains very similar results if the period 1955–65 is considered as a whole (graph 2).

Graph 2: Increase in enrolment rates and in the population of the corresponding age groups from 1955 to 1965

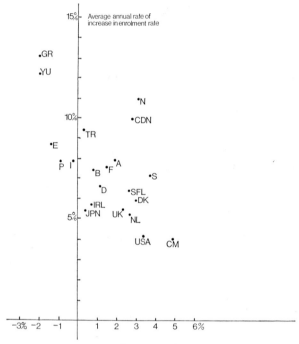

Average annual rate of increase in the age group population

	x-axis	y-axis		x-axis	y-axis
D (Germany)	1·1	6·6	NL (Netherlands)	2·7	5·2
A (Austria)	1·9	7·9	P (Portugal)	−0·9	7·8
B (Belgium)	0·8	7·4	UK (United Kingdom)	2·3	5·4
DK (Denmark)	3·0	5·9	S (Sweden)	3·7	7·2
E (Spain)	−1·4	8·7	CH (Switzerland)	4·0	3·9
SFL (Finland)	2·6	6·4	TR (Turkey)	0·5	9·4
F (France)	1·5	7·6	YU (Yugoslavia)	−2·0	12·2
GR (Greece)	−2·0	13·1	CDN (Canada)	2·8	9·9
IRL (Ireland)	5·7	0·7	USA (United States)	3·4	4·1
I (Italy)	−0·1	7·8	JPN (Japan)	0·4	5·4
N (Norway)	3·1	10·9			

The fact that the growth of both the numbers of students and the rate of entry into higher education depends to large extent[8] on developments previously recorded in the area of secondary education, must obviously be taken into account: thus the progress achieved at this level between 1950 and 1965 has varied considerably from year to year and from country to country.

Sub-divisions in Student Populations

Up till now, this analysis has concerned the whole of the student population, without taking into acount the differences to be found in the sub-divisions which make up this population. The following section will be limited to rapid definition of the specific developments of female participation in higher education, and also of that of the foreign student.

In all of the OECD countries the number of female students has increased at a distinctly higher rate than that of male students. Since the two sexes are subject to similar variations (at least with regard to the age group relative to higher education), the rate of enrolment for females has therefore increased more than that for males: and the influence of demographic expansion on the growth of the student body has been less in the case of women.

But even if this growing involvement of female students has assisted in accelerating the world-wide expansion of higher education between 1950 and 1965, we are still far from achieving equality of educational opportunity between the sexes at this level: in 1965 women still had two to three times less chance than men of entering higher education.

Interesting though it would be to know with some accuracy the movements of students between the various countries at a time when the migrations of the heads of the most qualified professions appear to be developing, the present state of our statistical information would not allow the drawing up of an overall chart of these movements. Nevertheless, the fragmentary information gathered shows that, in the majority of OECD countries, the proportion of overseas students has nearly always diminished, generally from 1960 onwards, even though their total numbers have increased considerably from 1950 to 1965: this is particularly true for those countries which, traditionally, counted a high proportion of foreigners amongst their student population: Austria and Switzerland, and to a lesser extent Germany, France and the UK. Several countries, as a result of the extremely rapid development in national demand, have been obliged to limit the number of places offered to foreign students. On the other hand, some countries, which were accustomed to seeing a considerable proportion of their students departing to enrol in foreign universities, have considerably increased the number of places offered in their own institutions of higher education, thus remedying one of the principal causes for the departures:

such has been the case, amongst OECD countries, in Greece, Norway and Turkey. A similar development is characteristic of many countries of the third world.

With the exception of these countries, as also Iceland and Luxemburg, the other OECD countries lose less than 5 per cent of their total student population to foreign institutions.

Has this reduction in the flow of student exchanges had any effect on the whole range of courses, or is it limited in its effect to only the initial courses? In fact, at postgraduate level it is possible to discern an opposite tendency, but the reality of this cannot be established for lack of sufficient statistical information.

In 1965, the percentage of foreign students in proportion to the total student body in postgraduate education was 25 per cent in the universities of the UK, and 8·1 per cent in the United States (which, with 100,000 foreign students enrolled in the various institutions of higher education within its territories, is the principal host country, even though this figure represents less than 2 per cent of the total student population).

Demographic Prospects for the 1970s; Possible Consequences for the Future Development of Systems of Higher Education

Table 1 indicates the probable development of the age group eligible for enrolment in higher education during the next ten years (the period 1970–1980). From a comparison of the factors of variation of this group from one decade to the next, it would appear that the majority of the countries under consideration will experience during this period a very different development from that recorded during the previous ten years:

> In half of these countries, a reduction in the relevant age group should follow the rapid growth period of the 60s: this must be regarded as the consequence of the reduction in the birth rate following the 'bulge' of the immediate post-war period (this reduction is particularly marked in Japan).

> In the other countries, the age group in question will remain stable or, under the most favourable circumstances, will grow at a much slower rate than in the preceding years.

> Canada, Austria and Germany will, however, prove the exception, these last two countries having experienced the recovery of the birth rate ten years later than the other countries.

All other things being equal, we should therefore expect in most of the OECD member countries, a fairly definite slackening in the growth of the student body in higher education during the 1970s.

Such a reduction in the 'pressure of numbers' would have the certain advantage of allowing these countries to enter into a phase of consolidation and restructuring of their systems of higher education: they could under these circumstances carry out those qualitative reforms whose urgent nature has been even more clearly demonstrated by the explosion in numbers.

But the history of the last twenty years has shown that, contrary to what is happening in primary education and already, in a few countries, in secondary education, demographic changes are far from being the prime mover in the development of student numbers at this level of education.

With the exception no doubt of the United States and, to a lesser extent, Canada and the USSR, none of the countries can at present boast of offering its young people 'higher education for the mass'; the progress necessary to achieve such a goal is still immense if one remembers that in 1965 not one of the European members of the OECD achieved an enrolment rate in higher education of more than 15 per cent of the eligible population, that is still a rate lower than that achieved in the United States before 1950.

It is therefore possible that the rate of enrolment in higher education will continue to grow between 1970 and 1980 on a scale similar to that recorded during the 1960s, with the exception no doubt of the United States. This would in addition correspond with the forecasts or objectives laid down in those countries where the responsible authorities have sought to define the future development of their system of higher education.[9] Account must also be taken of the fact that the reforms introduced at secondary level during the 1960s will have their impact on higher education during the coming decade: these reforms will have a principal effect of increasing considerably the number of candidates possessing the necessary qualifications for entry into the institutions of higher education.[10]

On the other hand, it is more difficult to arrive at an estimate of the structural reforms that will be carried out in the systems of higher education during this period, and consequently of the influence of these reforms on enrolment: for example, the development of institutions providing shortened courses (either within the university or outside it) and a growing tendency among students towards this type of study (thus following the example of the United States) will without doubt lead to a change in the pattern of enrolment rates at this level of education, by reducing the average length of courses. Inversely, the development of courses at postgraduate level, together with the introduction of a more widespread system of permanent education, will introduce new factors for the expansion of student numbers in higher education.

But even if one considers a hypothetical forecast favouring the rate of growth already recorded for enrolment in higher education between 1955 and 1965, one can see that most of the OECD European members will still not reach in 1980 the same rate achieved in 1965 in the United States. This does not detract from the fact that all these countries should, taking into account the characteristics of their demographic development, find themselves in the next ten years in a particularly strong position from which to reduce the gap which separates them from the United States. The situation will be much less favourable when the children of parents from the particularly numerous age group born between 1940 and 1950 in turn reach the age of entry into higher education, that is to say about 1985–90.

NOTES

1. This chapter is based on a report of the OECD Secretariat entitled *Development of Higher Education 1950–67* (and more particularly Chapter II). This report is being published in two volumes: the first (published 1970) consists of a statistical survey on the expansion of higher education in the member countries of the OECD; the second volume (published 1971) provides an analysis of this survey.

2. Although information about the period 1965–70 is not yet complete, everything indicates that the average growth rate will be maintained for the last five years in many countries.

3. The term 'higher education' here applies to all post-secondary education: university or non-university. The age group studied includes 70–80 per cent of the full-time student population and therefore varies from country to country according to the number of years' study and the age of entry pertaining to the country. That is why it seems better than the age group of 20 to 24 years, which is generally taken as the age group for study in articles of this kind. However, since the age structure of the student population is modified in the course of time (for reasons not necessarily demographic) the ideal procedure would be to analyse this development for each individual year of age.

4. This revival had earlier begun in North America, in the Scandinavian countries and in the Netherlands.

5. This baby-boom was particularly noticeable in North America, Finland, the United Kingdom, the Netherlands and, above all, in France.

6. It would have been a third or less in 1965 in Greece and Yugoslavia – two countries where numbers in the relevant group decreased between 1955 and 1965 – and also in Norway, despite the fact that her population of relevant age increased by 35 per cent in the course of these ten years.

7. The rank correlation (in accordance with the Spearman formula) between the two categories is − 0·44, but is not greater than − 0·14 if one excludes the six Mediterranean countries.

8. Not entirely, however, for the proportion of qualified school leavers who go into higher education is liable to change during the course of time: on this subject see OECD, *The Development of Higher Education 1950–1967: Analytical Report*, Chapter III.

9. See on this subject OECD, op. cit.,

10. Several recent studies forecast for the 1980s a school attendance rate into education close to the maximum possible for the population between the ages of 5 and 19 in many European countries; in particular: *Possible Futures of European Education: Numerical and Systems Forecasts*, a study undertaken by the Institut für Bildungsforschung in der Max-Planck-Gesellschaft at Berlin, within the framework of the European Cultural Foundation's project *Europe 2000*.

11

Higher Education and the State

John Pratt

Relationships between higher education and the state in Great Britain today are neither orderly nor codified. They are the consequence of developments over a century or more. Sometimes arrangements have simply been left over from the past: others derive directly from some initiative. But however the arrangements have derived historically they have important implications for colleges and universities, for the staff in them, and for academic freedom, autonomy and democracy.

What happens in education is ultimately the responsibility of Parliament. A university gets its charter from the Privy Council and owes its existence, standing and continuation to the state, quite as much as a local authority technical college. It is the form of the relationship which differs. One of the striking things about the relationship is the absence of legislation. The University Grants Committee, for example, bases its operation not on any Act but on a Treasury minute. The great 1944 Education Act mentioned higher education only in passing. This is largely the result of British legal tradition. Once there is legislation in any area, the whole of that area is deemed to require legislation for any government action. It is quite in order for the state to give money to universities through the UGC, but any legislation about this would involve legislation about universities as a whole. This has meant that relationships between the state and higher education are the more obscure.

Already relations have been subject to subtle but growing changes. The UGC, which previously reported to the Treasury, since 1964 has reported to the Department of Education and Science. From the beginning of 1968 the Comptroller and Auditor General has had access to the books of both the UGC and the universities. There has been the growth of the research councils and its implications for university development. Finally, and importantly, there has been a very rapid growth of higher education outside the universities, under entirely different systems of administration, in the technical colleges and colleges of education. The government has been the main initiator here, and in 1966 for example announced its recognition of the 'binary' tradition in higher education and proposed to designate 30 polytechnics to head the public sector.

The issues between higher education and the state which have been emphasized by these changes are reasonably clear. The major conflict of interest is that between the demands of the academic community for freedom, autonomy and democracy on the one hand, and the legitimate public interest in its affairs on the other. We cannot discuss these without first making clear the nature and functions of higher education. Since the 1944 Act the emphasis has been placed on level: higher education has meant work taking the student beyond GCE A level or ordinary national certificate (ONC). In practice this implied that the student should be over 18 and there has been a widespread assumption that studies were normally full time. This view of higher education never did justice to the variety of its provision: it is basically the stage of education following primary and secondary, and may be full time, part time or sandwich, vocationally or academically based, in a university, technical college or college of education. For the objectives of this stage we can do worse than look at the Robbins Report.[1] They include 'instructions in skills suitable to play a part in the general division of labour' . . . the promotion of 'the general powers of the mind' . . . 'the advancement of learning' . . . 'the transmission of a common culture and common standards of citizenship'. He added that institutions themselves may vary. The vocational emphasis would be more apparent in some than in others. The participation in the life and culture of the community would depend upon local circumstances. But the system as a whole should provide adequately for all of the objectives. Many of us would probably feel that he could have added a further aim, that of meeting social demand. Whilst it is true that the Report, to its credit, took a social demand approach, this appeared as Robbins' own political judgment, not as an established aim of the system. Yet it is patently the case, particularly in parts of the higher education system outside the universities, where the creation of courses and awards in response to public demand has been a hall-mark.

Demands of the Academic Community

To turn to the issues – first, the demands of the academic community. Here again Robbins is probably the classic authority. He distinguished two main types of academic freedom – individual and institutional.[2] Individual freedom is a concept most of us are familiar with – the absence of discrimination on grounds of colour, sex, religion and politics, and the right to teach according to the teacher's own conception of fact and truth. Further, there is the right to publish and freedom to pursue personal studies or research. He recognized, of course, the need to perform necessary duties – to teach according to a syllabus, but recognized that the problems are generally soluble.

Institutional freedom, or autonomy, we are again familiar with, in theory at least. Autonomy seems generally to mean the freedom of appointment, freedom to determine curricula and standards, freedoms of admissions, etc.

To Robbins' concepts (only a few years later) we would probably wish to add two others. Both are in a sense freedoms of relationships. First the freedom *between* staff and students, which may boil down to the freedom to teach at all. I am thinking particularly of the instances at Guildford and Hornsey where staff entered buildings closed by an authority because they regarded their responsibilities to be to their students, and were sacked for it. Robbins' ideas offered no guide to these situations, and his comments at the time indicated that he did not accept this right. The other is the concept of democracy, the right of staff of all levels and students to participate in the government of their institutions, which even now may be very little exercised in most universities and colleges.

Public Interest

The other side of the issue, legitimate public interest, has two main facets. There is first the obvious interest of the community in what goes on in its institutions – however autonomous. It wants to avoid scandals. Even the public schools – financed almost entirely independently of the state (though there are of course hidden subsidies) – are subject to rigorous conditions and inspections in the defence of the children. But secondly there is the key issue of finance. With some £200 m. a year of public money going into the universities alone, the public concern is obvious. The state has to see that this money is spent effectively and productively and that costs are kept as low as possible. This is generally regarded as a right and proper duty of the state and was the basis on which the books of the universities were opened to the Comptroller and Auditor General.

The problem lies in the fact that finance implies control. The greater the amount of state finance, the greater the control, yet also the greater the need for assurances that the money is properly spent. To meet this problem a number of devices have been evolved and tried. Each of these attempts to ensure that expenditure is properly accounted for yet the needs of the academic community are met.

The first may be called independence. Here the emphasis is much more towards the academic community than accountability. This was more or less the situation of the two universities, Oxford and Cambridge, up to the middle of the nineteenth century. The disadvantage then was that the places became so corrupted, decadent and self-centred, that it took a whole series of Royal Commissions, Select Committees and Acts of Parliament,[3] together with the establishment of a rival set of colleges to reform them. There is again a move to establish an independent university. We can be sure that, however successful it may be at remaining free from state finance, controls of the scandal-avoiding type are inevitable and proper. And if the university is to meet even Robbins' modest aims fully, particularly the one about national needs, some sort of institution will be necessary to ensure this. One university alone may be able to satisfy the state that it has sufficient self-control to do these things. It is very hard indeed to visualize a situation where all the universities could be in that situation, so I do not propose to consider the idea any further here.

The second structure is the most familiar buffer between education and the state, the local authority. The technical colleges, the polytechnics and the colleges of education are protected by this. The success of this arrangement stems from the 1888 Local Government Act, which created county, county borough and the London County councils. There were for the first time competent authorities to whom powers and duties could be given, but who operated on a sufficiently local basis to meet the variety of local demands. Since then, the legislative framework for higher education outside the universities has remained unaltered in its general structure, but there have been a number of important changes in detail. Central to these changes is the role of another buffer – the governing body. Amongst the conditions of designation of the new polytechnics was one requiring local education authorities to delegate substantial powers to new boards of governors. The Weaver Report[4] and the Education (No. 2) Act of 1968 required local authorities to establish governing bodies with increased powers for colleges of education and colleges of further education.

The third arrangement also involves a buffer, the UGC. This was created in 1919, without legislation, to advise the Treasury on how its grants should be distributed to the universities. It has become in many people's eyes the symbol of freedom in universities consistent with accountability. Yet there is a growing claim that many of the freedoms are illusory.

Finally, there is direct grant status. This has had a mixed history. An odd assortment of institutions have come under the direct control of the Ministry or Department of Education. There are the National Colleges, specializing in the more obscure technologies (such as the College of Rubber Technology), who are now moving into the university sector. For a long time, Loughborough College was direct grant, as it was attracting over 90 per cent of its students from outside its local authorities' boundaries. The CATs became direct grant colleges from 1962 to 1965 and the Royal College of Art, which awards its own degrees, is also direct grant under the DES.

Each of these arrangements has different implications for the colleges or universities, and for the people in them. These implications are not always the most obvious and some are apparently paradoxical.

LEA Administration

Local education authorities are a very substantial buffer in higher education. They aid or maintain over 500 establishments of further education including the polytechnics, as well as colleges of education. Recently, the way they run these colleges has been changed by the 1968 Education (No. 2) Act, its subsequent circulars and the designation of the polytechnics. All this makes a complex situation more complicated, and it will be helpful if we distinguish the different types of college in the public sector before giving only a brief analysis of their relations with local government.

Local education authorities maintain nearly all colleges of further education. Most of these are technical colleges, but this group includes colleges of art and colleges of commerce, music, etc. The colleges vary in the amount of work they do in higher education. At the top of the hierarchy are the polytechnics. They have relatively powerful and independent governing bodies, as a condition of their designation. Then comes a range of colleges, some with a majority of work above A level or ONC standard right down to those with little or none. Their mode of government was the subject of the Education (No. 2) Act and Circular 7/70. In addition, most colleges of education are maintained by LEAs, though fifty are run by voluntary bodies and are aided by the local authority. Their government was the subject of the Weaver Report as well as the Act. Here, too, things are complicated by the role of the central government and the universities. The Secretary of State has general overall control of the number of students in colleges of education because this affects the numbers of teachers available for teaching in schools. The colleges are subject to the academic control of universities, who approve and oversee their courses. However, in most other aspects the local authority and the Secretary of State have the main control over their development.

For all maintained colleges, the LEA meets the running costs and building costs, at least in the first instance, by finance from loans or rates. For a long time, however, LEAs have been subsidized by central government. Before 1959, running costs were subsidized by a percentage grant (about 60 per cent). After 1959, this became a block grant negotiated in advance, to enable LEAs to have greater freedom in spending the money allocated to them. Also, in 1951, a 75 per cent grant was introduced for advanced work (i.e. above A level or ONC/D) which meant that LEAs had to find only a quarter of the recurrent costs of advanced courses. Arrangements for advanced courses became even more favourable after 1959, expenditure being met from a 'pool' to which all LEAs contributed. Cynics hold that any one LEA can thus expand in higher education at almost no cost to itself.

The effect of all the recent changes has varied according to the type of college, but in broad terms it has been to oblige LEAs to establish governing bodies for their colleges which have a certain measure of independence and powers to spend money under broad heads. On the governing body have to be represented the staff of the college as well as outside interests; the LEA need not have a majority. By and large, the more important the type of college the greater freedom its governors have – polytechnics having relatively powerful governing bodies, small FE colleges having ones with less independence. We can see the importance of these changes if we recall one of the points of the previous arrangements.

It is important to remember for example how little formal identity the colleges had. They were not legal entities and everything was done for them in the name of the LEA. A major effect of the changes was to stop college governing bodies from being a sub-committee of a further education sub-committee of an education committee of a local authority!

Even so, the ways in which functions are shared between LEA governing bodies and colleges vary. Normally, an authority will determine the general character of its college. Sometimes this is virtually imposed upon it from outside, e.g. the polytechnics. Governors generally have oversight of the curriculum, whilst the principal has responsibility for day-to-day management. All the arrangements depend a lot on personalities involved. There are striking instances where an enterprising principal, or even head of department, can dominate more or less the entire college, the board of governors and the LEA.

Then the LEA itself is not free. Under the 1944 Act the Minister has the duty to ensure that LEAs fulfil their duties. He does this by laying down standards and general requirements by regulations. They are concerned mainly with avoidance of wasteful duplication of courses, whilst ministerial approval is required for buildings and alterations for large items of equipment and for the provision of courses.

Finally, behind all this lies the figure of the District Auditor. Like all auditors he checks in detail that LEAs are spending their money properly, and by proper authority. His presence can be the final inhibition to development – he has powers to investigate even teachers' use of time.

In practice these arrangements give a distinctive flavour to administration in the colleges. The persistence of local authority procedures means that a lot of trivial decisions can get bogged down in bureaucracy. To get a window replaced may take weeks. Staff may have no say in their room decoration; there are all sorts of rules on the disposal of library fines and so on. On the other hand important decisions can go through on a bewildered nod. A computer may be obtained quicker than a coat of paint.

Probably the most fiercely fought of the battles in local authorities are over who appoints whom. Again, things have changed recently, and colleges often have almost total freedom of appointment within a broad financial constraint. Generally, the overall staff establishment is fixed by the LEA, after consultation with the governors. The latter usually have a noticeable say in the appointment of the principal, and he, in effect, appoints the rest of the staff. Detailed control here has often been formidable. For instance, even when a governing body was free to make appointments, they may have been (or may still be) subject to confirmation by the education committee. An appointing board might find itself able to offer a man a job, but unable to tell him his proposed salary. Where an establishment is rigidly fixed, this leads to problems, particularly of promotion. The most frustrating single curb is over the appointment of non-teaching staff – administrators, secretaries, etc. Here, the attempt to keep them on grade scales and in numbers comparable with those in all local authority departments has led to a simple dearth of competence in administration, an almost complete inadequacy of libraries and a continuing waste of staff time. The recent changes have often done little here, leaving non-teaching staff still subject to the establishments committee of the LEA. A polytechnic able to appoint without question some of the most eminent teachers in the country may find itself vetoed when seeking a car park attendant. The picturesque example of one post-war chief education officer who wrote all his letters in longhand helps to explain why local authority colleges, whilst often well equipped, are often grossly understaffed in clerical grades.

For colleges of further education, and the polytechnics, there are complex arrangements before they may start new courses, and which contrast sharply with the apparent total freedom of the universities. The initiative for new courses usually comes from the principal of heads of departments; sometimes the DES may approach an LEA to run a specialist course, e.g. in computing; sometimes industry makes formal suggestions to the college, perhaps through the governing body. In all cases the principal has to formally approach the governors and the LEA, though their approval is invariably nearly automatic. The course then needs approval from the regional advisory council (RAC) and the Regional Inspectorate. The RAC is supposed to co-ordinate courses within its area, whilst regional HMIs have formed a committee (under DES encouragement) to vet RAC decisions from a national point of view. After this, DES approval is needed for all advanced courses. Its main concern is with numbers; there are regulations for minima, which often encourage a large entry and high wastage rate. For courses requiring external validation, like those for CNAA degrees, then that body has to approve as well.

In colleges of education, course approval is different. In a sense, they offer only one course; certainly, they do not put on the bewildering variety that one might find in any technical college. Overall control of the number of colleges and students rests with the DES. For any changes in the balance of the course, of the main areas of study or the overall numbers, the approval of the Inspectorate and the Secretary of State is required. Often, the latter requires considerable detail, too, of the subjects, numbers and the resource implications of any proposal. The main academic control lies with the universities, or rather, in practice with the institutes of education, for normally university senates retain few of their formal powers, but merely approve and award the certificates or degrees in education. It is the institute which normally devises the courses; it does this with a greater or lesser amount of consultation with teachers in the colleges, though each college is represented on the institute. In general, teachers have very little contact with the university senate. Normally, too, if an institute approves a course, then the Secretary of State will grant his approval. The extent of control exercised by the university over BEd degrees, however, is usually greater than for teachers' certificates. In at least one case a university has not agreed a BEd course, but the college has been allowed by the DES to do one from another university.

In other aspects, all colleges in the public sector operate under the elaborate system of controls illustrated here. Up to a point this is inevitable, and even acceptable. It is inevitable because the 1944 Act did not foresee the great expansion of further education, and particularly its responsibilities in higher education. The Act and its ensuing administration retain the flavour of schools rather than institutions of higher education comparable with universities. Officials and councillors are certainly more familiar with the former than the latter, though this must not be overdone – many of the industrial magnates of the north are more than a match for an ambitious polytechnic director. These controls are acceptable, up to a point, because of the real responsibilities of officials and councillors towards their ratepayers and electors.

Overall, we can see pretty clearly that the local authority buffer has tended to emphasize the legitimate public interest, with many inhibiting and unproductive controls. Yet, despite all this, the sector of higher education outside the universities has been fast expanding and responsive to social and industrial demands. Since the time of the Robbins Report, the technical colleges and the colleges of education have expanded roughly twice as fast as the universities, and several times as fast as Robbins then forecast. In 1969/70, there were 118,000 full-time students in the colleges of education and 91,000 in the technical colleges,[5] compared with about 220,000 in the universities. In addition, the technical colleges were catering for about 120,000 part-time advanced students. Taking all students into account, the public sector already has a majority of the students in higher education.

This expansion has arisen partly out of the traditions of this sector. The colleges have always tried to meet social and other demands as they arise; in addition the universities did not expand fast enough to cater for all qualified school leavers, and much of the overspill went into the other sector. But the administrative arrangements also facilitate expansion. The 75 per cent grants for advanced work and the pool system of finance have encouraged local authorities to develop their colleges. Within the colleges themselves, the system of annual budgets has, by and large, reinforced this trend. This may seem an inhibiting arrangement at first sight, especially when compared with the quinquennial grants of the UGC. But the former system means colleges know what they have to spend in the one year; the future can, as it were, look after itself. With the quinquennial system, developments have to be planned over five years. When this is settled, some time before the start of the quinquennium, it effectively prevents most major changes over the next five years. No one will intervene; the UGC has given only earmarked supplements to grants for things like salary rises during a quinquennium.

The growth of the public sector has not relied only on university overspill. A major factor has been the initiative of the state, with the establishment of the binary policy and the new polytechnics. In the Woolwich and Lancaster speeches of Mr Anthony Crosland, then Secretary of State for Education and Science,[6] the government recognized an alternative tradition in higher education to the universities, and announced its intention to develop the public sector as a complement to the latter. The main institutions in this sector were to be comprehensive academic communities – called Polytechnics in the White Paper of 1966 – *A Plan for Polytechnics and Other Colleges*. About 27 of these polytechnics have now been created of existing colleges and designated by the Secretary of State, and another three are to follow.

State initiative has not been restricted to the establishment of colleges. The state has also been responsible for major academic innovations. One of the first of these was the national certificate scheme, which arose in 1921 from an initiative by the then Board of Education, and which offered a nationally verified and accepted qualification for courses created and examined in the technical colleges. This principle was repeated in the Diploma in Technology. The National Council for Technological Awards was set up by the Ministry of Education in 1955 to administer this award, for students completing four-year degree level courses in technical colleges. It incorporated the only really radical innovation in higher education this century – the sandwich principle – which has now been taken into the university sector with the former CATs. The principle of external moderation of internally created courses has been up-graded to full degree status with the translation of the NCTA into the Council for National Academic Awards. This is in fact the largest degree-awarding body in the country outside London University.

The UGC

The UGC is generally agreed to have two main tasks:
(1) To advise the Treasury via the DES on the total money to be spent on universities.
(2) To allocate the total between universities.
It operates for recurrent expenditures a famous system of quinquennial grants. Each university discusses its development in detail with the UGC and then makes estimates of its expenditure for each of the five years of the quinquennium. The UGC collects these and submits them to the DES. Here it is strictly advisory; though its advice is not made public and its discussions with the DES and those of the DES with the Treasury are entirely confidential. The government makes the final decision on the total allocation. The UGC then divides this between the universities and the DES by convention does not interfere. Individual universities can then allocate their grant at their discretion, though it is felt that it should bear a resemblance to the estimate, otherwise the UGC will take that into account in the next quinquennium.

Thus the universities have the first, if not the last, say in their general pattern of development. They create their own courses, appoint their own staff and set their own entry requirements.

Universities' problems are of a different kind from technical colleges and colleges of education. Whereas the latter two have rigid formal structures and an elaborate system of checks and balances to restrict them, and are in fact increasing their freedom of action, the universities have almost total freedom of action and are increasingly claiming that it is being eroded. One thing ought to be clear, however, and probably many people in the universities overlook this: namely that their freedom is rigidly constrained by money. The total grant is fixed by the state almost *ex cathedra*. What the UGC arrangement seems to result in is a lack of understanding where the limits are and why universities don't get money for this, but do get it for that. There are also implicit constraints, under the general national demand. Robbins proposed expansion as a national need and the universities, without exception, did so. All were free to refuse, yet none did. Afterwards when the problems entailed by expansion became obvious, many people reacted as if they had been forced into it. Similarly, salary scales were until recently settled entirely outside the universities' orbit, by the PIB (Prices and Incomes Board).[7] The present arrangements represent a rather odd two-stage compromise between negotiation and external settlement, where the staff side and the universities hatch a proposal between them, which they then jointly submit to the DES, the UGC sitting in on both sets of meetings. In the technical colleges and colleges of education there are formal negotiations between staff organizations on the one side and the

DES and LEAs on the other.[8] And within the national scales, the universities have far greater formal discretion to appoint, there are extra payments for special merit and facilities for increments to overcome difficulties in recruitment. Yet it has been in further education that the most free use has been made of salary scales, and in the universities that scales are claimed to be too rigid. And remember the outbursts when the PIB proposals were announced.

The most important drawback for the universities appears to be in lack of consultation. The universities put up their proposals for the next quinquennium and the UGC hands down a fraction of the money required. There are few collaborative discussions about estimates. The UGC visitations are extremely formal, and elaborate preparations are required in the arguments. Days of talks every five years, plus directives, exhortations or conversations in between, would seem to offer very little either for planning or for freedom. The former CATs felt this especially. The measure of academic freedom came for some of them when they were simply refused point blank the opportunity to develop in the social sciences, which they felt they would have been able to do both as direct grant or local authority colleges.

But in general it is hard for the universities to substantiate the bogy of state interference. The UGC itself was established to prevent this; and only because the universities were themselves unable to raise sufficient funds. Since the establishment of the UGC, they have been free to develop more or less in which direction they chose. The government has been continually faced with universities which will not develop in areas of national need, and about which it is powerless to do anything. Under the UGC, the universities have undoubtedly prospered. Since 1919, their number has doubled. Since the war about ten new universities have been created, owing their foundation almost entirely to the state.

Direct Grant

This is anathema to many university teachers – direct control by the government – absolutely impossible they would say, almost axiomatically. What did the CATs make of it? Well they rather liked it. Most people in the colleges look back on their direct grant days with pangs of nostalgia, the word honeymoon even crops up in their reminiscences. There are a number of reasons for this. It may simply be that the past is always nicer than the present, but this doesn't explain why they don't feel at all that way about LEA control. It may have been that they were specially treated. Certainly they were the peak of the further education sector and the pride of the Ministry. But that doesn't altogether help when you are thinking in terms of special institutions anyway. Certainly financial times may have been better. It was during the period of the run up to the 1964 General

Election that they became direct grant, and times for universities have been a bit hard of late. But what people say is that in many ways they were freer under the direct control of a department of state than they were under the LEAs or under the vaunted buffer UGC.[9] And the reason they felt freer, they say, is because they were consulted about decisions. The limits of their actions were explained in proper terms, they could as a group, through the Committee of CAT principals, evolve policy in time to deal with current problems. They were able if necessary to pick up a telephone and speak to the appropriate official in the DES. One CAT principal recalls how he was able to secure a £160,000 block of flats by doing just this. The administrative arrangements centred around the governing body yet again. Each college was administered by a governing body set up under trust deed. It was responsible for the conduct of the college and was the employer of all teaching and non-teaching staff. The Exchequer grants were calculated as deficiency grants after the receipt of fees, etc. The Minister's policy was to give governors the maximum autonomy consistent with efficient control of expenditure. Each year governors submitted estimates of income and expenditure to have them approved by the Ministry and to keep them within (known) amounts approved under various heads. Virement to the extent of five per cent of the smaller total was permitted, and more if the Minister approved. New courses still required approval, as did new buildings. But the limit of purchase without reference was doubled (£500 to £1,000) and the Minister approved only the establishment of senior staff. The Ministry dealt with both the principals and the governors of the colleges together. They were called to meetings twice a year, which discussed the pattern of development of the colleges. Long-term plans for students' numbers were settled as were long-term building plans. There was a sub-committee to discuss building standards. No doubt there would have been others in time. Details within the overall plans were settled between the individual college and the Ministry. The Ministry asked for the first estimate in October. By January it knew and told the colleges what the available total was likely to be.

Conclusion

One of the important points to note about the different arrangements is the way that the battles for resources are fought. Under LEA control everything is at arm's length, as it were. If LEAs can be said to be fighting other LEAs, they do it through the DES. There are no direct confrontations. This is true particularly of buildings. There has in the past been little visible constraint on current expenditure. If the students were to be taught money generally came in the form of rate support grants. Colleges rarely rival each other. The rule of thumb is if we do it for one we do it for all. You may not get what you want, but at least nobody else does. Only in the RAC is there serious inter-authority rivalry, for the approval of courses, and this leads to noticeable tensions.

Under direct grant arrangements, institutions are effectively fighting against each other. The CATs each knew the total money available and it had to be split between them; thereafter the general pattern of expenditure followed that decided in discussion.

Under the UGC, the battle for resources outside the universities goes on *in camera*. The visible battles are all inside the institution. Professors vie for their share of the cake; more social science immediately means less engineering. The experience of the CATs is salutary; under the LEAs and direct grant status, they had begun to develop in the social sciences, often to the chagrin of the engineering departments, whose fears increased at the thought of increased freedom under the UGC. But this turned out to be unfounded when the UGC denied the CATs' development in the social sciences and the imagined lost resources were again available to the other departments. The in-fighting in universities does go some way to explaining their elaborate power structure, with its endless committees; each group of people seeks a check that another is not gaining ascendancy and thus resources. A consequence is that academic initiatives become all the harder to develop.

All this shows that things are not always what they seem. Administration by local authorities can be extremely tedious and restrictive, but it is considerably improving. Whatever else it may prevent it need not prevent expansion nor innovation, for it has been responsible for the fastest expanding sector of higher education and the most innovative, and is likely to be responsible for the majority of students in the future. On the other hand, despite its many apparent advantages, there are fewer uniquely cogent arguments for the UGC, and some of its freedoms are not as free as they might be. Also, the direct control of a number of institutions by the DES was surprisingly agreeable to them. In the future, the role of governing bodies is likely to be central, at least to colleges in the public sector. Their importance may well increase, too, as a result of changes in the structure of local government, for colleges may seek greater independence from more powerful local authorities.

The main issue for the future is no longer to worry about the role of the state in higher education; this chapter has attempted to show that on balance it has been markedly beneficial. It is this: if we seek to maintain a system offering a wide range of types of higher education, then clearly a variety of methods of control and administration will continue; the question is to determine the balance between them, and we are now able to do this free of some of the assumptions about the relations between higher education and the state that have governed our decisions in the past.

NOTES

1. *Higher Education: Report of a Committee appointed by the Prime Minister under the Chairmanship of Lord Robbins* (Cmnd 2154, pp. 6–7, HMSO, 1963).
2. op. cit., Appendix four, part I.
3. e.g. *University Reform Acts of 1854 and 1856*, Royal Commission on the Universities, appointed 1872.
4. Report of the Study Group on the Government of Colleges of Education, HMSO, 1966.
5. Reported in *Hansard*, November 27, 1970.
6. Speeches made at Woolwich on April 27, 1965, and Lancaster on January 20, 1967.
7. See *National Board for Prices and Incomes*, Reports Nos. 98 and 145, Standing Reference on the Pay of University Teachers in Great Britain (Cmnd 3866 and 4334, HMSO, 1968 and 1970 respectively).
8. See various reports of the Burnham Committees.
9. See T. Burgess and J. Pratt, *Policy and Practice: the Colleges of Advanced Technology*, Chapter 8 (London: Allen Lane the Penguin Press, 1970).

12

Soviet Higher Education between Government Policy and Self-determination – a German View

Detlef Glowka

There is, at present, no movement in the Soviet Union pointing towards a substantial reform of higher education. There have been no cases of student unrest to indicate that something is basically wrong with the system. Soviet higher education approached the fiftieth anniversary of the October Revolution and the one-hundredth anniversary of Lenin's birthday celebrating its own perfection. The question arises though: how similar are the tasks and aims of higher education in the Soviet Union to those of 'capitalist' countries? And are the problems being handled more successfully in the USSR?

For some important aspects of higher education, about which public opinion in the West is still quarrelling, the Soviets undoubtedly feel that they have found their own satisfactory solution. The objectives in higher education seem to be clear. They are defined as highly qualified and specialized professional education and simultaneously as communist upbringing. No Soviet official would acknowledge the possibility that discrepancies could occur in his country between the higher education system, the state, society and the economy. In his opinion higher education is playing its optimal role in contributing to the construction of a communist society. Furthermore, correspondence between societal, in particular economic, needs and the expansion of higher education in both its qualitative and quantitative aspects would be claimed – as a result of communist policy in general and of successful educational planning in particular. The avoidance of wastage, another topic of discussion in the West, has been achieved to a substantial degree. A study course of ten months each year guarantees an intensive utilization of buildings and equipment. The intensive and detailed guidance of students keeps the drop-out rate low (about 10 per cent in full-time education). An extended system of instruction by correspondence – still to be developed in many other countries – functions well and produces more than 40 per cent of the graduates from higher educational establishments. It is true, equal opportunity for students from different social origins has not been achieved to ensure that the social composition of the student body corresponds to the social structure of society itself, but the so-called underprivileged strata are much better represented than in West European universities. Equal rights for women has become fully accepted in Soviet higher education; nearly 50 per cent of all student enrolments are women. This is not to suggest that in the Soviet Union the above-mentioned features have left higher education with no unsolved questions, but the problems seem to be less essential and more technical in character.

Some problems, found in higher education in the West, have no place in Soviet society. Concepts of the autonomy of a university and of academic freedom are not vital issues. Party and government have many channels at their disposal, through which they can effectively influence teaching, research and administration in higher educational establishments. Every student follows a prescribed curriculum and is appointed to a 'collective'. The impact of so-called individual demand in higher education has less influence in the USSR. For individual interests are always weighed against those of society as a whole. Individual interests do not determine the broadening of higher educational facilities, but conversely, individual aspirations are adapted to admission quotas, which are planned in accordance with manpower needs.

Compared with the West, the system of Soviet higher education is characterized by stability in the clarity of aims and in the regularity of development. But within this stable framework several important sections of the system are being subjected to processes of substantial change, which could lead to a general reform. Such dynamic zones will be treated below.

Dynamic Zones within Soviet Higher Education

Development of Higher Education and the Proportions of the Educational System

The Soviet authorities are proud to record the extensive expansion of higher education since the October Revolution. Official figures quote the following: the number of students per 10,000 inhabitants is 49 in the Federal Republic of Germany, 63 in England, to 88 in France, but 187 in the USSR; the Soviet figure is surpassed only by the USA with 226.[1] In 1958, the year of Khrushchev's educational reform, 456,000 freshmen students were admitted to institutions of higher education, 30 per cent higher than eight years previously. Only seven years later – due particularly to an expansion of part-time education – the number of admissions in 1958 had been increased by 86 per cent. But then the XXIIIrd Party Congress stated that to some degree the educational system had developed disproportionately. In connection with the economic reforms more qualified workers and technicians for each specialist with a higher education ought to be trained. The congress set up the following target figures:

Admissions

	1970 in percentages since 1965	1970 in absolute figures
To vocational-technical schools	156	1·8 million
To secondary specialized schools (technicums)	128	1·4 million
To higher education	106	0·9 million

The slowing down in the expansion of higher education is to continue in future. Simultaneously this development indicates a tendency to lower the supply of semi- and unskilled workers.

General secondary education has been the most quickly expanding section of the Soviet educational system. In 1970 two million pupils received their 'middle school' leaving certificates thus qualifying to apply to institutions of higher education; this represents increases of 2·8 times since 1960 and 9 times since 1950. During the seventies 'secondary education for all'[2] should be achieved. The upper grades of the 'middle school' have had their function changed fundamentally: instead of providing a preparatory course for an elite hoping to enter higher education they must now give the foundations for on-the-job training and for further lower and middle professional education. But the great majority of secondary school graduates aspire to higher education, which is accessible only to a minority of them. Competition for the limited number of places has increased and will continue to be keen. Improvement of selection procedures has become a main topic in discussions concerning higher education. Within the near future Soviet policy will have to deal with the contradiction between a wider accessibility of secondary education on the one hand and limited possibilities of obtaining higher education on the other.

Quality versus Quantity

One of the most important, if not the chief task, for Soviet higher education policy is labelled the improvement of quality. Notwithstanding the great and universally recognized achievements of Soviet science, the present state of higher education as a whole is still suffering from some of the problems which prevailed during the first decades after the October Revolution. During the last five years or so it has been declared that quality should take precedence over quantity.

With regard to the student body the aims are to begin by improving the selection of the most qualified and talented applicants and by taking measures to raise the level of secondary education. After the entrance examination a student should encounter competition rather than be spoonfed. Material incentives and rewards for higher marks on final examinations are being sought.

The main effort is being devoted to the improvement of material and personal equipment in institutions of higher education. Formally, all institutes are ranked as equal by the application of standardized norms; but in reality wide variations from the norm are found. The condition of the material facilities is a cause of much complaint. Faculty members are often criticized as insufficiently qualified, and at many institutes considerably more than half the faculty have not the required academic degree. A Party resolution of 1960 called for improved quality of doctoral dissertations and another resolution of 1966 initated a long-range programme of continued education for the teaching staff in institutions of higher education.

Teaching in higher education has recently become a subject for discussion and research. A central council has been established and numerous conferences and research units have been geared to meet the main problems in this field: fewer lectures in favour of more effective forms of instruction, independent work for students, the broader application of programmed instruction, the preparation of more and better textbooks and the modernization of curricula. These are tasks encouraging local initiative and the personal engagement of instructors. But measured against the importance of the study of higher education in a system in which teaching, staffing and curricular conditions are powerfully influenced from the centre, the present state of affairs is far from satisfactory. To date, no central research institute or journal has been established to promote systematic research in teaching in higher education.

The traditional backwardness of provincial areas compared with the big scientific centres will make improvement in quality a continuing and urgent theme for discussion.

Towards more Research within Higher Education

The Party's policy in the past caused a concentration of research at academies and their institutes; higher educational establishments, including to some degree the universities – with the only exception of the few biggest ones – became principally teaching institutions. But during the last decade the Party's opinion about the relationship between research and teaching has changed substantially.

It could be said that in the sixties Soviet leadership became aware of the immense importance of scientific research. Several Central Committee resolutions have stressed this issue. The slogan of the productive force of science and research became widespread. Raising productivity by material incentives – the principle behind the current economic reform – has been extended to research institutes.[3] In connexion with this development the 'discovery' had been made that the majority of very highly qualified personnel employed in higher educational establishments are not actively engaged in research. The recent call for more research within higher education is in accordance with the desires of faculty members, because this trend offers the chance of getting into close touch with practical economic and societal problems, of obtaining better equipment for laboratories and of casting off some teaching in favour of personal research interests. Furthermore, the educational relevance of research is being underlined. The involvement of students in research processes has become another principle of policy and is already in practice at new universities, as for example in Novosibirsk.

Higher educational establishments are experimenting in the search for new organizational forms for research within the traditionally teaching-oriented structure. More than four hundred 'problem laboratories' and around fifty 'scientific research institutes' – until now a monopoly of the academies – have been set up. The bulk of the research being conducted there is ordered by industrial enterprises and based on contractual commitments. The amount of such research has increased by up to ten times within the last decade. In 1968, the expenditures for scientific research at institutes under the jurisdiction of the Ministry of Higher Education, amounted to 350 million roubles; 78 per cent of this sum was paid on a contractual basis by industrial enterprises, and only 22 per cent for the state budget.[4] To some extent the research groups are permitted to dispose of their own profits and thus to improve their material facilities which are still a weak point and which it is hoped to raise to the level of the academies.

For a centralized administrative system operating with established standards for equipment and staffing and with far-reaching controls at its disposal, it is a delicate task to build some elements of a market economy into higher education. The transitional and difficult character of this situation keeps things in a state of flux.

Economic Aspects of Higher Education

The economics of education – which is, in its modern sense, a recent scientific innovation in the Soviet Union, too – has developed mainly in application to higher education. A real movement for the introduction of economic thought into higher education has arisen during the last five years. 'The scientific organization of labour' is one of the slogans under which conferences are being conducted and journals filled with articles. This view of higher education in terms of the economics of industrial enterprises deals with such themes as the determination of optimal sizes of higher educational establishments and their regional distribution, the rationalization of norms for teaching staffs, and how to make more effective use of personnel and material resources and so on.

At first glance it is surprising that the planning of higher education is getting new working foundations from this development, for planning has been practised for a long time. Prevailing planning procedures are now being criticized on the basis of new concepts. Long-range, scientifically based plans for the development of higher education are currently being regarded not as facts, but as desiderata. Not even now, at the time of writing, has an educational programme for the seventies been drawn up and announced, at least not publicly. Another widely discussed theme is the question of how to place graduates with a higher education more effectively within the national economy.

Party leadership has recognized that the economics of education is highly significant and supports its study. It is typical of Soviet higher education that it is wide open to the concept of its being responsible for its own economic efficiency. The introduction of the economics of education does not signify a reorientation but rather confirms an already predominating self-understanding. This process should not be simply taken as one of reaching decisions in education on economic grounds. There are also traits of emancipation: expenditures for higher education are no longer classified as being unproductive; it could be substantiated by facts and figures that material equipment is one of the main factors influencing the quality of education, and should therefore be improved; the criticism could be made that the growth of expenditures for higher education are not keeping pace with the growth of capital investment in the national economy. In applying the economics of education, the representatives of Soviet higher educational establishments are gaining a stronger sense of their own societal importance.

Specialization, Differentiation, Integration

The present structure of the Soviet higher education system was shaped during the late twenties and has remained basically unchanged since then. The orientation towards practical and professional requirements became its main feature. Out of nearly 800 higher educational establishments only 48 are universities; the others consist of so-called Higher Educational Institutes, many of which are relatively small and highly specialized establishments. The list of 'specialties' comprises more than 300 different diplomas for higher education; 65 of them are granted at universities. About 10 per cent of specialists with higher education are graduates from universities; a small part of them (around a quarter) go as teachers to secondary schools (the majority of secondary school teachers receive their professional education at Pedagogical Institutes).[5] Often the quality of instruction at universities is much better than at institutes. Therefore one of the main duties of the universities, especially of the leading universities in Moscow, Leningrad, Kiev, Novosibirsk and some others, is to provide the higher educational institutes and research establishments with instructors and scientific personnel. The smaller provincial universities rank considerably below the bigger ones; on the other hand, however, some of the institutes can compete with leading universities.

Around half the higher educational establishments are under the jurisdiction of the Ministries of Higher Education (either the all-union Ministry or a union-republic one), which also controls secondary specialized education. Other institutes are under various ministries, for example the ministries of education, of culture, of health, of agriculture, of transportation and so on; in this way higher educational establishments are directly geared to the practical needs of branches of the national economy. In theory together they form a unified system of higher education without differences of rank. But secondary school graduates know very well that there are real differences of quality of instruction and, as a consequence, of career chances; the ratio of applicants to vacancies at higher education establishments differs between one to one and fifteen to one. These differences are mainly due to a prestige scale of institutes and faculties.

The pedagogical and administrative structure of Soviet higher education was regarded until recently as successful. But lately some critics have called for a change. The rector of Novosibirsk university, Belyayev, a member of the Academy of Sciences, may be quoted here at some length. He makes two points:

> Our higher schools have developed from the system of polytechnical institutes and universities largely along lines of the differentiation and increasing specialization of the higher educational institutions, particularly the technical schools. This process is under way at present, and it is also facilitated to no small degree by the departmental insularism of the higher schools. Today universities with a broad range of specialties and higher polytechnical schools are only islets in the sea of narrowly specialized institutes. . . .
>
> Another trouble of our higher schools, in my view, is their rigid structure (the system of the formal equivalence of higher schools, the curricula, the periods of instruction, the rigid nomenclature of specialties and diplomas). The unification is illusory, since it does not reflect the actual possibilities and quality of the higher schools. After all, it is no secret that there are enormous gaps in the average level of the training of specialists who are all alike, formally speaking, but graduated from different higher schools. On the other hand, with the growing complexity of our national economy and the progressive social division of labour, we need specialists with different kinds of training even in posts that are formally the same. The concept of the diploma-bearing specialist has obviously become too general and indefinite.[6]

Belyayev supports a concept which has become a matter of discussion recently, namely the differentiation of higher education. This aims at a sequence of stages in the training of specialists – a first stage of more general education for the mass professions within a shorter period of instruction than now, a more specialized and higher level second stage and a third stage for the education of highly skilled research specialists. Other proposals aim at combining differentiation with a process of integration. For example, the training of technicians (specialized secondary education) and of engineers (higher education) should be brought together in order to give both a common basis of technical knowledge, to use laboratory facilities in common to enable talented *technicum* students to switch over to higher institutes, or conversely, to give students of higher institutes, who do not master the curricular aims, a technician diploma.[7] Another route to integration takes the form of regional co-operation between various higher education establishments for the purpose of making a more efficient use of laboratory facilities and of co-ordinating research. The assignment of higher educational institutes to various ministries proves an obstacle to closer co-operation.[8]

Trends and Political Preconditions

The five spheres of change within the Soviet system of higher education decribed above have two traits in common. First, the current processes promote a more complex integration of Soviet higher education with society. Soviet society, and in particular its economy, has become more complex during the last decade; higher education is going to keep pace with this development in order to meet more effectively social needs. Second, an adaptation by small steps instead of far-reaching reform is characteristic of this process. But the single steps are so significant that they easily could lead to a substantial reconstruction of the whole. Particularly the concept of a differentiated and simultaneously integrated system of higher education – a model just cautiously suggested in the Soviet Union but already widely discussed or even more or less practised in the West – could become a nucleus of innovation. The traditional relations between secondary and higher and between general and vocational education, between specialization and vocational training, between research and teaching, between the adaptation of the education system in terms of individual aspirations and its response to planning, would then become problematical and result in new relationships within a framework of comprehensive higher education.

Higher education and science develop under the leadership of the Communist Party – this axiom remains unquestioned. A series of Central Committee resolutions reveals the Party's activity in this field. What should be pointed out here is the style characterizing the role of the central political government. After criticizing Stalin's era because of the 'cult of personality' and Khrushchev's era because of its 'subjectivistic and voluntaristic style' the present development of society is supposed to be founded on rational and scientifically based decisions. In other words:

aims should not be simply deduced from political and ideological ideas; they should be based to a greater extent on objective information and insight about circumstances. This view leads directly to an increased demand for scientific research in the social sciences as emphasized in a Party resolution. In this, higher educational establishments are called upon to make their contribution. So the higher education system is going to turn from its role as the object of policy to one as a counsellor in policy making. 'The label "totalitarian" no longer fits comfortably' – this is the outcome of some studies devoted to Soviet policy making.[10] That is especially true of higher education. The dynamic forces which have determined the development of higher education during the last decade can be characterized as spontaneous and the result of the system's internal development. The expanding role of science, the increasing importance of quality, the necessity of economic considerations, the increasing complexity of organizational structures and the impossibility of functioning effectively without autonomy are traits of higher education, which did not originate as consequences of political decision making. The Party leadership, however, faced these trends and reacted hoping to stimulate them and gear them to economic needs. Soviet officials like to label this process 'democratization', having in mind some extension of the rights and decision-making powers at the lower levels of administration. With such indications a new statute for higher educational establishments was passed in February 1969.[11] The interests of the higher educational establishments and the Party's claim to lead are not permanently in harmony in this process of democratization. But both sides agree on their basic aim: to make the Soviet Union highly industrialized. For the Soviet higher education system such an aim corresponds to its traditional pragmatism and economic orientation, and for the Party leadership it reveals a basic trait in communist society.

A comparative look at East Germany as the most industrialized country in the communist bloc indicates in what direction Soviet higher education is developing. In the GDR a substantial reform of higher education has been going on since 1966 and is supposed to be completed in 1975.[12] The reform aims at making higher education an integrated part of a 'comprehensive societal system of socialism'. Professional training at higher educational establishments will be performed at three stages – in accordance with the above-mentioned principle of differentiation. Research is to be extended considerably, in the course of which the single higher educational establishments will 'profile' themselves according to the special demands of economy, the State and society. A concept of the large scale of science is outlined. Specializing their research the institutes and the newly established university departments will be combined into huge research organizations along the lines of concentration within industry.

For Soviet higher education the process of its further integration into society signifies at the same time a process of consolidation. Probably, because of the increasing importance of this social sub-system, its representatives – scientists, instructors and students alike – may identify themselves with this development and become more self-confident. Creativity may be stimulated as ideological commitment decreases. But that critical attitudes will become more overt and that discontent with the established political system will arise cannot be excluded. Comparisons in the communist world are possible. There have been cases of student unrest in Yugoslavia, and the movement for liberty in Czechoslovakia in 1968 and previously (1956) in Poland and Hungary was essentially supported by students and intellectuals. The Soviet Communist Party, too, has had to rebuke students 'for insufficient political and moral consciousness'. Recently the Communist Party has attempted to enforce ideological upbringing in higher educational establishments. The party's claim to lead politically and ideologically seems to be unchallenged. A tendency towards the reduction of ideology can be stated only in regard to practical and scientific requirements but not in general. At present nothing indicates – except as an abstract probability – that within the near future Soviet universities could become the source of concepts critical of communist society.

The development of higher education in the Soviet Union or in the GDR on the one hand and in the West on the other seems to be proceeding from different conditions but converging in its tendency. In the East the starting point of higher education is characterized by centralized political control, by a concentration on teaching, professional training and by pragmatic attitudes towards science. While in the West we find the idea of autonomy, an introduction to knowledge instead of profession training and the cultivation of knowledge for its own sake as basic traits of higher education. The trend is in the direction of more political control and an increasing participation by the public, of a professional education for enlarging student enrolments (probably the relative student enrolment figures in the Soviet Union will soon be exceeded by figures in the leading Western European countries) and of a more pragmatical approach to teaching and research within higher education. In this sense 'convergency' to a middle position between formerly opposite conditions could be predicted with some degree of confidence.

Of course, contrasting conditions should not be understood as mere differences of historical origin – the long university tradition in the West and the short Soviet tradition since the October Revolution which created the present higher education system. For example, the manifold problems concentrated in the concept of the autonomy of research and teaching are treated quite differently in East and West as a consequence of present political climates of opinion. These differences will continue and any convergence will remain partial tendencies. Traits of convergency will develop to the degree that higher education in the West is subordinated to the technocratic management of an industrial society. But in the West the technocratic tendency is opposed in universities by the current movement for democratization and the emancipation of society. This movement represents one of the main traits in our time by which higher education in the West contrasts with higher education in the Soviet Union.

NOTES

1. See *Statistical Yearbook of the USSR 1968*, p. 174. We do not propose to discuss here the definition of higher education.
2. In the Soviet version this comprises ten years of general education or combined general and professional education lasting eleven years.
3. See Central Committee resolution in *Pravda*, 23 Oct. 1968.
4. See *Vestnik Vysshej shkoly*, vol. 9, 1969, p. 52.
5. See B. M. Remennikov, 'Economic Problems of Higher Education', in *Soviet Education*, Vol. 11, 1369, No. 8–9.
6. See *The Current Digest of the Soviet Press* (CDSP), vol. 21, no. 38, 15 Oct. 1969, pp. 12 and 31.
7. See Briuchovets in *Izvestia*, May 20, 1970.
8. See *CDSP*, vol. 22, no. 1, Feb. 3, 1970, pp. 33–4.
9. See *Pravda*, Aug. 22, 1967.
10. Peter H. Juviler and Henry W. Morton, *Soviet Policy Making* (London: Praeger, 1967).
11. See bulletin '*Ministerstva vysshego i srednego spetsial*', nogo obrazovaniia SSSR, 1969, no. 5.
12. Die Weiterführung der 3. Hochschulreform und die Entwicklung des Hochschulwesens bis 1975, Beschluß des Staatsrates der DDR vom 3. April 1969. Deutsche Lehrerzeitung (Beilage), Nr. 17, 1969.

13

Student Problems*

B. R. Williams

Student discontent is not new. One can find in Turgenev and Flaubert descriptions of students' plots and attitudes which have a strikingly contemporary flavour. There have been serious student troubles in most countries at one time or another connected with political oppression, or with struggles for national freedom, or with unemployment. What is perhaps new is the strength of discontent in so many countries at the one time.

The international extent of serious student discontent may however be more apparent than real. We get more news, we get it more promptly, we get it presented in more dramatic forms. Demonstrations make good television copy, students are articulate, and the news media converge on student demonstrations as wasps on jam. The students involved, and the public, are easily led to over-emphasize the importance of many of the events televised.

Factors in Student Unrest

Between the student revolts with widespread political significance in Eastern Europe and Western Europe there is a world of difference in the underlying causes and in the risks taken by students involved. Between the student revolt in Paris and the student sit-ins for example in Birmingham, Bristol and the London School of Economics there is also a great difference. There may well be some common factors, but the differences are greater than the similarities.

The manifestations of student unrest have varied enormously throughout the world, depending mainly on the seriousness of grievances, the political institutions of the country, and the nature of the university processes. The causes of unrest have been equally varied. In several East European countries one of the main causes of unrest is State control of the universities and the use of that control to induce conformity to the 'established wisdom' and power of the ruling Party. In France, West Germany and Italy, staff and buildings are appallingly inadequate by

* Based on a talk to the Australian College of Education, July 1968.

Australian standards, the economic and social significance of degrees is greater and the failure rates are higher. In the United States, where in some ways student unrest has been most sustained, there are four factors of special importance – the Negro problem, the very high percentage of students in tertiary education, the method of financing expensive research, and Vietnam.

Education is of critical importance in the struggle for the rights of blacks in American society. The tensions involved must affect the universities, and those universities which try to do most for the blacks may suffer most. The very high percentage of the age group at college or university also creates problems. Very many students are not interested, feel captives of the system but are reluctant to drop out, and are very ready to join in demonstrations which offer a sense of community and involvement. Contract research has induced in many of the faculty an unhealthy degree of detachment from university problems, and in many of the administrators a temptation to forget the importance of maintaining detachment from Government and industry. The significance of Vietnam to the higher-education age group needs no elaboration.

That the differences are greater than the similarities should not turn us away from a search for common factors. That many of the causes appear to be external to the universities should not cause us to neglect their internal state of health. At times of trouble there is always a tendency to blame 'outside agitators'. There will always be agitators. The important question is whether their corn will fall on stony or a fertile ground. In many universities, in different parts of the world, the ground has been fertile and it is important to understand why it should be so.

I suppose that the two most popular explanations are the 'state of the world' and the generation gap. There is much wrong with the state of the world. We have in modern technology a wonderful power to control disease and to end poverty, but also a frightening power to destroy. Yet we lack either the will or the power to use technology for the good of mankind. It is natural for the young to assume that the difficulties can be surmounted and important that they should. Otherwise the will to overcome difficulties would be too weak. But I do not believe that we can explain the major part of 'the student problem' in this way. There was a quietism in the bulk of students not long ago, and I expect this mood to return before very long. To my regret I have not found in the literature of student power or student revolt much sign of an analysis or a style that would suggest staying power. The flavour of adolescent reaction, the evidence of naïve belief in instant wisdom, is too strong.

I am sceptical too of the generation gap as an explanation. The generation gap is a very old but very vague concept. (One modern form of it is that 'you cannot trust anyone over 25'. Many of us here, if ever caught in such an outrageously generalizing mood, would cut the age limit drastically.) Has modern youth a much more powerful sense of a frustrating gap than previous generations? Have modern methods of communication and marketing created a much more specific youth culture than used to exist? If so, how quickly is this youth culture outgrown and what succeeds it? Have the growth of knowledge and the rapid increase in the proportion of children completing secondary education and entering tertiary education created such a knowledge gap that children now feel that their parents are hopelessly out of date? Perhaps they have, but before we accept this as any sort of explanation we should ask why such a high proportion of student activists have well-educated parents, why their activism is directed against universities which have played such a conspicuous part in creating the new knowledge, why a high proportion of the activists have very little knowledge of or interest in the fields where knowledge has grown most. In many important ways there is a much bigger gap, and a faster-growing gap, between those who comprehend modern mathematics, science and technology and those who do not, than between the generations. In many students, I suspect, the attitude to modern science and technology, to the 'computer-card society', is based as much on a sense of deprivation, even of personal inadequacy, as on fear that modern technology will be used for wrong purposes.

In some respects the gap, or at any rate the conflict, between the generations has diminished because of a change in parental attitudes to discipline. Indeed, some of our student problems can be traced to this change, and its effect on student attitudes to 'authority' in universities.

The Societal Role of Universities

Universities have a distinctive role in society. Some of their administrative arrangements and codes of conduct derive from their distinctive role in communicating, testing and extending knowledge. But in some countries, from law or custom, universities have also acted in *loco parentis*. From the change in parental attitudes to discipline, and the increase in the average age of students, has followed a strong challenge to this role and to the disciplinary rules and procedures which follow from it. In this case through lack of change, universities created an internal conflict between the generations. It is, or was, common to hear students argue that disciplinary decisions 'lacked legitimacy', and this helps to explain why many students who did not approve, or even disapproved, disruptive activities, nevertheless rallied round the disruptors after they had been 'disciplined'.

From their nature universities are ill-equipped to deal with mass disciplinary problems. They depend on a complex mixture of formal and informal arrangements, and much that is most valuable depends on informality. But informality in large universities is very dependent on the moderation and good sense of its members and on their commitment to reason and argument. When faced with violence or threats of violence there is a very natural fear of counteraction which might threaten freedom of discussion and the spirit of critical inquiry and dissent. It is therefore possible for a relatively small number of students who are not committed to the fundamental purposes of a university to organize disruption, in the knowledge that many members of staff (some of whom will be terrified of being called conservative or old-fashioned or not with it) will argue the importance of entering into discussion with them, of mediating between them and the 'administration'. Able disruptors are then in a position to exploit liberal attitudes for illiberal purposes. The only lasting solution to these problems is to be found in a widespread understanding of the essential purposes of a university and of the forms of behaviour and organization which follow, the provision of effective channels of communication and the means for dealing promptly with problems that arise, clarity of thought about the basis of university discipline and a readiness to adopt procedures to contemporary conditions. Then prompt action to deal with force or threats of force and violence are likely to work and to discourage repetition.

Earlier physical maturity and the later age of economic independence have combined to create a greater 'responsibility gap', and I suspect that this is one reason why student demands 'to participate in all decisions that affect them' have become more widespread and strident. The manner in which many universities responded to these demands contributed considerably to student unrest.

To a remarkable degree universities have been caught at a time of change without a coherent philosophy. Few of us in universities thought about the basis of university discipline, of the extent to which disciplinary arrangements did not in practice derive directly from the needs of teaching and research, until disciplinary decisions were challenged. Few people thought about the basis of university government and administration, of the extent to which they derived from the needs of teaching and research, until student activists made demands to participate in all decisions that affected them.

Because of this lack of prior thought the process of adaptation has often been rough and accompanied by disturbances. Some of the demands for participation are based on the concept of the university as a mini-state from which it follows, it is argued, that all members should have equal voting rights.

I have no doubt that the concept of the university as a mini-state, as potentially a democratic mini-state, is incompatible with the essential purposes of the university. There are many issues on which members of the university who have proved their competence in scholarship and are in a position to relate their views to the continuing life of the university must be in a position to control the final decisions. This is true of the basic content of courses, the standards set for degrees, academic appointments and promotions, and research policies. This is implied in the traditional reference to the community of masters and scholars. A student's decision to enter the university should involve, as Ashby puts it, 'a voluntary acquiescence in the discipline of scholarship', and a willingness to accept a student/teacher relationship which moves progressively to a position of equality as the student acquires competence and becomes a master.

Universities should be very forthright about this. An effective way to maintain or to extend discontent is to appear to promise more participation than can reasonably be granted or is intended; to offer shadows not substance.

It is reasonable to ask why universities have been caught unready at a time of change which they have played a large part in promoting, and have at times appeared infirm of purpose, even fuddy-duddy. The answer to this question is complex and I will attempt only one part of the answer. Universities have been preoccupied with problems of growth in numbers at a time when they have been undergoing rather radical changes in their nature. This change in nature is due to a marked growth in the role of extending knowledge relative to communicating it.

In most forms of research, specialization is very productive and academic staff have tended to become more and more specialized. (Knowing more and more about less and less?) Related to this is what Jencks and Riesman describe as the rise of the academic profession. A profession is characterized by practitioners who are more 'colleague-orientated than client-orientated'. A significant proportion of academic professionals now have closer links with colleagues in other universities and countries than with colleagues in other disciplines in their own universities. Undergraduate education has suffered, and there are fewer 'university men' absorbed in the general problems of their university than there used to be. Size has been a contributing factor.

Universities have some hard thinking to do about their own affairs. Revolting students have forced us to look more closely at university processes. Even though many of the main causes of revolt are to be found outside the universities, we will continue to suffer from them, and at times suffer acutely, unless we put our own affairs in order and earn the loyalty of our students.

14

Social Class, Race and Access to Higher Education

Edgar B. Gumbert

Several nations in the fifties and sixties became aware that their schools and universities shaped the lives of many of their citizens in ways that were not always acceptable in democratic terms. It was discovered that inequalities in achievement existed along social class and racial lines and that educational institutions reinforced rather than alleviated them. Debates paid close attention to the concepts of race and social class and to their impact on education.

Racism

Racism seems to be a relatively modern phenomenon.[1] Prior to the fifteenth century the typical division of mankind was less into antagonistic races than into competing religions. In the eighteenth and early nineteenth centuries natural historians introduced the notion that men could be classified into five races and that they could be ranked into higher and lower orders. Biologists soon corrected this view, but the popular belief in the inferiority of some races persisted.

The ideas of racism and class control developed together and distinctions between them were not always made. The colonization by whites of Africa, America and India fed racism. The political and economic interests in this imperial movement were so strong that by the nineteenth century the belief in the inferiority of coloured persons was a regular and established doctrinal system. A profitable slave-trade developed. In America and elsewhere colour racism was used as a foundation on which whites based their social, economic and political privileges. In Europe in the nineteenth century, racism in the form of anti-Semitism was used, particularly in France and Germany, as a political weapon. Discrimination was not limited to coloured races, Jews, or 'mixed races'. In 1853 the doctrines of 'Aryanism' and 'Nordicism' were originated by a Frenchman, Arthur de Gobineau, to show the biological and psychological hierarchy within the white race itself in order to justify class rule. After the Franco-Prussian War of 1870, 'Aryanism' was extended from a doctrine of class supremacy to be, in addition, a doctrine of national supremacy.

Although these dogmas had no empirical foundations, they served as a rationalization for the hierarchical organization of many societies. Since World War II, colonization, exploitation and racism, the latter particularly in the United States, have received world attention.

Placement of blacks in the system of stratification in the United States frequently has been likened to a caste system. Theoretically, membership in a caste is by birth; upward mobility is not possible; and social intercourse with members of society outside of the caste is not permissible. But this was and is not the case in the United States. There was and is no prescribed and identifiable black style of life from which it was or is impossible to depart. Nor, conversely, was there one style reserved for whites.

The Just Society

This writer believes that it is not very fruitful to talk about caste or even about race in the United States, and, in principle, in other industrial nations. To do so diverts attention from more fundamental social and economic considerations. Race essentially is a conservative concept. An analysis using it enables the investigator to assess the assimilative powers of a social system but does not point to ways by which the system might be transformed. For instance, in the fifties and sixties in the United States emphasis on the race theme led social reformers to concentrate their attentions on breaking down barriers to the free movement of blacks into the mainstream of society. It diverted attention from the fundamental changes needed in order to create a more just society for all. An analysis and critique of the larger system was not undertaken. Drastic inequalities took a racial form, but this was caused less by racism than by support for the status quo by major political and economic institutions. Wealthier blacks were more concerned with integration; the poor were concerned with immediate and pressing economic and political problems. The 'War on Poverty' instituted by the Johnson administration was a modest move in the direction of legislation based on a class analysis of society. A concern with power emerged with the shift from race to class. Instead of trying to find ways of handling 'the Negro situation', it became at least possible to discuss ways to solve the general problems of the underclass – black and white – in the United States.

The social position of black people in the United States was one facet of the more general system of stratification. Of course, race and class are not identical concepts. Descriptively, some of the detailed problems associated with them are different. Nevertheless, a stratification system using race as a concept can be understood in terms of class. It is a particularly brutal form of class oppression, but it is a difference of degree, not of kind. A class system provides a single plan for placing every member of society. It can be thought of as an institutional force which presses individual behaviour into certain social roles. A qualitative judgment, class determines social chances. Occupation, income, beliefs, family background, educational opportunity are among the factors that need to be taken into account.[2] Regardless of details, all systems of stratification, wherever exhibited, are forms of hostility and aggression; they constitute an invidious assessment of individuals; and they contribute to a climate of exploitation. The solution to the problems of both class and race is the transformation of society.

Class structure is intimately related to the ideology and to the form and scope of the economic activity upon which the society is engaged. Circumstances shape the details of the system. For example, it is frequently pointed out that 'In Brazil, money whitens; in Haiti, culture does.' Even in the United States where racism developed early and black slavery was well established by the beginning of the nineteenth century, there were differences in opportunity and mobility between the urban-industrial North and the rural-agrarian South.

Marx claimed social classes emerged from the economic structure as one group in conflict with another. To neo-Marxists the central categories of empirical sociology are 'capitalism' and 'bourgeois society'. This writer, following Raymond Aron, thinks it is more fruitful when analysing education to see the categories as 'industrialism' and 'technocracy'.[3] The Marxian theory that industrial development brings about a pauperization of the working class and that inevitably there will be a class struggle between the owning and the working classes did not adequately predict the phenomena. The working class did not become more homogeneous; nor did it absorb and command the loyalty of other groups of the population. On the contrary, industrialism brought about greater job differentiation and social stratification. Professional, managerial, clerical and technical occupations increased. With the growth of a white collar salariat, the class struggle took on a different nature. Social power was at once more diverse and, in a limited sense, more equal. Control of education took on heightened importance.

In advanced industrial nations several elites are formed, e.g. political, intellectual, business and labour elites. Their origins, their skills, the people to whom they listen, their interrelationships, the ways in which they view the world and their codes of actions are major concerns. Reforms in the property system or in the functioning of the economy, while necessary, are not alone sufficient to alter the nature of the elites. Governing elites have different characteristics which theoretically can vary from place to place and from time to time. Pareto, for example, claimed that a governing elite might consist of 'Lions' and 'Foxes' and too few of one and too many of the other might create instability in the society. In such cases the mode of recruitment of leaders is paramount and educational reform may afford a better opportunity for altering society and its stratification system than economic reform alone. For the reform to attain desired consequences, the type of successful individuals in the elites and the educational channels through which they passed should be known.

Education and Technetronic Society

In a 'brain intensive' or 'credential' society, access to educational institutions provides the opening to movement in the larger society. In industrial societies, universities cease being the secluded preserve of a small ruling class. To be sure, they retain traditional functions. They train members of the different ruling elites and they legitimize certain kinds of traditional institutional power. But they also train a host of intellectual and technical workers to take their place in the middle levels of the industrial system. Moreover, no widely accepted agreement about the form or content of higher education appropriate to an industrialized society has emerged.

Max Weber saw the heart of the issue. He wrote,

> Behind all the present discussions of the foundations of the educational system, the struggle of the 'specialist type of man' against the older type of 'cultivated man' is hidden at some decisive point. This fight is determined by the irresistibly expanding bureaucratization of all public and private relations of authority and by the ever-increasing importance of expert and specialized knowledge. This fight intrudes into all intimate cultural questions.[4]

Zbigniew Brzezinski outlined the same struggle in a little more detail, and was more certain of the outcome. In the United States, he said, a new breed of 'organization-oriented, application-minded intellectuals' had exploited and harnessed the techniques and technological devices of the 'technetronic society'. This caused a shift in the balance of power in the intellectual community. Brzezinski claimed, with approval, that

> the largely humanist-oriented, occasionally ideologically-minded intellectual-dissenter, who sees his role largely in terms of proffering social critiques, is rapidly being replaced either by experts and specialists, who become involved in special governmental undertakings, or by the generalists-integrators, who become in effect house-ideologues for those in power, providing overall intellectual integration for disparate actions.[5]

The struggle to which Weber and Brzezinski refer is a struggle for power, but it is not in a Marxist sense a class struggle. People who do and who do not own the means of production are both sides. Nor is it a racial struggle. But because universities are indispensable feeder institutions for membership in the power elites in industrial society, and for the middle echelon jobs as well, the stratification system tends to be rooted in them. Battle for control of them and access to them is very nearly a battle of life or death – for blacks and whites alike. Power and class differentiating functions tend to displace the status differentiating function of the university.

Several writers provided philosophical rationales for attributing great power to education and therefore for politicizing it. Although obviously different in several important respects, Francis Bacon, Descartes, Marx and John Dewey linked knowledge to power and in the many nations influenced by their thought the tradition is still carried on. It is one thing upon which the parties in the struggle for control of the universities agree.

Since World War II the context within which universities have operated was set by an economic demand for high rates of economic growth and by a political demand for social justice. The war, the Cold War and, in Asia, Africa and Latin America, anti-colonialism provided impetus for these demands.

During and after the war human rights were widely discussed. In the post-war period most European nations implemented social welfare legislation. There were demands for higher educational standards of living. Questions were raised regarding access to education and how it was to be distributed.

Theoretically, a number of basic services can be provided on the principle of equal distribution to all irrespective of either ownership or social status or personal merit, e.g. criminal justice, public transportation, sanitation. Not all analysts agree that education can be distributed in the same way. Public and private claims on education may conflict if demands for equal access to all kinds of learning lead to uniformity. Even in conditions of economic abundance the equal distribution of education may not always be possible. It may be possible only in homogeneous communities where the cultural standards of classes do not conflict so much as to reduce social intercourse to a minimum. Security and belonging foster variety and creative expression.

However, industrialism constitutes a continuous challenge to community. Specialization of work activities is one of its by-products, and this fact influenced debates about the distribution of education. Moreover, the situation was further complicated in the United States where the post-war years were dominated by a rage to produce and by the hates and fears of the Cold War. Although the economic system had a staggering capacity for production, the fruits were not equally distributed. Little welfare legislation was passed; the nation turned its back on those who could not keep up; it did not turn its attention towards them until the sixties, and then only under the threat of violence. Blacks and whites alike were cut off from good jobs, decent housing and education, although the burden fell more heavily upon the former. Both were not so much exploited as ignored.

The University Response

The discussions about education in Europe and the United States involved questions about the aims and content of education and how far universities should go to accommodate themselves to external social demands. They also involved the criteria that could be used to determine the distribution of education. The relevance of aptitude and ability as criteria for deciding upon access to universities was widely discussed, as were the difficulties encountered in trying to identify and categorize students according to them.

The post-war expansion of higher education in Europe and the United States was conservative and took place well within the framework of traditional norms and institutions. In Europe an elite system was expanded. Although expenditures in higher education were increased, the benefits went largely to the classes that formerly had received them. Unequal chances and unequal distribution remained. In the United States higher education was expanded according to principles laid down in the land grant colleges in the 1860s and in the graduate research universities in the 1880s and 90s. Although more populistic than universities in Europe, vocationalism and professionalism still dominated their growth; little experimentation was undertaken. On the whole, classes formerly excluded were not admitted until the late sixties. As in Europe, benefits went to the middle classes which continued to provide the recruits for elite position.

How to provide the means to operate these systems and how to cope with the contradictions that emerged from their operations constituted the material for educational debates in industrial nations in the fifties and sixties.

Economic demands on universities were not always consistent with claims of social justice. While industrial societies were scientifically bold and technologically innovating, they were socially and politically conservative. The emphasis on science, computers, efficiency and a vocabulary about mass society made the technocratic rhetoric sound revolutionary. But while oriented towards the future with regard to technology, the future apparently was already here with regard to politics and social justice. The preferred model of society was derived from a Platonic-Aristotelean theory of elite control and paternalistic dominance over a hierarchical society. The scientific enterprise might generate new knowledge in the physical and psycho-biological sciences but technocrats did not look for discoveries in the social sciences about new forms of social and political participation. It was expected that these sciences would produce knowledge that would merely confirm and strengthen elite control. The conservative Platonic theory that the fate of the state is identical to the fate of the governing elite was widely held.

Furthermore, industrial societies for their survival had to associate higher education with the process of providing qualifications for work, and this reinforced elitist tendencies and class conflict. Jobs were neither regarded nor rewarded equally. Powerful incentives to move into the highest ones were devised. Many aspired to the universities and to the jobs for which they prepared, but only a few were selected. The discrepancy between aspirations and university places caused frustration and bitterness. The alleged inferiority of those not admitted to the university was keenly felt. Reminders of their failure were continuous, e.g. through the widely diffused and technologically improved communication media.

Obviously, strategies for social mobility needed to be devised by industrial nations. The means used to select the elites were vital issues in national debates. The movement up and down the social system and the recruitment of the elites had to be consistent with claims of social justice. A doctrine to legitimize the unequal distribution of education was needed. The most widely adopted covering principle in industrial nations was the principle of equality of opportunity. In advanced industrial nations, this functioned as a hierarchical, not an egalitarian, principle. Its operation helped to fill vacancies in the elites and created social and cultural gaps within the remainder of society.

Theoretically, according to the doctrine of equality of opportunity equal ability will lead to equal access to education regardless of social class background. In fact, when the doctrine is followed access to education normally is greater in the more favoured social classes at every ability level. Intellectual distinctions frequently turn out to be institutionalized class distinctions. Social class bias is built into the normal measures of academic achievement. Admission to universities is on the basis of grades and test scores and these are highly correlated to family income. It is difficult for low-income children to gain admission to universities. Minority groups of all kinds, particularly blacks in the United States, because they come from a sub-culture which frequently is at variance from the one found in the university, are at a disadvantage. In some cases they come from anti-educative sub-cultures. They do not have the stimulation and same motivational systems on which success in universities is predicated. Curiosity may not have been developed or may not have been channelled into exploratory activities that pay off in formal educational settings. Their activities and experiences while wide from one point of view might be restrictive from an academic point of view. One of the main gains of the twentieth century so far is the discovery of the subtlety and complexity of the forces that combine to favour or hinder academic success.

Several strategies for bringing new classes and minorities into the university have been devised. Scholarships and loans were the first solutions tried but they brought about few significant changes in the social composition of universities. Special programmes for 'disadvantaged' persons and for 'high risk' students were then developed.[6] In these programmes criteria for selection are less rigid. Promising test scores or some evidence of ability to handle academic work and signs of improvement in secondary schools are looked for. Perseverance, motivation, emotional 'toughness', willingness to accept personal responsibility, some signs of a feeling of self-worth, leadership potential are other qualities desired. Once in the university, remedial and tutoring programmes need to be set up. Special counselling sessions have been used.

Requests also have been made to abolish academic performance comparisons, e.g. letter grading and class standings, and to abandon the concept of academic failure altogether.

Some critics of the universities have argued that since it is an elite practice to admit only qualified candidates to them, the universities instead ought to admit everyone who wants to enter. People, they say, are more important than standards or the preservation of institutional power.

Short of open admission policies quota systems have been advocated, particularly in the United States. They propose that a certain percentage – say, 10, 12, or 15 – of selected minorities, based either on race, poverty, or ethnic background or some other criterion of minority status, should be admitted to the university regardless of intellectual distinction.

Supporters of this position argue that intelligence is not entirely or even significantly innate and constant. It is, they say, something that can be acquired. Thus, they argue that students, even of university age, should be given an opportunity to develop their intelligence.

To eliminate 'cultural schizophrenia' black students in the United States have demanded 'black studies' programmes.[7] Allegedly they help to provide 'ego identity and ethnic confidence'. They claim to be able to improve the understanding of blacks by non-blacks and to hasten integration. Political power is said to increase as a result of such studies. Social distances theoretically narrow because less emphasis is paid to white and to middle class values and experiences. Class rule by whites is supposed, therefore, to diminish.

Needless to say, many citizens of the industrial nations do not think the claims of equality should be pressed so far.[8] By trying to do too much, they say, the universities will lose their unique power and will not be able to be of any service to the community. They claim standards will be lowered by admitting students 'not qualified to profit'. They do not see how reforms in curriculum or in teaching methods, nor how any amount of money, could prevent a flood of unassimilable students from degrading the work of universities. Universities would become too large and impersonal. Higher learning would be vulgarized and the quality of life in general would be debased. Also, they say open admission policies or quota systems violate the principle of fairness, as some qualified students would have to be denied admission. Moreover, to them compensatory education does not belong in the colleges and universities. The crucial years, they point out, are the first eight, and particularly the first four or five, and that is where investment should be made if education is to facilitate mobility.

The Industrial Society and Resources

The contradictions in the industrial system in the twentieth century were revealed intensely in the universities, particularly since World War II.[9] Industrialism discredited as sources of expanded awareness institutions such as the family and religion and it offered universities as alternatives. At the same time, however, the work requirements of the industrial system forced on the universities specialized instruction that fragmented rather than synthesized knowledge and perception. While more people had time and freedom to question their existence, work became boring, meaningless, unchallenging and unrewarding. Caught between dreary jobs and unemployment, discontent was widespread. Professional and vocational needs conflicted with human and cultural needs.

The industrial system needed an expanded system of higher education, and most ambitious nations after World War II proceeded to provide just that. However, resources in the form of classroom space, libraries, laboratories and enough teachers to keep close teacher-student relations were not always provided. In the sixties students in France, Italy and the United States rioted against inadequate resources.

Even when first-rate resources for inquiry were provided, the conflict between the university function of teaching on the one hand and the functions of service and research on the other – the latter growing primarily out of the nexus with the industrial system – led students to claim that even the best universities offered an arid existence. The 'community of the educated' disappeared. In the sixties, the revolt of students at such universities as Columbia, California and Berlin indicated that there was no necessary connection between size, affluence or distinction of faculties and quality teaching. Professional requirements took precedence over decent treatment of undergraduates.

Because elite systems of higher education were expanded, highly intelligent and ambitious students were carefully selected. Frequently from homes committed to liberal doctrines, they had been brought up with freedom to criticize, debate and question. Their skills, confidence and expectations created great capacities for self-management. They expected that the life of the university would grow out of the background and interests of those who comprised the university community. The university claimed to carry on the tradition of free and open inquiry. However, in the United States and in several European countries students claimed that crowded conditions and the requirements of technological organizations for order and for discipline led the universities to authoritarianism.[10] Typically, students were denied opportunity to participate in making academic policies and to influence the development of the university. Instead, university officials required that the students obey rules over which they had no control. When they did express views about war, colonialism, hypocrisy or bureaucracy, they frequently were not heeded, or the authorities resisted them, sometimes violently.

The universities obliged the industrial establishment and removed outstanding young people from ties to family, community, productive labour, even class in the case of those drawn away from lower class origins. But by taking on custodial and extended manpower training functions, and by requiring that the students participate in a 'youth culture', the universities created what Kenneth Keniston called 'psychological adults' who were 'sociological adolescents' – adults who were not yet integrated 'into the institutional structures of society'.[11] This created a privileged but powerless youth which was a potential threat to the society which fostered it.

The successful academic revolution that made the universities the servants of the managers of the industrial system left many of the incipient members of the industrial elites discontented and opposed to them. In some cases they turned against established governmental, military and academic elites.

The conventional wisdom in Western Europe and in the United States since World War II was that the fundamental conflicts and contradictions of the industrial system could be contained within the framework of existing political and educational institutions. Students challenged this assumption in the sixties in virtually every industrial nation. They taught many people that political equality does not necessarily bring economic or social or educational equality; and that political democracy does not prevent class rule. They showed also that questions of education are really class questions, not in a narrow sense that education can palliate the effects of a class system, but in a broad sense that all educational activity is related to the class structure of the larger society. Their aims and their actions led many people to see that if equality is only possible in an affluent society, affluence alone does not guarantee equality. Under industrial conditions, inequalities constantly were reproduced and in some cases were rendered extremely acute. In the end many people thought again about the promises of democracy and how best to keep them.

BIBLIOGRAPHY

1. For a comprehensive coverage of the race question see, UNESCO, *Race and Science* (New York: Columbia University Press, 1961).
2. T. H. Marshall, *Citizenship and Social Class* (Cambridge: University Press, 1950) p. 106.
3. See for example, Raymond Aron, *Progress and Disillusion: The Dialectics of Modern Society* (New York: The New American Library, 1968).
4. Quoted by Burton R. Clark, *Educating the Expert Society* (San Francisco: Chandler Publishing Company, 1962), p. 3.
5. Quoted by Noam Chomsky, 'The Menace of Liberal Scholarship', *The New York Review*, January 2, 1969, Vol. XI, No. 12, p. 30.
6. See Robert Williams, 'What We Are Learning From Current Programs for Disadvantaged Children', *The Journal of Higher Education*, April, 1969, pp. 274–85.
7. W. Todd Furniss, 'Racial Minorities and Curriculum Change', *Educational Record*, Fall, 1969, pp. 360–5.
8. A comprehensive statement that summed up European and American opposition was made by Vice President Spiro T. Agnew in a speech in April, 1970, reprinted in *The Chronicle of Higher Education*, Vol. IV, No. 28, April 20, 1970, pp. 1–2.
9. I learned much about the educational conflicts from a manuscript of a book on politics and community by Dr Vincent Watson, particularly from Chapter III, 'Education, Culture and Social Change'.
10. See for example the 'Charte de Nanterre', reproduced by Lawrence Stone in 'Two Cheers for the University', *The New York Review*, August 22, 1968, pp. 21–2.
11. Kenneth Keniston, *Young Radicals: Notes on Committed Youth* (New York: Harcourt Brace and World, 1968).

15

The Level of Education and Training

Edmund King

Earlier articles have shown that the accepted idea of the university in some countries precludes the concept of 'training' as that is understood in English-speaking countries. Furthermore, in systems where some training is accepted as part of higher education's responsibilities, that function may be hived off into non-university institutions. These may be given names indicating inferior status (e.g. 'further' as distinct from 'higher' education). Alternatively, the more practical and *training* sectors may be lower in the intellectual and career hierarchy than the more academic sectors. In some traditions of higher education the only careers systematically trained for have been those of medicine and law; and even here the amount of practical training and expertise may be nugatory by 'Anglo-Saxon' standards.

The Concept of Training

This hierarchy in higher education is no mere reflection of the present socio-economic system, though it does perpetuate it. The problem lies deeper – in the very roots of language and ideology. Some languages have no word for 'training' appropriate to the level of the university, except as a recent importation. Moreover, the very idea suggests an apprenticeship to the traditional skills and the approval of others – a conditional level. Our word 'profession', with its connotation of great knowledge, growing research, and public service (all autonomously invigilated by a responsible learned body), is still sometimes a foreign concept. Scholars are 'scientists' working on their own, being almost as independent as the universities themselves.

In many countries, the concept 'science' includes realms as abstract as philosophy and classical studies. People using the English word imply experience of practical work, field studies, and considerations of applicability to daily life or further experimental learning. English speakers presume that such procedures are integral to the learning process in any 'science', even if their interest is diverted from 'applied science' or technology as such. Thus some kind of know-how or training is acquired on the way, and is implicit in our notion of a 'discipline'. Yet in some other countries schools and higher institutions (even formally concentrating on 'science') may partly or entirely lack facilities for experimental learning by students. A demonstration bench for the professor and his assistants suffices. Thus professional *training* would be difficult, especially in view of the numbers enrolled. Some practical consequences will be reviewed later; but the point must be made here for conceptual clarification.

For the reasons just given, the English word 'training' is widely inclusive. It is used to include the acquisition of theoretical knowledge and factual information during the process of becoming a teacher or doctor or priest, without special emphasis on professional skills. By contrast, the corresponding word in other languages focuses on vocational techniques – usually at a lower level, as we might imply by making a distinction between a technologist and a technician. For higher education this difference of idiom and ideology is important. Talk of 'training' or expertise challenges not only higher education's responsibilities to students and manpower needs but the present hierarchy of function and status among university teachers. Most overseas professors do not do the sort of thing implied by 'training', and may never in their lives have felt called upon to be good at it. If they continue in public practice outside the university (a common thing), that may be highly specialized in purview and isolated emotionally from the teaching responsibilities of a professor.

Most professors outside the 'Anglo-Saxon' world are part-time pluralists who do not consider they have global responsibilities for making sure their students know the multiple aspects of a field of knowledge – let alone the practical skills of science and the forensic applications of learning. Even if they admit that such a teaching role inheres somewhere in the university, the concept of all-round information or all-round training is restricted by the autonomy of faculties and the still more fragmented self-sufficiency of 'academic freedom'. Established teachers cover what subjects they will as and when they will. Coverage of theoretical or factual knowledge is therefore patchy; and general competence or specific 'training' is a concept for someone else to think about.

If some responsibility for general coverage is accepted in principle, who will discharge it? And where? Once again, the local language of life may preclude it. A 1966 survey of Italian established university teachers (*professori di ruolo*) showed that nearly one-third of them were over the age of 60, while nearly four-fifths were over the age of 46. Other university teachers are 'unestablished', and dependent upon their 'feudal barons' (as the slang phrase has it) for whatever courses they can pick up. Including these junior colleagues together with the 'private teachers' (*liberi docenti*; *Privatdozenten* in other countries), a full professor may have fifteen or twenty assistants in some sort of compliant dependence, if not abject bondage. Their livelihood depends partly upon professorial bounties, partly upon teaching in secondary schools, partly too upon other callings such as being a journalist or librarian or small administrator. Few indeed are in business, technical occupations, or active research. Italy is mentioned here; but the comments are appropriate to most continental countries and to those throughout the world which have followed their example.

The two major ambitions of the trained and qualified person in most countries are to teach (theoretically) in universities, or to be an administrator. Political ambitions may be combined with either of these. One consequence is that, in addition to the transatlantic 'brain drain', there may be an internal flight from the bench or laboratory to the swivel chair. People ostensibly classifiable as 'trained' technicians or researchers are following no such calling; few are up-to-date all-rounders; even if they were, fewer still would be available to help train undergraduates. In any case, if you visit a practical centre of some sort, you will very often find three distinct kinds of animal: the professor proceeding along like a cardinal or a hospital consultant with his team; the demonstrator actually doing the thing; and smartly dressed students writing it down in clean notebooks.

The concept of 'training' is a tender plant in such higher education systems. Indeed, it is amazing that so much training is acquired incidentally. The best of that is often gained *outside* the institutions enjoying the highest prestige. The German *Technische Hochschulen* are now superb institutions of international renown, and some are multi-faculty; but they owed their origin to the refusal of conventional universities to house studies of more practical than academic interest. (We must not forget that the local translation for those concluding words would be: *'scientific interest'*.) In much the same way, the Scottish universities declined to have any part in teacher-*training*; they kept academic studies of education but banished training to the colleges of education. That phenomenon has repeated itself in some new English universities. Its extension is now being talked of among older universities, where titles such as 'educational studies' are now preferred.

This criterion is of great importance – the more so because, as Dr Frank Bowles showed in *Access to Higher Education* (1963), university systems which include teacher preparation can be conveniently classified as of the newer and more polytechnical 'North American' style, in contrast to the older European tradition which teaches a narrow range of academic interests destined to serve a few 'liberal' professions recruited from a slim band of the social spectrum. Within this general distinction (conceptually based) we find structural or hierarchical distinctions between faculties and subjects. Where faculties such as those of agriculture and commerce have been established (only in recent years, as a rule), they stand lower in the hierarchy of esteem and attract fewer and weaker students. Furthermore within a faculty of science, for example, an internationally famous biologist may locally be of little consequence because of the nature of his subject. He may indeed be a very junior member of the staff.

All these conceptual idiosyncrasies have marked practical results, not least in the matter of training. Recruitment is lopsided. Arts studies (e.g. in the faculties of 'letters' or 'philosophy') may account for half of all the enrolments. On the more practical side enrolments may be quite un-economic in terms of job expectation; for example, in 1969–70 seventeen thousand were enrolled for medicine in France, when only about one-third of that number could hope to find employment as doctors. A similar situation prevails in many countries. As for providing *training* as well as instruction, the complications are obvious; yet competence is everywhere demanded today.

Thoughts about Structure

This conceptual clutter from the past has left us with a hierarchy of in-stitutions, usually with more theory at the top and more practice below. But not always. In Britain one may find architects, engineers, and men of the law taught in universities; one will also find them taught-and-trained at comparable levels outside, not only in technological universities and polytechnics but also in learned corporations or societies as well as firms employing such professions. Until the Robbins Report on *Higher Educa-tion* (1963), the professional education of most teachers, architects, journalists, accountants, lawyers, bankers, and businessmen was categorized as 'further' (not 'higher') education. Much of it still is, though previously impenetrable barriers have now become permeable membranes – or have disappeared. There is much more two-way traffic in and out of universities, colleges, research centres, industries, and trading corporations.

There thus develops a tendency to forget about the old insistence in Britain on continuous and well-channelled studies within one institution, planned from the very start of the undergraduate course. Intercollegiate and interdisciplinary co-operation is more common, permitting the cal-culation of a student's progress by 'units' or other devices indicating approved equivalence. (Of course, these have long been familiar in North America.) Though this might seem a purely operational feature, it is mentioned here because of its structural implications. Most obviously, higher education can be structured to allow of 'sandwich' arrangements. This term indicates alternating periods of 'more theoretical' and 'more practical' study, which may take place in alternating institutions of higher education or be divided between such institutions and industrial or com-mercial apprenticeship.

The more technological institutions of higher education were the first in Britain to adopt this procedure, which became an essential feature of the former Diplomas in Technology (now transformed into full technological degrees). In any event, those technological diplomas crowning more than 100 different courses from 1955 onwards were very soon granted the kind of academic equivalence which enabled their possessors to proceed to PhDs in regular universities. Likewise, other kinds of diploma gained by practical rather than theoretical approaches to professional competence are now accepted by many universities as of 'graduate equivalence' for the purposes of postgraduate study leading to masters' degrees or doctorates. So we already find not merely the co-operative partnership of the sandwich course but a recognition that in some cases at least an approach through *training* may lead to academic respectability.

Nor is the traffic only one-way. Since many firms have much more money to spend on research and facilities than universities, and may more readily endow non-university institutions of learning than universities for purely administrative reasons, academics are readier to move in and out of practical life during their careers. In some fields academic nomadism is obviously preferable to the 'windowless monads' criticized by our colleagues in Western Europe, when speaking of their contemporaries' 'chairs'. Certainly in Eastern Europe, many diploma courses (roughly equivalent to American masters' degrees) include a project of study which is not merely of practical significance but based upon practical training experience. This is quite additional to any 'polytechnical' ingredient or 'socially useful labour' incorporated for party or general education reasons.

Structural reorganization of this kind brings higher education into much more feasible relationship with training possibilities, especially as universities are over-preoccupied with increasing enrolments, with students from unfamiliar backgrounds, and with shortage of teachers in scientific and technological subjects. The administration of universities, problems of student unrest, the growth of postgraduate and post-doctoral research, and the academics' own problems of research all make it imperative to shed some of the load by differentiating functions somehow. Can there be better division of labour?

Operational Considerations

The academic life itself on the purely intellectual side is undergoing a crisis of conscience in the matter of competence and training. If we speak of training for professors and junior staff we generally think of university teaching, and training for it – as is occasionally done in the United States; but from the scholarly point of view itself there is need for fresh thoughts about academic competence. The scholar once picked up the elements of his trade like the gentleman amateur. He was not trained to know and explore the map of knowledge, use bibliographical resources, handle statistical evidence, beware of its pitfalls, or avail himself of computer services. The scholar had to be a jack of all trades, learning them on the way. Up to a point, some basic disciplines (notably mathematics) lent a kind of preparatory training for new academic ventures; so good mathematicians almost inadvertently found themselves specializing in increasingly quantified psychology and sociology. As long as students of these subjects were required to exercise omnibus skills of computation themselves, mathematical training was as prerequisite for them as Latin used to be for many university studies. Nowadays, however, girl computer programmers and other technicians take care of less intrinsically academic research exercises. Today's preparation for becoming a scholar-teacher in a university depends more upon knowing the distribution of academic activity and the skills of teamwork than upon being a one-man band.

Remaining responsible for academic supervision overall, professors and deans increasingly have to depute responsibility for the continuous accumulation and redistribution of knowledge, and for building up the skills requisite to the preparation of a scholar. At the more strictly empirical or training level, technicians or American-style 'teaching fellows' can certainly be very useful to undergraduates as well as the professors whom they support. In technology and industry it is generally calculated that each expert needs the support of about five technicians or subsidiary workers; though most academic enterprise exists on a shoe-string, the great expansion of research for higher degrees does introduce a similar possibility. Studentships and research associateships sponsored by universities or funding organizations outside may either demonstrate important skills or communicate them indirectly by participation in seminars. Furthermore, at least some senior university teachers are becoming less Olympian, while distances on the academic hierarchy are less marked than before – if only because of so much mutual interdependence.

In these circumstances some of the better features of the British tutorial system can be re-adapted to training in research techniques and the more practical aspects of any professional preparation, from teaching and medicine to interviewing and salesmanship. Shifts in the pattern of instruction help in this direction. In the first place, more use is made of case-studies with discussion; secondly, no one is ever taught or trained once and for all, but must follow up throughout life with in-service re-education and re-training. Thus teaching and training must inevitably depend upon widely diffused partnerships. We all rely more on communicating distant experts' information and skills by means of film, TV, and other aids (still unfortunately novel in most universities). This both facilitates and necessitates tutorial follow-up. Indeed, this newer deployment of teaching resources seems likely to have a better future than the old *ex cathedra* and occasional exposition of some professor in a great hall, or the close but uneconomic class of a scarce scholar closeted with ten or a dozen students. These procedures have their unassailable place; but today's emphasis must be on more profitable use of personnel and plant, and on training rather than sitting at Nellie's feet.

In summary, greater partnership between learners and teachers, research procedures and training requirements, between theory and practice, seems not only called for but inevitable because of rapid changes in the world of learning. Knowledge expanding at unprecedented speed and in unimagined variety must be continuously acquired and reviewed, appraised by continuously evolving techniques, and continuously reconsidered in relation to utilitarian application and its social implications. Thus, whereas the traditional dichotomy between 'academic' and 'applied' studies (or 'education' and 'training') permitted a divorce between universities and the world, and between universities and technological or commercial colleges, that dichotomy is now demonstrably outmoded.

Instead, it is clear that changes in knowledge and society suggest a triangular relationship between *aspects* of learning: (a) theoretical or fundamental inquiries; (b) applied aspects and operational skills; (c) social studies and evaluations, incorporating decision and feedback. This triangular relationship is interdependent and reciprocal. Between 'science', 'engineering', and 'the new humanities' there is henceforward a partnership which makes nonsense of old distinctions between 'general' and 'vocational' education, and of all the institutional and social hierarchies associated with them.

Questions of Level

This article began with a reference to institutions and studies considered to be inferior because they had to do with training and practical interests. We soon discovered that it was not really a question of *levels* so much as a problem of local esteem. Nowadays we recognize that many formerly disdained institutions and studies should be thought of as parallel to those formerly awarded top place in the hierarchy, not as inferior *per se*. That is obviously true of engineering in its many branches, and all the derivatives of physics. We do well to remind ourselves that many of the now esteemed 'humanities' were once second-rate outsiders in relation to Latin and Greek. Nowadays the social sciences are still in an ambivalent position, and business studies or anything to do with practical human contacts may struggle hard for recognition in Europe, although in the United States the professors in these fields are usually much better paid and surer of promotion than those in the traditional curricula of higher education. So we see that, instead of 'levels' or 'standards', we have been talking about idioms no longer justifiable now that the actual content of learning has expanded immensely in new fields which social demand has enhanced in importance. In any case we now know that theory, expertise, and humanity are complementary parts of that 'universe of understanding' which it is the task of universities everywhere to promote.

Yet manifestly there are different levels to be considered – those of attainment and states of readiness in any one field, for example. It would be ridiculous to expect the same amount of knowledge or skill from a mere beginner as from a well-taught undergraduate working in a favoured institution. Likewise the postgraduate is expected to be more advanced (at least in some areas) than the undergraduate. Yet these two examples remind us that present attainment is not by itself an index of intelligence or potential (which is a kind of readiness); nor does the quantity of information acquired necessarily place its possessor on a higher level than someone with deeper penetration or a more justifiable map of the terrain of knowledge. Thus a quantified appraisal or a well-filled transcript does not necessarily tell the whole tale, especially about levels.

These rather theoretical truisms are suddenly invested with practical importance. Higher education enrolments are doubling and trebling from decade to decade in many countries. When no more than 5 per cent of the age-group could be admitted anyway, it did not matter very much how the unsuccessful were excluded, provided that those admitted were of reasonable promise. Now considerations of manpower (demanding cultivation of all resources) combine with social demand and political claims for justice to ensure that no one is unfairly turned away – and that if one is turned away now there will be a later opportunity when scholastic aptitude and adequate attainment can be proved.

In Western Europe especially there is a nearly unpredictable expansion of school enrolments between the ages of about 15 and 20. (Though in Britain and the USA admission to higher education usually takes place about the age of 18, most Continental systems in practice round off school at the age of 19 or 20.) Some of these newcomers seeking admission to higher education have had good teaching in distinguished schools, and in precisely those fields on which they hope to concentrate at the university. Other newcomers from poorer backgrounds may have been further handicapped by the shortage of expert teachers of mathematics and the sciences, for example. On top of that they may have none of that unquestioning confidence that enables privileged children to claim their academic birthright promptly. So the higher education intake may really be at different levels at the time of admission. Longitudinal studies show poor correlation between intake level and attainment in degree examinations; but that does not negate the need for attention to different levels among freshmen.

Furthermore, secondary school systems throughout the world are in a spate of reform. A common practice is to establish a common 'middle school' or 'first cycle' between the ages of about 11 and 14, 15, or 16. Between the end of that cycle and the time when higher education can begin is a critical time for school and university policy. In the first place, pre-university schools were founded and conducted on the assumption that they would bring a minute proportion of the age-group to the threshold of the university. In 1963 that meant 4 per cent in England and 5 per cent in Scotland. Even after the great expansion of the 1960s and the redefinition of higher education the British proportion of entrants to any higher education is under 10 per cent. In Germany it is 8 per cent. The pressure for vast expansion is already mounting. If we look at those still in full-time education during the last pre-university year we find the following proportions of the age-group: Britain about 18 per cent; France and Italy about 25 per cent; Belgium about 38 per cent. These figures represent approximately a doubling in a decade. The next decade may double them again, since Japan already has about 80 per cent in this position and the United States about 90 per cent. So the business of teaching all these young men and women from different backgrounds, in different subjects, and with different career expectations of higher educa-tion or employment, implies a revolution in the content and method of upper-secondary school activity even if there were enough good teachers and other learning opportunities to go round.

A second consideration here is that of finding suitable premises to house them all, equipped with laboratories and library facilities and the sort of physical layout which lends itself to an alternation of private study and discussion around the formal instruction. This is of vital importance for our thoughts about levels in higher education, because a number of school systems are developing intermediate institutions which they may call 'junior colleges', 'sixth-form units', *collèges universitaires, instituts universitaires de technologie, Höhere Fachschulen*, and the like. These differ from junior colleges in the United States by being partly secondary, partly 'further' or 'higher' education – not only in age-range but some-times in content and subject-coverage too. A number of pedagogic and administrative considerations have led to these innovations. Whereas the 'common school' or 'common trunk' of the first cycle of secondary education was (and still often is) followed by a tripartite structure of upper-secondary institutions, there has been a tendency for the separate compartments to merge (as in Sweden) or at least to share some common facilities and general courses.

On the other hand, even those convinced of the need to house these various opportunities for the 15–20-year age-range in one establishment do not claim that the participants are all at the same level at any given age. Instead, they often point to the late success (perhaps at age 20 or even later) of someone who has matured late or has come back from being a drop-out. The transfer to an academic centre for young adults undoubtedly gives a fresh start to many. Administratively it permits concentration of scarce teachers, such as *agrégés* or mathematicians, and also (as in England) encourages the use of college lecturers (who are better paid and have good promotion prospects) for special services to the new upper-secondary and lower-tertiary population.

It is noteworthy that, in draft recommendations for a new Education Act in the 1970s, all the main teachers' organizations in Britain and the representatives of the local education authorities concurred in suggesting that secondary education should be common until about 16, followed by what they did not hesitate to call 'tertiary' education beginning at that age and going on to the age of about 20 or later. This idea is far from being a British peculiarity, but notionally combines elements from the college tradition in the United States as well as from other intermediate, pre-university schools like those in pre-war Japan. No doubt, 'high fliers' could go early into studies at a genuine university level; others could come later when possessed of prerequisite knowledge or skills (as in mathematics); some would never get there at all, though they might move on to less ambitious colleges at a 'further' or 'higher' level.

Some re-definition of frontiers between school and higher education in the United States seems inevitable when the Carnegie Commission on Higher Education completes its five-year survey in 1972. The fifth interim report in November 1970 recommended reducing the undergraduate course from four to three years, with the corollary that a higher level of educational attainment would be achieved in school before the age of 18. It foresaw a wider and more systematic use of community colleges (18 to 20) and of lower college divisions covering the same age-range. New relationships with work experience should evolve, perhaps between school-leaving and college enrolment. New kinds of apprenticeship and business preparation should be worked out as alternatives to formal studies now identified with 'higher education'. The latter should be expanded to a greater number of enrolments than at present (perhaps reaching 9 million in the 1980s) but not as an automatic consequence of graduating from high school. A new pattern of higher education should be more general and broadly based during its early stages – proceeding by two-year phases along a more systematic road to genuinely 'higher education'.

Formal equality as 'higher' education on paper by no means confers even courtesy equivalence. Post-secondary institutions are all called 'universities' in Japan and 'higher education' in the USA; but no citizen of those countries is in any doubt about the existence of an impressive pyramid of institutions from the most modest (overlapping the secondary curriculum proper) to the most distinguished by any international criterion. In fact, Dean Francis Keppel declared that the graduates of some American colleges were barely fit to begin undergraduate courses at others. This unofficial hierarchy was systematized by the California Master Plan of 1960 and others subsequently in other states; thus the best-qualified school-leavers are admitted to the campuses of the University of California, the moderate students to the state colleges, and the weakest to the junior colleges or community colleges. Where such formalization has not occurred, there are nevertheless manifest devices (such as the College Entrance Examination Board, or formally stated prerequisites) to ensure differential admission – the best-equipped students going to designated institutions.

At the same time, a continuous upgrading of all post-secondary institutions takes place as previously humble institutions (like teachers' colleges) expand their curricula and develop particular excellences. Thus they progress to become 'state colleges', and then 'state universities' or just 'universities'. Since financial support by states or benefactors is sometimes generous, such institutions can sometimes attract distinguished teachers and researchers, or become famous for specialized enterprise of some kind. The main point here is not to think of purely American events but to recognize the fulfilment of Tappan's plan for Michigan (1851) or Sidney Webb's plan for London (1904), both echoed in the Robbins Report in 1963.

Reform and Development in Higher Education

There can be no stopping the evolution and proliferation of higher education. Eager and well-qualified students cannot be turned away. If one institution will not have them, another will. Subjects and career interests unacceptable in one place will be welcomed in another. Reformers are affronted when they see that a venerable university is reluctant to house the social sciences, managerial studies, and the like; but they may find that electronic engineering or space research is well developed there already. Conversely, the *Technische Hochschulen* and Britain's technological universities are becoming centres for humane studies as well as some of the older professions, just as some American Institutes of Technology have done.

So much for institutions which are clearly of university standard. What of others? At a somewhat lower level and on a broader base, Britain is developing about thirty 'polytechnics', formed from the former regional colleges of technology to be 'comprehensive academic communities' which are 'to complement the universities and the colleges of education' by providing for technology, commercial careers, and the like. A recently established Council for National Academic Awards gives degrees for nearly 100 courses of study in the polytechnics.

Even in the period after World War II, many European higher education systems have been the battleground for conflicting claims – those of expansion (quantitatively and by diversification) and those of maintaining levels of attainment or quality of life. The Swedes took the radical step of abolishing the *studentexamen* in 1968, preferring to look for guarantees of student fitness by other means (records and continuous assessment). In France, Recteur Capelle demanded an *examen bilan* (or all-round 'balance sheet' of fitness for higher education); others, like Dean Zamansky and many scientists, refuse to accept the *baccalauréat* itself as a sufficient guarantee of fitness. The preparatory year (*propédeutique*) has been now favoured as a sifting device, now rejected; but with 200,000 students in Paris alone two years after the May 1968 disturbances, who dare exclude too harshly? Who, indeed, dare channel some of the 20,000 students reading Arts and Law at Nanterre into studies with a more obviously utilitarian outcome? But if no sifting is done, what of the national economy's needs? And what of standards?

One traditional way of ensuring standards has been that adopted in Britain – the pre-selection of academic specialists from the secondary schools for well-defined (if not absurdly narrow) courses in the university. In England especially these have been 'Honours' courses in single subjects or perhaps a pair of closely related subjects; other studies around the central honours course have been cognate, but very much subsidiary. The general education of the student in other fields or personal qualities has been left to him. High standards have been so maintained, and the failure rate has generally been about 14 per cent – exceedingly low by world standards, since in most countries as many as 40 per cent or 50 per cent drop out altogether, and the majority of the rest take from one to four years longer than they are officially required to. This small wastage in Britain, combined with careful pre-selection, has enabled the system to award exceptionally generous grants to students, and to encourage them to study far from home.

The whole pattern is now being called into question on several grounds. Rapid expansion is straining the finances of the universities and of the exchequer, so that the question of providing loans instead of grants is earnestly discussed. Economies might be sought too by providing a less favourable tutorial ratio. But the most serious criticism in the long run is that aimed at underlying educational assumptions. Nobody nowadays thinks that even the best of specialized courses can prepare a physicist or historian for lifelong academic sufficiency, let alone for professional and personal adaptability. Instead, many university curricula are being restructured to provide a broad foundation in several cognate but distinct disciplines before specialization develops during the later years; and, in addition, a judicious blend of humanistic perspectives is introduced into as many disciplines as possible.

The 1970 recommendations of the Carnegie Commission in the United States (referred to above) reflect both the need to economize human and financial resources and the wish to combine adaptability with efficient specialization. By reducing the present 1,600 fields of 'major' specialization to about 160 broad areas of preparation, 'emphasis on narrow certification' would be avoided. Many vocationally oriented students might seek an earlier qualification than now, or perhaps not go to college immediately – or at all. For those who do go to college there would be a progression from broad and adaptable foundations as follows: associate of arts, bachelor of arts, master of philosophy, and doctor of arts or philosophy – each degree being separated by about two years' study. To avoid restrictiveness, further opportunities for education and change should be kept open throughout life. 'Society would gain if work and study were mixed throughout a lifetime, thus reducing the sense of sharply compartmentalized roles of isolated students versus workers and of youth versus isolated age.'

Though such innovations are far from representing today's diffuse college programmes in the United States or the general curricula of the first two years in Japanese universities, they do come closer to the establishment of two-tier university systems with a general course up to the bachelor's degree, followed by specialization at the master's level, with doctorates for specialists later. Trends in the growth of knowledge encourage this tendency. The interdependence of studies in physics, chemistry, biology and so forth now turns people away from hitherto departmentalized specialisms. Complementary biological studies draw upon those constituent disciplines for consecutive broad courses at the cell, organism, and community levels, even though specialization may gradually develop. Interdisciplinary or regional studies in Arts and social studies as well as science support the preference of many for general undergraduate curricula; and the fact that postgraduate research and in-service review are expanding so rapidly favours the adoption of a more provisional attitude in undergraduate courses. There is, however, a serious problem of avoiding 'mush', and of ensuring that students not only learn something well but also acquire self-discipline and the skills of learning.

Conclusion

This paper has done no more than select a few topics relevant to contemporary discussion of universities' roles, with special reference to levels of education and training. The fact that levels should be discussed so earnestly itself shows widespread demand for an examination of conscience by all institutions of higher education. Universities were once the welcoming haven for the scholar in his privacy, the dilettante in his private enjoyment, and (to an unacknowledged extent) the careerist eager to climb the social ladder. They were exclusive by caste rather than by level of knowledge or skill, and had little need of or responsibility to the taxpayer. Most subjects familiar today were once excluded, and so were the concerns of most contemporary careers. Aloofness of this kind was equated with 'standards', by the simple method of considering other vocations and interests 'banausic'.

The scientific and industrial revolution, exploited for the control of the environment and the manumission of so many people and skills, has allowed all kinds of claimants to demand that the universities satisfy and help them – with knowledge, learned apprenticeship, and access to new-style professional careers. Since most of this expansion must be met from tax resources, and is itself the direct consequence of tax-supported secondary schooling, the activities of higher education have been brought under official scrutiny conceptually, institutionally, and operationally. What was formerly lauded without question as a 'liberal education' has been recognized as a 'badge of office' for the ruling classes and the privileged professions. Even for these, a more justifiable content in 'education' and a more realistic *training* have been gradually insisted on. With the growth of knowledge and the expansion of learned careers, both the separate disciplines of higher education and the entire institutions housing them have found themselves with new partners whose claims and opportunities it is perilous to ignore. Apart from the intrinsic excellence and public utility of these newcomers, their very presence and growth have been necessitated by the great flood of entrants to higher education and the growing array of jobs awaiting graduates.

The institutions of higher education, faced with these quantitative and qualitative changes and also being expected to serve governments and other enterprises systematically transforming the human condition, are experimenting with new patterns of recruitment, new structural forms, new partners, new means of communication, and new attitudes towards the lifelong careers of graduates (and others). All these changes demand a more flexible attitude to studies and students, and a stronger sense of the interdependence of 'pure', applied, and human sciences. Thus high levels of attainment in scholarship and research (and also in teaching and service) are matters of conscience. Today questions of scholarship, teaching efficiency, and competence in training are interdependent and moral questions for the universities, to which ancient prescriptions for education and training give no answers.

16

Forecasting Demand for Qualified Manpower: Some Problems and Difficulties

Maureen Woodhall

It is now regarded as self-evident that a country's economic prosperity depends not only on the supply of natural resources and the amount and utilization of physical capital, but on the education, training and productive skills of its workers. The interdependence between the supply of qualified manpower and the rate of economic growth is universally recognized, and this recognition, together with the world-wide emphasis now given to maximizing economic growth as one of the main, if not *the* main objective of government policy, explains the recent popularity of what is often called the 'manpower forecasting approach to educational planning'. Basically, this approach rests on the attempts of economists or statisticians to forecast the future demand, or needs, of the economy for qualified manpower, and the attempts of educational policy makers to gear the development of the educational system to future trends in employment and economic needs.

Previous volumes of the *World Year Book of Education* have examined different approaches to educational planning, and the relationship between the economy and education.[1] But it is appropriate that a volume concerned with changing policies in higher education should look again at the question of whether future manpower requirements can, and should, serve as a guide for decisions on the expansion and development of higher education.

Clearly, one of the most important functions of a university is the training of highly qualified manpower, without which no economy can operate. Therefore, it is emphasized that the pattern of university development should take into account the future needs of the economy. But equally clearly, this is by no means the only function of higher education. It is not the purpose of this contribution to weigh and balance the vocational, cultural and social functions of a university but simply to review some of the main problems and difficulties of forecasting manpower requirements in order to see how useful such forecasts might be in formulating national policies for higher education. The theoretical and technical literature on this subject is now vast, and a number of detailed case-studies and evaluations of actual manpower forecasting experience are now available.[2] This chapter does not attempt to do justice to this literature, but simply to provide the non-specialist with a brief over-view of some of the most crucial problems of manpower forecasting.

Different Types of Manpower Forecast

Manpower forecasting is now practised in both developed and developing countries, including countries committed to centralized economic or educational planning, and those which aim to provide maximum opportunities for market forces and free individual choice. Therefore it is necessary at the outset to distinguish between different types and purposes of manpower forecasting.

In countries which have adopted centralized economic planning, the preparation of forecasts of future levels of employment, and the occupational and educational characteristics of the labour force, constitute an essential part of economic planning. So, for example, manpower forecasting in the Soviet Union, or in France, despite fundamental differences in the nature of the economic plan, is an integral part of the preparation of the economic plan and the educational system is treated as one of the sectors of the economy for which levels of employment and output must be forecast, as well as the source of supply of qualified workers for all other sectors of the economy.

On the other hand, many countries which have no economic plan nevertheless produce forecasts of manpower requirements as a guide to educational planning, or as a basis for decisions of manpower policy. These forecasts may be intended to influence decisions about the future scale of the educational system, or the balance between different faculties, or to influence the educational and career choices of school children or the behaviour of employers. For example, for over twenty years the provision of places in colleges of engineering and medicine, in India, have been based on forecasts of the demand for engineers and doctors. In Britain, on the other hand, since the publication of the Robbins Report, the development of university education has been based on projections of 'social demand', that is the individual demand of qualified school-leavers, rather than on explicit forecasts of manpower requirements, but there has been some attempt to regulate the balance between science and arts faculties, on the basis of 'manpower needs'. At the other extreme, some American and Canadian manpower forecasts have been prepared mainly to help assess the need for labour retraining and mobility programmes, or to assist school vocational guidance counsellors, rather than to influence decisions on broad educational policy.

Fundamental distinctions must also be made between forecasts which attempt to predict future levels of demand or supply of manpower, forecasts which aim to influence demand and supply, by drawing attention to impending shortages or surpluses, forecasts which state the requirements for manpower, if a particular target is to be achieved, and simple projections of existing trends. Such distinctions are crucial if we want to evaluate manpower forecasts of different kinds, and such differences of objectives will also influence the forecasting techniques that are adopted.

To take an obvious example, a forecast which attempts to *predict* future employment patterns must try to take account of likely changes in production techniques, and future changes in the educational qualifications demanded by employers when filling job vacancies. On the other hand, a forecast which aims to show that unless the current policies of employers are revised, there will be a shortage of science graduates in ten years, will be based on existing employment patterns, but will hope consciously to change these in the future.

Such distinctions may seem obvious, but unfortunately one of the main problems and weaknesses of manpower forecasting, in the past, has been that the purpose and objectives of forecasts have all too often not been made clear, so that it is impossible to be sure whether a particular forecast is stating what *is likely* to happen, by a given date, or to state what *ought* to happen, if a particular target is to be achieved. Many manpower forecasts begin with a target rate of economic growth, set by the agency or Ministry responsible for economic planning and which represents an optimistic target which is only likely to be achieved if conditions are extremely favourable. In such cases, forecasts based on this economic target, represent no more than statements of the implications or prerequisites of a high rate of economic growth and are entirely conditional upon success or failure in attaining the target. But it is all too easy to forget this crucial fact, and for policy to be based on the assumption that the forecasts represent a likely picture of the future. So, for example, Indian forecasts of engineering requirements have frequently been based on very optimistic assumptions about the future rate of growth of national income, and have therefore emphasized the danger of a shortage of engineers. In practice, the rate of economic growth has hardly ever matched the targets set in the Five-Year Plans, while the provision of places in engineering colleges has been in accordance with, or even surpassed, the targets sets on the basis of optimistic assumptions about economic growth. The inevitable result is unemployment of engineering graduates.

This suggests that manpower forecasts are not likely to be useful guides for educational policy, unless the objectives and assumptions of the forecasts are made crystal clear, and understood by those responsible for educational decisions.

The Time-scale of Manpower Forecasts

Much controversy still surrounds the appropriate time-scale for manpower forecasts. If such forecasts are to form the basis of plans for the expansion of higher education, it is obviously desirable to have long-term forecasts, covering ten to twenty years, even if detailed planning of expenditure requires only short- or medium-term forecasts. It takes time to design and build new universities and the training period for highly qualified professionals, such as doctors, or scientific specialists, is sufficiently lengthy to require long-term planning. Therefore, if such planning is to be based on forecasts of future manpower needs, we need to be able to predict accurately at least ten to fifteen years ahead.

No one would deny the value of having long-term estimates of future needs or demands, but the crucial problem is one of accuracy. For the reliability and accuracy of most forecasts are likely to be in inverse proportion to the length of time-period. Certainly this is true of the demographic and economic forecasts which are built in to forecasts of manpower demands. Many manpower forecasters recognize this, but nevertheless maintain that it is desirable to try to look ahead for ten to fifteen years, even if such forecasts are liable to substantial margins of error. For example, one of the leading advocates of manpower forecasting, H. S. Parnes, argues 'When one considers the time involved in constructing new school facilities, in training new teachers, and in filling up the educational pipe-line in order to expand significantly the number of university graduates, it becomes clear that the educational planner must have in mind the prospective patterns of manpower requirements at least a decade or two in advance. Thus the need for long-term forecasts of manpower needs.'[3]

On the other hand, the usefulness of such forecasts is highly questionable, when one remembers the large margins of error to which they are subject. Blaug argues: 'The question is not whether to forecast or not to forecast, but rather whether to forecast inaccurately as much as ten or fifteen years ahead, or to forecast three or four years ahead with a much better chance of being accurate.'[4]

The question of accuracy is crucial if the forecast of manpower requirements offers only a single estimate of future needs. Since most forecasts are conditional upon some target rate of growth of national income or level of output, single-valued forecasts are particularly vulnerable, while those which are based on alternative assumptions, and therefore offer a range of possible values corresponding to high, medium or low rates of growth, would seem to be preferable. But even these leave unsettled the question of which alternative is the most likely, so that once again the dangers of inaccurate prediction undermine the usefulness of the forecasts for planning purposes.

Knowledge About the Labour Market and Manpower Utilization

One of the most difficult problems in forecasting manpower requirements is to obtain adequate information about the current stock of qualified manpower and its utilization. In some developing countries it is difficult enough to find accurate statistics on the number of graduates, by field of specialization, but even countries with the most developed educational statistics lack detailed information on the lifetime employment patterns of graduates. Most forecasts of manpower requirements are based on classifications of the labour force by occupation or educational qualifications. But detailed information on the occupational distribution and educational level of workers is usually available only for a few selected census years, and even then is rarely sufficiently detailed. For example, the 1951 Census in Britain gave information on the terminal education age of the population but no data on types or levels of qualifications, and the 1961 Census gave information only on higher scientific and technological qualifications. If, as so often happens, a forecast of manpower requirements for the next ten or fifteen years is based on statistical data which are insufficiently detailed and precise, and which are already out of date when the forecast is prepared, the results may be worse than meaningless. This is particularly serious when the forecasting exercise is long-term. For example, one forecast of demand for engineering graduates in India in 1985 was based on the results of a sample survey among engineers in 1955. In a country like India, where the pace of economic and technological change and also educational development, is so rapid, to assume that fundamental manpower patterns will remain constant over thirty years seems a remarkably unrealistic assumption.

Some forecasts of manpower requirements are based on international comparisons of employment patterns, in the hope that one country's experience may prove useful in forecasting future manpower patterns in another. For example, a forecast of manpower requirements in Puerto Rico, produced in 1957, made the assumption that by 1975 the level of productivity, and the educational attainments of the labour force in Puerto Rico would be broadly similar to the pattern prevailing in USA in 1950. Quite apart from fundamental difficulties about whether different countries do in fact follow similar 'manpower growth paths', given wide differences in natural resources, price levels and economic and educational structures, and whether one country's pattern of manpower utilization, which is usually admitted to be far from perfect, can serve as a guide for another country, at a different point in time, there is the problem of obtaining data on education and occupations on an internationally comparable basis. Differences of definition or classification may be crucial when preparing forecasts based on international comparisons.

The question of how occupations are classified is particularly tricky, even if we confine ourselves to one country. Many systems of classifying occupations, used in analysing census or sample survey returns, depend partly on data about the educational qualifications of workers and partly on the nature of the job itself. All too often it is impossible to know whether a particular job is classified as 'professional' because of the nature of the work, or the characteristics of the employees. Yet these occupational classifications are used as the basis for analysis of the relationship between occupation and education, and for forecasts of future manpower 'requirements', in terms of educational qualifications.

Another common method used in preparing forecasts, namely the extrapolation of past trends, is particularly vulnerable to the lack of reliable statistical data on manpower patterns. In any forecasting exercise, past trends may be an unreliable predictor of the future, since technological change may fundamentally alter techniques of production, or consumers may experience a radical change of tastes and demands. But at least the extrapolation of many economic trends is made possible by the existence of time series data. In most countries very little historical data are available on the employment of qualified manpower, changes in occupational patterns, and the relationship between the education and training of workers and the level of output in different industries or sectors. Such data as do exist are not usually sufficiently detailed to allow extrapolation of any but the broadest trends of employment for general categories of manpower, such as 'professional' or 'clerical' occupations. But planning the development of higher education on manpower grounds requires much more than very general forecasts for broad categories.

These are all problems which can be partly solved by the collection and analysis of better and more detailed data on current manpower patterns. More fundamental is our ignorance about certain crucial relationships, for example between the skills necessary for certain occupations and the formal educational 'requirements' demanded by employers, or between the education of workers and their productive performance. What is meant by the term 'educational requirements' applied to jobs? It is easy enough to ask employers what standards of education a worker will require to perform a particular job satisfactorily. This assumes that employers have far more information about the actual standards and syllabus of different courses than they actually possess; it also assumes that they have actually analysed jobs in terms of function, skills and techniques. Few firms have yet attempted detailed job analysis, so that the statements of employers about the educational 'requirements' of a job are likely to be very imprecise, and simply to reflect current hiring policies. Do current standards and hiring policies represent anything more than conventions reflecting present and past supply trends? One study of the utilization of highly qualified manpower in the engineering industry in Britain found that when the educational 'requirements' for different jobs, as stated by employers, were compared with the actual qualifications of the workers performing those jobs, there were very wide discrepancies.[5]

Does it make sense to talk at all about educational 'requirements' without bringing relative salaries into the picture? There are many jobs that may be performed better by graduates, but whether or not it will be profitable for employers to recruit graduates will depend on relative salaries. However, information on salaries is seldom used in the preparation of forecasts of manpower requirements and the very use of the word 'requirements' suggests that certain numbers and types of manpower are necessary, in some absolute sense, in order to produce a given quantity of goods and services, irrespective of the price that has to be paid.

However, experience shows that it is possible for different firms to produce the same level of output using different techniques and different combinations of inputs of labour and capital, formal education and on-the-job training. The choice will depend on both availability and price. If this is so, then the assumption of forecasts of manpower requirements, that there is a unique relationship between education, the occupation of a worker, and his productivity, and that it is possible to measure 'manpower requirements' as though this were a technological concept, is immediately suspect. Manpower forecasters may recognize that there are alternative ways of producing the same output, or of preparing for the same occupation, but nevertheless, the whole rationale of using manpower forecasts as a guide to educational policy is, in the words of one leading forecaster, 'the rather rigorous link that has been assumed between productivity levels and occupational structure on the one hand, and between occupation and educational qualifications on the other'.[6]

A great deal of research is still going on in many countries, to collect more information on these relationships. This is taking the form not only of analysis of employment patterns, and the occupational and educational characteristics of workers in different firms, industries, and countries, but also studies of the degree of substitutability between different skills and types of training and between formal and informal education, detailed job analysis, in relation to analyses of the actual knowledge and skill content of different educational courses, and studies of the performance of workers with different types or levels of education. All this research will provide more information on the interactions between the formal educational qualifications and subsequent training, careers, productivity and utilization of highly qualified workers. Meanwhile, the assumption of 'rigorous links' between education and occupation, or between the education of workers and the level of output in an industry, remains open to considerable doubt.

The Value of Manpower Forecasts for Educational Policy Making

The last few pages have provided a catalogue of problems and difficulties associated with forecasting manpower requirements. Some of these problems simply reflect a shortage of adequate statistical data. This will be remedied in time. Some of the problems, however, are much more fundamental, and reflect ignorance and uncertainties about the way the labour market operates for educated workers, the factors that govern the demand for, and utilization of qualified manpower, and the relationship between education and productivity. Some of this uncertainty will also be remedied in time. Meanwhile, is it sufficiently serious to invalidate manpower projections? This is a question on which there is still considerable controversy. It is therefore not surprising that there is disagreement about the value of manpower forecasts for educational policy.

Those who are engaged in producing forecasts of manpower requirements usually admit that their methods of forecasting are crude, that their data are inadequate, that present and past conditions cannot and indeed should not form the sole basis for decisions about future patterns of manpower utilization, but nevertheless they believe that even crude forecasts provide some help for educational planning. They argue that even if forecasts are inaccurate, some estimate of future demand for manpower, based on current patterns and trends, is better than nothing and may help to identify possible shortages or surpluses. So, for example, a recent review of experience in British higher education, since the Robbins Report, pointed out the problems involved in estimating manpower needs accurately but concluded 'Estimating these needs is certainly very difficult but it seems inevitable and desirable that it should in the long run come to play a bigger role in educational planning than it could in the Robbins Report.'[7]

On the other hand, critics of manpower forecasting question the validity of the assumptions underlying the forecasts, as well as drawing attention to methodological weaknesses. Almost all forecasts of manpower requirements assume, either explicitly or implicitly, that there is a fixed relationship between input, in the form of educated workers, and output in an industry or in the whole economy. Many manpower forecasts simply consist of the translation of a target level or rate of growth of output into occupational and educational requirements, on the basis of constant labour-output ratios. Thus, 'shortages' or 'surpluses' of manpower are defined in terms of this supposedly fixed relation between the supply of educated workers and the level of production. This implies that there is one, and only one, combination of inputs which is necessary in order to achieve a desired output.

It is this fundamental assumption that lies at the heart of the controversy about the value of manpower forecasting. Those who attack manpower forecasting as a basis for educational planning do so because they believe that the possibilities of substitution between different types of manpower, between formal education and on-the-job training and between manpower and physical capital are so important that any forecast of future demand based on the assumption of fixed input-output coefficients is likely to be misleading. It is emphasized that there are many possible techniques of production, and combinations of inputs, and that the one chosen by an employer will depend on the relative supply and price of each factor. But the element of price (or salary level, in the case of educated manpower) is usually missing from forecasts of manpower 'requirements'. This means that any forecast which ignores the possibility of substitution between input factors is likely to be inaccurate, quite apart from the problems of predicting technical change or shifts in demand, which are common to all long-term forecasts.

Blaug, for example, after reviewing the problems involved in long-term forecasting of manpower requirements concludes 'Surely, there is some point at which the penumbra of doubt associated with a forecast becomes so large that the forecast itself misleads rather than informs? There is little point in continuing to waste resources on long-term pin-point forecasts whose results are suspect even by the forecasters themselves. These resources could be much more profitably invested in improving our knowledge of the current stock of qualified manpower and disseminating this knowledge to students and employers'.[8]

Thus, the question is not whether there should or should not be forecasts of manpower requirements since governments and planning agencies will obviously continue to try to predict the future and to identify possible critical shortages or surpluses of manpower, but whether the present state of forecasting is sufficiently advanced to allow educational policy to be geared to estimates of manpower needs. Differences of opinion will still exist on this but the answer surely is that despite over twenty years of forecasting activity around the world, there is no country with a record of medium- and long-term forecasts of manpower requirements that are sufficiently accurate to form the sole basis for educational decisions.

Obviously the manpower implications of alternative policies need to be taken into account. No one would quarrel with the belief that 'Since one of the functions of the educational system in a society is to provide its work force with the abilities required for productive activity, it follows that the system must be reasonably well geared to the production requirements of the economy.'[9] What is at issue is whether it is possible to predict these requirements sufficiently far in advance to provide accurate estimates of the demand for qualified manpower.

Ultimately, the question revolves round the issue of flexibility in educational and manpower planning. If it were possible to predict manpower requirements accurately, that is to say, if there were a perfect relationship between occupations and education, and between education and productivity, then it would be possible, even if not wholly desirable, to make the achievement of these manpower requirements the sole criterion for policy in higher education. As it is, we still need to know far more about the relation between education and occupation, the possibilities of substitution, the ways in which employers adjust to changes in the supply or the salaries of educated workers, before manpower forecasts can provide unambiguous signals for educational policy. In the absence of such signals, the policy must be sufficiently flexible to allow for alternative patterns of manpower utilization.

A similar conclusion about the importance of flexibility was reached in 'A Technical Evaluation of the First Stage of the Mediterranean Regional Project' – an OECD project which remains one of the most ambitious attempts to base educational planning on manpower forecasting:

> Educational strategy should be formulated with the uncertainties engendered by technological change clearly in mind. For this reason, objectives of labour force flexibility might, for example, receive more stress in the planning of educational structure and content. Certainly manpower estimates should be presented in a way which reflects to some degree these underlying uncertainties. Manpower requirements estimates which conceal these uncertainties, by presenting single value estimates of requirements rather than ranges or alternatives, may do great disservice to formulators of educational policy.[10]

Conclusion

The aim of this chapter has been to draw attention to some of the main problems and difficulties involved in basing educational policy on manpower forecasts. This is not in order to prove that such forecasts are worthless, or that educational policy should not attempt to take account of manpower needs, but simply to show that our state of knowledge about the utilization of educated manpower is not yet sufficient to provide accurate forecasts of manpower requirements. Much of the on-going research in the economics of education is designed to increase this knowledge. For example, the Higher Education Research Unit at the London School of Economics, and the Research Unit in the Economics of Education at the University of London Institute of Education are currently co-operating in a series of 'post-mortems' or evaluations of manpower forecasting in various countries, including Britain, USA, Canada, France, Sweden, India, Thailand and Nigeria. The Research Unit in the Economics of Education will go on to study in detail the way in which the labour market for scientific and technical manpower operates in Great Britain. The results of such research may be to suggest ways in which some of the problems discussed in this paper can be overcome. It may also show how the results of manpower forecasts may be combined with other types of information, such as the rate of return to higher education.

Meanwhile, a 'manpower approach' to planning higher education demands that the higher education system should be sufficiently flexible to adapt to alternative patterns of manpower demand and utilization, and also that the universities should try to assess the implications of alternative policies for the supply, and relative salaries, of educated manpower. It is by attempts to examine and study the relationship between higher education and manpower supply, rather than by rigid adherence to forecasts of manpower requirements, that the future needs of the economy may best be reflected in the formulation of educational policy.

NOTES

1. See, for example, the 1967 *World Year Book of Education*, devoted entirely to Educational Planning.
2. See the section on manpower forecasting in M. Blaug, *The Economics of Education: A Selected Annotated Bibliography*. Second Edition (Oxford: Pergamon Press, 1970).
3. H. S. Parnes (ed.), *Planning Education for Economic and Social Development* (Paris: OECD, 1964), p. 73, reprinted in M. Blaug (ed.), *Economics of Education Vol. 1, Selected Readings* (Harmondsworth: Penguin Books, 1968), p. 264.
4. M. Blaug, 'Approaches to Educational Planning', *Economic Journal*, June 1967, p. 283.
5. M. Blaug, M. Peston, A. Ziderman, *The Utilization of Educated Manpower in Industry* (London: Oliver and Boyd, 1967).
6. H. S. Parnes, *Forecasting Educational Needs for Economic and Social Development* (Paris: OECD, 1962), p. 51.
7. R. Layard, J. King, C. Moser, *The Impact of Robbins* (Harmondsworth: Penguin Books. 1969), p. 28.
8. M. Blaug, 'Approaches to Educational Planning', *Economic Journal*, June 1967, p. 285.
9. H. S. Parnes (ed.), *Planning Education for Economic and Social Development* (Paris: OECD, 1964), p. 73, reprinted in M. Blaug (ed.) *Economics of Education Vol. 1*, op. cit., p. 263.
10. R. Hollister, *A Technical Evaluation of the First Stage of the Mediterranean Regional Project* (Paris: OECD, 1967), p. 74. A summary of the main conclusions is provided in the article by R. Hollister in the 1967 *World Year Book of Education*.

17

Changes Influencing the Development of Higher Education in the U.S.A.

Jacqueline Scherer

Economic – the Level of Training and Education

> I see no signs of any relaxation of the bonds that tie education to occupation. On the contrary, they appear to be growing stronger. The ticket obtained on leaving school is for a life journey. The man with a third-class ticket who later feels entitled to claim a seat in a first-class carriage will not be admitted even if he is prepared to pay the difference.[1]

Over twenty years have passed since T. H. Marshall spoke of the training function of education as it relates to citizenship and social inequality. In this period the compelling influences of political, economic and social issues have combined with normative conflicts over both the means and ends of developing the manpower resources necessary for survival in a turbulent global environment to add new dimensions of complexity in debates about vocational training.

In the United States the ideology of equal opportunity for all on the one hand[2] and the social realities of the current scene on the other have created a tense atmosphere in which anxious and divided participants disagree over the fundamental assumptions which had traditionally maintained the educational system.

Education and Social Questions

Higher education is at the centre of American life for several reasons. To illustrate as simply as possible how the American scene differs from others, we can note that a nurse, a policeman, or a computer programmer obtains his vocational training in institutions of higher education, and the possession of an academic degree is an essential for promotion to responsible positions in almost every occupation.[3]

In the American context, higher education holds a critical place in occupational recruitment, preparation and development. It is the focus of attention for industry and government and the direct concern of the general public by virtue of its size, importance and vocational dominance. Inevitably, the demands of sections of the population, such as women or black citizens, for greater participation in all areas of American life lead to direct confrontations with the system of higher education. Thus a system which is basically a fragmented, decentralized and large-scale collection of diverse units is expected to meet many different types of needs in a complex society. The system is required to provide *mass* higher education for all young people over the age of eighteen. (It is estimated to involve 9·6 million people by 1976.) It is an example of an *open* system at work, and it is quickly affected by diverse environmental factors. The boundaries are so fluid that they are difficult to define and the pressures on the system so diffuse that many observers fear that the system will be unable to cope with all the demands made upon it. Debates over priorities are intense: should scholarship and excellence be the primary aim of higher education, or should these institutions be put to the service of society at large? Should individual competence or social needs be the basis of allocating resources? These questions, always current in academic circles in one form or another, take on a new significance in the American context where the financial and personal investment is on a scale undreamed of elsewhere. Moreover, unlike planned societies, such as the USSR and China, the training function of higher education in the United States takes place in a democratic and pluralist context in which individual commitment to social goals must be sought.

Only when one appreciates the central social role of American higher education can one understand why some debates are different from those found elsewhere. One instance can be found in the distinction between student protests in the United States and elsewhere. American students are not the articulate spokesmen of a silent majority as in Czechoslovakia, nor the intellectual forefathers of revolutionary theoretical transformations as in France. They are expressing the popular and mass dissatisfaction with American society. The issues may be the growing difficulties of urban life, the deterioration of the physical and social environment, the political problems of Vietnam and social programmes, particularly welfare, but the significant point is that higher education is the *centre* of the governmental-industrial-military complex which must deal with these issues.

The interrelationship of these factors is best discussed in relation to three themes: (1) the vocational tradition in American higher education, (2) the social facts and societal changes which are transforming the educational scene in spite of the ideological lag in recognizing them, and (3) the global problems which face all training programmes in the post-industrial[4] phase of civilization.

The Vocational Tradition in American Higher Education

American educators have been more ready to acknowledge the training function of higher education than their colleagues working within elitist traditions, for several reasons. This is partly due to historical circumstances. European universities evolved in large part from medieval religious centres and the kinds of curricula which developed within them – classical studies, liberal arts – reflect the historical development of these institutions. It is also axiomatic that these institutions served the needs of the kinds of societies in which they existed: more stratified, established and stable than that found in the new American nation. The classical tradition was tempered in the American context by the absence of such historical precedents, the practical needs of a frontier society, and the open acceptance of economic well-being as a legitimate goal for education, politics and society.[5] Although British influence upon colonial colleges was strong and religious colleges did in fact continue the classical curricula, the adoption of the German university model in the late nineteenth century, with the combined stress upon objective scholarship, specialization and graduate education, became a more potent force in the subsequent growth of American higher education.

Yet the critical turning point which changed the system from one in which a small minority participated into a mass system for all came comparatively recently in the Service Man's Readjustment Act of 1944 (the GI Bill). For the first time, thousands of returning veterans were encouraged to attend institutions of higher education to improve their vocational skills and thereby ease the economic readjustment of the nation. In 1971 the children of these veterans alone would be sufficient to flood American institutions of higher education, but the fact that higher education is so important in vocational terms has also led to an unprecedented increase in first-generation students.

True, some of the highest-quality American undergraduate education is still to be found in prestigious, four-year liberal arts colleges, but under-graduate studies have increasingly become preparatory years for vocational training beyond the BA degree. In a similar vein, the American requirement for general education during the first two years of college is regarded as a necessary background for specialist study in the last two years. This arrangement guarantees that the American student does not limit his programme narrowly at an early age, but also, in a system without uniform entrance standards, ensures a minimal general knowledge.[6]

Vocational competence, broadly defined, is the foundation of an evolving national policy towards higher education. The increase in federal investment from three billion dollars in 1961 to ten billion in 1966 reflects this trend towards a national policy. Federal assistance has been given directly for manpower training in critical priority areas (science, mathematics, nursing, languages) and indirectly, by incorporating training provisions in other legislation to train specialists to teach others (i.e. the Peace Corps Act, the Area Redevelopment Act, the Economic Opportunities Act, and the Civil Rights Act).[7]

Government research contracts, however, have been the most significant instrument in Federal influence in higher education. The government contract has stimulated the growth and power of graduate education (and thereby diminished, in effect, the importance of undergraduate programmes). It has also encouraged specialization among both faculty and students, and raised central issues about autonomy, academic freedom, institutional goals and values. By virtue of the political and economic implications generated from large-scale governmental participation in research finance, selection and direction, these questions can no longer be classified as predominantly educational problems. They have direct social, economic and political reference for the whole of American society.

In addition to stronger links with governmental structures, ties with private enterprise are close. Corporations give generously to financing institutions of higher education; university staff openly seek research contracts; many institutions develop specific instructional programmes to meet business needs; and the co-operation between educational and economic leaders, which is now bitterly attacked by critics of the system, is cited by defenders as one of its most beneficial characteristics. Business leaders hold authoritative positions as trustees, alumni association leaders and advisers, and represent a powerful voice in administration. This power has been crudely used in many minor institutions to dictate policies, but, as recent student uprisings revealed, is effectively and subtly wielded in the most prestigious institutions (e.g. Columbia, Harvard, MIT).[8]

Even more significant than business ties or national legislation in the development of the American tradition of vocational training as part of higher education, is the general overall acceptance of the belief system which equates economic development, personal and national, with the expansion of higher education. It is an article of faith among many Americans that talent and skills are the foundation of wealth, and that American productivity has resulted from educational improvements.[9] Although this belief has been increasingly attacked by economists, sociologists and radical educators,[10] the link between GNP (Gross National Product) and GPA (Grade Point Average) is frequently given as the final justification for continued growth of the bureaucratic educational establishment.[11] It is because most black Americans and other pressure groups completely accept the basic premise that higher education *should* perform a training function that they are determined to win access to these institutions. They appreciate the social significance of the consequences of admission. This is also why business and government leaders are intimately involved in debates that may be superficially thought of as academic problems. It may be that the student cry for 'relevance' is related in the American context more closely to this instrumental view of education than it is to the demand of radical critics to direct higher education into wide-scale social reforms. It is perhaps significant that the vocationally committed students – engineers, teachers, business students, for instance – have not been very active in student protests.

To summarize, the American tradition of vocational training in higher education, always a strong *characteristic* of the system, has become the central *focus* of the system. Unlike societies that provide vocational training in separate institutions (e.g. colleges of education and technological institutions in the United Kingdom) or 'on the job', the American approach to advanced training has tended to give institutions of higher education almost a monopoly. Many critics advocate alternatives to this monopoly as the only way in which the system can become oriented to other educational goals, demanding a divorce between education and schooling; and between training and education. Yet the issue is not clear-cut. It is highly significant that in a comprehensive survey of graduates, J. W. Trent and L. L. Medsker concluded that 'the evidence suggests that the work world is not conducive to the open flexible disposition and spirit of inquiry that is so important to the attainment of identity, acceptance of others, understanding of the environment and the fullest realization of potentials'.[12]

Thus, any simple prescription to divorce training from higher education would have serious consequences both for the development of students, the support given to higher education, and the erosion of public control over one of the most critical aspects of society. The reality of the situation is that the interrelationships between the various parts of society are so complex and difficult that any dramatic changes in one sphere would have equally impressive repercussions for the others.

Societal Changes

(a) *Demographic Changes.* In the past decade changes in American society have had such profound implications for the development of institutions that the foundations of the entire social structure are under critical examination. It is a social fact that no less than 40 per cent of the population is under twenty years of age. The implications of this demographic reality upon university and college enrolments, and the resultant importance of higher education as a political and economic question cannot be underestimated.

(b) *Economic Changes.* Another social reality is the economic well-being of most Americans, which has led to the consumption of more goods, increased individual leisure-time, and rising standards of health, education and comfort. This well-being has also produced serious contradictions within the traditional belief system. An ethic based upon immediate personal satisfaction and self-fulfilment travels uncomfortably with the basic precepts of the traditional Protestant ethic. Similarly, an educational system which regards success by vocational accreditation is not likely to be receptive to student demands to abolish examinations and grading. Young Americans are also quick to note (with personal guilt and social bitterness) that the system that provides such magnificence for so many is still unable to cope with poverty and injustice for others.[13]

(c) *Increased Urbanization.* A third social factor affecting all American life is the increasing urbanization and nationalization of the population. Eighty per cent of Americans live in 'urban' areas, but the central population core in the largest cities consists predominantly of minority groups and the 'poor'. For example, over one-half of New York City has been statistically classified as poor. Yet the governmental structures of the US, originally founded in a rural land, exalted faith in local control, individual autonomy and private initiative – all characteristics which tend to restrain political solutions to social problems.[14] As these groups become more articulate and seek to gain power in various ways (demonstrations, confrontations, organizations), they come into direct conflict with many institutions of higher education over issues of land acquisition, housing and the allocation of public resources, and indirectly the central political question of influencing public decisions.

The painful realization that these social facts will require fundamental changes in the vocational function of higher education is only slowly being accepted by most educators. The complexity of resolving most issues is overwhelming and bewildering even to the deeply concerned. Unlike systems which are nationally directed and controlled, each unit in the American scene must adopt independent policies and programmes. Participants in the system are caught amidst many different kinds of pressures. These include the need to retain an image which will attract qualified students, staff and financial support among the established sections of American society, and the need to improve and restructure training programmes to meet rapidly changing technological needs. The most difficult task is that of transforming ingrained attitudes among both faculty and alumni, administration, staff, students and the general public regarding priorities in higher education, and the imperative demands of a society which looks to education for service in eliminating inequality, poverty and a deteriorating environment.

One issue which highlights some of these tensions is in relation to the demand of minority students for vocational training and the issue of academic standards. Students denied access to institutions of higher education because they were not academically prepared in secondary schools, are then denied the opportunity to receive higher education in a society which requires degrees for any measure of economic success. But to many American educators who devoted themselves to raising academic standards and to the striving for excellence in the post-Sputnik era, the criteria for developing prestige are college entrance scores, increasing numbers of graduate students, more research contracts and demands for higher academic achievement from candidates. 'Open admissions' becomes a threat to these hard-won gains.[15] Furthermore, there are genuine divisions among educators regarding the wisdom of separate courses in *Black Studies*, community control of administration, and other proposals which, although designed to eliminate inequality, often result in unexpected difficulties.[16]

To illustrate how social factors combine with educational concerns in matters of vocational training, one need only examine the changing work-force of most large American corporations. In Los Angeles, 42 per cent of first-entry hires made by the Bank of America were from minority groups. This figure was 48·9 per cent at Illinois Bell Telephone Company in Chicago, 46 per cent at Chrysler in Detroit, 46·5 per cent at Prudential Life Insurance Company in Newark, and 51 per cent at the New York City Telephone Company. To prepare these employees for responsible positions under present conditions will require that they participate in higher education.

Some experimental programmes have already been undertaken. For instance, in a Manpower Development Training Program in New York City a remedial course conducted for low-income women wishing to qualify as 'practical nurses' resulted in the group passing the New York State qualifying examination in six weeks instead of the usual one year. A combination of strong motivation in these mature students and a thorough remedial training scheme to overcome traditional educational obstacles in basic items, such as arithmetic and reading, made these significant gains possible.[17] Many institutions have inaugurated special programmes similar to the one at Rutgers University in New Jersey in which six hundred students from ghetto schools are enrolled in a special year-long programme to obtain remedial assistance so that they can continue on to a regular college programme. The trends towards 'compensatory education' at an advanced level are likely to increase.

The most successful development in meeting the vocational needs of youth in urban areas has been found in the expansion of two-year junior colleges which provide terminal vocational training programmes and academic courses for transfer to four-year colleges.[18] Within most junior colleges there is a constant tension between these two functions: transfer students seek more academically oriented courses, whereas terminal students require practical training. But junior colleges can enable the system to provide 'marketable skills at widely terminal points chosen by individuals'.[19]

The Carnegie Commission on Higher Education has recommended that five hundred community colleges be established in major metropolitan areas by 1976.[20] But critics of junior colleges point out that these may become second-class educational centres, providing training for under-privileged urban students who cannot afford the increasing tuition costs in prestigious four-year institutions. Furthermore, junior colleges are pro-bably the institutions tied most closely to local governments, and are therefore victims of the financial paralysis which currently exists in most American cities. Thus, those colleges located in middle-class areas are better equipped to perform the training functions desperately sought by the underprivileged sections of the population.

(d) *National Trends.* A fourth social fact which is changing American higher education is the powerful trend towards national homogeneity. Increasing staff-student mobility;[21] the control over licensing exercised by national professional bodies; a developing national culture encouraged by efficient and rapid communications, transportation and mass media; and a large well-established body of educational opinion that fundamentally accepts an instrumental view of higher educational goals persists in maintaining general role requirements throughout the system;[22] all have brought about this 'nationalization'. According to Warren Bryan Martin:

> External variety and surface change have concealed the conformity and rigidity in fundamental values even as false confidence that differences in external forms and appearances must result in varied internal assumptions, or from another theoretical perspective, that differences in structure and function are always manifestations of differences in values, have diverted attention from that prerequisite to significant change-examination of the deep values.[23]

Thus one can conclude that the problems are national, complex and interrelated although the structural means of resolving issues is diverse, formally unconnected and confused.

Technological Factors in Vocational Training

It is axiomatic that the rapid technological change which is taking place throughout the world demands corresponding educational transforma-tions. Most educators, however, have not actively digested what they have intellectually accepted: that vocational programmes become obsolete almost before they are inaugurated, that the knowledge explosion has created overwhelming problems for student, staff and curricular changes. And above all, that the new issues in higher education must be discussed in economic, political and social terms. Charles Frankel notes that technology is a 'mental style', carrying with it a distinct 'ethical outlook towards the environment'.[24] The effect of this new mental style is revolutionary and is at the heart of the debate over teaching versus research, problems of levels of training; specialization versus general education. The immediate impact of technology has been the vast increase in information to be assimilated, but the long-term effects are only dimly perceived. For example, manpower projections show that the economy has passed into a service-oriented, technological era. There will be a 160 per cent increase in the demand for technicians (from 405 thousand in 1964 to 1,074 thousand in 1975), and a 53 per cent increase in social workers, but a gradual reduction in production managers and agriculturalists. Yet what is the long-term effect of space programmes upon scientific manpower, or the implications of the biological revolution with regard to reproduction control, longer-life expectancy and changing life-styles? The vocational needs of female, white-collar and minority students must be considered along with the changing needs of product developments, changing markets and international product competition.

What is clear is that in a technological society, those institutions which provide advanced vocational training will be powerful political agents. American higher education has monopolized the training function, manifestly by co-operation with business and government; and latently, by trying to raise the general level of educational achievement among the majority of young adults, thereby helping employers to seek higher levels of formal education. Undoubtedly a technological society requires trained, adaptable workers and by delaying the entrance to the occupational sphere of people until over the age of twenty-one has helped in the reallocation of labour. It has also created grave problems. One lies in the increasing political effects of policy decisions in higher education. (For example, the demand for black admission quotas in many state institutions.) Another is the increasing problem of stimulating young adults within a collegiate ethic based, as they see it, upon paternalism, adolescent rules and isolation from world activities. Hence, the rebellion against *in loco parentis*. Most significant of all, however, are questions about whether the university should give first priority to its training function instead of focusing upon new and perhaps more socially significant needs of mankind in an entirely new world.

Summary

Laden with heavy, and at times conflicting, social, political and economic expectations of a society whose values are increasingly pluralistic and whose technological needs are imperative, the higher education system is the subject of many different kinds of controversies in American society today. It is in this wider context of the central function of higher education in American society that the narrower question of vocational competence has to be understood.

The vocabulary of today's higher education debates contains words like 'commitment', 'action', 'relevance'. The decade before was characterized by a vocabulary which used words like 'excellence', 'standards', 'objectivity'. The shift in the terms used in the debates is highly significant, reflecting as it does the trends of a decade in which higher education has moved into the central arena in the struggle to reformulate the bases of social institutions in American society.

NOTES

1. T. H. Marshall, 'Citizenship and Social Class', in *Class, Citizenship and Social Development,* Anchor Book Edition, 1965, p. 119.
2. 'Open admissions' is the term educators use to refer to the policy of providing a place in higher education for any secondary school graduate wishing to continue formal education. This has been adopted by several state institutions, and is the recommendation of the Carnegie Commission on Higher Education to be adopted nationally by 1976.
3. C. Jenks and D. Riesman estimate that higher education directly affects the lives of 4 per cent of the entire US population (*The Academic Revolution,* New York: Doubleday and Co., 1968).
4. K. Boulding describes the post-industrial society as one so far advanced technologically that the general characteristics of traditional industrial societies are no longer operative (*The Meaning of the Twentieth Century,* New York: Harper and Co., 1965). Since the US is the largest and most complex society to have entered this stage, the problems are the most glaring. Another critic, Peter Drucker, uses the term 'knowledge society' to refer to a situation in which human capital has been doubled due to benefits in health, longevity and an increase in educational standards, and in which the US faces critical discontinuities at all organizational levels (*The Age of Discontinuity: Guidelines to Our Changing Society,* New York: Harper and Row, 1970).
5. Benjamin Franklin extolled the practical uses of higher education in colonial Philadelphia. The best documentation of this position in early America, however, was the Morrill Act of 1862 which set aside 30,000 acres of land for the development of 68 land-grant colleges to encourage agricultural and industrial training. These institutions now enrol 40 per cent of the college population.
6. Every educational system adopts some criterion for judgment and evaluation of participation, either implicitly or explicitly. In the British system, 'excellence' is given as the justification for rigid selection procedures (cf. Boris Ford's review of some recently formulated goals in 'What is a University?', *New Statesman,* 24 Oct. 1969); French educators refer to the difficulties of degree examinations, Germans to the length required for ultimate doctoral success. It should also be noted that in a system with open selection as in the US, competition steadily increases as the student moves up, so that more students begin a degree programme than graduate; fewer obtain a Master's degree, and fewer yet a doctoral degree. Furthermore, throughout the system the student must constantly prove himself: he is subject to frequent examinations rather than final examinations at the end of the programme; he can fail a particular course at any stage in the programme; and even at doctoral level, must prove himself competent. Thus, he has little personal security and is constantly evaluated throughout the process.
7. See Richard M. Schrader, 'The Growth and Pitfalls of Federal Support of Higher Education', in *Journal of Higher Education,* Ohio State, Dec. 1969, for a comprehensive discussion of this topic.
8. One indication of the concern with which educators and administrators view student disturbances is the need to explain to alumni details of the eruptions and the administrative perspective on these matters. For example, Columbia has sent several letters, a detailed report in the *Alumni* magazine and even campus representatives around the world to allay alumni misgivings.

9. The specific comparison is as follows: the United States with 6 per cent of the world population and less than 7 per cent of land and natural resources, produces one-third of the world's goods and services. Of the population of 200 million, $3\frac{1}{2}$ million attend institutions of higher education, and it is estimated that the figure will rise to 9 million by the seventies. For a contrast with the United Kingdom, see Lord Robens, *Human Engineering* (London: Jonathan Cape, 1970).

10. For instance, Ivan Illich states that educational institutions should not mother, certify or indoctrinate youth, that the schools must be demythologized and new forms of education found; see 'Commencement at the University of Puerto Rico', in *The New York Review*, 9 Oct. 1969. See also the comments of John H. Schaar and Sheldon S. Wolin, 'Education and the Technological Society', in the same number of the *New York Review*.

11. Jencks and Riesman, *cit. sup.*, make this estimate. The Grade Point Average is the means whereby American students are ranked, combining their achievement grade with the point value of the course studied.

12. James W. Trent and Leland L. Medsker, *Beyond High School: A Psychological Study of 10,000 High School Graduates* (San Francisco: Jossey-Bass, 1968), p. 177.

13. Poverty is of course a relative concept and the statistical definition of poverty in the US would be considered a fair salary in most western European nations.

14. For an over-view of urban institutions, see J. Martin Kloysche, *The Urban University* (New York: Harper and Row, 1966). An important characteristic of these urban institutions is the large number of part-time students.

15. One of the clearest illustrations of these conflicts occurred at City College, New York City. This highly regarded academic institution, known as the 'poor man's Harvard', has served as a centre of scholarship for the intellectually gifted in New York City, but because of high academic standards for entrance, became predominantly a white institution operating in the middle of a predominantly coloured population. Reluctantly, the administration agreed to admit a higher proportion of black students although such students could not meet the academic standards which have previously controlled admissions. There were serious protests from alumni and faculty regarding this decision and to many the prestige of the entire university seemed threatened.

16. Jencks and Riesman, *cit. sup.*, contend that the increase in numbers in higher education has not led to more equality, but rather that in the race for excellence, institutions have had a change in the basis of status.

17. Evelyn Sussman, 'Manpower Development Program', in *The Educational Forum*, November 1969, XXXIV, i, p. 8.

18. See Leland Medsker, *The Junior College: Progress and Prospect* (New York: McGraw-Hill, 1960), and Patricia Cross, *The Junior College Student: A Research Description* (Princeton, New Jersey: Educational Testing Service, 1968).

19. Paul Larkin, 'The Challenge of Higher Education of National Manpower Priorities', in *The Journal of Higher Education*, Ohio State, March 1970.

20. Carnegie Commission on Higher Education, *Quality and Equality. New Levels of Federal Responsibility for Higher Education* (New York: McGraw Book Co., 1968), p. 37.

21. Increasingly students do not complete their degree at the same institution in which they began to study. Under the American course and unit system, it is possible to transfer credits from one college to another, and there is a growing increase in junior college transfer students into four-year colleges. The ability of faculty members to receive research funds directly from either the government or industry has also meant that staff mobility is a serious problem.

22. 'The cooling-out' function of junior colleges is well noted. By this is meant that these institutions tend to redirect students not academically suited for a four-year degree programme or unable financially to go further by providing the institutional means of attending some kind of higher education. For a discussion of this, see Burton R. Clark, *Educating the Expert Society* (San Francisco: Chandler Publishing Co., 1962).

23. Warren Bryan Martin, *Conformity-Standards and Change in Higher Education* (San Francisco: Jossey-Bass, 1969), p. 210.

24. Charles Frankel, 'Education and Telecommunications', in *The Journal of Higher Education*, Ohio State, vol. XII, Jan. 1970, p. 3.

National Policies

Brian Holmes

In this section an attempt was made to bring together articles representative of countries in the major regions of the world.

In the outline sent out, contributors were invited to analyse present-day national policies related to the development of higher education. In particular they were asked to review recent legislation affecting the growth and orientation of the universities and other institutions of higher education. Such legislation, where it exists, probably reflects more accurately than any other single source the general intentions of public policy. In some cases, however, where legislation is not available, other sources of information have to be found. It is therefore not surprising that these articles reflect national styles of discussion regarding higher education as well as describing the evolution of policies.

In most countries expansion is inhibited by the costs of financing higher education. Sources of revenue differ and new ways of raising money are sought. In general, however, private and local provision is giving way to national financing: at what cost to concepts of autonomy and control of higher education is difficult to judge. The finance and control of higher education have created problems which in several countries are being solved by the creation or reinforcement of binary systems of higher education. Into which of the two sectors – the university or non-university – new or developing institutions should fit is a question of some moment.

In England and Wales the position of the colleges of education (Hewett, pp. 240–250) is much debated. In France the disturbances of 1968, the creation of the new technological universities within recent legislation (Williamson, pp. 251–264) has raised questions of comparability, forced academics to re-examine emerging policies more critically than in the past. In the German Federal Republic many universities retain practices closer than in many countries to the traditional concepts of university freedom to teach and learn. Present attempts (Goldschmidt and Hübner, pp. 265–283) to give new structures and reorganize the German universities have had a mixed reception. In the USSR (pp. 284–297) the differences between universities and other institutions of higher learning are perhaps less than in many countries, nevertheless the evolution of policy in that country, too, illustrates some common issues.

Canadian (Edwards, pp. 317–333) and Australian (Cowen, pp. 357–367) developments have perhaps been influenced by both the USA (Nash, pp. 298–316) and the UK. In both cases the systems are emerging from a highly selective pattern based on that of England to expansionist policies. Japan (Kobayashi, pp. 368–375), India (Mukherjee, pp. 376–383) and African countries (Michael and Mnthali, pp. 348–356) faced pressures to expand shortly after the end of the Second World War. The former nudged by American educationists, the latter by the euphoria of independence. In Brazil (Abu-Merhy, pp. 334–347) policies designed to democratize higher education have a long and eventful history. A comparison of these national policies suggests that in spite of differences the universities continue to dominate the sphere of higher education and on their response to present-day pressures will depend in most countries the future of higher education in the last quarter of this century.

18

Contextual Change in the Education of Teachers – England and Wales

Stanley Hewett

The teaching profession of England and Wales has always suffered under the handicap of having first- and second-class members. The status has nothing to do with professional competence and expertise but depends entirely on the routes by which the teachers reach the profession and the qualifications with which they enter it. First-class membership is given to university graduates and until only very recently the degree was such a talisman that subsequent professional training was not a requirement. The second-class members are the non-graduates qualified by the award of the Certificate of Education after study in a college of education. While in theory equality of professional opportunity exists, in practice it does not. Professionally the race is to the graduate.

The Background

This distinction, rooted in the sharp pre-war division between secondary and elementary education, is a mischievous anachronism in a post-war situation which recognizes primary and secondary stages in the educational process rather than superior and inferior levels. The second-class members and the institutions created to produce them have been lifting themselves laboriously by their own bootstraps against considerable downward pressure throughout the period of their existence. Given a relaxation of these pressures and a modest helping hand over the next decade, the class distinctions which have for so long divided the profession can disappear far more rapidly than is generally imagined.

The colleges of education, or training colleges as they were then known, were established by the bodies which provided the schools so that employers of teachers could be assured of the number and kind of employees they wanted. Before 1902 the providing bodies were voluntary organizations representing, for the most part, the various religious denominations. After 1902, these were joined by local education authorities as providing bodies. Both local authority and voluntary bodies had one thing in common where their colleges were concerned – they regarded them as extensions of the school systems for which they were responsible. From the first moment of their existence the colleges were cast in a peculiarly restricted mould and were administered accordingly.

From the beginning, the use of central government funds brought central government into partnership with the providing bodies in the control of the colleges and the long tale of divided responsibilities began. Central government, acting through the Board of Education and Her Majesty's Inspectorate, controlled the standards of work while the providing bodies administered the institutions. Whatever differences of opinion the dual masters might have had, they had enough in common to keep them in working partnership. Both had a vested interest in limiting the function of the colleges and assuring themselves of a captive and docile audience from which to staff the elementary schools. Both had a keen interest in holding costs down to the minimum consonant with existence. The unholy alliance of bishops, aldermen and HMIs saw to it that future elementary school teachers did not get ideas above their intellectual and social station while at college.

Given this parentage and upbringing the colleges could not at any time in the nineteenth century or the first quarter of the twentieth century aspire to status as institutions of higher education. They were small, closed, isolated and inward-looking units. The curriculum was limited to that which its students would be likely to teach: the régime was illiberal, restrictive and authoritarian to a degree. The course was a two-year intellectual imprisonment: Dickens did not exaggerate with Gradgrind. It was hardly surprising that when university colleges began to struggle into existence, the thought of building on or developing existing training colleges seems never to have been entertained. The colleges, and thus the bulk of the teaching profession, were isolated from developments in the field of higher education by common, if tacit, consent. The responsibility for the maintenance of the cloister and country house concepts of teacher training must rest with those who controlled the colleges.

The first stirrings came after the first world war. The authority exercised by the Board of Education over the curriculum and standards of work in colleges was seen as not altogether conducive to professional freedom and intellectual initiative. It was felt that since universities existed to set intellectual and professional standards untrammelled by any vested interests (except their own) they ought to be involved in helping to establish standards for the teaching profession. Consequently in 1926 joint boards were established in which syllabuses and examinations were administered by university delegacies, though responsibility for certifying competence in teaching remained with HMI. The impact on the colleges was not dramatic – the largely anti-intellectual tradition in which they had been reared was formidably strong and the restrictive controls to which they were subject were still extremely powerful. In the inter-war years the character of the colleges changed very little. They remained physically small and isolated and the intellectual and social consequences of these environmental constraints were inescapable.

Wars concentrate the mind wonderfully and planning the post-second world war education system led the wartime coalition government to set up the first thorough inquiry into the supply and training of teachers. The McNair Report,[1] published in 1944, was a devastating indictment of the arrangements which central and local government and the voluntary bodies had made between them for the training of teachers. It condemned in the harshest terms 'the trail of cheapness' which characterized these arrangements and the consequences this penurious and restrictive attitude had on the staff and students working within the colleges.

The McNair Report

The Report made sweeping and liberal recommendations which were, however, only partly implemented. The course for the Teacher's Certificate remained of two years duration and the colleges were still restricted to training teachers. Nevertheless the colleges were associated firmly with universities by becoming constituent members of University Institutes of Education. Responsibility for the award of the Teacher's Certificate and all matters academic and professional were given to these Institutes of Education with college staffs represented on the Institutes' Boards of Studies, Academic Boards and Committees of Management. Universities were, in fact, given the sole responsibility for underwriting the standard of entrants to the teaching profession. Providing bodies and central government retained responsibility for financial and administrative arrangements, thus separating academic/professional ends from the financial/administrative means by which those ends could be achieved.

Despite the fact that they had now three masters instead of two, the colleges welcomed the McNair Report since it accorded with their views by clearly stating that the education of teachers belonged in the realm of higher education. Those responsible for the administration and finance of the colleges were less happy, for the Report was hardly a vote of confidence in their past efforts and would certainly encourage the aspirations of the colleges and thus make them more impatient with the restrictions placed upon them.

Those recommendations of McNair which were implemented had a profound effect upon the work of the colleges. The curriculum was liberalized, the quality of work improved and the colleges found new confidence. With their aspirations reinforced they became more resentful of the fact that key recommendations had not been implemented. Though the colleges had taken a major step towards integration with the rest of higher education, substantial barriers still existed. The course for the

Teacher's Certificate was still only a two-year course. The admission qualifications (five subjects at Ordinary level) were markedly below the minimum entrance qualifications to universities. The colleges were still restricted to training for teaching and the degree of self-government they enjoyed was a long way removed from the degree of autonomy which characterized institutions of higher education. Despite their very real gains they were still 'captive' institutions servicing a captive audience. Indeed the degree of development they had achieved put them in an extraordinarily uncomfortable position. As a result of their association with universities via the Institutes of Education they were expected by the universities to function as part of the higher education system while in the eyes of the rest of the partnership, the Department of Education and Science and the providing bodies, they were still extensions of the school system.

The struggle by the colleges towards full integration with higher education reached its next milestone in 1960 when the course for the Teacher's Certificate was extended to three years. Before it was introduced, the National Advisory Council on the Training and Supply of Teachers realized that instead of a slackening in the demand for teachers which it had earlier envisaged there was likely to be an acute shortage throughout the sixties unless active steps were taken to meet the crisis. The colleges expanded to meet the demands of a longer course and followed this by a further expansion to meet the crisis in the supply of teachers. The net result was a decade of continuous expansion which raised the student population of the colleges from 36,500 in 1961/2 to around 110,000 in 1970/1.

The Robbins Report

At the same time the Robbins Committee[2] was reviewing the provision of higher education and including the colleges of education in its deliberations. Two of the main recommendations for the colleges were that the abler students in them should have the opportunity of graduating with the degree of Bachelor of Education, and that the colleges should be merged with the universities as part of Schools of Education and should be financed through the University Grants Committee. The first of these recommendations was implemented, but, to the bitter disappointment of the colleges, the government of the day would not accept the second. The pressure from local government to retain control of these institutions and the desire of central government to keep tight reins on teacher supply combined to maintain the *status quo*. Steps were, however, taken to give colleges a greater degree of autonomy in the management of their academic affairs.

Following on the Robbins Report the government evolved the binary theory of higher education with public (Further Education) and autonomous (university) sectors. With their public finance and their university links the colleges had their feet in one camp and their head in the other.

The events of the sixties changed the colleges more than the whole of their previous history. In purely numerical terms they now represent a major sector (27 per cent) of higher education. There are 160 colleges and 7 departments of education in polytechnics containing 110,000 students, a steadily increasing proportion of whom are graduating BEd after a four-year course. They have greatly increased their provision for the professional training of graduates. The range and level of work undertaken has changed enormously in a very short space of time. They have in fact substantially improved the quality of their work while coping with an unprecedented expansion – an unusual combination. More has meant better rather than worse. The colleges have become, by a happy combination of circumstances, institutions of higher education associated with universities where the level of their work is concerned but still isolated by virtue of the fact that the minimum entrance qualification (five 'O' levels) is markedly lower than that required for admission to universities. Their financial and administrative arrangements are still on a fundamentally different basis from those which operate in the university sector with which they wish to merge. Until these last remaining barriers are removed the colleges will remain isolated within the field of higher education and first- and second-class members of the teaching profession will continue to exist.

The Future

The assumptions on which existing policy for the supply and training of teachers is based appear to be no longer valid in the rapidly changing patterns of secondary and higher education. The present system requires commitment to teaching before entry to college to take a course leading to either the Certificate of Education or the degree of Bachelor of Education. Since the second world war adequate numbers have been assured by the shortage of places in other forms of higher education, particularly universities, which had the effect of channelling candidates towards the colleges. This pressure is declining as provision of other forms of higher education is extended. More university places are now available, but it is the rapid expansion of degree courses on the public side of the binary system in technical colleges and the new polytechnics which has most radically altered the situation by providing alternative routes to higher education. At the same time as these new opportunities develop, there seems to be an increased desire on the part of young people to keep their career options open and to delay commitment until they have completed higher education. Membership of the captive audience of student teachers looks increasingly less attractive, particularly to men, and the external pressures to join it are far less strong than they were. This combination has depressed the numbers of acceptable applicants to the colleges. The annual intake to the colleges has been set by the Department of Education and Science at 39,000. In 1969 the colleges' intake was 37,949. In 1970 it fell to 37,384. Applications for entry in 1971 are 4 per cent lower than in 1970.

At the same time there is evidence that present policies force the colleges to recruit from lower levels of academic attainment than they did even ten years ago. The percentage of candidates entering the colleges with 'A' level qualifications has held steady over the last five years – 65 per cent have had one or more 'A' levels, 37 per cent have had two or more 'A' levels. The percentage of school leavers who obtain these qualifications has, however, been steadily rising and the attainment of college entrants may be said to have declined relative to the qualifications of school leavers. (In 1961/2 the colleges recruited their students from the 105·1 thousand pupils, 15·4 per cent of the relevant age group, who obtained five 'O' levels. In 1971/2 it is estimated that 105·3 thousand pupils, 15·7 per cent of the relevant age group, will obtain two or more 'A' levels.) The present supply policy no longer secures the required numbers nor ensures that they are drawn from the top 15 per cent in terms of academic attainment. If the teaching profession is to be adequately served it appears that there is an urgent need for a radical reappraisal of the whole basis for the supply and training of teachers. It must be done within the context of higher education as a whole for the problem cannot be dealt with in isolation. Indeed in contributing to a solution of the problems which confront higher education over the next decade the colleges may at last solve their own long-standing difficulties.

With bold and imaginative thinking and resolute action, the needs of the colleges and the needs of the universities could be made to coincide to their mutual benefit and to the advantage of the national systems of higher education.

College Needs

The first necessity for the colleges is to safeguard the quality of entrants to the teaching profession. One way of doing this is by setting minimum entrance qualifications which will ensure that entrants to the colleges are drawn from the upper levels of academic attainment among school leavers. Since it is estimated that by 1971/2 15·7 per cent of the relevant age group will obtain two or more 'A' levels and that the percentage is expected to rise to 24 per cent by 1981, the colleges should raise their minimum entrance qualifications accordingly and move with all possible speed to establish the same minimum entrance qualifications as universities. They would thus admit students direct to undergraduate courses. In doing so they would not only maintain the quality of entrants to the profession, they would also remove one of the remaining barriers which prevents them being fully integrated with the university sector of higher education.

The second necessity for the colleges is to abandon the requirement that admission is restricted to those who intend to teach. The captive audience principle no longer guarantees supply and the isolation of intending teachers from those preparing for other careers is a damaging and unhealthy limitation on their education. The colleges should become open institutions offering a variety of courses and develop as multi-purpose institutions without abandoning their main job of preparing teachers.

Thirdly, the colleges need to be fully integrated into the system of higher education by being financed and administered on the same basis as other institutions of higher education. Until this happens the distinctions which now exist between college and university students will never be fully removed and the distinctions between first- and second-class membership of the teaching profession will remain.

A proportionate share in the expansion of higher education is a precondition for the development of the colleges as multi-purpose institutions. Without additional numbers the colleges could not ensure the output of a sufficient number of teachers to staff the schools and at the same time cater for students whose interests lay elsewhere. The achievements of the colleges over the last decade in raising their standards to meet the requirement of undergraduate and postgraduate teaching have given them sufficient standing to tackle with confidence new areas of work. The increased numbers of students who will be seeking higher education over the next decade could give them the material with which to do so. This combination of circumstances gives the colleges an opportunity for development which has never before presented itself.

The Future of Universities

The universities also need to come to terms with an entirely new situation. The increased number of school leavers qualified for and desirous of higher education will, it is estimated, necessitate doubling the provision of higher education over the next ten years. The problem is not merely quantitative though most current thinking concentrates on the physical expansion and its economic implications. The more difficult problem is determining what kind of higher education should be provided. What is currently available in universities at undergraduate level was designed for highly selected elite groups and consists largely of highly specialized honours courses in traditional academic disciplines to which candidates commit themselves before entry. There is considerable evidence already accumulating that many students are ill-served by the inflexibility inherent in the system and in the narrowly specialist nature of the courses, which are akin to Procrustean beds to which the occupants must be fitted willy-nilly. A wider and more flexible range of possibilities is already needed. The need will become more urgent as an increased percentage of school leavers enters higher education. The more varied needs and interests of students will necessitate the extensive revision of course structures and course content. There is likely to be a demand and a need for curricula which permit more broadly-based courses involving increasing amounts of interdisciplinary study and which permit students to change the direction and emphasis of their studies as their interests and abilities develop.

Universities with their powerful faculty and departmental structures would not find it easy to adapt themselves to extensive revision of the range of undergraduate courses and it is here that the colleges could make a distinctive contribution to the range of offerings within the university sector of higher education. Adapting their experience and existing strengths they could develop grouped and integrated courses using thematic and task-centred approaches to unify a number of disciplines.

Courses in Colleges of Education

Education is, in itself, an interdisciplinary study in which the focus is provided by the professional goals of the course. The linking of Education with other Main Subjects and Curriculum Studies has provided the colleges with a wealth of experience of broadly based courses involving interdisciplinary study, grouped courses, practical orientation and different levels of work, which is capable of being put to good use in fields other than teacher education.

Similarly the constant interplay between theory and practice, which is implicit in a course of professional preparation, gives college courses, at their best, a purposeful relevance which can illuminate and make meaningful generalizations and abstractions which might otherwise remain inert and cold. This constant reference to the world of reality outside the lecture room is a device which could be developed into social and behavioural fields extending well beyond educational studies. Field-work elements analogous to the present school-based experience could be developed as essential components of courses and provide the focal point for theoretical studies. This would lend itself to the development of workshop techniques with an emphasis on problem-solving activities which would put knowledge to work in a way that is comparatively rare at the moment.

Another area in which the colleges have strength capable of further development is in the field of the creative and performing arts. Professional schools of art, music and drama do, of course, exist, but only in the colleges does one find art, craft, drama, physical education, movement, dance and music available within the same institution at specialist and non-specialist levels. The creative and performing arts have been traditionally neglected within university curricula and where they exist they have been available only to the specialist and so weighed down with academic respectability that the creative aspects have been underplayed and left for student societies and individual initiative to provide. The colleges could make a powerful contribution via this area to the range of offerings within higher education.

Within the traditional subject fields, colleges have developed approaches and experimented with content in a way that is not possible in more traditionally academic institutions. For a time the need to prove academic 'respectability' led the colleges to raise their standards along fairly traditional lines and this was done with some success. With success came confidence and there is now a greater willingness to experiment and a growing realization that within the boundaries of any given subject different emphases are possible in pursuit of different goals. One student can successfully complete a course by a very different route from another and at a different level.

The colleges have at the moment curricula, approaches and teaching methods which would form an admirable base from which to develop a range of possibilities which is not as yet present in higher education but which it will badly need. They could develop a variety of courses within which it would be possible to cater for students committed to teaching from the outset, for students who began without commitment but developed it at some point in their course, for students who began with commitment to teaching but changed their minds, for students who sought a general education before professional training and for students who wanted a first degree and no more.

Recognition of the fact that 'a course' is, more often than not, a satisfactory combination of courses rather than a single inviolate entity, is the conceptual base on which the colleges can build flexible, multi-purpose curricula. Colleges could devise a unit-based curriculum which would allow students a greater measure of control over their courses than they have at present. The size of units would need careful consideration since the larger the unit the less the choice and the smaller the unit the greater the possibility of incoherence and fragmentation. Similarly, restrictions on combinations would have to exist, both 'horizontally' in the units which could be taken at any one time and 'vertically' in the sequence in which certain units would have to be taken. There would also need to be overall prescriptions to ensure that where professional qualifications were given the required units for professional competence were taken. Most, if not all, the ingredients are to hand already. All the colleges need is the opportunity to allow students to mix them for themselves.

Federated Groups of Institutions

Such a development would not create a chain of liberal arts colleges in which the professional training of teachers became overlaid and denigrated. The colleges' major commitment would be to prepare teachers and the greater flexibility possible within the curriculum would enable this to be done more effectively than it is at present. Students would have the opportunity to adjust the emphasis of their courses to suit the kind of teaching in which they hoped to engage. Students hoping to work with young children could spend more time than they do at present on courses in the social and behavioural sciences and less time in subject studies. Potential secondary specialists might want to have the emphasis in the other direction. At the moment they are all dividing their time in much the same way between Education and Main Subject(s). The liberal arts would exist, as they should in any teaching institution, but they would not override in importance the existing bias towards the social and behavioural sciences. A multi-purpose institution is ill-served by having a single label tied around its neck.

Modification of the present structural relationship of the colleges to their universities is implicit in these proposed developments. Instead of being constituent colleges of an Institute or School of Education the colleges would in effect become campuses of multi-campus universities preparing students for degrees awarded by the university. There would be a federated group of institutions under a single administration within which the different institutions rationalized the use of their resources and the functions they performed. Transfer of students between institutions to enable them to undertake work appropriate to their needs and interests would be possible at certain defined points in their undergraduate courses and after graduation.

At present college-university relationships are confined to twenty-two universities. If the remaining universities were to be involved with the colleges in the closest proximity to them, the federated groups would be smaller in size than the existing Institutes of Education and the relationships within the group that much closer. Since the colleges vary considerably in size and resources, it is unlikely that they would all develop the same range and level of work. One of the functions of the central university administration would be to rationalize the resources and functions of the member institutions to make the most efficient use of their potentialities.

There are distinct mutual advantages. The colleges have always needed the universities and in the restructuring of higher education to which events are moving us the universities must come to realize that they need the colleges for the variety and flexibility which they can contribute to the range of offerings in higher education.

In assessing the colleges' capability for such work it is fruitless to base judgment wholly on existing resources, staffs and student bodies (though many would bear such scrutiny with equanimity), but to consider what the colleges would be like if they were to expand their numbers considerably and were to get a fair share of the resources available. They would, by 1981, be drawing from the twenty-four per cent qualified for higher education and direct entry to undergraduate courses would be the rule rather than the exception. In a multi-purpose role they would be appointing staff on rather different criteria from those which they must now apply in their present restricted function and there would be more opportunity for staff to specialize. The colleges have shown that they can teach at the level demanded by an honours degree in Education. They would not find it beyond their capacity to extend this to other fields since all BEd courses include a Main Subject component.

To those who believe that the pressures for a comprehensive system of higher education will eventually prove irresistible and that in the course of the next twenty years the binary line will cease to exist, the developments suggested above should commend themselves. Comprehensive higher education is likely to emerge through a network of related and varied institutions, covering a given area, between which movement and interchange would be possible. This network might be federated under a single title as is the case with the sixty-seven separate institutions which form the State University of New York. If this is the long-term goal the first stage must be to get some variety into the pattern now. If the colleges do not integrate with the university sector of higher education they will merge with the Further Education sector and the distinction between the two sides of the binary system will be such that bringing them together at some point in the future would be virtually impossible. On one side would be the universities in complete, if not splendid, isolation. On the other side would be a vast and varied network of institutions. Trying to bring together such disparate partners would be an exercise in applied incompatibility and the binary line would be there for ever. Continuing and extending the relationship of the colleges to the universities would produce broadly similar patterns on both sides of the binary line and thus preserve a balance between the two sections until such time as they can be regarded as a single unified system and obliterate the class distinctions which, at present, bedevil far more than just the teaching profession.

NOTES

1. Report on the Supply, Recruitment and Training of Teachers and Youth Leaders, HMSO, 1944.
2. *Higher Education*, HMSO, 1963.

19

Innovations in Higher Education: French Experience before 1968*

Ann Williamson

This chapter attempts to examine some of the reasons why innovations were introduced into French higher education and to assess their effects. A superficial examination of the reforms may create the impression that they were fundamental and extensive but this impression is due largely to the simultaneous publication of a number of decrees. In fact the French system of higher education has been undergoing a series of important changes throughout the twentieth century ever since the major reorganization of structure and administration in 1896. These changes, brought about gradually and involving new subjects and the examination system, were in fact more fundamental than the most recent changes. The main difference between the earlier reforms and the more recent ones lies in the general agreement that the latter were necessary.

A variety of factors led to this agreement: there was a widespread feeling, shared by the government, administrators, teachers and students, that there was a crisis in the university which was not meeting the changing needs of society, although the analysis of the crisis differed from group to group. There was also concern about the growth in numbers and the visible pressure on buildings and facilities and lastly there was a feeling that recruitment to the university ought to be democratized.

Since the agreement among the groups stretched only as far as the need for reform and not to the analysis of the situation, nor to the reform measures themselves, it is not easy to assess the effectiveness of the innovations which were introduced since there is no universally accepted criterion of success as there might be in an enterprise other than education where lower costs or increased profits would be an acceptable measure of successful innovation. It is possible, however, to examine more closely the fears about the increased number of students and also to see how far higher education has been made more accessible to students of working-class origin.

---

* This review article is based on a case study commissioned by OECD and prepared by C. Grignon and J. C. Passeron. It is printed by kind permission of OECD (Paris: OECD, 1970).

The Growth in Enrolments

The growth of enrolments in higher education is common to all developed countries nor is it likely that the increases will cease. An OECD publication in 1966 said the rate of increase 'has surpassed even the boldest forecasts. In France, for example, the 1962–3 enrolments in higher education were 14 per cent higher than had been foreseen a few years earlier; the figure foreseen by 1970, which had until recently been considered extravagant, will be attained by 1966–7.'[1] These increases led to the feeling that the problems were such that reforms were required. Current statements about doubling of student numbers since 1962–3 led to statements about the breakdown of the system which extended even to those faculties where the problem of numbers was not felt.

The reforms, therefore, were seen as attempts to modernize the system to enable it to cope with new demands. In fact the pressure of numbers should be examined with greater care and distinctions should be drawn between the reforms which were directly provoked by increases in numbers such as those in the sciences and arts and the reforms in law and medicine which were not the result of increases in the numbers of students.

It is evident for instance that there may be special circumstances making for the acceptance of reforms in law and medicine. The teachers in these faculties would also be practitioners and closely in touch with professional opinion outside the university and would be more willing to listen to demands for reform from outside the system. Thus the first degree in economics in 1959 was intended to provide the training in law and administration needed by industry. The university hospital centres, also, were established to meet the needs of people concerned about the slow progress of medical research in France. Outside demands do not impinge nearly so strongly, except in the pressure of numbers, on the faculties of arts and sciences where the courses are determined inside the university.

It cannot be denied, however, that the feeling that the numbers were unmanageable has popularized the idea of general reform even though the problem of numbers has been over-simplified. Furthermore, it is also the case that the increases in the numbers of students in higher education has illuminated problems which existed previously but which could be avoided as long as higher education catered for a small elite.

The intentions underlying the reform are ambiguous which also makes it difficult to evaluate them. The reforms are seen by some as a means of promoting the growth of enrolments while rationalizing education, while others expect the reform to slow down what they regard as the excessive increase in student population. The difficulty facing the advocates of a policy to restrict or slow down enrolments is that they have to present a *numerus clausus* policy while appearing to proclaim the same principles as the expansionists. Their argument, therefore, states that the universities should be preserved for the best students and that the rest should be directed to other establishments which will be set up. This policy amounts to closed higher education in its existing form.

Content of the Reforms

In the faculties of arts and sciences, the system of certificates (four or six certificates, according to the subject, made up a *licence*), to which had been added, since 1948, a preparatory year called *propédeutique*, was replaced by a system in which the preparatory year has now been suppressed and which comprises:

(*a*) a first two-year course, leading to the university diploma of literary studies (DUEL) or to the university diploma of scientific studies (DUES).

(*b*) a second course leading after one year's study to the *licence*, or after two years of study to the *maîtrise* which can be obtained with either four certificates or two certificates and a dissertation.

In short, the main changes introduced are the suppression of the *propédeutique*, the organization of the first course by years of study and the institution of the *maîtrise*.

The reduction of the *baccalauréat* to a single examination and the abolition of the *propédeutique* imply an increase in the flow of qualified applicants, while on the other hand, the reorganization of the first cycles of higher education is designed to ensure more severe selection and thus restrict the entry into the later cycles.

In fact the history of the changes in the faculty of arts and sciences since 1950 may be seen as an attempt to build barriers against increasing numbers. The *propédeutique* and the ruling that it could only be attempted four times and the introduction in 1966 of the two-year cycle leading to the DUES or the DUEL follow the same logic as a probationary period between secondary education and higher education proper. In the new style *propédeutique*, class attendance is compulsory and students have to choose a speciality at the beginning of the course. But even though access to the second and third cycles may be tightened up this will not offset the increased numbers applying for the first cycle in the arts and sciences.

There are two possible outcomes of this policy: there may be diversification of higher education establishments and in particular the introduction of university Institutes of Technology more quickly than originally planned, or secondly a *numerus clausus* policy may be introduced to restrict the number of students hindered only by the unpopularity it would incur if it were to be too openly declared.

While these reforms in the arts and sciences represent a negative approach to the pressure of numbers, the creation of new faculties and colleges offers a more positive approach. Between 1960 and 1967, seven universities were established, representing 25 faculties distributed among the various disciplines. At the same time, 25 university colleges or isolated faculties were also created. In spite of this increased provision, the size of faculties is increasing and although evidence about the ideal size or even the optimum range of sizes of faculties is not conclusive, a tendency towards a reduction in the size of faculties would seem to be a more desirable state of affairs.

Reform and the Democratization of Recruitment

Everyone seems agreed about the value of education but there is considerable confusion in the arguments between duty or political value of democratization and its economic profitability. According to the arguments, not only ought all children to have equal opportunity, but it is asserted that talent should not be wasted in an industrial society, although the economic argument is now used with greater caution than previously. It is evident, nevertheless, that the ideology of equal opportunity is very strong and is certainly given as the reason for reforms by governments even though changes in university organization and curricula seem to have very little effect in broadening the basis of social recruitment to the universities. It is also evident that in some cases mere increases of numbers going into universities is confused with democratization whereas an increase in enrolments may almost exclusively benefit those social groups which were already favoured.

Table 1 reveals that there has not been a significant increase in the numbers of working–class students entering the university, but what it does not reveal is the differences between the faculties in respect of democratization.

Science studies are often regarded as being the best for working–class students to enter since aptitude for literary studies may depend on a certain sort of family environment which is not common to working–class families. The study of science is assumed, therefore, to be more acceptable for working–class students since there are fewer handicaps to overcome than there are in literary studies. The greatest proportion of working–class students in fact were found in the faculties of science both in 1961–2 with 16·6 per cent and in 1965–6 with 21·3 per cent.

These figures would seem to indicate a slight trend towards greater democratization but it should also be taken into account that during the period 1962–6 the proportion of middle-class students fell while the proportion of upper-class students remained almost constant. Furthermore, the figures for the science faculties are somewhat deceptive because of the existence of the *Grandes Ecoles* which relegate the science faculties to lesser institutions.

More significant changes are to be found in the faculties of arts where the proportion of working–class students rose from 14·8 per cent to 19·2 per cent while the proportion of upper-class students fell during the same period by 4·2 per cent. Although recruitment to the faculty of arts is still a long way from the critical level beyond which its composition would be radically different from that of the other faculties since the various social groups are still represented in inverse proportion to their representation in the total active population, it may nevertheless be regarded as less bourgeois than in the other disciplines, including science. However, in so

TABLE 1

SOCIAL ORIGIN OF FRENCH STUDENTS BETWEEN 1961–2 AND 1965–6
PERCENTAGE BREAKDOWN

Social origin	1961–2	1962–3	1963–4	1964–5	1965–6
Farm workers	0·6	0·5	0·6	0·7	0·6
Farmers	5·6	6·5	5·4	5·5	5·8
Service industries	0·9	1·0	1·0	1·2	1·1
Workers	6·4	7·9	7·6	8·3	9·4
Total working class	*13·5*	*15·9*	*14·6*	*15·7*	*16·9*
Craftsmen-tradesmen	13·7	13·4	12·3	13·3	12·2
Office workers	7·9	7·4	8·6	8·2	8·6
Middle management	17·8	17·4	17·8	17·7	16·7
Total middle class	*39·4*	*38·2*	*38·7*	*39·2*	*37·5*
Professions					
Senior executives					
Businessmen	*32·5*	*29·3*	*32·5*	*33·1*	*31·5*
Not gainfully					
employed (other					
categories)	14·6	15·1	14·2	13·0	14·1

Source: Informations statistiques, Nos. 53–4, 69, 76 and 86, and the Central Department of Statistics and Economics of the Ministry of Education.

far as the social structure of the student population has remained much the same, the slight increase in the proportion of working-class students in the faculties of science and arts can hardly be interpreted as the percursor of a general trend especially as the social structure of recruitment into the faculties of medicine and law shows the opposite tendency.

Between 1961–2 and 1965–6, the medical faculties were narrowing down their intake: the proportion of upper-class medical students rose from 39 per cent to 43·7 per cent, while the proportion of working-class students remained about the same at 7·9 per cent as against 7·6 per cent in spite of changes in the system of instruction, new examinations and new subjects.

TABLE 2

TREND OF EDUCATIONAL OPPORTUNITIES ACCORDING TO SOCIAL ORIGIN AND SEX BETWEEN 1961-2 AND 1965-6

Father's socio-occupational group	Objective opportunities (probability of access)		Conditional probability											
			Science		Arts		Law		Medicine		Pharmacy			
Year	1961-2	1965-6	1961-2	1965-6	1961-2	1965-6	1961-2	1965-6	1961-2	1965-6	1961-2	1965-6		
Farm workers														
M	1·2	3·0	44·0	53·3	36·9	26·4	15·5	16·3	3·6	3·3	0	0·5		
F	1·0	2·3	26·6	33·7	65·6	55·4	7·8	8·6	0	3·3	0	1·2		
Combined	1·1	2·7	34·7	45·0	50·0	38·0	12·5	12·0	2·8	3·3	0	0·8		
Farmers														
M	3·8	8·5	44·6	45·0	27·2	24·4	18·8	20·3	7·4	7·9	2·0	2·2		
F	3·0	6·7	27·5	31·8	51·8	48·5	12·9	10·9	2·9	3·9	4·9	4·6		
Combined	3·4	8·0	37·0	39·2	38·1	35·0	16·2	16·1	5·6	6·2	3·1	3·3		
Workers														
M	1·5	3·9	52·5	50·0	27·5	24·8	14·4	17·8	5·0	6·6	0·6	0·6		
F	1·2	2·9	29·3	31·0	56·0	54·4	10·4	10·2	2·6	2·7	1·7	1·4		
Combined	1·3	3·4	42·8	41·7	39·9	37·0	12·3	14·6	3·6	4·9	1·4	0·9		
Office workers														
M	10·0	17·9	46·0	37·7	17·6	21·6	24·6	26·7	10·1	11·8	1·6	1·7		
F	7·8	14·3	30·4	22·3	44·0	53·4	16·0	14·3	6·1	5·7	3·5	4·0		
Combined	9·0	16·2	39·4	31·1	28·6	35·5	21·1	21·5	8·6	9·2	2·3	2·7		

TABLE 2—cont.

| Father's socio-occupational group | Objective opportunities (probability of access) | | Conditional probability | | | | | | | | | | |
| | | | Science | | Arts | | Law | | Medicine | | Pharmacy | |
Year	1961-2	1965-6	1961-2	1965-6	1961-2	1965-6	1961-2	1965-6	1961-2	1965-6	1961-2	1965-6
Employers in industry and commerce												
M	14·6	25·0	40·3	37·2	24·9	17·1	20·5	26·6	11·0	15·4	3·3	3·3
F	13·3	21·2	21·8	22·4	55·7	47·4	11·7	15·7	4·8	7·6	6·0	6·7
Combined	13·9	23·2	31·8	30·5	39·1	30·6	16·4	21·6	8·1	12·0	4·6	4·8
of which: Businessmen												
M	52·8	74·0	28·5	34·3	25·2	11·6	22·0	32·3	20·0	17·8	3·9	4·0
F	56·9	68·6	13·2	18·4	57·8	42·5	11·2	19·8	10·8	9·8	6·8	9·2
Combined	54·4	71·5	21·1	26·6	41·1	26·0	17·0	26·5	15·5	14·0	5·3	6·4
Middle management												
M	24·7	38·2	38·3	41·2	30·2	21·0	21·0	23·2	8·5	12·6	2·0	1·6
F	25·4	31·4	22·2	25·5	61·9	52·6	9·1	11·3	3·4	6·4	3·4	3·9
Combined	24·9	35·4	30·5	34·0	45·6	37·2	15·2	18·0	6·0	9·8	2·7	2·7
Professions and senior executives												
M	38·7	61·0	40·0	35·7	19·3	13·7	21·8	26·8	14·7	20·1	4·2	3·5
F	36·9	51·2	25·7	22·8	48·6	43·5	11·6	15·0	6·5	11·1	7·6	7·4
Combined	38·0	58·7	33·3	30·0	33·2	27·0	16·9	21·5	10·8	16·2	5·8	5·2

Thus the increase in the proportion of working-class students in the faculties of arts and sciences may even be interpreted as a sign of the increasing relegation of these students to certain types of study that have gradually been abandoned by students from the wealthier classes.

A calculation of the opportunities of access to higher education and the conditional probability of undertaking is not only the best way of quantifying the range of educational opportunities in a given country, it also explains the reactions and attitudes of the various social groups to the university.

The trend of opportunities between 1962 and 1966 shows an increase for all social groups. The rates for 1966 are all higher than those for 1962. It should be emphasized, however, that this increase in the opportunities for all groups is not in itself a sign of the democratization of higher education if democratization is defined in the strict sense as equal opportunity of access to the university of a student from the different social groups. So that if instead of the extreme differences the differences between social groups are observed then the gaps between middle management and senior executives widened between 1961-2 and 1965-6 rising from 14 per cent to 23 per cent. Similarly the gap between operatives and office workers widened from 7·7 per cent to 12·8 per cent. So from a strictly numerical point of view, workers' sons' chances of access to higher education more than doubled over the period, but doubling a low number does not have the same significance as doubling a number which is so much higher as is the case with the sons of other social groups.

In short, the trend of educational opportunities between 1962 and 1968 has, through the general rise in rates of probability of access, confirmed the educational privileges of the upper classes so that a worker's son has a 3·9 instead of a 1·5 chance out of 100 of going on to higher education which means that in spite of increased probability of access the rate is still sufficiently low as to make it very unlikely except in exceptional cases.

In addition it should be noted that the statistical groups which had to be used for calculation purposes are almost all sufficiently heterogeneous to contain wide disparities: apart from the 'farmer' group which is patently heterogeneous, the 'farm worker' group includes both ordinary labourers and the managers of large capital intensive farms. A large number of workers whose children continue their studies probably belong to the category of foremen. A more detailed analysis would no doubt reveal still greater disparities (especially if regional inequalities were taken into account) than those detected by an analysis based on conventional statistical groups.

Several things, therefore, become apparent when examining the figures. First the increase in higher education enrolments went hand in hand with a high degree of stability in the social structure of the student population. Furthermore the distribution of the different categories of students among the various types of faculty remained much the same: the faculties of arts, and to a smaller extent the faculties of science, were still the refuge of a higher proportion of working-class students, while law and especially medicine continued to be reserved territory.

Secondly the general rise in objective opportunities of access to higher education between 1962 and 1966 has not led to the democratization of university recruitment; for the working classes the probability of access is still low enough to be regarded as nil, while it is becoming sufficiently high in the case of the upper classes to strengthen their privileges, making entry to university almost a certainty.

Where women are concerned although the figures for access to higher education in France are higher than in many other countries and has stabilized at about 42 per cent it appears that the price of access for women is a particularly severe restriction in their choice of studies.

The reforms, therefore, have not overcome inequalities due to social class nor have they overcome secondary disparities such as those between the sexes. And as it is only the lowest levels in the higher educational system which have been subjected to any extensive reform, while the *Grandes Ecoles*, the preparatory classes, the *agregation* and the state doctorate remain intact, it looks as though the traditional university system has made a minimum concession to income and planning requirements in return for the right to preserve the social characteristics intact.

Differences in the Reforms

Certain things are apparent in the reforms. There is unevenness both in the ways reforms have been introduced and the way in which they work. The reforms in laws and medicine for instance differ sharply from those in arts and sciences. The main innovation of law study reform was the creation of an economics degree which had been arranged several years earlier with the first moves to introduce economics and sociology into the traditional curricula. Similarly with medicine, the institution of university hospital centres is likely to transform medical studies as a whole at all stages of the student's career and even the career of the teachers. Considerable changes have been made in the distribution of subjects, the time spent on observation and the time spent in clinical work. So that the reforms of medicine and law studies are general reforms involving a systematic redefinition of the organization of studies, and introducing new subjects and even new disciplines. The increased proportion of hospital work also involves changes in teaching method. Whereas in the faculties of arts and sciences the creation of new examinations and degrees such as the DUES, the DUEL and the *maîtrise* involves changes of title and not a break with the old teaching organization and still less with traditional attitudes.

The reforms differ not only in the way they are applied but in the way they came into being. They do not derive from the thought and action of the same instigating bodies. For instance, the reform of law studies seems to have been prompted by the pressure of changes in administrative employment and managerial jobs. The reform of medical studies was the work of a committee of experts convened by the government, more as a result of the desire to make French medical research competitive at international level than because of the pressure of public or professional agencies which were not greatly interested at that time in the problems of research. In arts and science, the decisions were prepared in comparative secrecy by negotiation between ministerial departments and university pressure groups, although approved or made subject to reservations by many groups or unions, they did not stem directly from a movement of opinion.

The Dual System of Higher Education

To appreciate the significance of reforms which affect only the teaching side of the faculties and sometimes only at certain levels, as in arts and science, it is necessary to remember the place and role of the faculties in French higher education, i.e. in a system dominated by the dichotomy between the faculties and the *Grandes Ecoles*. If one accepts the formal definition of their function, the *Grandes Ecoles* in France are vocational training institutions, whereas the faculties in principle enjoy the privilege of deferring consideration of future occupational requirements to the benefit of a system of instruction whose sole purpose is the transmission of knowledge or the preparation for research. In a society where 'education for its own sake' is held in the highest esteem and where the disciplines which are least directly usable in the professional world are given pride of place, it might be expected that the faculties would rank first in the hierarchy of university prestige. But this is not the case. The *Grandes Ecoles* represent what might be called the 'higher education of higher education'. *Grandes Ecoles* students are not only selected by the competitive entrance examination but also preselected when accepted for the preparatory classes attached to the *lycées*. This double-screening system enables the *Grandes Ecoles* to recruit from among the best 'products' of secondary education; this educational elite is recruited on the basis of university criteria and is perfect material for shaping into a social elite. It is not surprising that recruitment for the *Grandes Ecoles* is even more bourgeois than recruitment for the faculties.

Furthermore there is no doubt that the dual nature of the French higher educational system is responsible for the inflexibility and overlapping which hamper progress in research. By selecting the best students, the *Grandes Ecoles* tend to sterilize research in the faculties. In these circumstances, it is not surprising that throughout the history of the French higher educational institutions new bodies specializing in research have been constantly set up and that this phenomenon has accentuated the division between research and the university system proper.

Reform and Changes in the Structure

The reforms have affected only the faculties and, in science and arts, the lower levels of university studies without affecting the rest of higher education preparatory classes for the *Grandes Ecoles*, the *Grandes Ecoles* themselves or such rewarding diplomas from the professional and social point of view as the *agregation*. These limitations mean that the recent reforms are condemned to introducing into the university system only those innovations which are unable to change its structure. In a university structure that has remained fundamentally the same because of the three poles around which it is built (faculties, *Grandes Ecoles* and special research institutions) and which have retained their functional weight, innovations are obliged to take the direction forced upon them by that structure. It may, therefore, be questioned whether the introduction of a fourth type of institution in the form of the *Instituts Universitaires de Technologie* really constitute a change in the basic structure of higher education.

The creation of the university institutes of technology was one of the kingpins of the reform of higher education. By creating a greater variety of university streams the reformer instituted to substitute the possibility of 'rational' orientation based on aptitudes for the policy of negative selection shown by the trend towards the multiplication of barriers. However, in view of the small number of Institutes created – 22 in 1967–8 – they are at present quite obviously incapable of transforming the structure and operation of an educational system which is still based on faculties and *Grandes Ecoles* and which is characterized by the absence of any real higher technical educational system.

Historical precedents moreover provide many examples of innovations designed explicitly to meet explicit demands and which were nevertheless diverted from their declared purpose by the specific logic of the educational institution. Technical educational establishments therefore tend as a general rule to give up their function of vocational training progressively in order to provide science courses at an ever higher level, and some of them have even managed to acquire university status. So that although it is the reformers' intention to adjust the university institution by means of the *Instituts de Technologie* to the economic demand for skill and the social demand for training, it cannot be assumed that the reform will work as the reformers anticipated.

It is, no doubt, too soon to anticipate the future evolution of the *Instituts*, but it is already apparent that they tend to operate a selection process from the start; thus less than a third of the applicants in 1967–8 were accepted.

It need only be pointed out that it was precisely by introducing a severe student selection process that the former technical schools generally triggered off the process of 'updrift' and 'deprofessionalization' by which they have been characterized hitherto.

TABLE 3

APPLICATIONS AND ADMISSIONS TO IUT IN 1967–8

	Applicants	Applicants accepted	Actual entrances
Number	15,130	4,938	4,125
Per cent	100	32·6	27·3

Other Factors Limiting the Reforms

Other factors which act as brakes on the reforms are the lack of diversity in French higher education and the recruitment of teachers. The lack of diversity prohibits the local adjustments, developments or experiments that are possible on a university scale but are no longer possible on the scale of a State institution: the French universities differ from each other only by their degree of conformity to a single model represented by the Paris faculties. The *de facto* subordination of the provincial universities to the University of Paris is just as much responsible as the Napoleonic tradition of administrative uniformity for the persistent tendency of every faculty to become a fully-fledged faculty offering the whole range of degrees like the Sorbonne.

Secondly the protected status of university teachers is regarded as increasingly unfair by other professions. It would be useful to analyse the real mechanisms which ensure the security of university teachers independently of performance. The method of recruiting teachers is also highly traditional. The thesis required of teachers is not regarded as a contribution to research but as the foundation and qualification for a teaching career in the hope that it will bestow life-long protection.

If it is easy to demonstrate the limited scope of most of the aspects of the reforms, this is because the measures of reorganization have left unimpaired the major institutional equilibrium maintained between the faculties, the *Grandes Ecoles* and the research institutes. Even the establishment of the new University Institutes of Technology has not altered this balance.

It is only by implementing a systematic policy of sociologically justified innovation that there would be some chance of reaching the critical level beyond which it is impossible to reinterpret innovations in terms of traditional logic. Educational innovations cannot be reduced to a simple modification of the course of study or curricula.

At the present time, however, with current ideas and concepts no coherent pedagogical ideology exists which would be capable of supporting the changes in function and operation that the political situation might on occasion make possible. So that seminars devoted to university reform, including the Amiens Seminar which explicitly concerned teaching, have not got much further than declarations of intention as regards the definition of the pedagogical reform of the university institution.

P. Bourdieu outlined an analysis of the 'system effect' as applied to the educational system which should make it impossible to consider the consequences expected from an innovation, without at the same time studying the significance of that innovation in relation to the system in which it is to be placed.[2] Thus, if it is true that the various aspects and levels of the educational system are particularly interdependent and closely related, it is also true that this interdependence is usually concealed from both agents (students and teachers) and administrators, who are only connected directly with the system's legal organization, and if the reinterpretation of change of which the university system is consequently capable always owes more to the system's logic than to the reformer's intentions, then the theoretical and practical problem to be considered concerns the *nature* and *place* of the key links defining the university system as such, i.e. both its strength of resistance to blind innovation and its possible vulnerability to scientifically prepared measures of action. Do *critical levels* exist beyond which innovation cannot be reinterpreted in terms of the old standards? Which points of the university system are especially sensitive to action to initiate a changeover from one system of operation to another? These are the questions that educational theorists cannot evade without provoking purely superficial effects whose importance must be peremptorily asserted or repercussions which they have neither foreseen nor intended.

From this point of view, the implicit or explicit analyses current today on the tactics of reform might be classified in terms of their increasing awareness of the problem of an applied strategy. Three analyses may be used. Least helpful is the empty phrase 'innovation for innovation's sake'. This attitude accounts for the largest proportion of the literature on reform. The essentially superstitious belief in a sort of intrinsic efficiency of innovation is in fact very widespread in technical advanced societies which have developed a 'tradition of novelty'. The sort of terms associated with this attitude are 'radical challenge', 'fundamental upheavals' and so on.

Secondly research based on psychology or psychosociology hardly seems capable of transforming a system in which the functions and operational principles are so closely linked with fundamental social and economic equilibrium, and in particular with the historical configuration of relations of strength between the social classes.

Lastly there is the determinism associated with increasing numbers of students. Thus some people expect the rise in the numbers of students and the increased size of the system to produce upheavals which will automatically define the new aims of education.

It is clear that the analysis of the social mechanisms which support and perpetuate the values of university culture in its traditional form, need to be taken further. If this article suggests that there are decisive links in the educational systems depending on such things as the recruitment of teachers and most important on the social origin of students, it is because these mechanisms define the educational system as a social system functionally related to all other social systems.

NOTES

1. In *Curriculum Improvement and Educational Development* (Paris: OECD, December 1966), p. 28.
2. P. Bourdieu, 'Systèmes et Innovations' in *Pour une Ecole Nouvelle* (Paris: Dunod, 1969), p. 347.

20

Changing Concepts of the University in Society: the West German Case

Dietrich Goldschmidt and Sibylle Hübner

The Problem

During the past decade, the majority of the world's non-socialist, industrial states have faced large-scale student unrest. To all outward appearances, these disturbances often resemble each other so closely that one might be inclined to believe that their causes are also basically identical. The widely apparent solidarity among students was forged on the basis of protest against the Bomb, the Vietnam war and racial discrimination. Yet behind these clear-cut political demands lies a deep dissatisfaction with the educational situation, a dissatisfaction which has institutional causes that vary from country to country. Japanese universities have a different relationship to the country's employment system than, for example, do those in France or England. The problem of drop-outs from America's tightly structured colleges differs from that of West German students who break off studies which are relatively loosely structured.

For all their differences, universities throughout the world are faced with the same question: as Clark Kerr recently put it, 'Is the University still viable?' It would be fair to assume that he chose such a provocative formulation in order to stimulate arguments that would justify the university's continued existence in terms of the future, and not simply on the basis of venerable traditions. For it can be said that constantly growing specialization has made an ideological farce of the notion – implicit in the traditional understanding of the university – that there is a oneness uniting all scholarly pursuits and scientific disciplines, and inhibiting any meaningful reform in teaching as well as future-oriented research. Be this the case, then it would be necessary to give up this notion once and for all and create something altogether new in its place. If, however, one feels that precisely because of this methodological and thematic differentiation a sense of unity is all the more important in order to help people learn to master their society's historically developed technostructure in a rational fashion, then it will be necessary to rethink what the university is there for and organize it in such a way that, in the future, co-operation may be ensured between presently diverging branches of science and scholarship. Both alternatives are easily justified. In the following pages we shall discuss the relative merits of each on the basis of an analysis of the German university as it looks one hundred and sixty years after the reforms initiated by the great scholar and statesman, Wilhelm von Humboldt.

The Current Status of Higher Education in West Germany

Throughout West Germany, both internal and external controversy about the university as institution reached a remarkably high point during the sixties.[1] While student groups employing various political tactics were struggling to bring about an internal democratization of the universities and create socially relevant forms of education, government authorities were in the process of legally redefining the organizational framework in which education will be provided for ever growing numbers of students in the decades ahead. In several federal states – most notably Social Democratic Hamburg, Hesse and Berlin – new legislation on higher education was passed, giving junior faculty, tutorial assistants and students a considerable voice in university administration from the departmental level up, thereby forcing the creation of new forms of co-operation between faculty and students. For the first time, professors began to organize in order to drum up public support for their own specific interests; the establishment of their *Bund für die Freiheit der Wissenschaft* in November 1970 has not only contributed to the polarization taking place at West German universities among conservatives and progressives of whatever hue, but also serves as a revealing indicator for what is meant by 'academic freedom' and the 'university's self-definition'. In the appeal published to mark the founding of this association the university was characterized, for example, as 'the weakest institution' in West German society, threatened to be 'paralysed and destroyed' by 'unlimited student co-determination' in university affairs. Even the state, it went on to say, could soon be threatened with the same danger of destruction if it should fail to intervene in time to secure 'academic freedom'.[2] Anyone who is unwilling to accept this appraisal and forecast is automatically declared an opponent of the all but unbroken high ideal incorporated in Germany's academic tradition – an ideal that proclaims the scholar's or scientist's autonomy as essential to the search for pure truth or, in other words, his freedom from paternalistic intervention on the part of non-academic authorities. Not only is the sceptic or dissident seen as a traitor to this academic ideal; he is also stamped as an opponent to the democratic form of government established in West Germany. To equate opposition to the university with opposition to the state, as these professors do, may seem correct to the small group of radical students organized into 'red cells' at the universities. But on a more general level, it would be wrong to accept uncritically the view held by members of this Association for Academic Freedom that a firm nexus exists between the principles of democratic representation and the traditional professorial right to admit to their ranks only those selected by their corporate group. The ideal this interest group takes as justification was formulated under the rule of those absolute, though enlightened monarchs who, when faced with a German bourgeoisie that in the wake of the French Revolution began to strive for political power, relegated this class to the sphere of cultural and intellectual pursuits. The contention that this ideal is compatible with political realities and the demands of modern society still remains to be proved. It is quite possible that the deep pessimism voiced by many professors results from the fact that students have been anything but gentle in showing that the 'professor-potentate university' – the traditional preserve for personal power – is no longer adequate to the educational needs of our present, not to mention future society, in this era of university expansion.

Objectives and Function of the Traditional Ideals

In 1809, Wilhelm von Humboldt – then head of the Prussian public instruction administration – drafted an educational conception for the University of Berlin which was to serve as model for future universities in what was then the Kingdom of Prussia. Although it established the criteria on which all subsequent discussion on university reform in Germany has been based, Humboldt's conception has recently been shown to have a contradictory function, brought face to face with the actual performance of today's universities. Gradually, its underlying assumptions and objectives have degenerated into empty slogans, however much they progressively anticipated the mode of 'scholarly instruction' practised around the turn of the eighteenth to the nineteenth century[3] and for a certain period exerted a positive influence on the development of higher education in Germany. Yet, to recognize a discrepancy between what the university claims to be and its reality, does not necessarily lead to a renunciation of the original ideal. What is needed now is to re-examine that ideal for its intentions and measure them against the substantive changes that have taken place (concrete situation and new requirements) in order to establish to what extent the ideal is realizable.[4]

Critical observers of the present plight of German universities note that these institutions are no longer able adequately to fulfil their functions in education, research and administration. Attention is drawn to the following facts:

– Many departments lack the capacity to accept all qualified applicants; the restricted admissions policy, previously applied only in the Department of Medicine, is now being extended to cover other fields such as pharmacy, architechture and psychology.[5]
– In all fields, the student-faculty ratio is considerably poorer than in the Anglo-Saxon countries.[6] In general, neither students nor faculty find satisfaction in

lectures and classes that take on the character of mass meetings. Such over-filled courses fail sufficiently to stimulate the student and draw out his intellectual potential.

– Curricula are frequently poorly co-ordinated and demonstrate little long-range planning. Moreover, consideration is rarely given to providing even a minimal representation of the various academic and scientific approaches.

– On average, students require 50 per cent more time to complete their studies than officially stipulated as the minimum period. The number of students who leave the university before graduation runs to approximately 25 per cent of any given first-year class on an all-university average.

– Administration work is steadily increasing. In the traditionally structured university, this increased burden leads professors to neglect research and delegate teaching to junior faculty and tutorial assistants.

– The higher a teacher's position in the hierarchy is, the more seldom do students and faculty come into direct contact. Person-to-person discussion often does not come about until the student faces his professors in his final, oral examinations. Considering the general German tendency to keep one's distance, this particular situation poses the danger of arbitrariness.

These functional defects can be partially or even totally eliminated through institutional reorganization, but not without breaking certain taboos connected with the traditional ideals and expressed in terms of 'academic freedom', 'education through academic training', and of a 'unity' or 'oneness' of arts and science, of research and teaching, and of educators and those being educated. Torn from the social and political context in which they developed, these programmatically framed ideals and modes of orientation have, as it were, taken on a life of their own: they have cemented traditional academic privileges without preserving and reinforcing the sense of obligation formerly associated with such privileges.

Freedom and Responsibility under Changing Conditions

The principle of academic freedom or 'freedom of research and teaching' – once aimed against state interference – was clearly seen by Humboldt to 'relate closely to everyday life and the needs of the state'; according to him, the university – as a place for 'guiding youth' – was involved in an altogether 'practical business'.[7] In his classical text, freedom is not taken to mean the right simply to do as one pleases in research and teaching – in other words, to remain indifferent to what students expect from higher education. On the contrary, Humboldt felt that the university should not be an end in itself and that the freedom granted was the best instrument for indirectly promoting the aims of the state.[8] 'Education through scholarship' was designed to maintain this congruity. 'For only scholarship, which stems from within and can be imbued, transforms the character as well,' writes Humboldt, 'and the state is as little concerned as mankind with knowledge and discourse, but rather with character and active conduct.'[9] Without saying as much, Humboldt was proceeding from the fact that the universities as they existed around 1800 primarily served to educate clerical and governmental officials – in other words, academic freedom was of advantage to the state since it was from the universities that government recruited its administrative personnel. Universities at that time had an average enrolment of 500 students and the Faculties of Law and Theology were given a pre-eminent position, so that most graduates could count on entering a career in one of the representative institutions.[10] Only secondary importance was attached to training students for an academic career. In essence, therefore, 'education through scholarship' meant nothing more than power through academic training. University education gave the children of the bourgeoisie the opportunity to qualify for professions which hitherto had been reserved for the scions of the nobility or which were being newly created with the development of an industrial-bureaucratic culture. In this way, the etatist state assimilated the intellectual elite and incorporated it into its own structure, and was thereby imperceptibly transformed.

Under the pluralist, party-dominated type of government formally established in Germany after 1918, academic and scientific 'freedom' cannot even indirectly be placed in the service of the state in the same way it was under the etatist, monarchical system that gave way to the democratic order. The state is no longer, by definition, the incorporation of the nation – however understood – as long as it is constituted and governed according to the principle of majority rule. Why, then, does the state grant the universities and those working in them their 'academic freedom'? Warned by the experience of Gleichschaltung during the Third Reich, when universities were forced to conform totally in commitment to the chauvinistic and racist ideas propagated by the national socialist regime,[11] post-war authorities in West Germany were more inclined to encourage an individualistic art-for-the-sake-of-art attitude in research and teaching than run the danger of giving the impression they were exerting some normative, controlling influence on developments in the arts and sciences. Nonetheless, the value of 'academic freedom' has to be proven on the basis of the social relevance of the achievements accomplished in its name. As a training place for highly qualified manpower, the university exists in constant interaction with the country's employment system; furthermore, its role as an institution for research means that it administers considerable public funds. For both these reasons, members of the academic community are invested with a social responsibility that extends beyond their immediate interests, be they aware of the fact or not.

The Three Principles of Unity under Changing Conditions

The traditional idea of unity of students and educators implies a community of interest in which both groups should bear equal responsibility for determining what subject matter is to be selected for discussion and research. Since, as Humboldt maintained, science and scholarship have nothing to do with absolute knowledge and must always be treated as an open question, never to be settled for once and for all,[12] the only valid relationship between professors and students must be a collegial one. As long as research, understood here in the sense of 'search', is carried on primarily in the form of discussion among the groups involved, it is possible for all participants to work together on an equal basis, regardless of differences in intellectual qualifications. With the rapid advance of science, medicine and technology, however, there is an ever-growing demand for the kind of complicated experimentation that requires a more complex technical and organizational apparatus. This produces sharper distinctions according to function – in other words, hierarchies are created on the basis of specialized training.[13] The resulting professionalization of research has irrevocably shattered Humboldt's classical image of the university as the place where all branches of scholarship are united. In its place, a capitalistic 'university-enterprise' is developing,[14] which – in order to function rationally – requires a large and industrious junior faculty which does not have the same privileges as full professors enjoy.[15]

Reform-minded people are emphatically denying the contention that departmental hierarchization – to the extent that it serves no scientifically functional purpose – is an objective necessity. The Federal Ministry of Science and Education has adopted this critical view with the result that, in its latest draft proposal for legislation on the organization of higher education, actual function and no longer formal qualification is to determine rank of university staffs.[16] On the level of the individual states (*Länder*) as far as legislation has already been enacted, various modes of proportional representation amongst all those involved in teaching and research have been established. The university law passed by the Hessian state legislature in May 1970 is now being questioned at the Supreme Court level by a group of 194 professors who maintain that their constitutionally guaranteed right to teach and carry on research without impediment and under their own responsibility is being threatened by the fact that junior faculty, students and non-academic staff now have a voting representation in the university's policy-making bodies.[17] One paragraph has caused particular offence: 'All university members have to bear in mind the social consequences of scientific knowledge. Should they receive knowledge of even non-university research findings for which there are grounds for doubt, they are obliged to bring this to the attention of the public.'[18] A few professors fear that this could block scientifically important research projects and that interesting commissioned research might be increasingly siphoned off to private institutes. This may well apply in certain cases, primarily in technological research.

On the whole, however, it is undoubtedly the demand for greater organizational efficiency that has produced the growing exodus of large-scale research from German universities – a tendency noticeable since the turn of the century. Modern research is often too costly in terms of manpower and equipment to be carried on in university institutes as they are presently set up. Scientists there generally have their hands so full with teaching and administrative duties that only a very few hours remain per week for pure research – and this only sporadically.[19] What has happened as a result is that the highly proclaimed 'unity of teaching and research' has been broken at the universities, where an antiquated organization has permitted research to be crowded out by administrative duties, so that it now has largely shifted to external institutes.[20]

One prominent example is the Max Planck Society, successor to the Kaiser Wilhelm Society, founded in 1910, which now sponsors numerous independent research institutes devoted to basic research in various scientific fields.[21] Financed by more than 90 per cent by state and national government subsidies, this society is pledged to the same principle of academic freedom to which German universities have been committed since Humboldt's time. Apart from the field of Big Science, experience has shown that research carried on outside the universities need not necessarily be less independent of outside control than that conducted under university auspices. Such independent research facilities have an advantage over traditionally structured universities in that they are relatively free of departmental rivalry and thus are in the process of becoming a focus for the kind of effective interdisciplinary research the universities, compartmentalized as they are, have not been able to promote. A start has been made in this direction, on such problems as the inequality of educational opportunity, pollution, the causes of illness, and the mechanisms involved in settling martial conflict, to name a few.

The University Structure – Old and New

By tradition at German universities, chairholding professors have been invested with personal responsibility for all research and teaching done within their sphere, and thus for all research funds allocated. This led to the situation whereby each professor, together with his staff of academic underlings, conducted his research in complete isolation from all others. It lay in his discretion to determine a project's scope and definition; one could say his very person was the guarantee for quality. Humboldt himself had emphasized that what ensured a well-functioning university was the 'choice of the men to be placed in action':[22] their moral and scholarly capacity was thought to guarantee the cohesion of scholarly endeavour. To him, the unifying factor bridging any inevitable methodological and theoretical differentiation lay less in the material itself than in the person involved. In the idealistic view prevalent in Humboldt's time, it was the loosely-knit corporative body of individually outstanding scholars that composed the cosmos seen in the *universitas litterarum*. This notion corresponded to reality as long as, by virtue of the professors teaching there, certain German universities remained a Lourdes for students at home and abroad. For a long time, the professor possessed an authority beyond that accorded by scholarly eminence in his field. Remarkably enough, the image that resulted managed even to survive *Gleichschaltung* during the Third Reich; although hollowed out, it was not destroyed until just recently, at the hands of radical students. Robbed of his nimbus, the professor is redefined as a 'specialization-idiot', meaning that he is neither willing nor able to see beyond the narrowly drawn confines of his specific field, and is so highly specialized that he feels competent to exert influence only in matters concerning his own discipline. As contemptuous as the epithet sounds, it does contain an important element of truth: the unifying force exerted by the cultivated individual no longer suffices to prevent the university from disintegrating into a 'multiversity', given the need for ever more specialized knowledge to keep pace with today's tendency to turn all social and life-sustaining processes over to scientific study and control. An institution like the university can only counter this economically determined demand for utilization by serving the interests of society as a whole – in other words, by dealing with precisely those questions and problems which organizations dependent on economic effectiveness cannot afford to tackle. In West Germany, efforts are being made to redefine the functions of the university in this direction, as the latest draft proposal for legislation on university organization shows. The federal government has declared this document to be the 'expression of a policy on higher education which breaks with the traditional German university system and is designed to integrate higher education to a greater extent in the general development of society.' Universities should remain 'the seat of unimpeded teaching and research', but at the same time will be expected to take on responsibilities of an altogether new nature and scope.[23]

In the light of this definition of the university in terms of its future function, politically responsible agencies and affected interest groups on all levels are concerned with working out ways for making reform organizationally possible. These considerations also take into account that, due to constantly rising professional standards, the envisioned organizational structure will have to integrate numerous training courses previously not ranked as 'academic'. According to plans, the so-called 'advanced vocational schools or colleges' of engineering, commerce and social work are to be affiliated with the universities in the framework of a comprehensive system of higher education – the *Gesamthochschule*. In this way, the German university will lose the primacy it has enjoyed for centuries as the centre of elite education. In future, it will form only a part – be it the most ambitious and demanding part – of a larger educational complex designed to promote interdisciplinary co-operation and provide better opportunities for access to different levels of training.[24] No longer will the chairholder serve as the cohesive factor by virtue of his person; the new organization of teaching and research will be centred primarily around problem spheres that require constant interdisciplinary co-operation and interaction. How this will work out in detail is still unclear. For the time being, the traditionally huge and complex faculties are being replaced by departments which should provide a new cohesion by grouping together a small number of disciplines on the basis of the subject-oriented practical problems they have in common.

Such a new organization also requires changes in teaching. Course content revision is only just beginning. Before a clearer picture can be given, teaching objectives need to be redefined and experimentation with methods must be carried out. Considerable numbers of students and junior faculty feel that a course of study that offers opportunity for reality-oriented project work and 'learning through research'[25] would be particularly well suited to replace traditional forms of university instruction in which didactic considerations often played no role – a main target being the mass lecture as the primary vehicle for transmitting knowledge. There is also discussion about doing away with the conventional course structure, which was rigid and narrowly circumscribed to each major field, in favour of easily combinable 'building blocks' composed of didactic units.[26] Even in the nineteenth century, the quality of university education was supposed to be measured against the practical efficacy of knowledge as well as the theoretical effectiveness of its transmission. Since, however, the student population was small and theoretical considerations played a negligible role in matters of a practical nature, these criteria were of little enough consequence to justify leaving it to the professor's individual 'style' as to how they would be met.

Today, the rush to the universities is on and teaching staff is expanding rapidly. In this situation, only a standardization of generally applicable didactic rules can guarantee the student an education which, within a reasonable period of time, will provide a 'practically useful orientation for life situations' as well as the technically essential information needed to make given processes utilizable.[27] For it is in reflecting on the processes by which knowledge is transmitted that one finally becomes conscious of what education was always, though unconsciously, intended to do:

establish a connection between the possibilities for emancipatory action inherent in a profession and the expertise this profession requires.

Didactic blueprints are a newcomer to the field of West German university planning. They are expected to facilitate a more rational organization of instruction, bring about increased motivation, help cut down the length of study and reduce the drop-out rate, thereby promising a fairer basis on which to gauge university performance. In view of the steady yearly increase in the number of school leavers who go on to the university,[28] it has become essential to put the definition of teaching objectives on a sound scientific basis.

With the expansion of the university into a mass institution, problems are emerging which stem not only from the current effort to redefine the boundary lines between the various fields or from the lack of adequate space, equipment and personnel. Reasons are also to be found in the social background of students and in the changing picture of the professions. In the traditional 'elite university', students were drawn primarily from the aristocratic or bourgeois classes – from families whose wealth and property generally guaranteed at least minimal financial security during the period of study and in the initial phase of getting started in professional life. Today, on the other hand, most students come from a middle-income, white collar or civil service background. Although more and more of their fathers have had academic training,[29] they often have little or no assets beyond their monthly earnings. If one compares the social composition of the student population on the basis of the 1928–9, 1951–2, and 1967–8 statistics, one can see that students from a civil service background have lost their once clear preponderance, whereas white collar workers' families are being represented at an ever-increasing rate. The proportion of students whose fathers are in civil service has sunk in this period from 47 per cent to 38 per cent and, further, to 30 per cent; on the other hand, white collar representation has risen from 12 per cent to 23 per cent to 31 per cent.[30] This development should not be taken as evidence for any basic equalization between the two strata in regard to educational opportunities. It only reflects Germany's changing employment structure: while the relative proportion of civil servants has remained constant, the number of white collar workers has increased from about 15 per cent in 1928 to a level of 30 per cent of the total employed population.[31] Now as ever, children from professional, civil service and academic families are considerably over-represented at the university, whereas working-class children are grossly under-represented in relation to the general population picture.[32]

Socially discriminated and privileged groups continue to exist in West Germany despite the constitutionally guaranteed right of 'equal educational opportunity'. Little can be expected to change in this respect as long as it is still left basically to the family to determine whether the child will go on to the university and to finance his studies if he does. What is needed for any effective educational reform geared to the realization of democratic goals is a programme of publicly-funded financial assistance to ensure the possibility of university study irrespective of family circumstances. Without such security, university study becomes for many students a 'balancing act without a net', as the high drop-out rate and increasing symptoms of psychological stress demonstrate.[33] Money problems, combined with difficulties in regard to career orientation, deeply affect the daily life of many students.[34] To be sure, a considerable group of entering students still make their choice of studies dependent on the parental wish that they uphold the father's professional status and/or maintain the family's accumulated property by assuming his professional function. So it is that, of all doctors' children studying, half major in medicine – and the same holds true for the children of pharmacists and farmers.[35] But the majority of students have no such clear-cut obligation to fulfil, and the choice of career tends to be based on more individual criteria, although – as in the case of academic families – the initial decision to go on to the university may well be strongly influenced by the status-preservation factor.[36]

Little is presently known about the mechanisms involved in the process of career socialization, particularly during the decisive judgment-forming phase. Yet what many a student goes through during the course of his studies seems to indicate that, today more than ever before, it is in this period that students attempt to free themselves of the examples they had uncritically accepted – often a long and involved, conflict-ridden process. The costs are considerable, both to the individual and to society as a whole. Selection processes, still strongly traditional in nature, tend to inhibit self-realization and militate against any creative change in the social roles the individual is preparing himself to assume. Great efforts – and not only of a financial nature – are going to be necessary if improvement is to be brought about. Elementary schools must provide for compensatory educational counselling. And as soon as the first comprehensive schools and universities are established, it will be necessary to introduce practical and psychological counselling services at the secondary school and college levels, as well.[37] There is no question that such a scheme could provide the means for manipulating future student generations. Yet in a society that has still to realize the goal of equal opportunity, this danger can be seen as the lesser evil when measured against the 'natural' pressure to conform which the family exerts on practically all young people, regardless of social background.

Any attempt to eliminate what all parties concerned consider the intolerable defects of the traditional university system can easily produce the temptation to create a 'streamlined university',[38] one which would be so thoroughly rationalized that frictions may well not occur – but neither would creative innovation. The students and progressive professors who in the sixties agitated, demonstrated and went on strike to bring about university reform in West Germany have meanwhile become somewhat hesitant and sceptical in regard to the reform programmes brought forward by the government and educational bureaucracy. They fear that along with the old university's easily recognizable faults its less obvious advantages will be eliminated as well – what Habermas has called the 'remnants of those agreeably archaic freedoms'.[39] One such remnant was the students' 'academic freedom': their liberty to determine for themselves how long and what subjects they would study, and transfer from university to university at will. In many cases, this undoubtedly led students to feel disoriented and encouraged irresponsibility among professors. Yet on the other hand it has also helped quite a number of students to become more mature by stimulating the processes of self-reflection and self-criticism.

The kind of organization of studies that encourages emancipatory processes while at the same time eliminating time-consuming and unproductive detours would make it possible to integrate positive features of the old university into the framework of the new one. In view of the way higher education and, in accordance, university administration have been expanding, the question remains whether the conditions that have facilitated academic freedom are not changing as well. There is a tendency developing in West Germany to distinguish between undergraduate and postgraduate studies along the Anglo-American pattern, meaning a tightly regimented course of studies in the first phase and a freer, more flexible programme at the advanced level.[40]

The End of Deutsche Bildung

From its re-establishment at the beginning of the nineteenth century up into the twenties of our century, the German university was world-famed as a model institution – the purveyor of *Bildung*, a concept that embraces not only education and scholarship, but also culture, breeding and refinement and, hence, a system of values which reflects an elitist, upper-middle-class mentality. No wonder, then, that after the débâcle of the Third Reich this concept could not remain for ever unchallenged.

Recent efforts to redefine what education means have involved a serious appraisal of other educational systems. This can be traced in part to the influence exerted by the occupation powers after 1945, as well as to the enormous post-war need to catch up with developments in all fields and to the exchange of information with other industrialized countries, which has been developing constantly in the last two decades. In addition, an important impetus was provided by the realization that, by international comparison, West German education comes off badly in terms of scope and responsiveness to the needs of underprivileged strata.[41]

Shortly after World War II discussion got under way about reforming the educational system, and above all the universities. Two recommendations – both drawn up on British initiative – deserve particular mention. The one, known as the 'Blue Paper', was prepared by a 'Study Group on University Reform' which had been called into being by the British Military Governor to clarify the need and possibilities for university reform. With the exception of Lord Lindsay of Birker and the Swiss professor, Jean Rudolf von Salis, this commission was made up only of German scholars, most notably the physicist Carl Friedrich von Weizsaecker. Their conclusion was that a reorganization of teaching and research at German universities would be worthwhile since they had not kept pace with 'the structural changes going on in society';[42] at the same time, they considered the universities as upholding a 'fundamentally sound' tradition that deserved to be maintained.[43] This concession basically relativized everything that followed in the way of reform proposals. Nothing substantial was done to break down the status hierarchy which, in fact, was reinforced by proposals, following in the wake of increasing demand, to create new positions of lower rank alongside the existing faculty structure-positions mainly occupied with teaching – a solution that was finally institutionalized.[44] This particular case illustrates how the Blue Paper provided a necessary justification for those who needed it, not to carry out sweeping reforms in the university's structure until very recently.

Developments might have taken another turn, if the report prepared by the British Association of University Teachers on a reorganization of the German university system had had any decisive impact.[45] This report, published in May 1947, concluded that the German academic institutions' greatest problems lay in the inner connexion that existed between their structure and their ideology, in the composition and educational ideals of their faculties, all of which failed to meet the conditions for a democratic society. The much-praised 'academic freedom' was felt to amount in practice to 'anarchy, mitigated by professorial tyranny'; moreover, a 'strong feeling of intellectual superiority towards the work of most other European nations' was said to prevail at German universities.[46] These English critics touched on a fatal phenomenon which could be observed again and again at German universities: individual intellectual arrogance and nationalistic enthralment connected with a narrow-minded identification with an exaggerated caste-image. That such traits were widespread even before Hitler came to power was pointed out by Max Weinreich in the introduction to his book on *Hitler's Professors*.[47] Most of those who continued teaching at German universities after 1933 let themselves be swept up in the wave of nationalism and accepted the sacrifice of academic independence and integrity. This left Germany's professorial community morally compromised – thus signalling the beginning of the end for *deutsche Bildung*.[48]

For all their specific national flavour, the French notion of the *homme cultivé* and the British standard of what a gentleman should be, are educational ideals that are open and attainable even for foreigners. Such is not the case with the traditional German ideal which, in the term *deutscher Geist*, infuses intellect with an almost mystical, spiritual quality. Ever since it was evoked as a symbol of national identity in the face of the Napoleonic invasion, *deutscher Geist* has had an exclusive quality, barring effective access for anyone not of German mother tongue. In the plan he put forth in 1807 for establishing a university in Berlin, Fichte wrote, 'Whoever may be of another nation fails for loss of language to qualify for living with us in mutual exchange.'[49] He further specified that the German language should become the medium of instruction for all disciplines taught at the university. His reason for proposing this innovation was that one could only think creatively in a living language – not, for example, in the Latin of an 'extinct people'.[50] This view fit in well with the experience of other European nations, which found their spiritual identity only after Latin had been replaced as the literary language. In the case of Germany, however, centuries of division into a multiplicity of individual states and principalities had the effect that such emphasis on the use of the national language served to promote the development of what would later prove to be a disastrous political ideology.

In having developed into an intellectually unifying force, the German university became a symbol of national identification and revival.[51] Even though a united nation did not exist, people at least wanted to cultivate whatever they had in common intellectually and spiritually and through education help prepare the coming generations for the task of creating national unity. The product of the educated bourgeoisie, these notions were initially sustained by a good measure of liberal pathos. With the failure of the 1848 Revolution and Germany's growing economic and political power, however, unity became a matter of chauvinistic self-assertion. Unification finally came about in 1871, on the heels of the defeat of France. The new German *Reich* was founded on three ideological pillars: faith, fatherland and education.[52] This Germany – in comparison with its neighbours a 'late-born nation'[53] – became obsessed with an imperialistic megalomania which within a matter of only a few decades led to World War I and produced World War II. The result for Germany was social and economic chaos.

In 1945 it seemed as if all the pillars of national identity had been knocked away, making it possible with the help of the victorious powers to start off anew on a democratic basis. New governmental structures were developed in both West Germany and East Germany, each bearing the imprint of their respective occupying powers. In West Germany, the idea of supranational, European integration gained ground and for a time was even adopted with enthusiasm. On closer examination, however, it becomes evident that in West Germany, in particular, traditional cultural and economic structures managed to survive the great collapse in one form or the other. Unchanged above all was the 'unpolitical' sphere of education, apart from some surface features. As the British Association of University Teachers stated in 1947, 'If a new spirit is to be infused into the German universities, much will depend on the numbers, powers and status of the non-professorial staff of lecturers'[54] – in other words, all university teachers below the rank of full professor. But nothing effective happened to drive out the traditional *deutscher Geist* for once and for all. Although the radical Nazi professors were removed from their posts, the faculty's structure and philosophical outlook remained unaffected. Thus, the old system of *deutsche Bildung*, anchored in the professors' attitudes, ideals and behavioural patterns, could re-establish itself unhindered.[55]

It was as a result of the protest of a student generation that has grown up without experiencing the German hubris and its catastrophic consequences, that people recently have come to recognize that the universities cannot possibly do justice to what will be demanded of them in future unless they renounce the philosophical and structural legacy inherent in the concept, *deutsche Bildung*. All recent legislation on higher education gives junior faculty wider powers in teaching, research and administrative matters. At the same time, professors, instructors and students are engaged in the task of developing a new understanding of what their academic work means in the present-day social context – an understanding that will not only take into account the technocratic society's need for implementable knowledge but simultaneously represent a challenge to all involved to take an active part in making this society ever more just and humane. This challenge to scholars and scientists to measure their academic work against new social and political criteria – in West Germany, an urgent prerequisite to any successful reform of higher education – is for the first time coming out into the open as an issue in other Western societies, too. What matters everywhere is that academic education is to be understood not as an elitist privilege, ensuring for the few the right to live out their lives in an ivory tower, but rather as a democratic responsibility to be shared by the growing numbers of teachers and research workers.

In the same vein, the aim of establishing 'comprehensive universities' has ideological significance apart from any instrumental value it may have in increasing the system's efficiency. The idea of an integrated 'comprehensive university' is not new; it came up during the period of the Weimar Republic, which lasted from the end of World War I until 1933. But the university establishment of the time rejected this notion in terms that were altogether in keeping with the traditional hierarchical order that prevailed, overtly or not, among both academicians and the disciplines they represented. The professor of German literature, Gustav Roethe – at the time rector of the University of Berlin and president of the German Universities Association – gave a speech in 1924 at ceremonies commemorating the founding of the Berlin Institute of Technology, in which he said: 'Heaven preserve us from any gigantic comprehensive university that would mix everything that only vaguely smacks of College into one huge primordial stew. That would be un-German, through and through. For the strength of the Germans lies in the fusion of one's altogether autonomous, individual powers. . . . The unfolding of the single power is something the sound German takes care of from within himself.'[56] It is precisely the reverse concept that underlies present efforts to create, in the 'comprehensive university', an institution which will embrace and interconnect all sectors of higher education and make transitions easier for both teachers and students. The objective is to remove the basis for the development of university hierarchies, thereby creating maximal conditions for the development of democratic structures and for the provision of equal opportunity, without losing sight of the necessity for functional and scientifically justified differentiation.

The end of *deutsche Bildung* also means that an end has been put to isolationist, elitarian policy in the realm of higher education. This can be seen as a positive indicator for the beginning of what may well prove to be a more general and fundamental democratization process in West Germany. The centuries' old bourgeois premise according to which *Bildung* and democracy are, in principle, mutually exclusive,[57] blocked the development of democracy in Germany again and again. This premise has been destroyed – we may all hope, for good. Education, freed of all ballast, is the prime requisite for the realization of democracy.

NOTES

1. cf. D. Goldschmidt, 'The Current Status of University Reform in Western Germany' in *Students, University and Society; a comparative sociological review*, ed. by M. Scotfort-Archer (to be published), London.
2. cf. *Frankfurter Allgemeine Zeitung*, Nov. 6, 1970.
3. cf. F. Paulsen, *Geschichte des gelehrten Unterrichts auf den deutschen Schulen und Universitäten vom Ausgang des Mittelalters bis zur Gegenwart*, Berlin and Leipzig, 1921.
4. cf. H. Schelsky, 'Die Universitätsidee Wilhelm von Humboldts und die gegenwärtige Universitätsreform' in *Abschied von der Hochschulpolitik oder: Die Universität im Fadenkreuz des Versagens*, ed. H. Schelsky, Bielefeld, 1969, pp. 151 f. and J. Habermas: 'Zwangsjacke für die Studienreform' in *Der Monat*, vol. 18, no. 218, 1966, pp. 7 f.

5. In winter semester 1970–1 there were places for only 36 per cent of the applicants for study in these fields. Cf. *dpa-Dienst für Kulturpolitik*, no. 47, Nov. 23, 1970.

6. The ratio of students to chairholders is 113 : 1 in the Faculty of Economics and Social Science, 97 : 1 in the Faculty of Law, and 87 : 1 in the Humanities Faculty. Cf. Table 4 in W. Baumeister, *Die berufliche Lage der Nichtordinarien; Untersuchung über Arbeitsbedingungen und Rechtsstellung der habilitierten Hochschullehrer ohne Lehrstuhl*, Göttingen, 1970.

7. W. v. Humboldt: 'Über die Innere und Äußere Organisation der Höheren Wissenschaftlichen Anstalten in Berlin' in *Die Idee der Deutschen Universität*, Darmstadt, 1956, p. 384.

8. ibid., p. 381.

9. ibid., p. 379.

10. F. Paulsen, op. cit., p. 129.

11. cf. *Die Deutsche Universität im Dritten Reich; Eine Vortragsreihe der Universität München*, Munich, 1966.

12. op. cit., pp. 377 f.

13. cf. H. Plessner, ed. *Untersuchungen zur Lage der Deutschen Hochschullehrer*, vol. 1, *Nachwuchsfragen im Spiegel einer Erhebung 1953–55*, Göttingen, 1956.

14. M. Weber, 'Wissenschaft als Beruf', in *Gesammelte Aufsätze zur Wissenschaftslehre*, Tübingen, 1922, pp. 526 f.

15. cf. Plessner, op. cit., p. 39. Of all teachers regularly employed at West German universities in winter semester 1953–4, 48 per cent were non-qualified, and another 7 per cent qualified *Assistenten*, or instructors. See also D. Goldschmidt, 'Teachers in Institutions of Higher Learning in Germany' in *Education, Economy and Society; a Reader in the Sociology of Education*, H. A. Halsey, J. Floud and C. A. Anderson, eds. London, 1966, pp. 577 f.

16. cf. *Entwurf eines Hochschulrahmengesetzes*, Bundesrat publication no. 689/70 of Dec. 18, 1970, Bonn, p. 17.

17. Junior faculty includes *Assistenten* with or without the doctoral degree, as well as *Assistenzprofessoren* with or without the *Habilitation*. The right referred to is Article 5, § 3 of the West German constitution, which states: 'Freedom is guaranteed for the arts and science, research and teaching. The right to teach in freedom does not suspend loyalty to the constitution.' On the case itself, see *dpa-Dienst für Kulturpolitik*, no. 51–2, Dec. 21, 1970.

18. 'Gesetz über die Universitäten des Landes Hessen' in *Gesetz- und Verordnungsblatt für das Land Hessen*, section I, no. 23, § 6, p. 325.

19. H. Schelsky, loc. cit., p. 161.

20. cf. J. Hirsch: *Wissenschaftlich-technischer Fortschritt und politisches System; Organisation und Grundlagen administrativer Wissenschaftsförderung in der BRD*, Frankfurt, 1970.

21. This society currently encompasses about 50 such institutes, most of which are involved in scientific research, although some projects are being carried on peace and educational research.

22. W. v. Humboldt, op. cit., p. 380.

23. *Entwurf eines Hochschulrahmengesetzes*, op. cit., p. 14.

24. *Empfehlungen zur Struktur und zum Ausbau des Bildungswesens im Hochschulbereich nach 1970*, published by the Wissenschaftsrat in three volumes, Bonn, 1970.

25. 'Forschendes Lernen – Wissenschaftliches Prüfen; Ergebnisse der Arbeit des Ausschusses für Hochschuldidaktik', *Schriften der Bundesassistentenkonferenz*, no. 5, Bonn, 1969.

26. cf. 'Entwurf einer Baukasten-Gesamthochschule', issued by the SPD-Landesverband Baden-Württemberg, Stuttgart, 1969.

27. J. Habermas, 'Vom sozialen Wandel akademischer Bildung' in *Mitteilungen des Philologenverbandes Rheinland-Pfalz*, vol. 5/6, 1970, p. 6.

28. Alone at the universities, the number of first-year students has increased from 25,609 in 1952 to 63,764 in 1969, i.e., from 3·5 per cent to 8·7 per cent of the whole age group; taking together all institutions expected to fall into the sphere of the comprehensive universities, the total entering population has grown during the same period from 44,385 to 106,355, i.e., from 6·2 per cent to 14·4 per cent of the whole age group. Cautious planning estimates figure that by 1980 the comprehensive universities' capacity will reach 244,800, or *c.* 25 per cent of the given age group. Cf. the *Empfehlungen* issued by the Wissenschaftsrat, op. cit., vol. 3, p. 65 (table 24) and p. 108 (table 47).

29. 8 per cent of all students have university or college-trained fathers employed in non-civil

service white collar jobs. In 1951–2, this figure was only 4·7 per cent, and in 1928–9, a mere 1·2 per cent. The number of students whose fathers are in the civil service category (including teachers in Germany) with college or university training, has dropped slightly from 13·5 per cent in 1928–9 to 11 per cent in 1967–8. On the other hand, recruitment from the group of independently employed professionals with college or university education has all but doubled from 6·5 per cent in 1928–9 to 12·1 per cent in 1967–8. Cf. G. Kath: *Das soziale Bild der Studentenschaft in der Bundesrepublik Deutschland, Wintersemester 1967–68*, Bonn, 1969, p. 46 (table 18).

30. ibid.
31. ibid., p. 48 (table 19).
32. Whereas *c.* 53 per cent of West Germany's employed population are blue collar workers, only 6·7 per cent of the student population come from this background. Cf. Kath, op. cit., p. 48.
33. cf. G. Kath. C. Oehler and R. Reichwein: 'Studienweg und Studienerfolg' in *Studien und Berichte*, vol. 6, published by the Institut für Bildungsforschung in der Max-Planck-Gesellschaft, Berlin, 1966; also, D. Goldschmidt, 'Psychological Stress; a German Case Study' in *Student Power*, J. Nagel, ed., London, 1969, pp. 59–72.
34. G. Kath, *Das soziale Bild*, pp. 69 f.
35. ibid., p. 55.
36. In 1967–8, 33·5 per cent of all students at institutions of higher learning had fathers with a college or university degree. ibid., p. 46 (table 18).
37. See the *Empfehlungen* of the Wissenschaftsrat, op. cit., vol. 1, pp. 46 f.
38. J. Habermas, 'Zwangsjacke für die Studienreform' in *Der Monat*, loc. cit., p. 13.
39. J. Habermas, 'Universität in der Demokratie – Demokratisierung der Universität'in *Merkur*, vol. 21, no. 5, 1967, p. 424.
40. *Empfehlungen* of the Wissenschaftsrat, vol. 1, pp. 72 f.
41. Cf. R. Poignant, *Das Bildungswesen in den Ländern der EWG; eine Studie zum Vergleicq mit den Vereinigten Staaten, Grossbritannien und der Sowjetunion*, Frankfurt, Berlin and Munich, 1966.
42. 'Gutachten zur Hochschulreform', issued by the *Studienausschuss für Hochschulreform*, Hamburg, 1948, p. 3.
43. ibid., p. 3.
44. *Empfehlungen des Wissenschaftsrates zum Ausbau der wissenschaftlichen Einrichtungen* (issued by the Wissenschaftsrat), section I, Bonn, 1960, p. 63.
45. cf. 'The Universities in the British Zone of Germany' in *The Universities Review*, vol. 19, no. 3, May 1947, pp. 203–22.
46. ibid., pp. 211 and 221.
47. M. Weinreich, *Hitler's Professors; the Part of Scholarship in Germany's Crimes against the Jewish People*, New York, 1946.
48. cf. *Bekenntnis der Professoren an den deutschen Universitäten und Hochschulen zu Adolf Hitler und dem nationalsozialistischen Staat*, 1934, presented by the Saxonian branch of the Nationalsozialistischer Lehrerbund Deutschlands on the occasion of the Reichstag elections.
49. J. G. Fichte, 'Deduzierter Plan einer zu Berlin zu errichtenden Höheren Lehranstalt, die in gehöriger Verbindung mit einer Akademie der Wissenschaften stehe' in *Die Idee der Deutschen Universität*, Darmstadt, 1956, p. 187.
50. ibid., p. 185.
51. F. Paulsen, op. cit., vol. 2, p. 265.
52. As reflected in the title of the selected writings of Paul de Lagarde from the years 1878–91: *Deutscher Glaube, Deutsches Vaterland, Deutsche Bildung*, Jena, 1914.
53. *Die verspätete Nation*, title of the second, 1959, edition of a book by Helmuth Plessner, originally published as *Das Schicksal Deutschen Geistes am Ausgang seiner bürgerlichen Epoche*, Zürich and Leipzig, 1935.
54. loc. cit., *The Universities Review*, p. 212.
55. The agitated and undetached debate that went on in the immediate post-war years on this issue is recorded, for example, in the *Göttinger Universitätszeitung*. See also W. F. Haug, *Der hilflose Antifaschismus*, Frankfurt, 1968. Haug criticizes the inadequate attempts of prominent German professors between 1964 and 1966 intellectually to 'overcome' the

universities' Nazification. They failed to grasp the fact that their own idealistic understanding of the world was enmeshed with the organicism of the Nazi era.

56. *Die Technische Hochschule zu Berlin 1799–1924. Festschrift*, Berlin, 1925, p. 34.
57. '*Demokratie und Bildung schliessen sich genau ebenso aus wie Demokratie und Freiheit*'. Paul de
Lagarde, *Ausgewählte Schriften*, 2nd ed., Munich, 1934, p. 141. See also F. Stern, *Kultur-
pessimismus als politische Gefahr; eine Analyse nationaler Ideologie in Deutschland*, Berne,
Stuttgart and Vienna, 1963, pp. 99 f.

21

Higher Education in the Soviet Union

Igor Ekgolm

Under the Soviet government, significant changes have occurred in the development of public education, science and culture. The citizens' right to education is guaranteed and ensured by an extensive network of schools, free tuition at all levels, instruction in local languages, availability of trained teachers, a wide network of secondary and higher vocational schools, government grants for students, a system of part-time adult education, and a ramified network of cultural and educational centres. The Soviet system of public education is built on the following principles.

Being a national system it rules out the element of chance in the siting of educational institutions and the contents of the education being provided, as well as ensures adequate educational facilities.

The Soviet Union has an integrated system of educational institutions consisting of pre-school establishments, primary schools, eight-year schools, ten-year secondary schools or specialized secondary schools, and higher schools. Each successive stage is a natural sequel to the one preceding it.

Every stage and type of school is open to all irrespective of nationality, parents' rank or circumstances, colour of skin, or religious belief. There is a wide network of correspondence and evening schools of general and vocational education. Eight-year education is universal and compulsory (the shift to compulsory secondary education is under way now). School is completely separated from the church, education being fully secular. The principle of equality of the sexes in the sphere of education and the connexion of education and practice is applied throughout.

The system of public education terminates in institutions of higher learning which supply all branches of the national economy and culture with highly trained specialists and take part in the training and retraining of the researchers and teachers the country must have.

As of January 1970, there were 78 million persons in the Soviet Union undergoing some form of education, over 49 million of them attending schools of general education.

In the 1968/9 school year, 4·5 million finished eight-year school, and 2·5 million finished secondary schools of general education, with over

450,000 receiving eight-year education and over 600,000 receiving secondary education at young workers' schools and village youth schools while continuing in their jobs. Appointed to work in the national economy were 1·6 million young specialists graduated from higher education and specialized secondary schools, including 565,000 with a higher education and over a million with a specialized secondary education. In 1970, establishments of higher learning and specialized secondary schools admitted 895,000 and 1,312,000 students respectively. At the beginning of 1970, the number of scientific workers exceeded 870,000 including 220,000 Doctors and Masters of Science.

Government Policy

Government policy in the field of education began to take shape with the early decrees of the Council of People's Commissars, signed by Lenin. They were: 'On Instituting the State Commission for Public Education', 'On Separating the Church from the State and School from the Church', 'On Stamping Out Illiteracy Among the Population of the RSFSR', and the 'Rules for Organizing Public Education in the Russian Republic'. These documents offered a concrete programme for bringing education within the reach of every Soviet citizen from eight to fifty. In carrying out the programme most careful consideration was given to the wishes and needs of each group of people in the multinational state.

Just before World War I, in 1914, Russia had 105 colleges and universities taking care of 127,400 students. These institutions were concentrated in 16 cities and towns while by far most of them were situated in St. Petersburg and Moscow. There were only four colleges in the whole of vast Western and Eastern Siberia and the Far East.

There was not a single college or university on the territory of the present Union Republics of Byelorussia, Uzbekistan, Kazakhstan, Azerbaijan, Kirghizia, Tajikistan and Armenia. Russia trained less graduate personnel than most European countries.

Pre-revolutionary Russia, which accounted for about 4 per cent of world industrial output, had merely about 190,000 trained experts; in 1970, the Soviet Union accounted for over 20 per cent of world industrial output while altogether nearly 16 million experts with a higher or secondary technical education, including six million with the highest qualifications, were employed in its national economy.

Among the urgent problems the Soviet government tackled from the very first was that of raising a new people's intelligentsia whose interests would concur with those of the people. Lenin wrote in April 1918: 'Without the guidance of experts in the various fields of knowledge, technology and experience, the transition to socialism will be impossible, because socialism calls for a conscious mass advance to greater productivity of labour compared with capitalism, and on the basis achieved by capitalism.'[1]

To produce such a body of specialists, it was first necessary to renew the composition of the student body. Under a decree of the Council of People's Commissars, issued on August 2, 1918, the colleges and universities opened their doors for the first time in history to the mass of the workers and peasants. Free tuition and financial support for needy students were introduced. Since by far most of the working people lacked secondary education, preliminary courses were arranged at colleges and universities to help prospective entrants improve their educational background.

Raising a thousands-strong army of university teachers has been a major achievement which took years of concentrated effort.

The creation of a force of college teachers was an important point in reforming the institutions of higher learning. For some time after the revolution the more reactionary-minded university professors stiffly opposed the radical reorganization of the system of higher education. But the effort launched by the Soviet government to achieve an upsurge of public education, science and culture won the support of a large section of the Russian intellectuals, world-famous Russian scientists K. A. Timiriazev, N. D. Zelinski, V. I. Vernadski, N. E. Zhukovski and other well-known figures among them. In pointing out the paramount importance of enlisting their participation and utilizing their knowledge Lenin stated that in order to create a socialist system of higher education a strong force of university teachers hailing from the ranks of the workers and peasants should be made available.

The measures the Soviet government introduced in order to regulate the social composition of the student body, to open the way to knowledge for workers and peasants, were a major step towards creating a new force of scientists and lecturers. The organization of workers' departments at colleges and universities, conducted at Lenin's suggestion, was one such measure.

Another important step towards providing the necessary scientific personnel was made in 1925 with the institution of postgraduate courses. The 'Post-Graduate Course Regulations' endorsed by the government on March 31, 1939, established the postgraduate course as the principal form of training scientists and teachers, which continues today. Over 60 per cent of Soviet scientists having a Doctor's or a Master's degree have passed through a post-graduate course.

In the 1969/70 academic year there were about 100,000 post-graduates in the Soviet Union. More than 56,500 of them were trained at colleges or universities, 35,892 studying full-time and 20,653 taking part-time courses. Today post-graduate courses are functioning at 585 universities and colleges and 1,323 research centres.

There has developed in the Soviet Union a large and essentially new system of higher education. In the 1969/70 academic year 4·5 million students were trained at 804 institutions of higher learning in a wide range of specialities, notably in the fields essential to current scientific and technical progress, higher levels of socialized production, and the flourishing of science, technology and culture.

The System of Higher Education

The system of higher education comprises universities and various institutes, polytechnical or specialized, with periods of study ranging from four to six years. The aims, content and methods of teaching and the organization of the process of study at universities and at specialized colleges have much in common, although there are some distinctive features as well. The universities, which train students for research activities in the first place, lay particular stress on scientific training, and the institutes, while providing a good theoretical grounding, concentrate on the application of the results of research to practice.

The training of graduate personnel is carried on in the Soviet Union by institutions of higher learning of various types. They may be tentatively divided into three principal traditional groups, viz., the universities, polytechnical institutes, and specialized (or branch) colleges. Most establishments of higher learning belong to the state and are maintained at government expense, funds being supplied from the state budget. (A few institutions of higher learning belong to co-operative and other organizations.)

The universities have emerged historically as major scientific centres carrying on large-scale research and simultaneously training specialists for work at research centres, industrial establishments, cultural and educational institutions, secondary schools and colleges, and in state administration and public organization.

University education embraces nearly all the natural sciences and humanities, viz., mathematics, physics, chemistry, biology, geography, geology, philology, journalism, history, philosophy, economics, law, and so on.

Under the Soviet government, the number of universities has risen to 53 (as of 1970) against 12 in 1913. Universities have been set up in all Union Republics. More recently universities were opened in the Mordovian, Daghestan, Yakut, Bashkir, Kabardino-Balkarian, Chuvash, Kalmyk and North Ossetian Autonomous Republics, and in the towns of Novosibirsk, Donetsk, Kaliningrad, Tomsk, Krasnoyarsk, Kuibyshev and Vladivostok. Among the largest and oldest in the Soviet Union are Moscow, Leningrad, Kiev, Odessa and Kazan Universities.

University education in the Soviet Union is based on profound and extensive general theoretical training and on an organic combination of research and study. Concentrated at universities are large bodies of scientists and teachers working in the field of natural and exact sciences, such as physics, mathematics, chemistry, biology, geology and overlapping sciences, which form the theoretical foundation of technological progress in all branches of the national economy. University laboratories account for many a brilliant discovery from which new branches of science and technology have sprouted. A great number of Master's and Doctor's theses are annually defended in universities. Some universities – Moscow, Leningrad, Kiev, the Urals, Tashkent, Kazan University, etc. – have lately furnished the base for the training of teachers for refresher institutes and teachers of the social sciences, and for refresher courses for teachers of philology, chemistry, mathematics, physics, and so on. The universities also play an important part in training versatile specialists in the humanities. Liberal education is also widely represented by teachers' training and library colleges, schools of law and economics, and numerous arts colleges – conservatories, theatrical and art schools, and so on. In a socialist society, such colleges play an ever greater role in supplying experts.

The scientific-technical revolution and the attendant giant growth of industry, transport, communications and construction determine the significant place of technical colleges in the system of higher education.

An important place among the technical colleges belongs to polytechnical institutes, which are establishments preparing engineers in a great number of lines. The Leningrad Polytechnical Institute, for example, has eight departments – the Physicometallurgical, Mechanical Engineering, Electronic-Mechanical, Hydraulic Engineering, Electronics and other Departments – and graduates engineers of 62 specialities.

Another type of technical educational establishment is represented by branch (or sectoral) colleges which usually train specialists for some one branch of industry with related metallurgical, mining, building, chemical engineering, transport and other colleges. The number of departments and specialities is usually smaller in such colleges compared with polytechnical institutes. The Sverdlovsk Mining Institute, for example, which trains engineers for the coal-mining industry, has the Departments of Geological Prospecting, Mining, Geophysics, and Mineralogical Chemistry. There are technical colleges in more than 70 cities and towns.

Agricultural colleges, numbering a hundred, make a distinctive group. They train experts in agronomy, in stock breeding and veterinary medicine, and in mechanization of farming. The syllabuses and curricula of these colleges reflect the problems of particular interest to the areas in which they are situated. Agricultural colleges increasingly develop into research centres rendering effective practical aid to the collective and state farms.

Medical workers are trained at special medical colleges offering courses in therapeutics, pediatrics, sanitation, stomatology and pharmacy.

Lastly, there are physical culture and sports colleges training doctors and teachers in the field of physical culture.

Over 70 per cent of full-time students receive monthly stipends, those coming from elsewhere being accommodated at hostels. The average cost of tuition per full-time student, covered from the state budget, amounts to 1,066 roubles a year.

The training of specialists in any line is based on the natural and social science subjects which are in the forefront of science. The content and limits of subjects taught largely depend on the bias of the college, the perspectives of the development of science, technology and culture always being taken into consideration. For this reason as far as the natural sciences are concerned the students study not only what has been or is shortly to be introduced in practice but also that which has not yet emerged from the theoretical stage. Science and technology are developing at such a fast rate that many theoretical subjects inevitably provide the means for handling applied problems (e.g., the theory of numbers, nuclear physics, and so on). Studying the natural sciences and their theoretical divisions is absolutely indispensable to developing in students a creative way of thinking and an ability to look ahead.

Much attention is given to the study of new branches of science and technology on whose practical application scientific-technological progress depends. It is, above all, computer techniques which help solve the most difficult of theoretical and practical problems in technology and economics, chemistry and biochemistry, medicine and history, control and automation. Therefore all students get a thorough grounding in modern computer methods. A prominent place in the system of higher education belongs to specialized subjects.

A more profound understanding of physics, chemistry and other natural science subjects is achieved through a study of Marxist-Leninist philosophy, pedagogics, psychology and physiology; the study of economics is helped by a knowledge of philosophy and mathematics while knowledge of chemistry, physics and mathematics helps master biology. Therefore in the process of study close links are established between the natural and social sciences and specialist courses.

Problems of world outlook and methodology form a component part of each course of study. Much attention is given to ideological and political education. In the process of studying the social sciences, students master the teachings of Marx, Engels and Lenin and the dialectical method and learn to conduct social activities.

Development of college education in recent years was dictated above all by the requirements of the current scientific-technological revolution which has penetrated literally into every sphere of society, making an impact on production, politics, culture and everyday life. Its distinctive features have greatly influenced college education.

Its first distinctive feature is the organic connexion and interpenetration of science and technology. Today science creates a margin of knowledge, preparing the ground for technology's further advance, cutting new paths for it. In turn, technological progress has a powerful effect on scientific thought, stimulating it, providing science with the necessary up-to-date facilities and advancing new tasks. All leading branches of scientific knowledge, the entire scientific activities, their organization, technical equipment and regulation have been involved. At the same time the whole technological basis of society has been revolutionized.

Its second distinctive feature is that science is turning more and more into an immediate productive force of society. It is not unusual today for applied, and even fundamental, research to form an organic part of the very process of production while research institutes and laboratories are part of the production apparatus. All this is accompanied by definite social changes, by the growth of the number of engineers and technicians and of the share they take in production. While in 1960–7 the number of industrial workers in the Soviet Union increased by 26·7 per cent, the number of engineers and technicians increased by 63·3 per cent over the same period.

A third distinctive feature of the current scientific and technological revolution is that under its influence there is taking place a fundamental change in the development of machines which not only free men from physical labour but increasingly take over the functions of production connected with thought, the logical and control functions above all. Production is being automated and computerized on an ever-growing scale.

A fourth distinctive feature of the scientific and technological revolution is the introduction of chemistry in production, creation of new branches of the chemical industry, and the emergence of new sources of energy.

All this required that the Soviet state should pay increasing attention to the training of graduate personnel. Colleges and universities recruit students through various channels, such as schools of general education, specialized secondary schools, and two- or three-year vocational schools providing an equivalent of secondary school in general education. Boys and girls employed in the national economy complete their general secondary education at evening (shift) schools or correspondence schools. They enjoy a number of privileges granted by the state, viz., a shorter working week and four-to six-days' paid leaves to take their examinations. Students of evening and correspondence departments or colleges enjoy similar privileges.

Preparatory departments launched in 1969 help to increase the entrants' standards. In the 1970/1 academic year such departments functioned at 500 Soviet colleges.

In the 1970/1 academic year the Kharkov Institute of Aircraft Engineering started a preparatory department for full-time day students (who do no other job). Admitted to the department are those who have completed secondary school and have been recommended by a factory, a building project, a transport or communications office, a state farm or a forestry project, etc., and who have had at least a year's experience of work. Students of preparatory departments receive hostel accommodation and draw grants to the same amount as first-year students. Those successfully passing the examinations at the end of the course are admitted to the first year of college without having to take entrance examinations.

Teaching Methods

The establishments of higher learning use diverse forms of organization of the process of study and varied teaching methods, constantly perfected so as to stimulate the students' activity, develop their creative capacity, and put theory into closer contact with practice. Along with traditional forms and methods of teaching, such as lectures, discussions, students' essays, graduation papers, laboratory work, practicals and so on, programmed aids, educational television programmes, audio-visual aids and electronic apparatus are being introduced on an ever-wider scale.

Apart from classes, students have the opportunity to extend their knowledge and improve their skills in Student Scientific Societies, Young Lecturers' Schools, Departments of Public Professions, amateur drama and opera groups and various creative associations.

To encourage students to engage in original scientific effort, a three-round National Competition for the Best Student Paper has been instituted. In October 1970, the Third All-Union Competition in the social sciences was completed.

The competitions have assumed a truly mass scale. In some higher schools, for example, Donetsk University, the Zaporozhie Teachers' Training Institute and the Kuban Medical Institute, 90 per cent of the students participated in the Third Competition. A total of 713,000 papers were sent in.

Eighty-five thousand students participated in the First Competition. Over 60 per cent of papers came from technical colleges and science departments. Most papers drew on local material. One of the distinctive features of the Third Competition was that it attracted many evening, correspondence and military academy students. A considerable number of papers were contributed by foreign students studying at Soviet colleges.

In recent years such forms of social student activities as participating in building teams, staging marches at the sites of military and labour glory and All-Union mass-propaganda marches have assumed a permanent nationwide dimension.

As part of the plan of work of Soviet higher schools, students participate in the people's constructive effort during the summer vacation period, constructing dwelling houses, farm buildings, schools and hospitals, helping to build railways, draining marshland, giving performances, lectures and so on in the field.

The higher schools conduct systematic quests for young talent. In 1970, the N. K. Krupskaya Teachers' Training College at Kherson started a young mathematicians' correspondence school to assist village school-children in matriculating to mathematics departments. The first year the school enrolled 130 pupils. Workers' Departments, run by many colleges with the help of their senior year students who act as teachers, serve a similar purpose.

Soviet universities and colleges educate youth in the spirit of friendship among peoples and in the spirit of international solidarity with all the progressive forces of our times. Soviet young people dedicatedly work at numerous building projects in Asian and African countries, at Cuban sugar plantations, in Young Pioneers' summer camps in the Congo (Brazzaville), at Somali schools. Young Soviet doctors conducted a campaign for vaccinating the population in the liberated areas of Angola. A large group of medical workers, mostly medical college seniors, went to Peru to aid earthquake victims. During two months the young doctors attended nearly 45,000 Peruvians. These are only a few instances of the practical expressions of solidarity by Soviet youth.

Soviet students resolutely come out against the revival of fascism, neo-nazism, militarism and aggression and against fascist dictatorships. They attach the greatest significance to the solution of the problem of European security. Together with the entire Soviet people, the students support the Vietnamese people staunchly resisting US aggression. This solidarity finds concrete expression in giving thousands of Vietnamese young men and girls the opportunity of obtaining an education in the Soviet Union and in supplying schools, technical secondary schools and colleges in the Democratic Republic of Vietnam with relevant equipment and teaching aids.

Cultural co-operation of nations has a long historical tradition. Marxists view international cultural co-operation as an objective necessity to the progressive development of all nations, big and small. This necessity issues from the tendency towards the internationalization of the production of spiritual as well as of material values. Marx and Engels wrote: 'The intellectual creations of individual nations become common property. National one-sidedness and narrow-mindedness become more and more impossible.'[2]

Lenin wholeheartedly supported the development of extensive inter-national cultural co-operation.

International Collaboration

At different stages, co-operation between the Soviet Union and foreign countries in the sphere of education has fulfilled different functions. When there was need of it, the Soviet government sent experts to foreign countries to study their experience or receive technical education there, or it invited prominent foreign engineers and scientists to help train Soviet personnel.

The Soviet Union co-operates with other countries all over the world in the sphere of culture and education carrying on a reciprocal exchange of students, teachers, literature, scientific documents and so on.

The Soviet Union maintains lively contacts with the peoples of develop-ing countries, above all by way of training native personnel at numerous Soviet institutions of higher education. Soviet teachers, engineers, doctors, geologists, power engineers and other experts also train local personnel.

In February 1960, at the desire of progressive public and government circles of Asian, African and Latin American countries, the Patrice Lumumba Friendship University was set up in Moscow. Its principal aim is to aid Asian, African and Latin American countries by training qualified specialists from among their own citizens and providing easier access to education for young people, above all for the children of poorer families.

The University has seven principal departments, that is, Engineering, Physics, Mathematics and Science, Medical, Agricultural, History and Philology, and Economics and Law. The University has also a preparatory department where students acquire sufficient Russian and have their general education brought up to standard.

In ten years the University has developed into a large scientific and educational centre. Its annual enrolment amounts to 600 foreign and 225 Soviet students. In the 1969/70 academic year it was attended by over 4,000 students while 90 graduates of its Medical Department were gaining supervised practical experience in Moscow clinics. Apart from that, 150 Soviet teachers of Russian as a second language were trained at the Refresher Department and 25 persons attended the refresher courses for machine-building engineers organized at the request of the UN.

In the 1969/70 academic year there were 3,092 students from abroad representing 84 countries. There were 964 students from Latin America, 832 from Africa, 524 from Asia, and 770 from the Arab East. The largest single groups came from Chile (186), India (210), Syria (143), Mexico (109), Nepal (99), Kenya (81), and Sudan (95). There were 447 women among the foreign students.

Over 700 lecturers distributed among 82 chairs in 149 subjects conducted scientific work. Among them were 84 professors and 388 assistant professors. Of the teaching staff 76·8 per cent were young scientists and scholars under forty. The leading lines of research correspond to the requirements of Asian, African and Latin American countries.

In the sphere of petrographic mineralogy, for example, they study the problems of geology and magmatic formation and methods of surveying and prospecting for useful minerals in Africa and Hindustan. Physicians study the epidemiological and clinical features of infectious diseases in tropical countries and methods of treatment. The plan of research embraces 18 fields and 21 problems amounting to nearly 150 research topics. Much attention is paid at the University to training scientific workers, primarily in the fields of physics, mathematics, economics, history and philology, for colleges in Asia, Africa and Latin America. The Soviet Union also maintains contacts with Western countries in the sphere of higher education.

In the 1969/70 academic year the Soviet universities and colleges had on their staff 307,800 scientific workers and lecturers including 272,300 professors and teachers, 9,600 of them having a Doctor's degree and 87,600 a Master's degree (or 3·5 and 32·1 per cent respectively of the total number of college teachers). The number of Doctors and Masters of Science employed at universities and colleges is steadily growing. To enable more teachers to win a Doctor's degree, those preparing a Doctor's thesis are granted paid leave, or are put solely on research, for which purpose a thousand appropriate places are annually made available to the universities and colleges. This method has proved highly successful.

So also have refresher departments and institutes for college teachers which have been set up at major Soviet institutions of higher education in order to enable every college teacher to add to his knowledge, renew it by obtaining information on current achievements in science and technology, and improve his teaching skill.

The system of advanced training also includes periods of practical work for lecturers in specialist subjects in leading industrial and agricultural establishments and research institutions. It also includes ten-month and two-year refresher courses for teachers of foreign languages, and permanent regional, city and district seminars for teachers of social and other sciences as well as national, inter-college and college conferences, meetings and so on.

In the 1969/70 academic year, there were 115 Refresher Departments at universities and colleges attended by 17,800 teachers undergoing advanced training. During the 1968/9 academic year 11,800 college teachers improved their qualifications. Altogether more than 20,000 college teachers and lecturers have attended refresher departments and institutes since 1967.

At present steps are being taken both to extend the programme of advanced training for college teachers and improve its standards.

The guidance and management of the system of higher education in the Soviet Union is based on national planning and forecasting of development of the economy, science and culture. In working out the draft plan for training experts for 1971–5, the USSR Ministry of Higher and Specialized Secondary Education started from the basis that their task would fully meet the country's requirement for experts. Jointly with other ministries, they examined the situation in every economic branch to see how well it was provided with graduate personnel, defined the types of specialist training, and estimated the need for graduate personnel, taking into account at all times the substantial changes that have occurred in the siting of universities and colleges over the past few years. Development of the productive forces and growth of population have made it necessary to organize dozens of new colleges, branches and departments, and to stream-line the whole system. In future, main attention will be paid to specializing colleges according to economic branches, developing and improving their facilities, and improving the structure and management system. At present establishments of higher education are found in every Union and Autonomous Republic.

Guidance and management of scientific research being conducted at universities and colleges will be pursued in the context of the tasks posed to the higher schools by the Resolution of the Central Committee of the Communist Party of the Soviet Union and the USSR Council of Minis-ters, endorsed on September 24, 1968, on measures towards increasing the efficiency of research organizations, which outline concrete steps to be taken towards accelerating scientific and technological progress. The things to do are to revise the system of university and college research centres, estimate the effect of their activities, determine the range of research in each case and bring its results to a stage where they can be introduced into practice.

Future Developments

Further progress of scientific research conducted by universities and colleges will be promoted through the organization of university and college scientific centres. Already under way is the North Caucasian Centre which will develop fundamental research in natural and social sciences with a view to furthering the economy and productive forces of the North Caucasus; co-ordinate research in natural and social sciences; and pool the effort of institutions of higher education in that part of the Soviet Union. The experience of the North Caucasian Centre will furnish the pattern for a system of university and college scientific centres.

To provide for better guidance and management of institutions of higher education, many ministries of higher and specialized secondary education of the USSR and Union republics have set up Scientific-Technical and

Method Councils with sectors for various branches of science and techno-logy. The Scientific-Technical Council of the USSR Ministry has 39 such sectors which supervise the activities of scientific centres functioning at universities and colleges, submit proposals on introducing their findings into practice, compile surveys of the more significant results, and help organize interdepartmental conferences.

These measures are to make the institutions of higher learning more efficient. They are concrete expressions of government policy, in the sphere of higher education whose success few will deny. However, the Soviet achievements are not connected solely with the sphere of higher education or, more precisely, with institutions of higher education. These institutions, their purposes and results are in themselves derived values. The impetus lies in the fact that Soviet people have not merely dreamed of an ideal society but have been actively creating it.

Marxism-Leninism solves the problem of the ideal society from the standpoint of the interests of working people. Ideal society or true democracy consists above all in providing genuine freedom of labour, abolishing exploitation of man by man, and stopping sources of inequality and oppression.

Democracy and all the features of an ideal society we have mentioned above, are inherent in the very nature of socialism, being the product of its economic system. Socialism, which manifests itself first and foremost in the sphere of social relations, implies that all the good things of life, educa-tion among them, belong solely to the working men and women who produce them. This social system makes it possible for society to use its material means in order to pursue and achieve humanitarian aims, provid-ing for the all-round development of the individual. Soviet state policy on higher education originates entirely from this principle and is directed at making education serve the producers of material and spiritual goods.

Karl Marx described men of the communist future as *rich* – certainly not in the primitive Philistine sense – and, at the same time, being in *need* of enjoying a full life. These propositions by Marx have formed the basis of the Soviet Party and Government policy in the field of economic and cultural development. A definite role in it is assigned to higher education establishments.

The aim of communist education in the Soviet Union is the all-round development of man's mental and physical abilities and faculties. It embodies the education of the mind, polytechnical instruction, and moral, aesthetic and physical education. The universities and colleges employ every means at their disposal in order to bring about the achievement of this aim.

Education of the mind presupposes assimilation of mankind's generalized experience and spiritual culture on the one hand, and development on this basis of the cognitive abilities of the rising generation on the other. Mastering modern knowledge is a major condition of drawing the rising generation into the people's social and labour activities. It is also valuable because it lays the foundation of polytechnical and professional training, serving to bring out and develop the abilities of the individual.

In conditions of rapidly developing industrial and agricultural production, and the unprecedented progress of technology, an important means of shaping the versatile individual, and simultaneously providing the indispensable condition of eliminating the antithesis between mental and physical work, is polytechnical education which, according to Marx's definition, introduces the basic principles of all production processes to the individual while making him able to handle the simpler implements of every industry. Lenin connected the idea of polytechnical instruction with the principle of linking instruction to productive work.

The formation of moral feelings, notions and convictions and the development of the appropriate patterns of behaviour, are indispensable to the all-round development of the individual. A high moral code, good breeding and intellectual refinement, and an ability to combine private and public interests, are inalienable features of an all-round individual.

Communist morality is no figment of the imagination. It is an objective reality, one of the forms of the people's social consciousness, reflecting relations of co-operation and mutual assistance among workers free from exploitation. Communist morality is the sum total of the norms, principles and rules of behaviour of the builders of the new society. It germinated in the working class even under capitalism; the October socialist revolution provided the conditions under which it struck root and flourished.

Aesthetic education, which essentially consists in making the individual aware of what is beautiful in nature, society and human relationships, and capable of recognizing the surrounding world through the medium of art, and also serving to develop artistic tastes and faculties, is indispensable to producing a versatile personality. Physical education is necessary to make youth healthy, strong and hardy. Apart from improving the constitution and carriage, it develops courage, self-control and tenacity.

The Soviet universities and colleges have turned out millions of well-educated, cultured and active builders of socialism and raised a strong force of scientists, scholars, engineers and designers whose pioneering creative effort is embodied in the numerous remarkable triumphs of the Soviet people.

NOTES

1. V. I. Lenin, *Collected Works*, Vol. 27, p. 248.
2. K. Marx, F. Engels, *Selected Works*, 1962, Vol. I, p. 38.

22

The American University

Paul Nash

The American university is undergoing a remarkable crisis, manifested by acute tensions that have arisen between conflicting sets of values. These tensions are products of the accelerating rate of change in the United States. Changes in technology, bureaucratic organization, and urban problems provide the background for changes in the intellectual and emotional texture of everyday life. The individual often feels alienated and powerless in the face of the bureaucratic *massif*. The organization tends to take on a life and momentum of its own and become independent of its members, who feel excluded from participation in the decisions that govern its direction. Important changes are also taking place in the distribution of power. It has been estimated that by 1972 most Americans will be under twenty-one years of age and the median age of the voter will be twenty-six. Many concomitant changes will follow.

On the whole, education in America has failed to understand or come to terms with the implications of the increased rate of change. The university, in particular, has been maladaptive. University administrations have too often done nothing about the facts of change, interpreting their responsibility as merely to keep the mechanism operating. Archibald Cox, in his report on the *Crisis at Columbia*, attributed the roots of the crisis at Columbia University to widespread student and faculty dissatisfaction as a result of the administration's resistance to change.

Out of this background has arisen a situation in which traditional values are being continually threatened or challenged by emerging values. Sometimes the two sets of values appear to be in irreconcilable conflict, especially when simplistic or dichotomous thinking leads to strong polarization. At other times, it appears that a creative synthesis of the dialectical struggle can be achieved, especially when communication, listening, and dialogue are present and in good repair. Often some form of co-existence appears to be the best that can be hoped for. But at all times the emergence of new values presents a tension. Some of these tensions will be presented here as an organizing framework within which the condition of the American university can be analysed.

Scarcity and Affluence

The basic value tension in contemporary America is between those whose values were developed in an economy of scarcity and those whose values have been shaped in an economy of affluence. Among the first group can be included a large proportion of the adult population. Even those who are affluent today include many who carry harsh and vivid memories of the Depression of the 1930s or of youthful hardship in European or American slums and farms. Their attitudes and values have been permanently affected by these experiences. In the university this first group is heavily represented among the senior faculty, the administration, and the trustees. In addition, they are especially strongly represented among older alumni and taxpayers, who constitute major sources of financial support for private and public universities respectively. In the second group can be counted a large proportion of middle class youth and people under thirty, born during or since World War II and raised in white, affluent suburbs of large cities. They constitute a significant section of both the university student body and the younger faculty.

The tension between these two sets of values focuses on the price one is willing to pay for the satisfaction of material wants. People who grow up amidst scarcity are readily reminded that there may not be enough to go round. Hence, they are easily moved into a competitive stance towards their fellow men. Similarly, they can be convinced without undue difficulty that it is prudent to be polite, obedient, and inoffensive towards those who have the power to affect one's economic or vocational fortunes. These children of scarcity may also find it difficult to project values that go beyond the satisfaction of material wants. Such wants are capable of great extension, and this extension has perhaps proceeded further in the United States than anywhere else. It is possible, presumably, to aspire to have a television set in every room. But these wants are not capable of unlimited extension. More than one television set in a room becomes dysfunctional. There comes a point, with affluence, where continued increments of things cease to satisfy. People are then apt to seek satisfaction in other values.

This is the world in which most of these middle-class students and younger faculty grew up. Having always experienced a world of material affluence, they are easily convinced that there will always be enough. Hence, there is no justification for focusing one's life on the task of earning a living. There is a strong assumption among these young people that the material aspects of life will be taken care of somehow and hence it would be foolish to make significant concessions, in terms of other values, to the task of money making. Many of them reject totally the consumer-oriented society that finds its ultimate values in the salesroom and the supermarket.

They refuse to be what Erich Fromm has derisively termed the 'eternal sucklings' of a commercial culture. They fight against being manipulated by advertisers in the cause of higher profits for shampoo, deodorant, liquor, and cigarette manufacturers.

Those who espouse scarcity-values (even though they may now be affluent) usually resent being shown what a high price in human terms they have paid for material success. Long-established habit has accustomed them to responding quickly and obediently to the crack of the whip of threatened scarcity or material loss. They do not take kindly to the spectacle of a rising generation of young people who appear to be immune to such threats and who refuse to jump in response to this particular whip. The young with their affluence-values look critically at the culture their elders have created, with its rewards of a comfortable suburban home, a respectable bourgeois existence, and an ever greater consumption of goods, in return for fitting into the bureaucratic demands of the organization, pleasing the boss or teacher, not speaking out controversially, and not behaving provocatively. And they say: the promised life is dull, uninteresting, and shoddy; and the price of slavish conformity is too high.

Puritanism and Hedonism

Another important tension in American life, clearly epitomized in the contemporary university, is between the long-established values of Puritanism and the newly emerging values of hedonism. American adult society is still largely dominated by Puritan values, which stem in part from the scarcity-economy in which most of the older people grew up. Puritanism is a kind of moralizing rationalization for scarcity: if you haven't got something and can't get it, then make a virtue of going without it. American Puritans have mastered the discipline of postponed gratification. Rising above the American urban landscape as the cathedral rose above the medieval city are the monstrous offices of insurance companies, which attest both to the companies' gigantic profits and to the future-orientation of American adults, the most over-insured people in the history of the world. The Puritan may – and usually does – acquire material goods, but less for enjoyment than for the psychological insurance of holding, stockpiling, and amassing.

In the university, this Puritan value position is held by most of the older faculty, administration, and trustees. The faculty, in particular, are likely to be strongly future oriented. Indeed, the whole academic programme can be seen as an exercise in postponed gratification. Students are not usually encouraged to ask themselves whether they are enjoying what they are studying: the focus is rather on the degree that will, at some date in the future, make their present efforts and sacrifices worthwhile. In its most extreme form, this attitude is exemplified in the view of academic study as a mortifying discipline: the best educational experience is gained through studying something in which you have no interest but that you are compelled to study. (The university version of 'It doesn't matter what you teach a boy as long as he hates it.')

Puritan values are also dominant among many student groups, including working-class, first-generation students, who are earnestly aware of the future cash value of their degrees; some of the more politically conscious of the radical students, including Maoists, Weathermen, and the Progressive-Labour wing of the Students for a Democratic Society; and those members of the Women's Liberation Movement who ironically combine emancipated views on many social and political issues with highly Victorian views on sex.

It need hardly be pointed out that Puritan values are under severe attack by many groups in American society. In the university, hedonistic values find expression primarily among those middle-class students who are products of an affluence-economy and who see little reason to barter present enjoyment for future reward, since their previous experience has led them to believe that the future will be at least as beneficent as the present. Their values are externally represented in such forms as colourful and sometimes bizarre dress, long hair, beards, beads, rock music, and casual attitudes towards drugs and sex.

The values and behaviour of these students strike jarringly against the traditional patterns of Puritan America. They insist on living in the here and now. They obtain things only for present use and enjoyment, not for the purposes of hoarding. They prefer to give things away and receive things as gifts rather than buy and sell (an attitude destined to strike despair into the heart of one whose life is based on commercial values). Their enjoyment is often expressed through gestures in the realms of drugs and sex that offer maximum provocation to an up-tight Puritan society.

A substantial element in the student protest movement, for example, has been the campaign to legalize the use of marijuana. Students argue that it is less harmful than liquor or cigarettes but that it is illegal only because it is not protected by big business interests, as are alcohol and tobacco. Sex is another focus of Puritan-provoking behaviour on the part of hedonistic students. The scientific endeavours of adult society produced antibiotics and the pill. The students now argue that these inventions permit them a degree of sexual freedom and enjoyment that their elders never had. Not unexpectedly, the older people feel a little resentful. If one has spent a lifetime acquiring what one calls the virtue of 'moral restraint' it is painful to be told by members of the next generation that it was really only fear of pregnancy or disease. Parietal rules are a favourite target for protest by hedonistic students. The student's refusal to accept the right of the university to control his sexual life is a direct challenge both to the traditional American notion of the university as a surrogate parent and to the idea that a Puritan society has the right to determine or limit his forms of enjoyment.

The Puritan-hedonist tension creates severe problems in the university, both in and out of the classroom. The Puritan professor is liable to be contemptuous of the hedonist students who refuse to follow unquestioningly the same hard route, without short-term rewards, that he himself traversed. For their part, the students consider it pointless to follow traditional courses of study. They will study if the experience is enjoyable in terms of present meaningfulness and personal relevance. If the formal curriculum cannot be made to yield these values, they will either drop out of the university or nominally stay in (for the alternative of the draft is even less likely to be hedonistically satisfying) and find their pleasures outside of the classroom.

Loyalty and Dissent

One of the major societal tensions that is reflected in the university is that between the value of loyalty and the value of dissent. The traditional American view of the role of the university is as the loyal and faithful servant of society. The widespread use of loyalty oaths for faculty members and even for students receiving loans has been a symptom of the view that members of the university community should subscribe to the values and political attitudes held by the majority of the American people. Despite a recent Supreme Court decision declaring many of these oaths unconstitutional, the attitude from which they sprang remains dominant.

Perhaps only in a nation so largely created by immigration could one so often hear the view. 'If they don't like it here, why don't they go back where they came from?' In the university, this is expressed as, 'No one forced you to come to this university. Since you freely chose to come, you should accept the way things are done here.' Such views are predominant among conservative taxpayers and *alumni*, who are conscious that they are paying part of the bill for students who too often appear ungrateful for their heavily subsidized education.

Within the university, however, it is widely held, especially among liberal faculty and students, that the crucial and indispensable role of the university is as society's honest critic rather than as her polite and loyal servant. This means that the university should judge and dissent from mainstream values whenever they seem vicious or pernicious. The text of the Resolution on Rights and Responsibilities, passed by the Faculty of Arts and Sciences of Harvard University on April 14, 1970, said in part:

> The rights of members of the University are not fundamentally different from those of other members of society. The University, however, has a special autonomy and reasoned dissent plays a particularly vital part in its existence. All members of the University have the right to press for action on matters of concern

by any appropriate means. The University must affirm, assure and protect the rights of its members to organize and join political associations, convene and conduct public meetings, publicly demonstrate and picket in orderly fashion, advocate, and publicize opinion by print, sign, and voice.

The right and the responsibility to dissent from ideas and practices that one considers harmful are viewed by many university faculty and students as central aspects of the appropriate role of the university. It is clear that dissent and protest, ranging from the carefully reasoned to the lethally violent, are endemic in contemporary student culture. Many protesting students see America as a dangerously self-righteous society, exacting a blind loyalty to all of its official actions and stated values. In their view, only a self-righteous nation could have conducted the war in Indo-China with the blind, missionizing zeal that has characterized the American campaign there, and then react with bewildered hurt when other nations do not understand its good intentions. Self-righteous authority, they say, is blind to the possibility that it might be wrong, or partly wrong. It is dogmatic in its justification of, and demand for loyalty to, its present course of action and is therefore largely closed to the possibility of correction and growth.

These liberal students see themselves, on the other hand, as essentially anti-dogmatic. They are open to the possibility of change in all areas of life. In place of a self-righteous confirmation of loyalty to present practices, they prefer the experimental approach to life. This means that they consider they have the right and responsibility to question all present theories, practices and assumptions, all social forms, all authority, all precedent, and all institutions. It is ironical, in the light of this attitude, to find among the protesting students a small minority of political activists who fall into a dogmatic style of protest that fits better with the rigidities of the establishment they are attacking than with the experimental attitude of most of the students themselves. 'Non-negotiable demands' hold little promise of lasting change, because they represent a righteous dogmatism in place of the openness to dialogue and correction that is a crucial ingredient of reform that persists.

The tension between the values of loyalty and dissent are perhaps most clearly epitomized in the conflict between those who demand uncritical loyalty to the American government's policy of war in Indo-China and those who demonstrate their opposition to this policy by violent means. An important debate has been going on in the university on the appropriate limits of the right to dissent, especially with regard to the use of violence. The Harvard statement previously cited went on to say,

The University places special emphasis ... upon certain values which are essential to its nature as an academic community. Among these are freedom of speech and academic freedom, freedom from personal force and violence, and freedom of movement. Interference with any of these freedoms must be regarded as a serious violation of the personal rights upon which the community is based . . . Interference with members of the University in performance of their normal duties and activities must be regarded as unacceptable obstruction of the essential processes of the University. Theft or wilful destruction of the property of the University or its members must also be considered an unacceptable violation of the rights of individuals or of the community as a whole.

It is a fact that violence has been committed by university members as a way of expressing their dissent. But several points deserve clarification in this regard. In the first place, the vast majority of dissent and protest by students, faculty, and others has been non-violent. Only a tiny minority of dissenters have committed violence. Moreover, it is important to distinguish between violence against property and violence against persons. Most often violence committed by student and faculty dissenters has been against property. Most of the violence against persons has been committed by police, National Guard, and other agents of university or government authority. To student threats to property these authorities have repeatedly responded by beating and shooting, often fatally. For their part, the dissenters usually share the hierarchy of values of those in the civil rights movement, who frequently committed crimes against property as a means of protesting against what they considered more serious crimes of violence against persons.

When students dissent violently one can usually observe that the commonest cause is frustration, stemming from the fact that they have not been listened to when they have tried to speak non-violently, to reason, and to offer evidence. Some faculty and students have been suggesting for many years that university reform in several respects is long overdue. The quiet, reasonable voices of these faculty and students have had little or no effect on complacent administrators or on equally or more complacent faculty colleagues. Now, however, there is an enormous spate of discussions, committee meetings, and dialogues, involving administrators, faculty, and students. Reform is in the air. Can the dissenters be blamed for pointing out that this reform, which seemed impossible before their frustrations exploded, is now accomplished with little difficulty?

Prime targets of faculty-student dissent and protest are the Indo-Chinese war, the draft, the Reserve Officers Training Corps (ROTC), and the complicity of the university in war preparation and research. In many universities dissenters have protested against recruiting on campus by the armed forces, the Central Intelligence Agency (CIA), and industrial companies heavily or visibly engaged in war production, and against the use of university facilities or the granting of academic credit for ROTC activities.

Loyalists inside and outside the university are shocked and angered by what they consider acts and attitudes of ingratitude and disloyalty on the part of the dissenters. They believe that the university should loyally serve the nation's purpose and hence see no reason why war research should not be part of the academic enterprise. The dissenters, on the other hand, want to separate the university from any activities that they consider immoral. They think the university should take a stand on moral and political issues and declare its position publicly, even when this leads to unpopularity. A still unresolved tension exists between those who urge that the university as an institution should espouse and work for political causes and those who believe that this should be done only by members of the universities as individuals, leaving the university itself as a place where all opinions are respected and where the dialogue is protected and nurtured.

Ideology and Existential Choice

In addition to the tension between those who want to change the American university and those who resist these attempted changes, there is a deep tension and often conflict among those advocating change. The two principal groups involved in this tension might be called the ideologists and the existentialists. Such a division has clearly emerged in the student-faculty protest movement in recent years.

Increasing attempts have been made recently to infuse the protest movement with an ideological dimension. Some of these attempts have stemmed from traditional sources, like Marx, Trotsky, Lenin, and the Industrial Workers of the World; others draw upon Mao Tse-Tung, the National Liberation Front, and Fidel Castro; still others constitute reactions to significant contemporary experiences, like alienation, secularization, and bureaucratization. An important group among the ideologists is the Progressive-Labour wing of the Students for a Democratic Society. They are distinguished from most university protesters by being not only politically ideological but also authoritarian, coercive, puritanical, culturally conservative (although politically radical), ready to use violence in achieving their aims (like the Weathermen), and often unobtrusive in appearance and dress. They are also committed to the cause of achieving a worker-student alliance, a cause that demands from its supporters an enormous capacity to resist discouragement, in view of the conservative position of American workers in general and trade unions in particular. These ideologists are ready to work and suffer to bring about 'the revolution', but their values are not really revolutionary. Observing them in action leads one to conclude that their 'victory' would merely be the replacement of one authoritarian, coercive, hierarchical establishment by another. They seek a change of leadership in society rather than a fundamental change of values.

Potentially more revolutionary, but (at least in the short run) politically less effective are the existentialists among the protesters. For the most part, existentialist protesters lack blueprints and avoid utopias. They have no comprehensive answers growing automatically from an ideological base. The answers, they argue, will emerge through action. Hence, they will typically seize upon a minor grievance as the best route to major reform. Their rationale is that by attempting to alleviate a minor grievance one becomes aware of the need to reform the whole institution or society. Similarly, they refuse to plot the future in detail for those who will come after them. They want students and others in the future to be continuously engaged in creating the pattern of their time, rather than merely carrying out a plan created for them by others.

Characteristic of the stance of these existentialists in the university is their demand to have the right to do their own thing, to make their decisions in the light of their perception of the existential situation and to bear responsibility for the consequences of those decisions. Only in this way, they argue, will they grow, not through obeying the demands of the prevailing ideology. This dominant ideology is represented, they claim, in the widespread view that the university should serve the needs of business, industry, the government, and the military. The existentialist protesters reject such a concept of the university, arguing that its appropriate role is to pursue free, open-ended inquiry wherever it may lead. In this way, they say, the university will better help society to cope with the facts of change than if the university is merely a reflector of a current ideology that is necessarily the product of a vanishing past.

Most of the protesters in the university tend towards the existentialist end of the spectrum. Their lack of theoretical base or ideological system-atization makes it difficult for them to consolidate their victories, which have to be won again in every generation, on every campus, in every encounter, by every individual. Protest in the university tends to lack a strongly political dimension, except when there is vigorous repression by the authorities, at which time the ideologists gain in strength and support, to the cry of 'Smash the repressive bosses!' The ideologists depend upon men like President Grayson Kirk of Columbia, S. I. Hayakawa of San Francisco State, Governor Ronald Reagan of California, and Mayor Richard Daley of Chicago, for without the short-sighted repression of such men it would be difficult to create the widespread resentment necessary to render the protest movement responsive to ideological sloganeering.

Authority and Participation

Some observers of the American university would consider the tension between the value of authority and the value of participation to be the central tension in contemporary academic life. There is no doubt that it has never been more difficult to advocate the claims of authority with impunity. Authoritarianism has never been so consistently on the defensive. Students and younger faculty of all shades of political opinion condemn authoritarianism and the abuse of power as heinous offences. Until recently, student protests against authoritarianism were directed usually against administrators. Faculty were generally exempt from these accusations, despite their frequently archaic and authoritarian pedagogy, unjust and arbitrary grading practices, personal aloofness and inaccessibility and thinly veiled contempt for students. But now this is changing. Students are becoming increasingly impatient with such behaviour. They are recognizing that administrators are often more willing to change archaic attitudes than faculty. The apparently divine right of faculty to freedom from accusations of authoritarianism has ended.

Not only is authoritarianism in any blatant form undefended in the American university, but authority in all forms is increasingly under attack. For clarity, it is necessary to distinguish at least between the authority of status or rank and the authority of expertise. For some time, students have demanded the right to participate with those of higher assigned rank (faculty, administrators, trustees) in certain decision-making processes. More recently, however, the legitimacy of authority itself (including the authority of expertise) has been challenged by radical groups on the campus.

It is instructive to observe how rapidly change has taken place in this matter. As recently as 1959, in a thoughtful analysis of policy making in the American university, Freeman Butts[1] presented the 'liberal position' on academic policy formulation. It was that in a democratic society it is essential that those affected by a decision participate actively in making it. But when he came to list the groups that might be involved in formulating university policy, Butts included 'the board of control, the chief administrative officers, and the faculty'. Students were nowhere mentioned as a concerned group. Butts' presentation of the 'newer and more liberal position' consisted of a polite request for merely more faculty participation in policy decisions. Such a view would be widely regarded as the most timid conservatism today.

The demand for participation in decision making and the concomitant questioning of traditional forms of authority enlist different degrees of support depending upon the nature of the decision to be made. Three broad areas can be distinguished. The first is the area containing decisions relating to students' personal and social lives. It is widely held that regulations are needed for the satisfactory conduct of social life in the university but a diminishing number of institutions today would deny students a major share in making those regulations. The doctrine of *in loco parentis*, so strong and healthy only a few years ago, has suffered rapid demise.

The second area in which students are seeking to participate includes matters of university governance and policy making. Major university reports have recommended that this demand for participation should receive affirmative response. The Cox Report on Columbia University insisted that ways must be found whereby students can meaningfully influence their own education and other aspects of the university's activities. The Muscatine Report on the University of California recommended the creation of autonomous campuses at that university and greater participation for students in decisions that affect the university community, at the departmental level, on important committees, and in advising fellow students. There is a recognition, moreover, that these changes should be made not merely to forestall more student unrest but because they are essential for the students' own growth in responsibility and in order for the university to behave in consonance with its own values. Charles Muscatine has written:

> An institution devoted to free inquiry, disciplined reasoning, and uncoerced choice cannot be governed by decrees or slogans without subverting its fundamental purposes . . . governance cannot be separated from education . . . Education . . . is the primary validation of increased student participation in governance.

The third and most controversial area concerns matters of curriculum, pedagogy, course content, the appointment, promotion, and dismissal of faculty, methods of grading, and the use and allocation of university income.

In other words, these are matters on which faculty or administrators consider they have special competence, or the authority of expertise, because of experience, training, age, or special responsibility. Students are already participating to a degree in some of these decisions, but faculty and administrators seem determined to hold on to ultimate decision-making power in this area. It is unlikely, however, that demands for wider participation can be arbitrarily halted by those in authority. The process feeds upon itself. A taste of power tends to whet the appetite. As students successfully assault convention after convention, they often find that what has been long accepted as essential turns out to be merely contingent. This discovery leads to a state of mind that is ready to question all customary forms of authority and to demand that they justify themselves in rational-pragmatic terms.

Hierarchy and Equality

Related to the tension between authority and participation in the university is the tension between hierarchy and equality. The American university is by tradition a hierarchical institution, with a board of trustees at the top that hires the president, the chief executive officer, who in turn appoints deans who govern over faculties who teach, evaluate, and control students. In tension with this traditional model is an emerging model, in which the university is conceived as a teaching-learning community, where all may at times be teachers and at other times (or simultaneously) learners and hence are in a condition of rough equality.

The modes of operation in the first model are giving orders, telling, lecturing, testing, examining, and the application of fixed or slowly evolving standards. The modes of operation in the second model are collaboration, dialogue, discussion, mutual inquiry, self-evaluation, and the creation of new forms of excellence. Clearly, the second model places on the faculty greater demands, especially for intellectual flexibility and emotional strength. It is not surprising that it is often resisted by faculty.

If standards become regarded as open to change, then important questions arise with respect to the admission of students to the university. Already the stronger universities apply a whole range of selective criteria that depart radically from the traditional Grade Point Average. These criteria include evidence of organizational leadership in high school, musical talent, divergent thinking, idiosyncratic hobbies, capacity for inventing, and skin colour.

This latter, of course, is the most important variable in the list of 'other criteria'. Stories abound of admissions officers from northern universities touring the southern backwoods in search of that invaluable commodity, the talented black. In many areas, it would appear that black pressure for special admission quotas for Negroes has succeeded so well that universities must compete with one another for the inadequate supply of available blacks to meet their unfilled quotas. This leads to questions about minimum standards of entrance. If these are relaxed for blacks, why not for disadvantaged whites? And who, in a sense, is not disadvantaged? Besides, does the democratic ethos not mean that all should have an equal right to a university education? In view of the well substantiated evidence that the best hope for gaining admission to university is to grow up and go to school in an affluent neighbourhood, should this economic advantage not be removed by an admission policy that ignores the academic fruits of a privileged schooling? Not surprisingly, in a country committed, at least constitutionally, to the notion that all men are created equal, the debate continues and the tension persists.

Intellect and Emotion

The standards that many in the American university are concerned to maintain are basically intellectual. Members of the faculty, in particular, are apt to see the special function of the university as nurturing the life of the mind. Many students, on the other hand, are becoming disenchanted with the fruits of intellect, especially as seen in science and technology, and some of them place greater trust in the evidence of their emotions. They view with loathing or suspicion the intellectual efforts that have produced the hydrogen bomb, destroyed the beauty of the earth, and dehumanized people. They *feel* that it is not right and they experience no compulsion to seek intellectual substantiation for their emotional conviction.

One of the benefits of intellectual endeavour in the university has been seen as vocational-professional effectiveness and success. This still holds a strong appeal for working-class students but many from more affluent backgrounds are seeking alternatives to middle-class values. One of the values they question is a preoccupation with vocational-professional achievement at the cost of the control and rationalization of emotions. Many students favour self-expression over self-control. Their affluence has emancipated them from preoccupation with vocational success. They want a rich and expressive emotional life. If this cannot be obtained in a particular vocation, so much the worse for that vocation. This development reduces the power of the university as a vocational-professional training ground. Students are becoming increasingly sceptical about intellectual 'standards' and vocational-professional requirements. This is already appearing in the questioning of established accreditation standards in the fields of education, medicine, law, social work, nursing, engineering, and architecture. Professional schools in these fields are increasingly being called upon to justify their intellectual requirements in terms of demonstrated relevance to performance in the field.

One of the principal causes of tension between faculty and students is that most faculty members appear to students to be primarily concerned with words and numbers, with abstract, intellectual concepts, while the students increasingly find their own meanings in the concrete world of particular human relationships, of emotion and action. Faculty often criticize students for being unwilling to submit to the rigorous discipline of intellectual inquiry and too ready to respond emotionally to calls of dubious worth. Students, for their part, often hold in contempt their professors' occupation with tidy bureaucratic pedantries and with playing the intellectual, academic advancement game, and hence with no time or inclination for personal relations with students. David Riesman and Christopher Jencks, in their recent study of the American university, *The Academic Revolution*, point out that few well-known university scholars teach more than six hours per week. Many bargain for less. In other words, they use their prestige and power to bring them the kind of intellectual life-pattern they prefer, which involves a retreat from the more emotionally demanding faculty-student relations that the students themselves value as a centrally important feature of their education.

Politeness and Honesty

A dark example of the hypocrisy that characterizes American society and the American university is, for the students, the treatment of the Negro. This treatment constitutes another prime source of tension. For example, the proposal to build, without consulting the local black residents, a new university gymnasium in a Harlem park was the immediate provocation that touched off the Columbia University revolt. The Cox Report subsequently condemned Columbia University for being apparently indifferent to the needs and aspirations of its poorest neighbours. Many students active in the protest movement obtained their training and experience in the Civil Rights Movement in the South, or later, in the black ghettoes of the North. When the Black Power Movement turned the whites away, saying, 'We'll solve our *own* problems: you go and solve *yours*', the white students sought other ways to express their dissatisfaction with a society that treated the Negro so abominably and to assuage their feelings of guilt towards the black man. The arena they chose for their redirected energies was the university.

These students want to make an honest woman out of the university, to 'legitimize' it, to separate it from its phony practices. Professors for years have been mouthing great liberal principles. It is not clear whether they expected anyone to take them seriously. The principles were to be copied down into notebooks and regurgitated at examination time. But now these students are not only taking the principles seriously but, even more alarming, *applying* them in practice.

In his recent study of some of these student activists, entitled *Young Radicals*. Kenneth Keniston attributed their radicalism partly to their upbringing by the first generation of 'modern' parents, who raised their children in the 1940s and 1950s, when permissive child-rearing and pedagogical practices were strongly in vogue. The activists coming from this kind of upbringing, Keniston found, are unusually stable, mature, and socially responsible. Moreover, they are *not* alienated from their parents, but are much closer to their parents than are nonactivists. They see themselves as carrying on from their parents a liberal tradition, which includes such values as racial equality, political freedom, and thinking for oneself. The difference is, however, that the parents are often liberals in *words only*; the children are liberals in action. That is, the children practise what the parents preach.

The university, these students argue, must make its own administrative practices consistent with the standards of honesty that it claims to uphold in the realm of scholarship. Hence, they would endorse the argument in favour of honest and open discussion contained in the Muscatine Report:

It is vital that the university conduct its own decision-making process with equal devotion to the principles it applies in scholarly contexts: open inquiry, reasoned justification of conclusions, and the submission of findings to public evaluation and criticism. Deviation from these norms undermines the character of life in the university by positing a double standard between the concerns of governance and the concerns of scholarship.

Objective Knowledge and Personal Relevance

An important tension in the contemporary American university arises out of challenges to the traditional academic goals of the search for truth and the transmission of this truth through teaching. In defence of this view, it is maintained that the university's central purpose is lost if it departs from the traditional procedures of seeking objective evidence, following the argument wherever it leads, suppressing personal bias and prejudice, and reducing subjective distortion as much as possible. Especially valued is the scientific approach of trying to make general laws out of particular instances, looking for universals, and creating generalizations out of individual experience so that transfer of the learning to other situations is possible.

Now, however, this traditional attitude is under attack for several reasons. Many students, for example, are opposed to pedagogy that hands down supposedly objective truth from above and as a corollary removes student initiative and stifles student criticism. They want to explore the world for themselves and they often have more confidence in personal knowledge, gained by first-hand experience, than in public knowledge gained by scientific inquiry. Science is thus viewed with scepticism because its enterprise is isolated from human emotion and it fails to concern itself with man as a whole being. It purports to be able to study man by abstracting and objectifying but, they maintain, this inevitably brings a falsity to the picture of man. Moreover, many students, especially on the Left, are suspicious of the supposed objectivity of the scientific method and they want to expose the hidden ideology in scientific teaching.

Another criticism of the established mode of the university is that it has become, in the eyes of many protesting students and some faculty, an academic ritual. That is, the educational process is regarded as a sort of academic game, in which the counters are credits, grades, and class attendance; the moves are (for the faculty member) getting through the curriculum, covering the ground, and, if possible, getting the students to do some of his research for him, and (for the student) 'psyching out' the teacher, making a good impression on him, and persuading him that you are brighter and harder working than you really are; and the prizes are promotion and more money for the faculty member, and a degree, and hence higher income, for the student.

In place of this dishonest and unattractive ritual these students want to institute educational relevance, in the sense that their educational experiences should carry personal meaning and significance in terms of their own lives in the concrete world. In addition, critical faculty and students claim that the university's impact is not sufficiently relevant to social, economic, political, and educational problems right on its own doorstep. For example, university administrations are rarely interested (unless they smell a prospective federal research grant) in the fact that the university lies in a racially segregated area, or amidst an urban slum.

It appears that this tension will continue to exist, especially between, on the one hand, those critical students who want their education to make a personal difference to their lives and to the solution of problems they consider crucial to the health of society rather than to be merely an age-old ritual that they obediently follow to the goal of a higher income, and, on the other hand, those defenders of the traditional academic point of view that the university best serves as an agent of creative change not by seeking relevance to individual lives or contemporary issues but by a steady loyalty to the quest for unbiased knowledge and objective truth.

Continuity and Change

The important value changes taking place in contemporary America and in the university affect different people in diverse ways. In general, young people are more amenable to these changes than older people. For the most part, the former are more flexible in their viewpoints and attitudes. Moreover, their experiences have been vastly different from those of their elders. For the latter, change has been something whose significance one could absorb gradually, like the invention of the airplane or radio. For young people, however, change has always been part of the constant current of their lives, creating a dynamic tension that affects everything they do.

Moreover, many young students hold a radically different notion of time from that which is conventional in the university. For most university scholars and teachers, what is important is the past: this is the source of all our knowledge, certainty, and wisdom. For many students, the important time is the present: this is the source of all our experience, awareness, and potentiality. Hence, while the focus of concern in the university has customarily been on tradition and continuity, the emphasis of a large body of the students is on change and innovation.

The university has concentrated on teaching about the past, and on persuading students to study, understand and respect the past. But the emerging value among many students is a primary concern with the here and now. Typically, the university bends its efforts and students to the tasks of studying, explicating, and making exegeses and commentaries on significant texts of the past. But an increasing number of students lack reverence for these texts. There is no *a priori* veneration in the attitude with which they approach the task of evaluating all texts, whether old or new, classical or obscure, foreign or domestic. They lack the antique collector's view of texts, that age enhances value. Unawed by the great names of past scholars, they want to submit all received truths, opinions, judgments, even the idea of the university itself, to the pragmatic test of present usefulness, relevance, and satisfaction.

In tension with such emerging values, the traditional values of the university are voiced by faculty who warn that change is not synonymous with progress, that it is a disadvantage to be moving fast if you are going in the wrong direction, and that there are serious and perhaps irreparable losses to be faced if certain vital continuities are broken. Yet an increasing number of students and younger faculty aim to use the university as a deliberate instrument of social change. Sceptical of the value of most past attempts to solve the problems that concern them, they often hold in higher regard some radical contemporary attempts, about which the university conventionally does not teach. Moreover, they want to be involved themselves in the enterprise of change. Not content to accept traditional notions of what the university is, they want to change it into an institution that they judge to have functional relevance to the amelioration or solution of significant present problems.

Conclusion

In the light of this analysis, what can be suggested about the future of the university in the United States? It seems highly likely that all the tensions discussed above will continue to exist and to exert their influence on the atmosphere of the university. Although this does not presage tranquillity on campus it holds at least a promise of creative change. Many of the emerging values described here seem to represent greatly needed correctives to traditional imbalances in the university. It is essential that the university explore new roles for itself, new uses of knowledge, and new syntheses of some of these tensions. The place of emotion in education, for example, seems inevitably to be going to receive more serious attention than in the past. Into the university from the field of human relations are coming important insights into ways to relate the cognitive and affective dimensions of experience and learning.

Furthermore, many young critics are presenting demands that constitute a reminder to the university of some of its most central values. Their emphasis on honesty, for example, can be seen as an echo of the traditional role of the university as the seeker after truth. Student protesters often feel alienated from many features of the contemporary American university. But the values they espouse are not alien: they stem from the finest elements of the Western cultural tradition. However, these values are often not practised. They are, admittedly, very difficult to practise. The students, in their disturbing way, are demanding that the university either start applying these values or stop getting free kudos by merely paying ritualistic lip-service to them.

But there are dangers in these encounters also. The greatest danger to the university – as to society – lies in increased polarization of these tensions. This happens most frequently when people take a simplistic view of their problems. Hence, one way to avoid greater polarization is to help both sides to face honestly the complexities of the situation. The alternatives are seen when polarization leads to loss of communication, which in turn leads to fear and hatred, the outcomes of which we have witnessed at Kent State University, Jackson State College, and elsewhere.

Change is essential for the very survival of the university. If the tension and dialogue between confronting groups do not lead to genuine change in the university, this will be a defeat for both sides, because the subsequent violence, chaos, and disruption on the campus will give federal and local law enforcement agencies apparent justification for moving in with sufficiently repressive measures to snuff out *all* protest and dissent. When that happens, the university as the principal home of creative, divergent, critical thought can hardly survive.

The survival of the American university is dependent upon the creative resolution of these tensions through genuine dialogue between those who safeguard the traditional values and those who are energized by the emerging values. The older members of the university community are mostly products of a pre-figurative culture (where children learn from adults). They conceive the present in terms of the past. But the younger members are mostly products of a post-figurative culture (where adults also learn from children), for the pace of change is now so rapid that we are all somewhat like immigrants in a strange land, where children are often the first to become in tune with the new situation and hence become the teachers of their parents. The young are often ready for social bull-dozing, wiping away all vestiges of what is, in order to make possible what should be. They are ready for radical breaks with the past and the creation of completely new forms.

However, in order to effect change without bloody conflict, there must be collaboration between those who hold power and those who seek change. No one has infallible answers to the problems facing the American university. Recognition of this can be the beginning of wise decision making, for the groups in tension can work together to find good answers if they will listen to each other. Many students are convinced that the university and society must be changed, but they usually lack the skill and knowledge to change them. This is the opportunity for a genuine collaboration between young and old, where both learn and both teach. The young, who are equipped by their age and experience to understand the nature of the contemporary world, can teach the old how to frame significant and relevant questions, while the old, who are equipped by their age and training to find answers, can teach the young the skills and knowledge needed to bring about the changes the world requires.

NOTES

1. R. Freeman Butts, 'Formulation of Policy in American Colleges and Universities', *Higher Education: The Year Book of Education, 1959,* (ed.) George Z. F. Bereday and Joseph A. Lauwerys (Yonkers on Hudson, New York: World Book Company, 1959), pp. 246–63.

23

Emerging National Policies for Higher Education in Canada

Reginald Edwards

The Dominion of Canada came into being on July 1, 1867, created by an Act of the British Parliament in Westminster, with the support and connivance of the Colonial Office of moves initiated within the British American colonies. Canada was to be governed by a Parliament in Ottawa, with the Queen, Senate and House of Commons as its three branches. It began as a federal, economic union among four colonies, the least number which could ensure viability. Those who worked to create Confederation had to take cognizance, on the one hand, of the culture, language, religion and institutions of Quebec, and, on the other, the suspicions of the powerful neighbour to the south, the United States, only recently emerged from a bloody civil war involving a constitution and the rights of individual states and already proclaiming 'Manifest Destiny'. Because of the former only a federal, and not a legislative union was possible; because of the latter, the central government had to be made much more powerful than the local governments, which, in turn, must not possess residuary powers. The powers of each, at the insistence of the Canadians, must be spelled out; in the drafting of the Act by the law officers of the Crown in Westminster the word 'exclusively' was introduced to make their respective functions quite explicit. Under this Constitution, as subsequently amended by Britain at Canada's request, by Canada, and by provincial parliaments, Canada still functions. Her obsessions are still those concerning Quebec and the United States.

The economic customs union was made possible financially by the relief of provincial debts and the payment of subsidies from central funds. These payments were on a per-capita basis, requiring a decennial census, to be carried out by the Department of Agriculture (for was not Canada destined to be an agricultural economy?). Local government was given exclusive control of matters not then thought important, including education, highways and public health and welfare. Concurrent legislative control existed only for agriculture and immigration, and here the legislation of the central government would prevail. The provincial government could not delegate powers to the central government though the central government might delegate powers to the provinces, but anything requiring a re-sharing of legislative responsibility would require a modification of the British North America Act, which, in this respect, remains largely as an Act of the British Parliament. In England Parliament is supreme. Its laws can be interpreted by the judiciary but not altered nor rejected. In Canada Parliament is not supreme and its own Acts might be declared *ultra vires* by its own Supreme Court, or, presumably, by a lesser court in the first instance.

Constitutional Provisions

A separate section of the Act, Section 93, dealt specifically with education, beginning as follows:

'In and for each Province, the Legislature may exclusively make laws in relation to Education, subject and according to the following provisions . . .'

Then follow clauses dealing with the rights of individuals to denominational, or separate, or dissentient schools, such rights to be protected by the Federal government, but with no further reference to Education, *per se*. In the work leading up to the Act, an attempt had been made, at the first meeting in Charlottetown, by the Lieutenant Governor of New Brunswick, to place the universities under the control of the central government. The modification with respect to religious minorities was introduced at the second, or Quebec meeting, which followed, and, at the London meeting which preceded the drafting of the Act, the four provinces had agreed to concurrent legislative powers over education, though this did not appear in the Act as presented to Parliament. Constitutionally the making of laws concerning education and schools lies solely with the provinces, and it is generally believed that it is respect for this constitutional provision which has prevented Canada from setting up any Federal Office of Education, notwithstanding that in the United States the precursor of the Federal Office of Education was created legislatively prior to Canada's Dominion status. Currently, descriptions of education in Canada tend to treat the similarities among provinces as evidence of a national character, with education in Quebec treated as an exception due to pre-Confederation historical causes, and that of Newfoundland, admitted to Confederation in 1949, due to the terms of the Union between Canada and Newfoundland at that time.

The major tenet of the Constitutional location of Education, Highways, and Public Health and Welfare under local control was the concept of local administration as a limited, fairly static operation, 'as little costly as possible'. Events were to prove otherwise. In 1867 these three, education, highways and public health and welfare, expended 12·7 million dollars, out of total (local and central) government expenditures of 25 million dollars. By 1937 these had risen to 648 million out of a total of one billion dollars, i.e. from approximate equality to the point where local expenditures almost doubled those of the central government. The financial arrangement reached at Confederation had been challenged almost from its inception; the remedy adopted then, the payment of subsidies, has become a continuing feature of dominion-provincial relations.

The validity of the concept of a viable economic union demands, for individuals, equal access to employment, and for provincial governments equal tax bases. Only then can a local government provide the services equal to those provided in other parts of Canada. Events have generally favoured the central provinces, particularly Ontario, as opposed to the Maritime or the Prairie Provinces. Currently British Columbia, Alberta and Ontario appear to be the 'have' provinces, the other the 'have nots', though to different degrees. Earlier, when the Depression years had brought the Prairie provinces to the verge of bankruptcy this was sufficient to produce the war time (1940) amendment of the British North America Act to place Unemployment Insurance among the classes of subjects under the jurisdiction of Ottawa, leaving the relief of the unemployables to the provinces and municipalities. Thus the government of Canada, with provincial consent, was able to both amend and retain the Constitution, but to re-adjust the respective financial burdens. A further subsidy was provided to the provinces in return for a provincial withdrawal from certain tax fields.

During the 1950s the financial needs of the universities, and the cost of a trans-continental highway system, and during the 1960s the continuing needs of all kinds and types of education, but more particularly post-secondary and adult, together with the needs for publicly subsidized health schemes (Medicare), have been raised at Dominion-Provincial Conferences again under the topic of fiscal jurisdiction and tax-sharing agreements. It is within such Constitutional negotiations that a Federal government must operate with respect to education.

It may not make laws concerning education, except for Indians, Eskimos, military personnel, the children of military personnel serving overseas, federal penitentiary inmates and inhabitants of the North West Territories. It is the protector of the legal rights of dissentient minorities. It may pay subsidies directly to a province without specifying their use; it may make funds available, and with the consent of the provinces, permit their use for specific purposes, including education. It may enter into arrangements with provinces to 'purchase' or 'rent' educational services. It may make grants of money to individuals and institutions for purposes of research; it may provide assistance to individuals, by bursary, scholarship or loan, which may be used for educational purposes. All these have been demonstrated. It is even conceivable that if a purpose could be defined which transcends provincial boundaries, the provision of the Act 'in and for each Province' may also be transcended and some form of Federal Office of Education, with accompanying powers, could also be created. Such transcending of provincial boundaries was obvious in the Federal payments made for the construction of a Trans-Canada Highway, and in the initiation of medicare schemes, though any province was left free to accept or decline the money available.

Historical Background to Current Debates

Historians looking backward may see events in perspective and postulate a continuity of development of which governments initiating legislation would have been unaware. Even politicians discussing legislation could only point to the past, then to the present legislation and by extrapolation raise sufficient doubts about the future as to cloud the present legislative issue. Governments for their part have election campaigns, Throne Speeches, Orders in Council, and Royal Commissions of Enquiry as means of creating a climate of public opinion favourable to their aims. Quasi-official bodies, created or supported by governments, may make pronouncements favourable to government intentions. The right of government appointment, a form of political patronage, may also work in directing the activities of 'independent' state-supported agencies in directions consonant with government desires. Favourable climates of public opinion facilitate the initiation of actions which governments desire but for which they previously lacked the courage to execute. There are two classes of legislation likely to affect higher education, that of Provincial and Federal Governments respectively. The latter is most likely to be financial in nature, and whilst Federal money has made possible the continued existence of some universities which might otherwise have disappeared, it has not otherwise seriously and directly affected the autonomy of the universities themselves. Such threats to autonomy are more likely to be perceived in Provincial legislation. In higher education the denominational nature of its provision in a college or university often precluded the institution from receiving financial aid from either government. The early non-denominational institutions, Dalhousie at Halifax (1818) and McGill in Montreal (1821), were equally precluded from obtaining such financial support by legislative decision of the two legislatures. On the other hand the endowment which the Royal Charter granted to King's College, York (now Toronto), in 1827 was revoked by the Assembly of the United Canadas in 1849 in order to create the non-denominational, publicly supported University of Toronto. Again, the Presbyterian inspired Queen's University at Kingston, was also granted a Royal Charter in 1842, but since 1912 has been chartered by the Federal Government in Ottawa. It is perhaps worthy of note that official reporting in the Canada Year Books prior to 1920 spoke of these four, McGill, Toronto, Dalhousie and

Queen's, as being Canada's only 'ranking universities'. Since Confederation the vast majority of universities have charters granted by their provincial government. Occasionally a denominational college in one province elects to be affiliated with a university chartered in another province, but does not receive financial support from the host province.

Federal presence in the field of education began with the creation of the Military College in 1876, the title Royal being added later. This was 'the first (military) academy to be established in the self-governing colonies, and one that emphasized a civilian rather than a strictly professional military education' for Canadian defence was the function of a militia rather than of a standing army. Emphasis was placed on the study of engineering and preparation for civil employment in business, law or politics after completion of the four year course. Today RMC is a duly chartered Ontario university, with the right to grant degrees in arts, science and engineering. Before the recent integration of the three Armed Services, all applicants for commissioned rank in the Canadian army had to possess a degree, as did most of those in the Navy or Air Force.

The establishment of a Royal Commission to enquire into technical education in 1910, and the Agricultural Instruction Act of 1913 (designed as a form of aid to agriculture where there was concurrent legislative power) were the first serious moves. Support for technical education came from the Act of 1919, and following an Order in Council giving power to the Federal Government to order 'treatment and training' to returning soldiers, extended this power amongst adults or those who had left school. The Rowell-Sirois Royal Commission of 1937 looked at the crisis in Federal-Provincial financial relations and led to the setting up of an Unemployment Insurance Fund. It rejected grants for elementary and secondary education and stated a case for a university's need for 'assurance of a moderately stable budget over a reasonable period of time', recognized that the 'provinces might welcome a small Dominion grant to their universities made contingent on the maintenance over a period of some years of the provincial grants to the same institution and on the preservation of high academic standards'. It did not recommend such payments, but thought of such grants being divided among the provinces in rough proportion to their populations, being spent at the discretion of the universities, possibly 'to provide scholarships and bursaries which would bring its opportunities within the reach of poor but able students'. It commented favourably on the Dominion government's educational work of organizing scientific research under the National Research Council and suggested that it would be an advantage to have a Social Science Research Council, which could co-ordinate work done in those areas. Finally it was prepared to be sympathetic towards the creation of a national library, which Canada at that time did not possess. Of course, it made no recommendations which would have contributed to the realization of such worthy objectives. Governments and universities are alike in their adherence to the Cornford dictum that nothing should ever appear to be done for the first time; in the context of education the Rowell-Sirois Report did nothing, but perhaps it did say things for the first time.

War-time and Post-war Developments

The emergency of the Second World War enabled many actions to be taken with respect to war preparations and training which strengthened the Federal presence in education. Physical Fitness, Youth Training, and Vocational and Technical Training were Acts which allowed both payments and some direction to be given to education. From the point of view of universities the most significant, but least publicized action was the Order in Council of October 1, 1941, which, *inter alia*, provided a weekly payment to any ex-serviceman beginning or continuing a university course, and payment, on his behalf, of the necessary university fees. Its effect was to produce a crisis in the universities, since numbers subsequently increased, operating costs increased and fees were insufficient to meet operating costs. Prior to this, fees, endowments and the occasional small subsidy had enabled most universities to meet operating budgets, except in the Depression years. Post-war legislation, incorporating the Order in Council, enabled the federal government to pay an annual subsidy of $150 for each student. Lest a university represented this as the fixed per student share of overheads, and used increased fees to pay operating expenses the law was subsequently modified to fix a maximum government contribution of $500 per year, fees and subsidy, per student. The universities were perceived as having rendered a national service, but the form of payment had precluded any one of them from improving its financial position.

Enrolment in the universities which had risen from 23,000 in 1920 to 36,000 in 1940, continued more spectacularly in the 1940s, reaching a peak of 83,000 in 1948. Of these some 35,000 were war veterans. The other portion of the increase was due to a general increase of population, and to a fact not then appreciated, the pressure of rising social expectations. During this period the average university expenditure per student enrolled fell from $515 to $433, despite inflationary pressures, which, until then had been held in check by war-time and transitional powers of the government. The financial task placed upon universities was greater than their resources could meet.

The government, in 1949, believing 'that it is desirable that the Canadian people should know as much as possible about their country, its history and traditions, and about their national life and common achievements;

that it is in the national interest to give encouragement to institutions that express national feeling, promote common understanding and add to the variety and richness of Canadian life', had appointed a Royal Commission to enquire into the activities of existing federal agencies which contributed to the national life, and asked it to make recommendations as to their most effective conduct. Under prodding from such bodies as the Social Science Research Council (founded in 1940 and supported with Carnegie and Rockefeller funds), the Humanities Research Council (1943, with similar support), the National Research Council and the National Conference of Canadian Universities, the Massey Commission, consisting of four academics and a civil engineer, agreed that the universities were too important a national institution to be ignored. They further agreed with the submission of the NCCUC. 'The work of the Canadian Universities is of vital and continuing importance to national development in the Arts, Letters and Sciences, to such an extent that this would be jeopardized or crippled if the activities of the universities were curtailed.'

On presentation of the report, the government decided to make a payment to the universities equal to fifty cents per head of population, to be distributed in each province among the universities in proportion to their enrolment. This ensured a payment for each student of about $120 to $130, the amounts varying from province to province. After the first disbursement the universities of Quebec were forbidden to accept the money, on the grounds that the action was an infringement of provincial rights. Despite this, the government continued to make such payments to the other provinces, but it took no other action on the Massey Commission report until 1956. At a meeting of National Conference of Canadian Universities and Colleges that year the Prime Minister, Mr St Laurent, announced that the per capita payments would be increased to $1, which brought the average per student payment to the universities to $220. He said that the NCCUC should hold Quebec's share until such time as Quebec would accept it, and informed the Conference that his government was to establish the Canada Council for the Encouragement of the Arts, Letters and Sciences, which it did on March 28, 1957. It appointed a former professor of law, and former Minister of Health, of National Defence, and Secretary of State, the Hon. Brooke Claxton, as its first chairman, a very fortunate choice.

At the same meeting the Prime Minister, in turn, was informed that university enrolment would double between 1954–5 and 1964–5 to about 130,000 students. This projection was based almost completely on the basis of earlier birth rates and increasing retention in secondary schools. In fact it doubled in seven years and by 1964–5 had reached 178,000. The present enrolment is about 355,000 and the projected figure for 1975–6 is 460,000. The average per student expenditure of the universities has risen from $1,072 in 1955–6, to $1,443 in 1959–60, to $1,550 in 1960–1, reached $2,968 in 1967–8 and is probably about $3,200 for 1970–1. Since student fees have been only slightly increased over recent years they represent a diminishing proportion of the total cost of a university education, currently about 20 per cent. Subsequently the per capita payments were to be raised, first to $1·50, then to $2·00 and finally to $5·00. Even so the average per student payment rose only to $283 and finally to $479.

When the Canada Council was established it was given two funds – one a Universities Capital Grants Fund, and the other an Endowment Fund, each of $50 million. The former, now fully expended, was to be used for grants to building projects, the university providing matching funds. Because of successful investment during the spending period this fund ensured over $120 million worth of buildings. The second fund could be invested in non-government stocks and bonds, and the income was to be used to provide support of the arts, letters and social sciences and humanities. It has been given funds also by other educational trust funds, by legacies, and by industry. The income has been disbursed and the capital retained intact. In addition it received in 1965 a government grant of $10 million, two thirds of which had to be spent in that year, and a further grant of $17 million for the following year. It currently disburses about $30 million in support of the arts, including music, painting and dramatic arts, the humanities and social sciences. It has been particularly effective in the support of doctoral students, as well as those in career appointments and senior university appointments. Fifteen per cent of all student support has gone to those studying history, 14 per cent for English, 11 per cent for economics, 10 per cent each to political science and philosophy, 8 per cent each to French and sociology, with 5 per cent to social psychology. Meanwhile the National Research Council and the Defence Research Board have subsidized research in the physical and biological sciences to an even greater extent. There is no doubt that the Canada Council has contributed greatly to the creation of many of the university teachers necessary to sustain the expansion of Canadian universities.

A number of the independent events of 1960 are significant in the emergence of a Canadian policy concerning higher education. In the first place the government of Quebec negotiated an agreement with the federal government, which secured from them funds for higher education, whilst maintaining Quebec's position on provincial autonomy in education. They did not accept federal money, but instead took several percentage points of the yield of taxes on corporations, a tax levied by both the Quebec and the federal governments. This released a great deal of money and set the scene for later dealings between the two levels of government. In the second place, after a change of government in Quebec following a provincial election, a Quebec cabinet minister attended a meeting of the

Canadian Education Association, the first such representation for over twenty years. It enabled the Ministers of Education to establish a Standing Committee of Ministers of Education, which was later to become, in 1967, the Inter-provincial Council of Ministers of Education, a formidable body designed to represent provincial rights in education. The third event was the federal modification of provisions for vocational training, the Technical and Vocational Training Assistance Act of December 1960. This made it possible to provide training facilities (buildings, physical plant, machinery and equipment) for 'the training of persons in technical or vocational courses given in regular secondary schools in the province where such training is given as part of the regular secondary schools programme'. Grants were either 50 per cent or 75 per cent of the cost. The Act was designed to remain in force for six years and gave a needed impetus to technical training in the secondary schools, particularly in Ontario which took liberal advantage of the scheme. The opposition to the Act, in Parliament, was not on the grounds of interference with a constitutional right, but on the grounds that it was designed for the relief of unemployment indirectly, rather than fulfilling a general election pledge for the rapid reduction of unemployment in Canada as a whole. The forecast expiry of the Act in 1966 was to become quite significant.

Commissions of Enquiry

On the provincial scene many provinces initiated enquiries, or Royal Commissions of Enquiry, into education generally or higher education specifically. Virtually every province reported one such enquiry between 1950 and 1968. Probably the commission headed by Monseignor Parent, reporting on education in Quebec, was the most thorough in its operation and the most far-reaching in its effects. The Byrne Commission and the Deutsch Commission in New Brunswick were responsible for the almost total remodelling of education in that province. On the national scene the federally appointed Royal Commission on Bilingualism and Biculturalism had a most vital part to play in suggesting means of securing national unity with cultural diversity, though its creation was attributed in political circles as part of a debt owed to a former Secretary of State, left undefended on other issues by his colleagues in the government. Out of its report has come the immediate creation of a $50 million fund for the teaching of minority languages in the officially designated bicultural areas, the fund being under the control of the Department of the Secretary of State. Whilst not an educational enquiry the Hall Commission enquiring into medical services has led to the creation of a $500 million fund for the provisions of facilities for the training of medical and para-medical personnel, and for medical research. Much of this will filter through the universities, and not merely their medical schools. But, on the other hand, rising expenditures on health could mean less for education. Current total expenditures on health are nearly $4 billion and on education are $6 billion some 15 per cent of the gross national product, a proportion which has more than doubled since 1930. Health care and higher education are likely to take up one dollar out of every six of the total increase in income in the next five years, and if the rate of increase of the past five years is extrapolated to the year 2000, these two would consume the whole of the estimated gross national product at that time.

Despite the importance of the foregoing, the report of the Commission set up in 1963 by the Association of Universities and Colleges of Canada (the successor to the NCCUC) on 'Financing Higher Education in Canada' has been even more influential. It was 'to study and report and make recommendations on the financing of universities and colleges of Canada with particular reference to the decade ending in 1975'. Its cost was largely borne by a grant from the Ford Foundation. Its report, issued in 1965, made the following five recommendations –

(1) That the Federal and Provincial Governments undertake to provide for the expansion of higher education in Canada on the scale of the Sheffield projection. (These figures have been given above.)

(2) That the Federal Government initiate annual discussions with the Provincial Governments to review the adequacy of the federal contribution to the cost of higher education; but that federal support be in a form which avoids any invasion of the provincial right, and obligation, to direct and control such education.

(3) That the Federal Government assign responsibility for co-ordination of assistance to universities from all its agencies to a Minister of the Crown.

(4) That such Minister establish a small advisory committee mainly consisting of senior professors from various regions and disciplines, and appoint a senior civil servant as secretary of that Committee and as organizer of the proposed annual discussion with the provinces.

(5) That the financial problems of the universities are so urgent that action to resolve them should be taken without delay.

Seldom, if ever, can the recommendations of a non-government, externally financed body have been accepted so readily. Each recommendation was implemented within the next twelve months, though the results may well be other than those intended by the commissioners. The probable reasons are certainly highly important for both federal-provincial relations and for the 'provincialization of higher education', as it has been termed, in Canada. They are to be found in the brevity and elegance of the report itself; in the date of its release in October 1965; the election campaign promises of the same month; the first and second reports of the federally appointed Economic Council of Canada of December 1964 and 1965, emphasizing the development of Canada's human resources and the part to be played by higher education in such development; the accession of strength in a nonetheless minority government, particularly in the form of three exceptionally able Quebec recruits; in the pressure of federal ministers and civil servants for some federal 'presence' to oppose the tactics of provincial Ministers of Education *vis-à-vis* information, accountability and power; and, finally, in the decision of the federal government to withdraw from shared cost programmes with provincial governments.

Government Action

The Throne Speech of January 1966 outlined the form of action which the government proposed to take, utilizing phrases, expressions and ideas from those various sources. The per capita allowance was raised from $2 to $5 and distributed on the basis of a weighted formula – the first change from simple proportional distribution. The importance and cost of graduate students and extra-provincial students were taken into consideration. Twelve Acts which affected higher education, directly or indirectly, were passed. An early one, the Government Organization Act, made the largest changes in the government of Canada in peace time. It created a Department of Manpower and Immigration, giving it control of 'the development and utilization of the manpower resources of Canada'; it established the Department of Indian Affairs and Northern Development, which was charged with 'fostering through scientific investigations and technology, knowledge of the Canadian north'; and in other sections encouraged research and development in many aspects of Canadian life, giving incentives for research in rural and urban life, industrial and agricultural development. A change in the duties allocated to the Secretary of State made her responsible for 'the encouragement of the literary, visual and performing arts, learning and cultural activities'. Parliament was asked if this was tantamount to creating a Federal Office of Education, as a pre-debate newspaper report had alleged. If so, members would have preferred it to be placed under the control of the Department of Manpower. Some observers suggested that it was placed with the Secretary of State to prevent too great an accession of power to the Department of Manpower.

The campaign pledge to create 10,000 university scholarships was vetoed by the Minister of Finance, but amendments to the Student Loan Act permitted students to borrow $1,000 per year, to a maximum of $5,000, with the government guaranteeing the loan and paying the interest charges until six months after graduation, at which point the student's liability for repayment began. Since Banks and Banking fall within federal jurisdiction this seemed to offer no problem, save that Quebec operated its own scheme with students dealing directly with its own Ministry of Education and not the banks. In Quebec the Minister specifies the universities at which attendance is acceptable for holders of bursaries or loans. At the undergraduate levels these are Quebec universities. Elsewhere in Canada there is no restriction on the part of the student as to the university he attends.

The previous minority government had believed that its activities had been characterized by 'flexibility'. Other observers spoke of weakness, of a lack of resolution, even of a 'creeping paralysis'. But at least for 1966 this was changed. Nowhere was this more apparent than in the decision to end shared-cost programmes, first made clear at the federal-provincial conferences, ostensibly on higher education, held in October 1966. The provincial premiers were reported to have left the meeting 'equalized in unhappiness'. Legislation introduced four days later transferred to the provinces 'four points of personal income tax and one point of corporate income tax to make it easier for the provinces to secure the revenues they require'. In return they took responsibility, or were required to accept responsibility, for higher education and for much of technical and vocational training. The fiscal transfer would amount to 50 per cent of operating costs, or for some provinces $15 per head of population. Although the grants were based upon operating costs, as defined in the agreement, and for the whole of post-secondary education, they were meant to provide capital costs also, as the Minister of Finance clearly indicated. Provincial returns of operating costs would have to be made to the Federal government. Internally, it might be possible for a university, with provincial consent, to borrow money for buildings and equipment and to amortize the total out of recurrent, provincial, operating grants.

Provincialism

This arrangement was part of a new 'co-operative federalism' without the initiative being specified. Some provinces saw it as a move for the federal government to dictate social policy and have the provinces pay for it, though the greater reaction on this score arose against a federal decision to pay 50 per cent of costs of approved medical schemes, the federal share being paid by a Social Development charge, a federal surcharge on personal income tax. Provincial governments were already involved in post-secondary education, especially higher education; they were not, at that time, with the exception of Saskatchewan, involved in Medicare. It might even be seen as the precursor of greater federal authority, as the provinces became increasingly unable to bear the costs – a return to a previous phase of dominion-provincial relations. To many it was only a fiscal transfer and not a genuine cost sharing; to one province at least it allowed universities to become involved in federal-provincial matters on aspects of education formerly completely controlled by ministers of education and their departments. Some academics perceived it as the first step in a process which eventually hands over undergraduate education to provincial ministries of education.

It would be foolish to pretend that the 'provincialization of higher education' began only at this point. To the extent that there had been any serious planning for higher education earlier, it had been done by universities or provincial departments of education, acting either alone or in concert. By and large, 'independent' universities which were to be found in Quebec and the east, and received little or no provincial support, fixed policies of admission in relation to income. Provincially controlled universities which were found largely in Ontario and to the west undertook the most rapid expansion with provincial support. Since 1960 each province has been forced to make plans for dealing with its one or more universities, so that now all provinces, save Saskatchewan and Newfoundland, which each possess only a single university, have a University Grants Commission or equivalent. Quebec has a Director General of Higher Education and has legislated for a Conseil des Universités, an advisory body, lay and academic, with all appointments made directly by the Minister. Ontario, which has gone the furthest in organizing these matters, created a Ministry of University Affairs as early as 1964. It has a Committee of Presidents of the Universities of Ontario, just as Quebec has a Comité des Recteurs et Principaux; it has a Committee on University Affairs, with academic and lay personnel. In Ontario the university professors have felt constrained to organize the Ontario Council of University Faculty Associations; in Quebec there is Le Fédération des Associations de Professeurs d'Université du Québec. Each province has a separate provincial student organization, though, until recently, the Ontario region remained affiliated with the Canadian Union of Students.

When financial support of the universities depends upon the raising of taxes some form of planning must exist. The first problem is one of deciding how much of a province's resources must be, or can be, allocated for higher education, taking into account all other responsibilities of government. The second problem is that of the expenditure and allocation of the money once voted. A third one, which took precedence in Canada, was how would the money be raised and who would raise it. The first is clearly not the function of the university, except for its continued need to press a socially and economically justifiable claim. The second raises the shibboleths of academic freedom, university autonomy and financial accountability. The first two are often expressed as 'the control of who teaches what, and to whom', or, if you will, appointment of staff, admission of students, curriculum and standards. University freedom also covers the determination of the balance between research and teaching, determination of policy related to the development of its own institution, and the internal allocation of funds once received.

Although these six aspects can be stated separately they are not independent of each other. Staff appointments are conditional upon the presence of funds, and the rank at which an appointment is made may be determined by the amount of funds available. This is particularly true of Quebec's universities at the present time. More recently, staff appointments have been subject to the influence of both a campaign to recruit more Canadians as university teachers and student pressure to be represented upon appointment committees, or even to control appointments, promotions and tenure. Standards for the admission of students are related to overall numbers and to funds available. A student's availability is also related to his possibility of obtaining a student loan or scholarship. Twenty-five per cent of Canadian undergraduate students are from families whose income exceeds $10,000, 45 per cent from those which exceed $7,000. On the other hand 9 per cent come from the poorest families earning less than $3,000 (a figure believed to mark the poverty line) and 22 per cent below $5,000. Forty-one per cent of students now have loans, but loans may well help those who need it least. Again, the loan programme may seriously deplete the number of female students from the middle and lower income families, since the necessity to repay to a bank an educational loan is regarded as a 'negative dowry' at marriage. There are moves to replace the loan plan by the creation of an Educational Opportunity Bank whereby every student on entering university is given an automatic credit for a certain amount of money each year, to be repaid by the addition of a 1 per cent (or more) surcharge on personal income tax paid during the next thirty years.

Admission standards are increasingly going to be related to educational levels determined by provincial ministries of education. The 1966 Act concerns the education of those possessing junior matriculation, which will have the meaning given to it by each province separately. There is also a move to abolish examinations related to matriculation requirements, and to set up a College Board type of examination for the whole of Canada, using Canadian rather than United States material, a move initiated by the Ministers of Education. Ontario has provided an alternate route to the university by two years' attendance in a non-university post-secondary institution instead of by attendance through Grade XIII; Quebec requires all students to have attended a two-year post high school course in a Collége d'Enseignement Général et Professionnel (CEGEP). University selection is being removed from universities to become almost entirely a function of high schools.

Curriculum and standards will be in some measure determined by the geographical location of the university within a province. Expensive courses will not be duplicated in adjacent centres, and this is becoming most apparent at the graduate level. At the undergraduate level it will encourage an American type course credit system, where 'credits' can be traded as between one university and another. At the graduate level large curriculum changes will need provincial acceptance, since universities will no longer be able to initiate courses they are unable to finance on a continuous basis. In the past universities have been able to secure private funds, from Foundations and elsewhere, which have been sufficient to initiate courses, but the eventual operation of these courses has become a charge upon general university funds. This will be very difficult in the future and may well make universities more conservative institutions than they are; on the other hand, better curricular planning may accrue when universities must consider more than the immediate present in initiating course changes. The more difficult decision might be taken to discontinue courses no longer relevant, but this could run head on into tenure and the teaching abilities of professorial staff.

Research and Teaching

Perhaps more important for the future of the university will be 'who determines the balance between research and teaching'. Research in Canadian universities, in the main, is to be federally supported, though provincial support is provided in some provinces. Such federal support ran to $106 million in 1967–8, and has increased since then. Post-secondary education is provincially supported, each province raising the whole cost through transfer of fiscal power and responsibility for taxation. When to this fact is added the increasing tendency of academics, singly or collectively in university decisions, to disparage the teaching of undergraduates and to stress their 'graduate courses' and graduate students and research, undergraduate instruction appears likely to fall almost completely under the control of a provincial Minister of Education. When, also, determination of salaries is becoming, increasingly, a matter of collective bargaining, norms of teaching duties might well be related to salary levels. Thus, levels of support, provincial and federal, might well prove divisive factors in academic life. The end result could be the splitting of post-secondary education into two parts – a tertiary level, including the undergraduate and post high school, functioning under direct control from ministries of education, and a quaternary level, the graduate school, the remains of the university as it previously existed, where teaching and research will continue, under university and federal control, but not free from provincial intervention. To the extent that such a graduate-school-cum-university must meet the demands of the society of which it is a part, it will be required to meet certain pressures for the production, through specialized education of medical practitioners and specialists, teachers for the tertiary level of education, scientists and engineers, as well as its own successors, as university teachers, and, increasingly, the future members of the higher civil service.

As a protection against the possible eventuality of diminished autonomy many members of the academic community favour 'formula financing' of universities. This is most highly developed in Ontario and appears likely to spread to other provinces. It arose from a joint meeting of the Committee on University Affairs and the Committee of Presidents of Universities of Ontario, and was approved by the Minister of University Affairs in November 1966. It set up a formula for the distribution of grants which 'presupposes that the amount available will be sufficient, together with other major sources of income, to enable the university system to function at least at its present level of excellence'. Eight categories of student are listed, ranging from a unit weight for all general arts and science students, via a weight of 3 for first-year graduate students in the humanities and social sciences, to a weight of 6 for all second and later years of PhD, weights being roughly proportional to operating costs. Each of the sixteen universities has a weighted unit total. The grand total is divided into the forecast operating costs, less student fees, to obtain a unit value. Each university then receives the product of its unit total times the unit value of government grant. Over the years the unit value has risen from $1,320 in 1967–8 to $1,530 in 1969–70. The crucial points are the determination of unit value, particularly the first determination, which is really a decision of the Minister of University Affairs, and the weighted unit total for any given university, which varies as its student 'mix' changes. There may be a temptation to adopt short run solutions, with teaching of first-year students in extremely large classes and a narrow curriculum in order to free resources and personnel for dealing with the 'six point postulant PhDs', which yields a poor student 'mix'.

In Quebec, where decisions on university financing have been taken by the Minister on the advice of his Director General of Higher Education, a peculiar situation exists. There are three large universities and three small ones, together with a newly emerging French language Université de Québec, a multi-campus operation related in conception to the State University of New York. As such, and as an emerging university founded in 1968, its financial needs are bound to increase rapidly and are considered separately. Of the six older ones, three are English and three French language ones, with total enrolments of about 22,000 and 30,000 respectively, for a population which is 80 per cent French speaking. In distributing provincial grants these political/demographic features are important. On any basis of formula financing the English universities would fare well, for, according to the widely read newspaper La Presse, administrative costs are lower, salary levels are lower and the staff/student ratio is poorer in the English universities. There is opposition amongst large segments of the public to the prestigious position of McGill, attributed to its long history, large endowments and good research grants.

The French universities need time and money in order to reach equal status. Thus special grants for 'rattrapage' have been made. Such a move is accepted as equitable and highly desirable by the whole academic community. But if the grants for 'rattrapage' become very large, the supposed inferiority of the French universities will be emphasized; if 'rattrapage' is small then the English universities will be favoured by equal per capita distribution of the remaining funds. In this nearly impossible situation, only a political decision by the Minister could effect the result desired, a much lower per student grant to English universities. For 1968–9 for the neighbouring universities of McGill and Université de Montréal the per capita figures would have been $2,175 for Montreal and $1,225 for McGill. Under formula financing, the larger graduate student enrolment at McGill would probably reverse these figures. Formula financing is not, therefore, universally acceptable.

In Canada as a whole the problem of financing universities is becoming increasingly submerged in the problem of financing the whole of education, and in particular, the non-university post-secondary component which is increasing exponentially. The major provinces have all made provisions at this level. In Alberta they took the form of regional Junior Colleges, one of which has already become a university, and another is following the same path. British Columbia, too, has its Community Colleges, whilst Ontario has its Colleges of Applied Arts and Technology. Only in Quebec is attendance at a CEGEP obligatory for two years after Grade XI before admission to a three-year university course. Quebec does not believe that a university is the only place for mass education, or that the majority of a population must of necessity attend a university. In setting up CEGEPs it has tried to maintain some equality of educational treatment through thirteen years of schooling, and to delay decisions about careers and vocations to a comparatively late date. It remains to be seen whether CEGEPs will prove effective in siphoning off demand for a university education into more technical and vocational channels. Elsewhere in Canada there is a trend to require twelve years of schooling followed by four years of university education. Ontario still maintains Grade XIII but without final external examination, and this does not necessarily imply thirteen years of schooling. Perhaps the best summary statement would imply more education for more people for longer periods. The proximity of the United States (most Canadians live within one hundred miles of the US), and its direct impact upon Canadian life extends to its educational system also. Diversity in Canadian education is provided by Quebec; it is provided by other provinces also. Only political regard for Canada's Constitution prevents a more vigorous federal presence, though even that would be no guarantee of a single national policy in higher education in Canada.

24

Emerging National Policies for Higher Education in Brazil

Nair Fortes Abu-Merhy

Emerging national policies of higher education in Brazil may best be understood against a brief historical outline of its growth.

Latin America has had universities since the sixteenth century, but Brazil was the last country to have an institution bearing that name although it possessed institutions of equivalent level in the Jesuit colleges of the sixteenth century and the Franciscan colleges of the eighteenth century. Early in the nineteenth century, the Portuguese monarch created two institutions of higher education for medicine in Brazil; in 1810 the Military Academy was founded from which two colleges for Civil and Military Engineering emerged and in 1816 the School of Art was created. These were isolated institutions and located in Rio de Janeiro where the Court established itself, except for a school of medicine in Bahia.

Political events hastened the independence of Brazil in 1822 and the first emperor founded Schools of Law in Olinda (later transferred to Recife) and São Paulo in 1827. In the 1834 Additional Act to the Imperial Constitution of 1824 the provinces (states) were made responsible for primary and post-primary education, and the central government for secondary and higher education.

During the Second Empire the Leoncio de Carvalho Law of 1879 permitted the creation of private institutions of higher education. After the proclamation of the Republic in 1889, the Constitution of 1891 created a Ministry of Public Education, Posts and Telegraphs, which was abolished in 1892, and secondary and higher education were again centralized.

Despite this the University of the Amazons was founded in 1909. Reforms were made in higher education although always with a centralized bias, but in 1911 freedom of education was restored and the University of Parana was created in 1912. These universities were short-lived. Not long after, in 1915 a less liberal reform once again gave the Union (Federal Government) power to create institutions of higher education. For the first time conditions were created in which universities could be effectively founded and the University of Rio de Janeiro came into being in 1920 (later to be known as the University of Brazil in 1937, and in 1965 as the Federal University of Rio de Janeiro). The model followed, modified to

Brazilian requirements, was French, and served an elite. Consequently, secondary education concentrated on a general culture after the French pattern.

In 1927 the state of Minas Gerais created its own university and this would have been a notable departure from the centralization of institutions had it not been obliged to follow the federal model. In the revolutionary year of 1930, the Provisional Government decreed that the University of Rio de Janeiro was the model to be followed by all other institutions, whether private or state; this legislation was in force from 1931 until 1961.[1] In 1934 the state of São Paulo created its own university with schools of philosophy, science and letters, and offered a number of basic studies as well as opportunities for research. This was the beginning of the public teachers' college.

In 1935 the Federal District created a university on the North American model, but because it did not conform to the existing legislation, it ceased to function in 1939. Some of the courses were integrated into the University of Brazil (now the Federal University of Rio de Janeiro) and thus instituted a school of philosophy, designed to train teachers for secondary schools.

During the period of totalitarian government from 1937 to 1945, several state and private universities and single-purpose institutions were created. But in 1946 a new democratic Constitution was introduced and subsequently, in accordance with the Law of Directives and Fundamentals of National Education, passed on December 26, 1961, the number of universities has increased rapidly.

In 1968 Brazil was divided into five regions: North, North-East, East, South and West Central. The population was estimated at 86½ million inhabitants. There were 302 institutions in 44 universities and 328 single-purpose institutions. The regions were regrouped in 1970 into North, North-East, South-East, South and West Central, when there were 50 universities, and the population had increased to over 95 million inhabitants.

The growth in education has been rapid. Over a period of five years enrolments in primary education increased by 25 per cent; in secondary education the increase exceeded 50 per cent and in higher education from 1934 to 1970 the increase was almost 400 per cent.

Emerging National Policies for Higher Education

Law of Directives and Fundamentals of National Education

This was the first general law on education which roused public discussion. Many amendments were debated in Congress. Educators, parliamentarians, teachers and students (chiefly from the school of philosophy) voiced their opinions. The law was under consideration from 1947 until 1961 and was promulgated in December 1961, but it lacked coherence since it had to include concessions to groups and parties with widely differing points of view. With all its defects, however, it can still be considered a stimulating and creative force in Brazilian education.

Although the 1946 Constitution from which the Law was taken proposed decentralization, laws from 1950 onwards had federalized the state universities and the single-purpose institutions. The State of São Paulo alone refused to federalize its university. The Law reorganized the Council of Education, a body first created in 1915 but which had undergone great changes in name and in powers, into a Federal Council of Education. And inspired by the debates on the Law, the Federal Government founded a new university in Brasilia, largely based on the idea of the North American campus, with general institutions and professional schools. The venture was a success and existing universities attempted to follow its example, and despite financial difficulties, the trend in university building has been towards integrated campuses.

The new Law devoted 21 of its 120 articles to higher education, i.e. over one-sixth. The following innovations were proposed:

(a) Courses were classified as (1) undergraduate, (2) graduate (for doctors' and masters' degrees), (3) specialized, and (4) extension and others.[2]

(b) The Federal Council of Education was authorized to recognize single-purpose institutions – whether federal or private – and public and private universities, except those in the state system which had been in existence more than five years. Under these conditions the respective states retained the powers of the Federal Council.

(c) The Federal Council was authorized to recognize state institutions.

(d) The duration of the academic year was to be at least 180 days, and an innovation was that basic curricula should be approved by the Federal Council but could be added to by institutions. Formerly the curriculum was standardized and laid down by federal decree.

(e) The provision of a minimum number of courses was prescribed for schools of philosophy, science and letters.

(f) The university was to be allowed to create university colleges providing high-school courses, preparatory to the university course. These tasks are difficult to integrate since university courses are usually semi-specialized and orientated towards industry, agriculture, commerce and teacher training for elementary and secondary schools.

(g) Free education was to be available for those in need – a principle not yet implemented. Federal and state universities were to charge only nominal fees and apply the income to student welfare. Private institutions charge very high fees but grant scholarships to those unable to pay.

(*h*) The autonomy of the federal universities was reduced. Formerly these had the privilege of being immediately accepted after their creation by federal law. Now they are able to initiate courses without government decree although not without the prior approval of the Federal Council. The autonomy of other universities which had not previously enjoyed such privileges was increased. The States of São Paulo and Guanabara, being the only states maintaining state universities, were permitted to authorize and recognize their establishments.

(*i*) The Federal Council of Education was to implement the National Education Plan.

(*j*) The Union was to devote at least 12 per cent of its annual budget to education, with the States, the Federal District and the municipalities contributing 20 per cent.

The main objective of the Law was to democratize education and to grant equal opportunity to all. Since the Federal Council of Education reserved the right to interpret the Law, its decisions became equivalent to law, a point on which much controversy arose. Indeed criticism of the Law, its application and the spread of new ideas and theories, led to general dissatisfaction on the part of educators, politicians and students who were at this period under strong political influence.

Higher Education Debates and Laws

The assault on the universities had begun. Briefly by 1963, three trends could be identified:

(*a*) Those who wished to change the social structure in order to achieve university reform (the leftists), and eventually transform the country into a socialist state, the only way, in their opinion, to open universities to all and to ensure the best interests of the community.

(*b*) Those who wished to maintain the *status quo*, a small right-wing minority, conscious of the privileges of class and the ease of teaching students coming only from the upper strata of society.

(*c*) There were those who wished to restructure the universities and single-purpose institutions in order to achieve a dialogue with the community as a whole. The institutions ought to have greater internal coherence and studies ought to be integrated, resources properly utilized, and other measures taken up to democratize institutions and to maintain them within the legal framework of the state. This was the majority view.

Increases in population aggravated the situation in that properly qualified candidates applied for vacancies which were not available. This gave rise to the problem of 'surpluses' (*excedentes*).

By now the students had formed a powerful body and in the existing unrest, representatives of the left endeavoured to unite students and workers to achieve their objectives. Political feeling found expression in leftist infiltration at the highest levels of administration. Popular reaction by the armed forces resulted in the revolution of 1964 which attempted to restore national order and create a climate for work and development.

A number of studies for the reform of the University of Brazil were prepared and a former professor there became Minister of Education and Culture, responsible for carrying out university reform. After formulating the Higher Education Statute (*Estatuto do Magisterio Superior*, Law No. 4.881–A/65) based on existing documentation and adding new measures of his own, the Minister sought the approval of the Federal Council of Education which decided to transform the Federal universities. This resulted in legislative action.

Meanwhile a so-called Extraordinary Ministry had been created to carry out the administrative reform decreed in the general Law of 1967. The first Revolutionary Government named this the Ministry for Planning and Economic Coordination. The Second Government confirmed its existence in the 1967 Constitution but named it the Ministry of Planning and General Coordination, which began to publish surveys and findings. The reform of the Ministry of Education and Culture took place in two stages, first the administrative reform (Law No. 200 of 25 February 1967) and the second in the academic year of 1970 (Decree No. 66.296 of 3 March 1970 and Decree No. 66.977 of 27 July 1970).

There already existed a good deal of documentation on the state systems on which to base further research, which was now dominated by the concept that an educational system is an adjunct to the social system and should incorporate many strands: demographic, economic, cultural, etc. The National Educational Plan of 1962 (revised in 1965) formulated by the Federal Council of Education could hardly be termed a plan but was merely a collection of qualitative and quantitative measures. It suffered because the 1967 Constitution revoked the obligatory contribution to education from the Union and the States which had been established under the 1946 Constitution and the Law of Directives and Fundamentals in 1961.

Lack of financial resources has seriously retarded the implementation of the Government's Ten-Year Plan elaborated by the Ministry of Economic Planning and General Coordination. It included the Sectional Plan for Education, entirely prepared by economists. On the other hand, the Directorate for Higher Education created the Forum for Rectors (27 February 1962). Later a Council of University Rectors was organized, a private body which nonetheless has influenced the course of higher education since it periodically brings the Rectors together to discuss matters of common interest. Its publications are able to highlight curricula problems and trends.

The Reform of the University

The story of the reform of the University is a long one; it will be analysed in terms of its origins in 1945 and the laws promulgated since 1966, which fall into two phases.

The first phase of reform originated in Decree Laws No. 53 of 18 November 1966 and No. 252 of 28 February 1967. The principal points in this legislation were:

(*a*) The reform was directed specially to the Federal universities or institutions created by the Federation, although the Union invited other universities to follow, intimating that those which did so would receive priority in the matter of financial support.

(*b*) The institutions were to consist of two equal sections for learning and research: those providing foundation courses and the others providing professional courses. Those giving foundation courses were permitted to develop their own professional interests.

(*c*) There were to be supervisory bodies with decision-making powers for teaching and research who would represent both the foundation and professional courses.

(*d*) The Faculties of Philosophy, Science and Letters were to be separated. From this decision arose the Faculties of Education providing courses which had hitherto been located in the Departments of Education.

(*e*) As a consequence of this, there would be a redistribution of teaching staff.

(*f*) A departmental structure of the institutions became obligatory. These were the smallest university units and included the relevant disciplines (this system had already been adopted by some universities and the practice now became general).

(*g*) Great importance was given to the Departmental Council which became more influential than the Faculty.

(*h*) Basic studies courses became identified as those supplying the fundamentals of knowledge: mathematics, physics, chemistry and biology, the geosciences, humanities, philosophy, letters and arts.

(*i*) The need was expressed that the university should help the wider community by extending its activities in the fields of education and research by supplying courses and services.

(*j*) Specialist institutes which had already achieved a high standard were allowed to continue.

(*k*) The duplication of resources for identical ends was forbidden in order to maintain the unity and structure of the university.

The reform was well received and all the institutions accepted the statutes and regulations. However, as this did not lead to a greater number of student places, public protests obliged the Government to create a working group to study how university reform could be expedited.

In the second phase several laws and decrees originated in the working group's report to the Ministry of Education and Culture. The salient points of these were as follows:

(*a*) The working group recommended a number of measures for the improvement of fiscal incentives, such as Law No. 5.525 of 5 November 1968 which created the Special Federal Lottery Fund, and Law No. 5.537 of 21 November 1968 which created the National Fund for the Development of Education, and finally Decree Law No. 872 of 16 September 1969 which is complementary to Law No. 5.537.

(*b*) As for university reform itself the principal legislation are the laws No. 5.540 of 28 November 1968 and Decree Laws No. 464, No. 655 and No. 749 and the decrees which regulated them. Two aspects of university reform at this stage need to be understood.

The Attempt to Control the Expansion of Higher Education

The idea began to spread that while economic growth creates a situation propitious to higher education, it is no less true that the university cannot alone support this development.

The great movements of population, particularly of males to the great cities, created a need for education in the hinterland but this in turn created problems through the lack of qualified teachers and lowered the standard of education. A problem was also created in that in the small towns the market for educated people was quickly over-supplied and the flight of professionally trained men from these areas left them in the same state as before the courses were established.

This problem will only be solved when manpower requirements can be equated with social needs, based on substantial research. Studies now being conducted must take into account the anthropological characteristics of the different geographic zones.

The economists applied an econometric model devised by Jan Tinbergen but their findings were not considered valid as they treated the cultural zones as homogeneous. In Brazil the zones are so heterogeneous that some may be classified as fully developed, some as semi-developed and others as under-developed. New institutions to be created in the light of manpower needs must take into account national and regional development.

It is this aspect which has been the subject of controversy due to the lack of research of the supply and demand of manpower. The Ministry of Planning and General Coordination, and bodies from the educational administration, are undertaking some research and publishing their findings and analyses. But there is much public disquiet. It has been said that Brazil has only four hundred thousand students but requires a minimum of a million in higher education, and therefore it is necessary to open schools to non-selective entry on the grounds that general studies, particularly in an under-developed country, can be adapted to various professions. On the other hand some argue that the problem of 'surpluses' in higher education is less serious than the problem of unemployment among qualified workers. There is also the fear of lowering academic standards.

Another potent factor which has retarded Brazilian development is the social status accorded to secondary (grammar) school graduates until recently. Few students were attracted to the technical high school but the new law decreed that the middle courses (*cursos medios*) should be completely equivalent as regards entry to higher education. Necessary measures are therefore being taken to modify entrance qualifications while the university supervises the examinations.

Social status in Brazil today is acquired through higher education and some courses enjoy a higher reputation than others: medicine, engineering, followed by law. The newer professions such as nursing, social service, journalism, secondary school teaching, are not as well paid and while the nation requires vast numbers of teachers and nurses, few follow these courses and even among those there is a big drop-out to private occupations where their standard of education guarantees a good position.

Structural Reform

The reform established long and short courses in higher education in response to the needs of certain professions: that is courses for technologists to meet the immediate requirements of industrial expansion, and courses for graduates with a deeper knowledge for continuing development.

One of the major difficulties of the Brazilian universities is to integrate technical and higher education, and the reform proposes that the entrance examinations should be at the technical level. The Brazilian tradition is identical to that of the French: i.e. the student possesses highly specialized knowledge on entry. Entry to the schools of engineering or medicine is highly competitive and for each vacancy there are ten applicants. The examinations are therefore of a high standard and for which the students prepare by an intense twelve-month 'crash' revision course. Some students may take the examination as many as four times. To change the entrance examination is very difficult.

One university bases its entrance examination on a secondary level of studies following the methods of W. Kenneth Richmond[3] and compiles a cultural profile of the student for guidance. However, the matter is undecided because, for example, it would be impossible to carry out such a lengthy process for all the 50,000 candidates to the Federal University of Rio de Janeiro. Thus, although the university reform decided on a uniform entrance examination, as recommended by Kenneth Richmond, the situation does not yet permit the implementation of such a system. It is one of the most controversial aspects of the reform.

The idea of a first cycle was one of the innovations of the reform, and for this it took as a model the 'senior college'. In order to achieve this, it will be necessary to shorten the existing secondary school course because the adoption of the first cycle would inevitably lead to the extension of the subsequent professional course.

The professional cycle has not been changed and so has necessitated the curtailing or simplification of the course. The nation cannot afford the cost of extending courses (six years for medicine; five years for law and architecture; four years for other courses). The creation and implementation of the first cycle requires a single campus – not yet possible in the majority of our universities, despite an accelerated building programme.

The reform allowed for the certification of specialists at undergraduate level which amounted to a recognition of technologists. Some universities have accepted this concept and are to develop courses at a graduate level, except in education which has barely been started. It is hoped that from 1971 some universities will provide graduate courses recognized by the National Federal Council.

It is recommended that universities should combine to set up Regional Centres in order to make the best use of available resources.

An important factor is the work routine of the teacher. The law allows part-time teachers doing 12 or 24 hours a week, or full-time teachers working 40 hours a week. Financial considerations oblige the universities to opt for the part-time teacher with a consequent deterioration in teaching standards. There is no doubt that finance is one of the greatest problems in Brazil.

The reform ended life-professorships and created professorial chairs. It was accepted that the *cathedra* had abused their privileges. The loss of status with no compensatory salary structure has encouraged many university teachers to leave education and take better remunerated positions in industry and commerce. But there are others who continue and uphold the traditions of their vocation. Present legislation has only slightly altered the structure created by Laws Nos. 53 and 252 already mentioned, by extending it to all universities and single-purpose institutions.

Conclusion

The university in Brazil is in a critical phase of reorganization. New concepts are embodied in profound economic change.

At the heart of the present state of civilization, as never before, is the confrontation between culture and technology, that is, the choice between a general culture with a specialist basis, and premature specialization with quick and ephemeral applications. In other words, should the university continue the pursuit of learning and encourage the acquisition of know-ledge or should it give priority to courses for material benefit and improve the economic development of countries such as our own? Can these two concepts be reconciled and to what extent?

Hence the dilemma, short courses or long courses? In Latin America today endeavours are being made to persuade public opinion to accept technical rather than general education, at the secondary level as well as in higher education.

It is, of course, true that Brazil needs medium grade technicians as well as more highly qualified personnel. Up to the present we have been pro-ducing people of a middle culture without attracting men and women to the semi-specialist courses while at the same time attempting to broaden the training of technologists at a higher level. The absurdity of producing more university-trained technologists than medium-grade technicians is comparable to raising an army with more generals than soldiers.

The problems of development are allied to administrative ones. Viewing the organization as part of the social structure, we realize that it must develop in harmony with the needs of society and to achieve this adequate planning must be carried out. To this end research, particularly under the auspices of the Ministry of Planning, is designed to correlate the demo-graphic, social and economic findings of the different regions of the country. The nation is now awake to the problem.

It is essential that we consider the consequences of such policies so that we may achieve the double objective of producing an integrated man and a skilled worker. The immediate problem is what type of university can achieve this. There are those who advocate a type of democratic planning in which all the national groups can participate, but under the special care of educators and educational experts. Others consider it the duty of the state to assume responsibility, and as economic development in the key-stone to it all, influential economists support the latter idea. So in Brazil the economist is exerting an extraordinary influence on educational planning. However, the universities are cautiously beginning to produce educational planners so that in future they can be integrated into Ministry of Planning teams. The vision of the educator is indispensable.

Today university reform is emerging from the theoretical to the prag-matic stage and is encountering serious obstacles. It is generally thought that short-term courses provide qualifications in the shortest time. This assumption must be carefully examined. The long courses differ and their duration may be four to six years. This is the case for medicine, all types of engineering, the social services, nursing, librarianship, journalism, dentistry, pharmacy, nutrition. Teacher training has been shortened to three years and even so it is considered to be too long. Experience shows that some teacher training institutes have opted for four years (eight semesters), consisting of 2,700 hours, while others complete the course in six semesters of 2,200 hours, or even in two periods of 1,100 hours. At the moment, all teachers training are considered equal but in the future, when undergraduates desire to enrol in postgraduate courses, they will have to reach graduate standard before being accepted by certain faculties.

This is a problem which will become more acute as the range of courses and professions develops. Another problem concerns curricula. Formerly curricula were standardized but now the National Federal Council sets down minimum requirements. Each institution is permitted to include complementary subjects and this may mean an overloading of available resources. In order to overcome this, the universities may adopt minimum curricula in a percentage of some courses while including relevant subject matter in others. It may even happen that the latter supplant the former. In courses which have a strong tradition this will not occur but difficulties may arise in new disciplines.

Another problem relates to the implementation of the first and second cycles in the new structure. The single-purpose institutions which merely provide one type of course are not obliged to provide the first cycle, they may initiate professional training from the first semester, although the course must take the same number of years. From this one concludes that professional training takes longer than the first cycle. Institutions offering more than one course are obliged to offer the first cycle as a general course included in the overall professional course and which occupies a shorter number of hours than the courses mentioned previously. There is no difficulty in organizing the first cycle where courses are interrelated but it is impossible to do so where they are totally different. Let us suppose an institution offering education, letters and mathematics. How can a general course be devised to be of use to the student of each? Should the curriculum be based on a general culture or on an initial exploratory professional basis? As the secondary school course lasts seven years, the last semester being highly propedeutic, how can a higher level course offer a course which is not propedeutic?

The universities are experimenting with curricula integration by area, that is bio-medical, technological, social science, etc. In order to implement the two cycles it is essential to have a university campus. Until this practice has come into general use the existence of the two cycles will be precarious, because it is not possible to retain teachers who are attached to other institutions. Therefore, these courses will have to be given in basic institutes while at the same time the initial professional courses are given in the specialist institutions in the region. Obviously such planning can only be effective when institutions are adjacent. The withdrawal of teachers from the basic institutes to the professional institutions has created difficulties.

Only further experience will enable an analysis to be made of the system and solutions found.

Yet another problem is that of the entrance examinations. The reform thought this would help the student to overcome the faults in his previous education while at the same time acquiring elements to permit him to follow his professional studies. In a nation which promises equal opportunity and can provide places for all who wish to follow higher education, this would be the ideal situation. Unfortunately, in Brazil, of a thousand pupils who enter primary school, only thirty-nine complete secondary school. The number of students attempting the entrance examination is insignificant. Such students undergo a preparatory year (outside the system) after completing the secondary course, since the entrance examination sets difficult papers in order to eliminate the majority of the candidates and there are ten for each place. Therefore it follows that students once admitted find the first semesters easy, and do not have to extend themselves. How can an average be arrived at when the standards maintained by schools are so different?

The reform would like to ensure that the entrance examination be restricted to standards achieved in secondary education, although this would arouse great controversy, particularly among the brighter students who achieve high marks.

It is proposed that a single entrance examination should be set for all courses and subjects. The orientation of students who have not followed an identical cycle course would, of course, be extremely difficult should this system be adopted, as has already been demonstrated. For example, if in bio-medicine a single entrance examination was established to cover medicine, pharmacy, dentistry, nursing, physiotherapy, nutrition and biology, it is reasonable to suppose that the candidates with the highest marks would be chosen for the medical course, and so on down the scale. A hierarchy in the profession would be created and social status would be conferred at the same time. Brazil needs more nurses than doctors and the problem is how to make good the deficit of the one over the other. The analysis of a research project undertaken into this problem in 1970 is awaited.

Still another problem is concerned with the teaching profession where there is no tradition of graduate courses. Teachers were selected through a system of competitive examinations, presentation of these leading to a doctorate, or by competing for the position of 'free-teacher' (*docente livre*, the German *Privatdozent*) and ultimately to that of a university professor, which was for life. The reform eliminated life professorships and consequently the *cathedra* and retained only full professors. To achieve this position the teacher begins as an assistant professor, is promoted to associate professor and then finally becomes a full professor. Selection is made by means of examinations, and paper and books published, and rarely by presentation of a thesis.

The idea of a university career teacher has only existed in Brazil since 1945 and only became general in 1965 after the Law No. 4.881–A on teaching was passed. This brought about a number of changes, for with the elimination of *cathedra* it was possible for career teachers to function. At the same time, life-professorships were attractive and a higher rate of remuneration would be a desirable incentive for professors. Unfortunately this has not yet occurred, and there is thus a tendency for teachers to leave the profession with a consequent lowering of teaching standards. To overcome this problem the Government is trying to allow universities to organize working hours. Financial considerations are of course paramount and the vast programme initiated by the Government for teaching adults to read and for implementing the primary schools attendance required by law is a very heavy drain. The population in Brazil is a very young one, about 50 per cent are below the age of twenty or 45 million not in the work force needed to be placed within the educational system.

The Government has decided to institute fees in the state universities and single-purpose institutions, a decision strongly resisted by students.

The reform established three categories of teachers in universities, 12 hours, 24 hours and full-time teachers. Decisive measures have already been taken by the Government on salaries for university teachers, for undoubtedly university reform can only be carried out if the position of its teachers is improved.

University reform is at last imbued with a new philosophy of which we select a few points. The working group understands that true university reform can only come from a dialogue between university and state, from the multiple forces of society and from the requirements of the student.

The university is the centre for social and cultural movements, it has a role as an agency for development and to cordinate within the system forces in which the state is the stabilizing element, thus justifying the stimulating and disciplinary action of the state. The working group accepts that the university reflects development but has not waited for social reforms to be fulfilled before reforming the university; the university is the cause and effect of development.

University reform must, in the opinion of the working group, fulfil its primary function of accepting the role as a pre-investment in the development effort.

In conclusion, we quote one of the most important pronouncements from the Report:

> . . . The Group sees the University as the focal point where a culture and a people of an era can attain the fulfilment of its auto-conscience. It is, therefore, one of its essential aims to promote the integration of man in his historical

setting, to supply him with the means by which he can seek and understand his cultural heritage. Seen in this light, reform has as its objective the raising of the university to the rational and critical level, turning it into the object of change in the condition and sense of development. It is the stage at which the university transcends the position of instrument of change into the creative force for spiritual leadership. In this perspective, the university fulfils itself in the variety of its functions, integrating knowledge in all its forms, and operates the synthesis of the theoretical *praxis* and not acting solely as the instrument of economic development but for the whole welfare and development of man!'

NOTES

1. This reform created the University of Education and Health, later the Ministry of Education and finally the Ministry of Education and Culture, an agency designed to promote the development of instruction and culture, to supervise such expansion and authorize and recognize educational and other institutions.
2. In Brazil undergraduate courses are called 'graduate', and graduate courses are called 'postgraduate'. In translating the text attention is given to meaning of these terms in the English educational system.
3. W. Kenneth Richmond, *Culture and General Education* (London: Methuen).

25

Political Independence and Higher Education in Malawi

Ian Michael and Felix Mnthali

This is an attempt to state the aims of a new university of unorthodox design, and to assess, after only six years, some of its intended and unintended effects on the society which created it. The account is written by the first member of the university to be appointed, who still has responsibility for it. An objective statement is therefore not to be expected, but some others of the original staff (here called the primers) have had an opportunity to exercise on it their established skill in checking egotism, complacency and self-deception. It remains, however, an account written by a foreigner. It is therefore followed by a comment from a Malawian colleague who did not know the university in its first years but has recently worked closely with the Vice-Chancellor and has seen something of the institution as a whole. He writes as one of those affected by the changes he is helping to make, and he too, though he writes personally, has consulted his contemporaries and colleagues.

Background

Malawi achieved self-government in 1963, independence in 1964, and became a republic in 1966. A university, though part of the political programme of independence, was not a new idea. It had been suggested by the vision of Dr Laws, who taught Greek and built a hydro-electric plant at Livingstonia in 1905, and it remained a passive aspiration until it was reactivated by Dr Banda on the break-up of the Central African Federation in 1963. During that year and in 1964 an international commission under the chairmanship of Dr Eldon Johnson, sponsored by USAID and the Americal Council on Education, had studied the educational needs of Malawi. Its recommendations included the establishment of 'one unitary national university . . . [with] responsibility for all existing postsecondary education and its future development'.[1] The main recommendations affecting higher education were accepted immediately and the British government at once agreed to help with the establishment of a university. The Vice-Chancellor was appointed in August 1964, and arrived early in November. A Provisional Council was set up by Act of Parliament on

12th November and met for the first time on 8th December. Nine months later, in September 1965, a hundred students were being taught.

Two influences of that time were, and have remained, particularly strong. The most powerful was the impetus of independence. It seemed a time for action, for speed rather than for caution, for achievement rather than for consideration. To say that the primers responded to the mood of the country (as well as to the instructions of the Prime Minister) is perhaps to flatter their inexperience. Their work would have been more carefully done if a year had been spent on drawing up an Academic Plan and another year preparing its implementation. Some early omissions, caused by haste, had persistently tiresome consequences. But at the time it felt right for the primers to hustle as they did. The wind was blowing in the direction they were to take: it would have been unpatriotic not to have raised a sail. The new university did not suffer by having identified itself with the mood of the nation.

The second most powerful influence was the imaginative suggestion of the Johnson report that the university should cater not only for professional levels of employment, for which a degree was a customary prerequisite, but also for what are less precisely called technician levels: the middle level of skilled manpower often neglected in developing countries. The implementation of this suggestion has been the focus of the university's planning, a main factor in national educational policy, and the basis of the economic justification for an institution which could not avoid being almost unbearably expensive.

Foreground

In 1971 there are in the university 1,000 students, of whom 390 are following degree courses in arts, science, social science, education, agriculture and law, and 610 are following diploma courses in agriculture, education, business studies, public administration, public health inspection, engineering, surveying and technical teaching. All students enter with a Cambridge Overseas School Certificate, the number and nature of the credits required varying with the course. Diploma courses last three years, courses for an ordinary degree last four, except in law and education which take five years. Annual entry to degree courses is limited to about 100, so there are many students on diploma courses who would be acceptable for degree work if places were made available. All courses are integrated in a single academic structure of Subject Boards, Group (i.e. Faculty) Boards and Senate. All students, whatever course they are connected with, are of equal status, as are all staff. If students wish to wear a gown it is the same for all. The university is, for historical reasons, organized in five colleges, four of them within ten miles of each other, the fifth two hundred miles away. Three colleges, and eventually all, work at both degree and diploma level.

This geographical dispersion, linked as it is to vocational and subject concentrations, is the greatest obstacle to the achievement of the university's aims.

Aims

In an account compressed almost to the limits of telegraphic pain it is difficult to state aims which are neither too general nor too local. It can be said however that the following aims were actively in the minds of the primers and had a conscious influence on their daily decisions:

(i) To respond to what was conveyed to the primers, by the government, by the then Prime Minister, by the Provisional Council of the university, as being national policy. It was not difficult to make such a response because national policy, in this respect, was at first stated very simply: that the university should be good enough to be accepted by other universities; that it should take the unitary form recommended in the Johnson report; that it should start work quickly.

(ii) To respond, in whatever was the appropriate way, to the fact that Malawi belonged, not to Europe or North America, but to a particular region of Africa. The primers, all of whom were foreigners and only one of whom knew Malawi, were ready to make the response and realized its importance; but they were uncertain of their judgment about what was appropriate. Could an institution be designed which fitted organically into the social structure of Malawi? Not easily by two groups of people, one knowing little about Malawi and the other knowing less about the working of a university; and certainly not in a hurry. The aim of relevance came therefore to be focused not on the design of the institution nor on its expression in buildings but on the curriculum and in the quality of student life outside the classroom.

(iii) To extend and strengthen the training for leadership provided hitherto by the customary practice of society, by a Western school system and a colonial system of government, and, for a very few, by higher education in English-speaking countries abroad. This obvious and difficult task is one at which Western universities have not, as a result of their own deliberate and distinctive efforts, been particularly successful. The primers assumed that it must be one of their aims, but several influences caused them to modify their preconceptions: governmental suspicion of any training for specifically political leadership; greater respect than is shown in the west for the authority of age and office; greater approval (than western societies think they have) for elitism; the lack in public thinking of any ideas derived from the academic and clinical study of human nature and human relations; an apparent lack, in any systematic and usable form, of the insights concerning human relations which traditional societies are supposed to evolve.

(iv) Through consultancy, national committee contacts, broadcasting and personal influence to make the university not only a teaching institution but also a disseminating centre which would make available skills and ideas drawn from other countries and other times. This is one of the aspects of university work which are lost to a country which sends everyone abroad for higher education.

(v) To encourage research, even with very limited resources, and especially research which is directly relevant to the social and economic development of the country. In 1970–1 fifty-three staff have received small research grants from university funds.

(vi) To put the new institution in a historical context: to make conscious the link with eleventh-century Bologna, eighteenth-century Princeton, nineteenth-century Massachusetts and twentieth-century Ibadan and Norwich.

(vii) To put the new institution in a geographical context: to establish its membership of a contemporary, world-wide academic community through which it could draw on the help of unknown colleagues in Sydney, Baghdad or Bonn.

(viii) To make good use, subject to severe limitations of time and resources, of the opportunity to innovate. The primers knew that the type of institution they were creating was unique within the British context and, as the *only* institution of higher education in the country, unusual by any other criteria.

Effects

It is much too early to say how far these aims have been achieved, but after six years there are presumably some changes or tendencies within society which are related to the establishment of a university. It would be surprising, and alarming, if there were none: it would also be surprising (and perhaps alarming) if they could be very precisely described. In order to describe them even imprecisely it is necessary to refer to some qualities as if they were particularly associated with, or derived from, university work and university people. If there were no such qualities a university could not have distinctive effects, but the qualities are not different in kind from those of ordinary people: they have stronger roots, they are more intensively cultivated. Ordinary people can run a little and jump a little: the athlete, by cultivating and concentrating on his unusual endowment of usual skills, raises them to such a height that they serve entirely new purposes in society. University people are trained educational athletes whom society employs for some of its specialized tasks. They can easily sound, and sometimes are, conceited, but this is a risk run by anyone discussing the specialized functions of his own profession.

On national consciousness The most widely spread effect of the establishment of the university, which had been a national aim linked to the achievement of independence, has been on the national consciousness. This is very much more than saying that the institution is a conventional symbol of prestige. Its impact is not made by splendid buildings but through its students and staff. An activity for which people used to be sent abroad is now available in Malawi. Even those who are in no position to judge the university see that it works, if only in the narrow sense that students go there, receive degrees or diplomas, and get jobs. Those who are more informed see that it works in the sense that its students are accepted for higher degrees abroad, that academic visitors and external examiners and international associations take it seriously. Although special pride is felt in the Malawian staff the feeling that the university belongs to the nation is not significantly affected by the fact that at present three-quarters of the staff are foreigners. This is hospitable and courteous, but it is also common sense: it is the students (to oversimplify things a little) who make the university, and the students are Malawians.

On national culture   The university is gradually, but too slowly, becoming a centre for the promotion of national culture. This is partly because universities naturally perform this function; partly because the primers and their successors had this as a particular intention; partly because in the university there is a concentration of foreigners who have felt in their own cultures the value of the arts and of scientific inquiry and therefore encourage the growing desire of Malawians to develop and interpret their own culture; partly because Malawian staff and students have, as never before, time, support and opportunity for drama, writing, sculpture, sociological, ecological and historical inquiry, painting, dance and music.

On village life   There has been little if any direct effect on village life except in the neighbourhood of the university's agricultural college. The indirect effects have been strongest through the training of students for agriculture, for teaching in day-secondary schools and for government service in the districts. Less immediate, but potentially as strong, are the effects of sociological and ecological teaching and research.

On the conduct of affairs   This is in some ways the most important of the effects on society, although it is impossible to measure it. It derives from three aspects of university life: analytical procedures; the ideal of comprehensive factual coverage; a tradition of independent thought for the individual and autonomy for the institution. The academic mind is almost boringly analytical. Its approach, whether in correspondence with a government department, or on a public committee, or in a radio discussion, can be tiresome if the matter is in fact straightforward, and useful if it is not. Since matters are seldom straightforward an analytical approach may be influential even when its proponent is a nuisance. It is not that civil servants, for example, lack the capacity for analysis: the conditions and conventions of their job lead most of them to give it less time than the academic is willing to give it. His approach is therefore different and complementary.

Similarly with information. The academic is trained to scrutinize every situation about which he expresses a judgment in such a way that he knows how far the relevant facts are accessible. He does not claim to possess the relevant knowledge so much as the relevant ignorance. He can frequently tell, even in matters about which he knows little, when relevant information is lacking. He knows what kind of information is needed and he expects to seek it. His position in a university, even a new one, gives him an assurance which it is a professional sin for him to abuse. He is, like the doctor, a member of an ancient international guild; his craft is the pursuit, the analysis and the handing on of knowledge. Independence of thought, and of expression in his teaching, he takes for granted. The autonomy of his institution matters primarily as it relates to his function as teacher and researcher. Such basic, functional autonomy is entirely compatible with loyalty to the nation, with dependence on public funds, and with a strong sense of public responsibility. But in all parts of the world and at most times governments (whether municipal, national or ecclesiastical) and universities have viewed each other with a biologically right and fruitful suspicion.

Society in Malawi has been influenced by all these factors. The traditional autonomy of a university has been warmly respected, but in a country where a high proportion of all activity is government sponsored a thoughtlessly independent air, whether individual or institutional, can be regarded as indifference. It is not enough for the university to avoid being self-centred and privileged; it must manifestly be seeking to serve the country. So long as that is so its influence on public life is great. This is perhaps happening in Malawi.

On employment The unitary nature of the university has already had an observable effect on society. Every year at least two hundred students enter the university who would not have done so had it been restricted to degree courses taught in a single college. These students, who would otherwise have gone to government institutions, and would have pressed for an expansion of undergraduate numbers, have received an education and a directly vocational training in a university. They get jobs in the middle levels of skilled employment at salaries which are small (compared with those of graduates) for their ability and for the education they have received. But more is being done by them for the economy than could be done by the much smaller number of graduates the country could afford to employ, and diplomates employed at the middle level have been educated in a way which should make them, in the long run, more effective than if they had received a shorter and more limited vocational training. There are already signs that their greater effectiveness is being achieved, but it has yet to be established, because it turns on their capacity to learn quickly from experience, to keep themselves in touch with new knowledge, and to adapt themselves and their work to a rapidly changing society.

I.M.

The Great Tradition

As the earlier part of this paper points out, the idea of a university in Malawi dates back to the nineteenth century. What is now left of Livingstonia shows that Dr Laws was thinking in terms of a university rather than a secondary, let alone primary, school. The legend of Laws shows that he was an unusual missionary who inspired his converts with as much zeal for the pursuit of intellectual excellence as for the Kingdom of God. . . . Indeed, the separation of religion from intellectual pursuits does not have a long history in Malawi. And, of course, there's the rub! The great tradition in Malawi is that of an education whose standards are as high as the early Scottish missionaries thought they ought to be. At the same time education is the sacred key opening the gate to everything; to the professions, to security, to righteousness, to the right partner in life!

Enter University of Malawi, Correctly

It is not surprising that the struggle for independence has never been quite dissociated from the cry for better, higher and more education. Indeed to many people the struggle for independence was the struggle for education. Malawi intellectuals organized a Nyasa College Association at the same time as they worked for political independence. This will explain why the few graduates there were at the time were all taken up by the movement for political independence. It also explains the involvement in the fight for independence of all the important schools there were at the time. Needless to add that many academically brilliant careers were irrevocably ruined.

The coming of the University of Malawi, then, fulfilled, or promised to fulfil, long-cherished ambitions and the ambitions themselves helped to give the university its form and direction. Malawi needed a centre for the pursuit of excellence in the realm of ideas at the same time as it yearned for utility and relevance in the realm of professional skills. These hopes had to be embraced in one institution and the concept of the 'umbrella' university was the best that man could devise at that time.

Form and Tendencies

In giving both degrees and diplomas the university meets the needs of the country at all levels, i.e. the level of the man who is useful because he dabbles in the world of ideas and the level of the man who is useful because he can immediately apply the skill gained in the university. In many ways what the university brought to Malawi is 'revolutionary' compared with what other universities have brought in other countries. By coming down to the bare needs of the country the university was making sure that it would not be the 'ivory tower' in the whole national effort towards development. The only problem at the moment is that the country as a whole is moving behind the university in this vision. Typical of this 'lag' is a remark I heard from a diploma student the other day, 'This university was created in such a way that it would provide the elite and the ready-made subordinates at the same time.' By 'ready-made subordinates' the student meant diploma students, and by the 'elite' he meant the degree students.

It seems to me that although everyone subscribes to the idea that the university is here to serve the needs of the country there is at the back of everyone's mind the feeling that somehow the university to be real must still correspond to European and American models. It hardly enters people's minds that Malawi can have something unique to contribute to the world. Although everyone would rather employ our diplomates sooner than our graduates hardly anyone ever thinks that they should be treated as well as the traditional degree-holders. One reason for this may be that nearly everyone involved in the great experiment, i.e. in the work of the university, has been brought up in the traditional western university where the prestige surrounding men of ideas does not always coincide with that surrounding practical and useful men. One either meets complete adulation for the man of ideas against the practical man or finds a period in which the man of ideas is never taken seriously. The two have never been nurtured together in the sort of symbiosis we are trying to create in the University of Malawi. But we have come to the point where we *know* and feel that what we are doing is the correct thing for the country, and that we are succeeding. Needless to add that the standards both at the beginning and at the end of our degrees and diplomas are rising every year. While this is a source for pride and hope it does point to a new development in the university.

Evolution towards the Ideal Model

Two of our colleges which from the start offered only diplomas now also offer degrees: the College of Education gives both diplomas and degrees; the College of Agriculture is also doing the same. The Institute of Public Administration gives degrees in Law and diplomas in Public Administration. What one hopes for is that the trend towards diploma courses evolving into degree courses will continue. If resources can be mustered the Polytechnic should become a School of Engineering. We are in no hurry to do away with our diplomas. At the same time the university should more and more provide the kind of personnel now coming to Malawi under the conventional label of 'experts'. No country is self-sufficient in the world of expertise. No country should be *totally* deficient in this commodity. The country cannot say to itself that it now has a university and at the same time continue to depend on imported high-level man-power in all fields. While the university cannot boast a medical school, because a medical school would be beyond the available resources which the country can put forward for the university as a whole, it is neverthe-less right and proper for it to be the first and foremost supplier of expertise in Agriculture, Engineering, Teacher Education, as well as in the general Arts and Sciences. It is making an impact on the country in these areas. For this impact to really reverberate across the country people must see that their experts in Agriculture, Education, Engineering, the general Arts and Sciences have been trained at home, although they may later have gone overseas. We are back to what I said earlier about people wanting their education to be as high as it can go and as easily accessible as it is high! It is both in the interest of the country and the university that what we do should be something on which the country can rely. I am not saying that we should have no more imported experts in Agriculture, Engineering, Education, the general Arts and Sciences but I think that to continue to import experts in these fields on a large scale would seem to indicate that the university's contribution in these areas is still limited. We should be able to provide varied levels of middle-level man-power as well as high-level man-power, and this would seem to indicate that the resources at the moment diverted to some forms of training overseas for all these levels should be concentrated in the development of the university.

One must put on record the fact that the country has been, in terms of available resources, extremely generous to the university. Education takes a lion's share of the country's budget and the university takes the lion's share of this lion's share. The only problem is that in terms of what we want to do, in terms of what our researchers would like to do, both for the country and for their own academic interest, this lion's share is small. The research done at this university is remarkable for its depth and relevance to the needs of the country. What is now needed is that it should filter down to more postgraduate training so that the expertise at the moment limited to university staff can be forever at the disposal of the country as a whole.

F.M.

NOTE

1. *Education for Development*, Report of the Survey Team on Education in Malawi, American Council on Education (mimeographed), April 1964, paras. 120 + 127).

26

Higher Education in Australia

Zelman Cowen

One of the instructions given to the first Governor of New South Wales, Captain Arthur Phillip RN, who settled the colony in 1788, was to set aside land to support a schoolmaster. Early attempts to provide education in the new colony, however, were hampered by lack of teachers and finance, and relied on whatever resources were available from state, church, and community enterprise. By the second half of the nineteenth century, the various early schemes for education, including state support to some religious schools, had extended primary education to many parts of the country, but had proven unequal to the task of bringing adequate education to most children.

In seeking ways to overcome this deficiency, the colonial governments were influenced by groups espousing a liberal system of education – which was expected to promote a unifying national sentiment and provide practical training for the new age – and by the peculiar economic and geographic situation in Australia, which required the financial and administrative resources of central government to provide social services for a widely scattered and sparse population. By the time the six colonies federated to form the Commonwealth of Australia in 1901, they had developed highly centralized secular systems of education supported by a 'surprisingly uniform body of legislation',[1] the strength of which is still apparent. The states have not acquired a monopoly of education: there is a large Roman Catholic education system, and other non-government schools, which teach syllabuses very similar in essentials to those of the State schools, and cater for about 20 per cent of pupils.

The Growth of Universities

Four of the colonies founded universities in their capital cities before 1901 (Sydney 1850, Melbourne 1853, Adelaide 1874, Tasmania 1890). Powers assigned to the Commonwealth by the federal constitution did not include those related to education; so it is not surprising that the universities established in Brisbane (1909) and Western Australia (1912), in much the same educational climate as their colonial predecessors, should resemble them in style, having faculties of arts and science and usually the professional faculties of law, engineering, and later medicine. In addition, unlike the tertiary institutions of some other countries, notably the United States of America, Australian universities were financed substantially from government moneys and student fees, with very limited private endowment. This situation still applies in universities and, with very few exceptions, tertiary colleges.

Except for extension into essentially professional faculties such as dentistry, commerce, architecture and agriculture, there were no major changes in universities until the mid-1900s. Rising population, increasing demand for higher education, and the Commonwealth Government's decision in the later 1950s to make very substantial matching grants to the States for university purposes, all led to a rapid growth in the size and academic range of the older universities and to the establishment of nine new universities. The capacity of the technical colleges to offer tertiary-level courses has also been increased; and more recently federal funds have become available to the States to establish and support colleges of advanced education which, in 1969, consisted of 43 institutions, some new, and some former technical or specialist colleges.

Population growth, and the increasing proportion of young people seeking higher education, are continuing to stimulate expansion. In 1920 there were only 8,000 students studying full-time or part-time at the six universities, while the country's population was 5·5 million. In 1960 there were 53,600 university students (population 8·3 million). In 1968 Australia's population was 12·2 million; 101,537 students attended universities and 59,484 attended Colleges of Advanced Education. Since 1951 the percentage of the 18-year-old age group attending universities has risen, for males, from 7·96 per cent to 17·22 per cent, and for females, from 3·07 per cent to 9·13 per cent. A leading demographer predicts that student numbers will rise between 1971 and 1981 from 122,000 to 155,000 (university) and 91,000 to 152,000 (other tertiary), with a rather diminished increase during the five years thereafter.[2]

Sir Robert Menzies, Prime Minister of Australia from 1949 to 1966, a staunch believer in the contribution to be made to national welfare by higher education, initiated Commonwealth planning to meet the increasing demand for places in tertiary institutions, and this has made available to higher education a much greater share of national resources than previously. In 1957, he announced the appointment of Sir Keith Murray, then chairman of the United Kingdom University Grants Committee, to head a committee to inquire into:

> ways in which the universities might be organized so as to ensure that their long-term pattern of development is in the best interests of the nation.[3]

The committee produced a report which has become a landmark in Australian university history, leading to the establishment, in 1959, of the

Australian Universities Commission (originally five members, now nine – four from universities, including the chairman, three from industry, and two from state public services) to make recommendations to the Commonwealth, after consultation with the States and the universities, on the needs of the universities.

The first report of the AUC, published in 1960, established the Commission as a major force in Australian higher education, with particular significance in the fields of finance, planning, and innovation. By receiving submissions, by making inquiries in all universities on their operations and proposed developments, and by rendering triennial reports (now four in number) to the Commonwealth, on the funding and development of universities, the Commission has performed an important service to the universities by maintaining a flow of reliable information about them to the Commonwealth Parliament and its officers; and, indirectly perhaps, it has also kept much better informed about their universities the state governments, which continue to bear about half the burden of their support.

A particularly important outcome of the Commission's first report was the recommendation that there be set up an advisory committee to examine and give expert opinion on various aspects of future university design.[4] Such a committee was appointed in 1961, under the chairmanship of Sir Leslie Martin, the chairman of the AUC, and comprised fourteen members drawn from the universities, industry and government. In 1964 the Martin Committee published its report on the future development of tertiary education in Australia.[5] The report dealt with the major types of tertiary institutions then in existence – mainly universities, teachers' colleges and technical colleges – and with the needs of higher education in many fields. The fact that all of the recommendations contained in the report were not immediately adopted by the Commonwealth and State Governments does not diminish the continuing effect of this expert and valuable document. The setting up in 1965 of the continuing Commonwealth Advisory Committee on Advanced Education (the 'Wark Committee', so described for its Chairman, Sir Ian Wark), the vigorous growth and development of the universities, and the more recent reorganization of teacher training in some states, are some of the outcomes attributable in varying degrees to the report. Its most important benefit, however, has undoubtedly been its usefulness to educators, planners and legislators as a detailed and comprehensive framework within which to examine and provide for the needs of higher education.

New Development in University Education

The six original universities were established primarily as undergraduate teaching universities, to prepare students for entry to the professions.

Associated research was conducted with very limited facilities. In 1946, the first of the nine universities set up in the last twenty-five years was established by the Commonwealth Government. This was the Australian National University at Canberra, which was at first wholly devoted to postgraduate studies and research. In 1960 the former Canberra University College became the undergraduate School of General Studies of the Australian National University; the six research schools of Medicine, Physics, Social Sciences, Pacific Studies, Biological Sciences and Chemistry now form its Institute of Advanced Studies. Doctoral students obtain their degrees in the Institute. It also provides a large number of short-term research fellowships (3 to 5 years); these are seen as a way of creating a pool of potential staff for other Australian universities, and for research and industry.

The universities of New England (1954) and New South Wales (1958) both developed from well-established institutions. The University of New England was formerly the New England University College of the University of Sydney (1938) and is unusual among Australian universities for the very high proportion of its students who live in colleges, which are mainly non-sectarian, on campus. The University of New South Wales was formerly the New South Wales University of Technology. These two universities and those previously existing, as well as some of the six established since – Monash (Victoria) 1958, Newcastle 1965, Flinders (South Australia) 1966, La Trobe (Victoria) 1967, Macquarie (New South Wales) 1967, James Cook (Queensland) 1970 – have rather similar course and faculty structures.

Bachelors' degree courses extend from 3 to 6 years depending upon faculty, and increase in length from degrees in science and arts through those such as law, agriculture, engineering, and medicine. Large numbers of Australian graduates have obtained their degrees by part-time study, and the universities of Queensland and New England, and Macquarie University, cater for substantial numbers of 'external' students who take courses by correspondence and in many cases by short-term attendance at the university. It is estimated that of the 109,000 undergraduates expected to be enrolled in 1971, 29,000 will be part-time students and 7,200 will be studying externally. The growing importance of higher degree studies is reflected in the increase in the number of higher degrees granted, from 207 in 1947 to 1,246 in 1968; the expected enrolment of higher degree students in 1971 is 12,000 in a total university student population of 121,000. During the period since the Second World War, the research PhD has been widely accepted, and more recently masters' degrees based on course-work rather than on presentation of a research thesis have been introduced in some universities. Those studying for the PhD and for various masters' degrees make up the bulk of higher degree students.

Faculties usually number over ten in the larger universities (e.g. Agriculture, Architecture, Arts, Commerce or Economics, Dentistry, Engineering, Medicine, Science; also Veterinary Science, Music, Education and Law) and are concerned with the content and quality of the degrees which, except for the PhD, generally take their names from the faculty. The teaching departments of the universities (numbering more than fifty in the larger universities) may often find themselves serving a number of faculties, and students enrolled in a particular faculty may be engaged more intimately with each of a number of departments having little or no apparent relationship to one another, than with the faculty itself. With the growth of universities, concern has been felt by both staff and students about the difficulty some students have in realizing themselves as individuals in this type of structure. In some of the newer universities (Flinders, Macquarie, La Trobe) related academic disciplines have been grouped in schools in order to encourage interdisciplinary co-operation and to make easier the student's understanding and appreciation of his university experience. At La Trobe, all staff and students are members of non-sectarian colleges around which much academic work is organized and which provide residence for a small proportion of their members. Elsewhere colleges fulfil mainly a residential function, generally with some tutorial work. At Flinders, the schools act in the same way as faculties to control courses. At Macquarie, the BA degree is the only undergraduate degree awarded; students enrol each year in one of the ten wide-ranging schools, and may choose to take a broad, general degree, including many disciplines, or a degree of a more conventional specialized pattern, usually containing about four subject areas.

Since 1961, the balance of interest in different academic areas in the universities has changed, as has the range of disciplines studied. Two main factors have been responsible. Firstly, demand by undergraduate students for professional and scientific courses has decreased, and a greater proportion have sought to study in the humanities and the social sciences. Between 1961 and 1968, proportions of students taking arts-type courses increased from 30·9 per cent to 39 per cent, while there were decreases in the proportion working in applied sciences, engineering, dental science, medicine, pharmacy and agricultural science.[6] Secondly, the AUC has responded to submissions made by universities by recommending the allocation of funds to allow new fields of study to be entered. Over the most recent triennia (1967–9, 1970–2) a number of additional universities have been given funds to create faculties or schools in natural sciences and earth sciences, and to introduce such studies as biological sciences, sociology, anthropology, Italian, Spanish, education, Asian languages, computer science, medical sciences and business studies. When formulating their submissions the universities take account of community and internal pressures; the AUC in making its recommendations takes account of the Government's desire to promote balanced and economic development in higher education; however, in approving academic development, it earmarks only those funds intended for major innovations.

New Developments in Non-University Higher Education

At the time of the appointment of a Commonwealth Advisory Committee on Advanced Education (the Wark Committee) in 1965, there were already well established in the States institutions wholly or partly engaged in non-university tertiary education. Some had been operating for over 50 years and most had built up courses well regarded in the industries they serve, leading to certificate, diplomate, or fellowship qualifications. Some were connected with secondary-level colleges or schools while others were wholly tertiary; some were concerned with a large number of courses while others specialized in particular areas. Their interests included many types of engineering, business studies, paramedical studies, pharmacy, agriculture, forestry, horticulture, mining, domestic economy, the arts, and building and architecture.

In the 1960s the states were finding difficulty in providing for the growing numbers seeking advanced education, and were faced with the Murray Committee's predicted increases from the 1963 enrolment of 34,000 to 55,000 in 1967, and over 80,000 in 1971.[7] In fact, enrolments for 1967 were 27,000; current (1969) prediction for 1971 is 60,300.[8] The Commonwealth Government provided capital grants in 1965 and 1966 to help relieve the States' difficulties. Following the submission of the Wark Committee's report in 1966, the classification 'college of advanced education' was applied to 43 existing and proposed institutions teaching at an advanced level (other than universities and teachers' colleges) which require completion of full secondary schooling as an entry standard, and whose students reach tertiary level of attainment. The strong Commonwealth support given these colleges has led to their rapid development. The states have increased their support, and public and industrial reaction to the scheme has been strong and positive.

In appointing staff to the colleges, account has been taken of both academic qualifications and industrial experience, and recent salary adjustments have improved conditions of employment so that competition with universities and industry for staff is increasingly strong. There is an emphasis on teaching; the colleges have been encouraged to release staff for consultancy and short periods of work in industry, and considerable use is being made of part-time teachers from the various professions and occupations. Although the Commonwealth has so far declined to include separate teachers' colleges among CAEs, it accepts teacher education as part of the function of the CAE, and in a number of states and in the Australian Capital Territory some pre-school, primary, and secondary teachers are to be trained in the colleges. In the last triennium the Commonwealth made a capital grant to the States for the construction of new teachers' colleges, and this has led to an improvement in teacher-training facilities.

The Functions of the Universities and the Colleges of Advanced Education

With the example before us of the development of binary systems of tertiary education in other countries, there has been a deal of interest in the evolution of CAEs, and their relationship with universities. There is some obscurity in the definition of the respective roles of CAEs and universities. It has been said that the colleges will have a strong technological emphasis; that they will be much concerned with practical and applied outcomes, while paying due regard to theory necessary to ensure scientifically based practice. It was said by the Wark Committee[9] in 1965 that in the colleges there would be:

- students with somewhat different types of interests;
- a greater concentration upon part-time studies associated with employment especially in scientific fields;
- a more applied emphasis;
- a more direct and intimate relationship with industry and other relevant organizations;
- far less attention to postgraduate training and research;
- a primary emphasis on teaching.

The distinctions are not clear-cut and many professional courses which require close relationship to on-going research seem certain to continue to be in the province of the university. In some areas, such as engineering and the paramedical fields, it seems likely that similar courses will be given by CAEs in some states and by universities in others.

In 1969, an inquiry into academic awards in advanced education[10] recommended the use of the terms diploma, bachelor, and master, suitably identified as CAE awards – e.g. BTech (Elec). Master's degree courses in the colleges would be designed to attract both college and university graduates. Some colleges have added bachelors' degrees to their range of awards and there has been put forward at least one proposal to introduce a master's course in management.

Legislation and Government in Higher Education

Because the changing role of the Commonwealth has made possible dramatic recent changes in higher education, attention has been focused on it. However, the universities, the CAEs, and the teachers' colleges (with the exception of the ANU, Canberra College of Advanced

Education, and the Defence Colleges) are established within the legislative frameworks of their respective states.

The universities are constituted under the provisions of separate state acts. Typically, these acts deal with such matters as establishment and property, the supreme governing body of the university (council or senate), the membership of the university, and the granting of degrees. They also usually contain quite general statements of the aims or functions of the university relating to teaching, examining and research, and permit the universities to make statutes or by-laws for which the approval of the State Governor in Council is generally required. In these the internal government of the university is delineated.

Most university governing bodies contain representatives of government, university staff, students, the graduate body and a number of *ex officio* appointees. Advice is received on academic and general policy matters from sub-committees of the council and from the senior academic board, sometimes composed of the professors and heads of departments, sometimes more representative. Faculties and schools have their own boards, on which academic staff and some qualified outsiders may sit, which advise the senior academic board. The growth of academic staffs has made many of these organs of government unwieldy, and it may well be that the older universities will need to reform their machinery. Both staff and students have expressed dissatisfaction with their limited involvement in university government, especially at the higher levels, and with the extent of outside membership of university governing bodies. Student bodies particularly have sought more participation in all levels of university government, and most universities are examining ways of creating more opportunity for student involvement.

Legislation for CAEs and teachers' colleges varies from State to State. Most of these colleges were originally under the direct control of the state departments of education; a few had governing councils recommending policy to education departments. Victoria (1965) and New South Wales (1969) created central boards to co-ordinate the affairs of CAEs and other states have taken similar action. The colleges are governed by councils made up of members of government, industry, and the public service, in most cases with staff representation, and in some cases with student and graduate representation.

In many universities and colleges, students operate a separate governmental structure in their student unions or student representative councils. These bodies represent student opinion to the university and college administrations, and on occasions to governments and other outside agencies. In some cases they also establish and manage student catering and recreational facilities, for which the AUC gives some capital support.

Finances

Triennially, the universities and the colleges of advanced education make, to the AUC and the CACAE[11] respectively, submissions on the funds they will require to finance staff and buildings over a three-year period. They take into account such factors as expected student numbers and likely course preferences, accommodation needs, salary and administrative and material costs. They also make proposals for the expansion of courses or the introduction of new academic activities, changes in staff-student ratios, administrative support, and student facilities. The Commonwealth bodies consult formally with the State Governments on relevant parts of the proposals; the universities and CAEs reach their State Governments through informal contact, government appointees to council, and in some states through boards of higher education. The AUC and the CACAE recommend to the Commonwealth the amounts to be made available to match money found by State Governments and from fees, on the basis of $1 for $1 for capital funds, and $1 Commonwealth to $1·85 State for operating costs. As well as receiving money from governments and from student fees, the universities receive donations and endowments for research and other purposes; in 1968, these were 5·2 per cent of total university income. Table 1 shows sources of university income for 1968:

TABLE 1

MAJOR CLASSES OF INCOME, AUSTRALIAN UNIVERSITIES, 1968[12]

Purpose of income	Source of income ($'000)					Total (rounded)
	C'wealth	States	Donations Special grants Endowments	Fees	Other*	
Specific capital purposes	20,923	14,976	610	–	174	36,683
All other purposes	67,875	57,879	11,374	22,210	8,284	167,623
TOTAL	88,798†	72,855	11,984	22,210	8,458	204,306

* Includes halls of residence, and interest from university investments.
† Includes ANU and Canberra CAE supported solely by Commonwealth funds.

Detailed figures are not available for CAEs. However, in the triennium 1967–9, total Commonwealth and State capital expenditure was over $40 million, and recurrent expenditure over $55 million.[13]

Present Trends

Rapid social change and student concern about education and social behaviour are phenomena with which Australian universities are now more concerned than they have been in the past. There is unprecedented public interest in all areas of higher education; industry is calling for personnel educated to a tertiary level and many students wish to qualify for industrial posts; a growing and rapidly urbanizing community is concerned about its own social welfare and quality of life, and requires graduates as informed citizens and specialized workers to help in the solution of its problems; students themselves are better skilled and more widely informed, questioning the quality of their education and making clear their expectation that their university experiences will be stimulating and relevant to their own diverse interests in society and academic work; the impending lowering of the age of adulthood from 21 to 18 gives students a new political status. There are implications for action by universities and CAEs: provision of a number of different course patterns and modes of learning which will satisfy the needs of both students and society; reorganization of large institutions to minimize the sometimes inhibiting effects of their size on the academic and social learning experiences of students; guidance of students towards courses appropriate to their capacity and interests; planning to take account of individual as well as physical and organizational factors, and to co-ordinate the work of the university and the CAE without infringing on the autonomy of either.

In the newer universities and CAEs, a wide variety in subject and course patterns is possible. Programme flexibility has been increased in some cases by the use of the semester system. Some universities and CAEs have service sections which offer lecturers preparation for, and advice in, teaching. There are also some with units providing technological support for teaching, or conducting research in higher education. Resources allocated to teaching support are generally minimal, however, and the older institutions particularly are burdened with many inflexible teaching spaces. Large classes of first-year students (some running into hundreds) are common, and there are few institutions where students can find local private study places to use casually between formal classes. The increasing formal and informal involvement of students in the government of higher education is bringing these problems more clearly to the notice of planners and the community; this may ensure that a greater share of resources is, in the future, given to improve and support teaching and to create institutions which are sufficiently flexible and virile to react constructively to student interests while maintaining their own academic integrity.

Planning for co-operation between universities and CAEs is being fostered by mutual representation on some governing councils, and informal discussions about course recognition. The Wiltshire report[14] on certification in the CAEs opens the way for establishment of machinery for interchange of students. In addition, the Tertiary Education Entrance Project[15] may free secondary schools to prepare students more adequately in the structure of the disciplines and to help in the guidance of interested students towards universities, CAEs or teachers' colleges. Progress in these two areas may help to place students in more satisfying courses and may create for those who desire it, a type of educational progression, perhaps by way of both university and college, which offers a liberal general education as well as specialist training.

NOTES

1. A. G. Austin, *Australian Education 1788–1900* (Melbourne: Pitman, 1961), p. 166.
2. Figures in this paragraph from:
   (a) *Yearbook of the Commonwealth of Australia – 1969* (Canberra: Commonwealth Bureau of Census and Statistics, 1970).
   (b) W. D. Borrie, 'Demographic Trends and Education in Australia' in G. W. Bassett, *Planning in Australian Education* (Melbourne: Australian Council for Educational Research, 1970).
   (c) Commonwealth Bureau of Census and Statistics.
3. *Report of the Committee on Australian Universities* (Canberra: Commonwealth Government Printer, 1958), p. 127.
4. *Report of the Australian Universities Commission* (Canberra: Commonwealth Government Printer, 1960), p. 75.
5. *Tertiary Education in Australia* (Melbourne: Government Printer, vols. 1 and 2, 1964; vol. 3, 1965).
6. *Fourth Report of the Australian Universities Commission* (Canberra: Commonwealth Government Printer, 1969), p. 17.
7. *First Report of the Commonwealth Advisory Committee on Advanced Education* (Canberra: Commonwealth Government Printer, 1966), p. 25.
8. *Commonwealth Advisory Committee on Advanced Education – Second Report* (Canberra: Commonwealth Government Printer, 1969), pp. 106–9.
9. *First Report of the Commonwealth Advisory Committee on Advanced Education* (Canberra: Commonwealth Government Printer, 1966), p. 23.
10. *Report of the Committee of Inquiry into Awards in Colleges of Advanced Education* (Canberra: Commonwealth Government Printer, 1969).
11. CACAE – Commonwealth Advisory Committee on Advanced Education.
12. *University Statistics 1968: Part 3 – Finance* (Canberra: Commonwealth Bureau of Census and Statistics), p. 7.
13. *Commonwealth Advisory Committee on Advanced Education – Second Report* (Canberra: Commonwealth Government Printer, 1969), pp. 9–10.
14. *Report of the Committee of Inquiry into Awards in Colleges of Advanced Education* (Canberra: Commonwealth Government Printer, 1969).
15. Bernard Rechter, *Admission to Tertiary Studies* (Melbourne: Australian Council for Educational Research, 1970).

27

Changing Policies in Higher Education – the Japanese Case

Tetsuya Kobayashi

'The diversification of higher education' is a phrase which characterizes the present trend of Japanese policies in higher education. The phrase was first used officially by the Central Council of Education of the Ministry of Education in its interim report on the reform of higher education, published in 1962. Since then it has been repeated by the Council in its reports on higher education of 1963 and 1970 and by the Ministry itself in policy statements on various occasions. At the same time the phrase has been raising arguments, both pros and cons, among those concerned with the nation's higher education.

The Central Council on Education argues that the new role of higher education in a changing society must be reconsidered in the light of the recent increase in student population as well as in the number of higher institutions, and of the rapid development in arts, science and technology. While the traditional function of the university in society – the conserving and upgrading of culture by its academic studies – is to be maintained as one of its important functions, the new emphasis is to be given to its teaching function, which should provide higher education, both professional and general, for a wider circle of citizens. However, the Council considers the present system of higher education inadequate to fulfil such functions, mainly because it is too uniform to meet the needs and demands of the different sections of society.

Thus the report of 1962 recommended the diversification of the higher education system into five types of institution differing from each other in function, organization and curricula. The first type of higher institution are graduate school universities, whose aim is to provide the highest level of professional training. The graduate school universities consist of graduate schools in different disciplines leading to the doctoral degree and an undergraduate college providing four-year courses, though they may lack the latter. The second type are to be called universities, which aim mainly at providing higher professional education. The universities consist of undergraduate faculties with possibly post-graduate training at the master level. The third type is the junior college, the aim of which is to give professional training, to provide knowledge and skills necessary for practical life, or to give general education. The duration of the course is two to three years. Under the fourth type come the technical colleges which provide professional training for graduates of junior secondary schools. The duration of the training is five years. The fifth type of higher institution includes colleges of fine arts which train professional artists in music and fine arts for a duration of four years, or seven years when they take students directly from junior secondary school.

The report of 1970 makes some modifications in the classification of higher institutions. The first type, the universities, provides the graduates of senior secondary schools with general and professional education for a duration of three to four years. The second type – the junior colleges – provides two-year courses. The third type are the technical colleges. These three types have the same characteristics as suggested in the 1962 report. The fourth kind of higher institution are called graduate schools; they provide the graduates of universities with higher specialized education for a period of two to three years and also function as in-service education or re-education institutions for adult students. The fifth type are to be known as research institutes and give research training at the level of doctoral degrees.

Before going on to analyse the questions involved in the suggestions of the Central Council on the 'diversification of higher education', it may be necessary to make a review on the development of Japanese higher education over the past twenty years, as this constitutes the background to the above recommendations.

Development of Japanese Higher Education over the Past Twenty Years

As Tables I and II show, the quantitative development of Japanese higher education over the past twenty years has been enormous. Between 1950 and 1968, the number of universities almost doubled, while that of junior colleges tripled. As for the number of students, the increase is five times in universities and sixteen times in junior colleges. In the case of newly established technical colleges, the number of the colleges has tripled over the first seven years after their establishment and the number of students has increased eleven times in the same period. Thus the percentage of students in the age group 18 to 21 which is in higher institutions has increased from 6·2 per cent in 1950 to 12·8 in 1968. Comparisons of the figures in 1940 and 1968 show that the number of universities has increased eight times and the number of their students fifteen times, while the higher institutions of the second level, that is, pre-war technical colleges and teacher training institutions and post-war junior colleges and technical colleges, have increased only 1·5 times in the number of institutions and 1·4 times in their students.

TABLE I
Higher Institutions in 1940

Universities	total	47
	Imperial	9
	governmental	10
	public	2
	private	26
number of students		81,999
Technical colleges	total	274
	governmental	105
	public	17
	private	152
number of students		153,291
Teacher training institutions (1943)	total	85
	governmental	85
number of students		69,057

TABLE II
Higher Institutions in 1950, 1960 and 1968

		1950	1960	1968
Universities	total	201	245	377
	state	70	72	75
	public	26	33	35
	private	105	140	267
number of students		224,921	626,421	1,270,389
Junior colleges	total	149	280	468
	state	0	27	23
	public	17	39	43
	private	132	214	402
number of students		15,098	83,456	255,262
Technical colleges	total		(1962) 19	60
	state		12	49
	public			4
	private		7	7
number of students			3,375	38,365

(The figures in the tables are quoted from *Annual Report of the Ministry of Education*, and Monbusho, *Monbu Nenpo*.)

Many factors help to explain these developments, among which the following three will be examined for the purposes of the present analysis.

The Egalitarian Policies of the Educational Reform of 1947

This educational reform of 1947 was carried out as part of the whole political and social process of democratizing a defeated Japan and transforming the character of the Japanese educational system, including higher education, from its traditional elitism, basically similar to that of Europe, to the egalitarianism of the American system. Four changes in the educational system made a special contribution to the development of higher education.

The first was the creation of the comprehensive junior secondary school, attendance at which was compulsory. This raised the school leaving age from 12 to 15 and increased the potential number of pupils who might later proceed to higher education.

Secondly, the establishment of comprehensive senior secondary schools made it possible for all secondary school graduates, regardless of their courses – whether academic or vocational – to proceed to higher education. As the enrolment in senior secondary schools has increased (from 45·5 per cent in the age group to 76·8 in 1968), the number of potential students in higher education has also increased.

Thirdly, the enforcement of co-education in the new system had its effect, particularly on the increase in the female population in higher institutions.

Finally, the policy which introduced parity among higher institutions contributed to the increase in the numbers of universities and their students. The old distinctions between universities and other second class higher institutions such as technical colleges and teacher training institutions, and among the former between the privileged Imperial universities and the others were all abolished by the 1947 reform. In the new system all higher institutions were called universities, although those giving shorter courses are now classified as junior colleges. They are, nevertheless, part of university or higher education as indicated by their Japanese title, which is, translated literally, 'short-term universities'.

The Economic Progress of Japan in the Fifties and Sixties

The rapid development of Japanese higher education over the past twenty years has been greatly stimulated by the improvement in the economic situation in the fifties and in particular by the economic boom of the sixties. The economic prosperity of the nation has in general provided the material and financial foundations for the expansion of its higher education. It has also made it possible for many parents to support their children over a longer period of education.

Furthermore, the expansion of industry and business has increased the need for highly educated personnel. This need has stimulated the aspirations of those in higher education on the one hand, and on the other has put pressure on the government to expand higher education. As early as 1952, the Japanese Union of Management Associations, an organization representing the interests of industry, made public its suggestions for improving higher education. These included (a) the expansion of science and technology faculties; (b) strengthening professional education in the curriculum; (c) diversification of higher institutions according to their orientation in research, professional education or semi-professional training and above all (d) the establishment of a technical college system with shorter but intensive periods of technical training.

The same opinions were expressed by various governmental agencies for economic development in the mid fifties. Thus in 1957 the Ministry of Education made a plan to increase the number of science and engineering graduates by 100,000 by 1970. In 1958 it also presented a bill to parliament to create technical colleges, and this was finally made law in 1961.

Private Universities

Thanks to the post-war liberal policy towards private education, the private higher institutions have been given an opportunity to develop. Responding more sensibly to the needs of the time, the private universities and junior colleges have increased their number as well as the number of their students. As the rates of increase have indicated, the expansion in higher education owes much to the growth of private institutions.

Problems Caused by the Expansion

The expansion of higher education has not been achieved without problems, however. The factors which have made a positive contribution to the expansion have also created problems.

By its egalitarian policy, the 1947 reform has succeeded in raising the general standard of education for a large number of students who would not have had a chance to receive higher education under the old system. However, it has failed to pay attention to a minority of gifted students who might have been given better education in the old selective system.

Another difficulty in the new system is its uniformity in curriculum structure. A university standard sets up a basic curriculum pattern which should be uniformly adopted by all universities. Each specialized faculty has further detailed standards, which again should be followed by all faculties of universities with that specialization. This uniformity was in a way necessary to maintain the academic levels of many of the newly created universities, but it is too uniform to meet the various levels of need and also hinders experiments in curriculum development.

Some of the faults in the new system have since been remedied by the creation of technical colleges in 1962, as well as by the liberalization of university standards in 1956 and 1970 which gives a certain freedom to each university to modify the basic curriculum structure. The faculties for teacher training, which were under the detailed standards for liberal arts faculties, had been given more distinctive features in the curriculum suitable for teacher education during the course of the fifties. A small number of state universities, most of which were former Imperial universities, have been given a privileged position by the government among state higher institutions as regards their graduate schools and research faculties.

Economic motives in the expansion of higher education have also created problems. The universities have been increasingly filled with students who have chosen universities for economic or professional reasons and these often conflict with the academism of the more traditional faculty members. This leads also to an attitude of apathy on the part of students towards liberal and general education. The industry's emphasis on professional education, which has gone too often at the expense of liberal education, has reinforced such a trend. The neglect of general education in the curriculum of technical colleges is an example of this.

The great increase in the number of higher institutions and in the number of their students over a relatively short period, to which the private institutions have made a great contribution, has raised problems as regards the quality of higher education, particularly among some private institutions. As their number increases, there is a wider difference in academic quality among institutions, faculty members and students. As the private institutions largely depend on students' fees for their finances, there is a tendency among them to admit students beyond their normal capacities. Higher tuition fees in private universities often prevent the able, but less well-off students, from entering them and this works negatively as far as an improvement in the quality of higher education is concerned.

New Policies in Higher Education

These are the background for the government's recent policy in higher education, which may be characterized by the phrase 'diversification of higher education'. The policy accepts a trend towards the popularization of higher education, or 'mass higher education', which has caused confusion in the dual function of universities, research and teaching. Thus instead of trying to find a happy combination of research and teaching in a university, the policy implies a diversification of the higher institutions into several types, each of which has a different degree of emphasis on research or teaching.

Until now, no legislation has been enacted to implement the recommendations of the Central Council on the reform of higher education, although occasionally it has been rumoured from governmental sources that a new university reform bill was soon to be proposed. On the other hand, a large number of the recommendations are in fact already being implemented. As has been observed, the present system has already developing in it distinctive types of higher institutions, such as junior colleges, technical colleges and teacher training colleges. Therefore this diversification of higher institutions in a way only justifies existing divisions. However, the distinction between graduate school universities and universities is new and has given rise to controversy. The idea is interpreted to mean the selection of some ten out of fifty state universities and the pooling of all material and personnel resources into these selected institutions for upgrading academic research and training, the remaining forty being concerned mainly with the education of undergraduates. The opponents of this idea regard it as a revival of the older distinction between the Imperial and the other universities, since it is obvious that the former Imperial universities which still possess their academic traditions and enjoy high social prestige will become the majority of those selected ten.

Having observed the difficulty in re-classifying the existing universities, a proposal has been made recently to establish new universities which should be organized along the lines of the recommendations of the Central Council. An education committee of the governmental Liberal-Democratic Party suggested in 1969 the setting up of some twenty universities in the coming twenty years according to the new ideas and structures. This proposal has since received some attention from both within the government and outside. In the same year the Ministry of Education appointed a preparatory committee for establishing a new state university in the north-east of Tokyo, Tsukuba Academic City, to be opened in 1973 as a new model university. In 1969 the government also set up a committee to study the plan of a radio and TV broadcast university, which may not fall into the above classification, but which is expected to show some fresh approaches to mass higher education.

Of course the diversification of higher institutions does not itself solve some of the problems mentioned above, notably those related to the quality of education in mass private universities. The Ministry of Education is aware of this and has been increasing its financial assistance to private universities, since its Council on Private Schools made a report in 1967 on the financial situation in private schools and universities and suggested a positive policy of state assistance to them.

In 1969 the Ministry decided to cover part of the expenses for teaching personnel. At that time some anxiety was expressed among private universities which feared that such financial assistance for teaching personnel might bring ministerial interference into their academic freedom. In this matter the Ministry seems to have been extremely careful and so far no complaint has been made by the private universities, but the new relationship between the state and the private universities will certainly have a great effect on the development of the private universities in the seventies.

BIBLIOGRAPHY

International Educational Research Institute, Hiroshima University, *Education in Japan, Vol. II, Educational System in Japan* (Hiroshima, 1967).

Japanese National Commission for Unesco: *The Role of Education in the Social and Economic Development of Japan* (Tokyo, 1966).

Kaigo Tokiomi, Terasaki Masao, *Daigaku Kyoiku* (Higher Education) (Tokyo, 1959).

Ministry of Education: *Education in 1955 ff.*, *Annual Report of the Ministry of Education* (Tokyo, 1957 ff.).

Monbusho (Ministry of Education): *Monbusho Nenpo* (Annual Report of the Ministry of Education) (Tokyo).

Monbusho (Ministry of Education): *Wagakuni no Koto Kyoiku* (Higher Education in Our Country) (Tokyo, 1964), translated by J. E. Blewett, *Higher Education in Postwar Japan* (Tokyo, 1965).

Monbusho (Ministry of Education): *Wagakuni no Kyoiku no Ayumi to Kongo no Kadai* (Development and Future Problems of Education in Our Country) (Tokyo, 1969).

28

The Indian Universities

K. C. Mukherjee

The origins of the present pattern of educational structure in India which includes the university as a characteristic type of educational institution can be found in the period of British rule. When significant territorial acquisition took place after the middle of the eighteenth century the British Government in India showed concern for education. The British Parliament was persuaded as early as in 1813 to authorize an expenditure of £10,000 annually for the 'revival and improvement of literature, and the encouragement for the learned natives of India, and for the introduction and promotion of a knowledge of the sciences among the inhabitants of the British territories in India'.

In those days there was no definite agreement on educational policy. The Anglicists in India intended to give priority to the development of higher educational institutions and the creation of an elite. But the Orientalists wanted to preserve and promote the traditional literary languages of India – Sanskrit, Persian and Arabic – while the Anglicists wanted English as the medium of instruction.

The conflict was finally resolved in the Anglicists' favour and Thomas Macaulay prepared his famous Educational Minute of 1835 in which he vigorously justified the cause of English education. Macaulay's views were sanctioned by the then Governor-General, Lord William Bentinck, who declared by issuing an Order in Council:

> . . . that the great object of the British Government ought to be the promotion of European literature and science among the natives of India; and that all the funds appropriated for the purposes of education would be best employed on English education alone.

By the middle of the nineteenth century, English schooling was established and had made considerable progress which necessitated a more comprehensive and planned educational policy. This need led the Educational Despatch of 1854 which among various recommendations suggested the establishment of the first universities in India – modelled on the University of London. Universities were accordingly set up in 1857 in Calcutta, Bombay and Madras, initially to prescribe courses of study in the colleges affiliated to them, to grant degrees and to examine students prepared in these colleges. This step was thus the first landmark of the modern university education which is found in the sub-continent today.

Post Independence Student Unrest

In 1947 when India received independence she had a total of nineteen universities. Since then the demand for secondary education has led to an increased demand for university education. The number of universities is increasing every year. In 1970 India had a total of seventy-two universities, the majority of which were of the affiliating type. Most of the affiliating ones provide instruction in their own teaching departments or in constituent colleges. Instruction in the non–affiliating universities are generally confined to teaching departments of associated colleges located within a fixed geographical area.

The problem of overcrowding is a major problem in Indian universities. Since independence there has been a spectacular rise in the student population in the colleges and university departments. The universities have not been able to expand their physical facilities or increase the number of teaching staff in proportion to the rise in the number of students.

The problem of student indiscipline for the last few decades has been the most disturbing concern to Indian educators. Throughout the last decade, news reports in the daily papers, can be found which read like the one in the *Daily Telegraph* of 26th February, 1970:

UNIVERSITY CLOSED – Calcutta University was closed yesterday after violent clashes between student groups armed with swords, bombs and pistols.

Student troubles in Western European and American universities are much more recent than in Indian institutions. The origins and solutions of the problem seem quite complex. But the problem is one that has vexed Indian educators for many, many years. Similar incidents to the University of Calcutta one quoted above were mentioned in Indian dailies ten or twenty years ago. For example a report in the *Hindu* of 14th May 1960 read:

STUDENTS ASSAULT COLLEGE STAFF, PATNA, MAY 12. A mob of about four hundred students today made a forced entry into the premises of the Patna Communal college and assaulted the Principal and four professors of the College, causing grievous injury to one of them. Three of the professors have been admitted to the Patna Medical College.

The trouble started following the expulsion of four student examinees from the examination hall for using unfair means during the annual examination in the college. One professor died later. Again on 18th March, 1970 one reads in the *Guardian* that in West Bengal, students participated in political violence in which at least twenty people were killed and sixty injured. Clashes broke out between supporters of the Marxist Communist and other political parties during a twenty-four hour strike called by the Marxists to protest against the break-up of the State's coalition government which they had dominated. Riot police in steel helmets and men of the Eastern Frontier Rifles patrolled several towns and cities as the Marxists students and their rivals fought with home-made bombs, spears, swords, guns and other weapons. Life throughout the state was paralysed. In one clash, police opened fire, and five people were killed with several injured. In another incident police used tear-gas when Marxist supporters fought with members of another party. In the industrial town of Burdwan, three people died and ten were injured in an armed clash between Marxists and Congress students. Armed demonstrators, many of them students, ransacked the Jadavpore railway station near Calcutta and crowds carrying spears and bombs attacked several factories. On still other occasions in Delhi, Agra, Aligarh and in many other parts of India the violence of the students were so severe and bloody that essential services in the university towns, including hospitals, electricity, water and train supply were paralysed, not to speak of the closed colleges and institutions.

Political cliques and anarchical groups exploit Indian students to such an extent that riots and strikes involving bloodshed and lawlessness are frequent. The most trivial incident can ignite a fire. Most writers realize that there is no single underlying cause and that the unrest has resulted from a number of problems. But overcrowding has a direct bearing on the conduct of the students and standards of education.

Expansion Problems

The expansion of higher education in India since independence has been the result not of planning, but of the social, economic and political changes that have taken place in the country. No one in India has seriously attempted to estimate how many universities and university trained scholars in arts and science will be required over a given period of time or how many different kinds of schools and colleges with what facilities and accommodation would be required. As a result an unbalanced growth of university has complicated the educational system of India. The student/ staff ratio in Indian universities is very high – in many cases as high as 100 : 2. The workload of the teaching staff is too heavy, approximately sixteen hours a week and involves each lecturer in too many subjects.

India's quantitative educational requirements during the present stage of her educational development necessitates a limitation of the expansion of secondary and university education and the attainment of universal primary education which has been officially recognized and stated in the provisions of Article 45 of the Constitution. This view of India's educational need is supported by the fact of widespread unemployment and inappropriate employment among the highly qualified and also by the acknowledgement of the country's highest educational leaders and foreign experts that excessive quantities of general secondary and higher education have been provided.

Rapid expansion of the universities has lowered the academic standards, both of the teachers and the taught. There is indeed a shortage of first-class scholars in many departments of learning and some of second-class men have been employed in university teaching posts. No doubt many books have been written and journals published by university teachers, but their articles are in most cases more pedantic than scholarly both in presentation and content. It is doubtful whether there has been any substantial increase in real scholarship. Doubts have been raised whether in India there are enough scholars and experienced teachers of higher intellectual calibre for students really to benefit.

The changes in the courses of study have been criticized mainly for two reasons. It has been argued that wide-ranging courses lacking specialization lead to superficiality. The liberal arts people have criticized the extent to which major importance is placed on scientific and technological studies while others, considering India's industrial needs, have held that to fulfil the Five Year Plans scientific studies should be given a major place in the universities. Others have expressed their concern about the universities' cherished autonomy and freedom. Again the scale of government expenditure on the universities and their unprecedented financial dependence is likely to curtail the wide freedom they previously enjoyed.

The number of universities is increasing so fast that they are coming to occupy a position in Indian society different from that which they had in pre-independence years. Before independence the universities were mainly the training grounds for selected fortunate students who represented the upper-class of society. These intellectuals and social elites came from a minority, the privileged upper classes who subsequently entered important posts in the country. But now the significant increase in the number of university places has led to a social revolution. It has also made the university, to a greater extent than ever before, the arbiter of school courses. The demands of the university influence the syllabuses and courses of study for the secondary and higher-secondary school studies. The influence of the universities is gradually penetrating more deeply into various aspects of Indian life pervading the entire fabric of education. The universities are now in a better position to influence the quality and direction of the country's life.

The Functions of the University

This unprecedented expansion leads us to consider the primary function and role of a university. In the past the main task of the university was to impress upon the minds of students a set of values essentially moral and religious in character. Secondly the university endeavoured to promote scholarship (without necessary research) and prepared the students for service to the country. The universities hoped to inculcate sound religion and true learning to produce good moral citizens. Later in life the majority of graduates were not very much concerned to experiment with new knowledge but were keen to preserve an ancient culture and hand it down undiluted to the next generation. The universities transmitted an ancient culture.

The mainly utilitarian and functional purposes of the universities were perceived; they also provided technical training for a clerical ruling class. That since independence there has been some change in the interpretation of the university's role is obvious. In his address to the University of Allahabad in 1947 Mr J. Nehru summed up the basic objectives of the university and its role in Indian life. He saw

> A univeristy stands for humanism, for tolerance, for reason, for the adventure of ideas and for the search of truth. It stands for the onward march of the human race towards even higher objectives. If the universities discharge their duties adequately, then it is well with the nation and the people.

Modern protagonists incline to minimize this literally traditional function, less certain of what should be preserved and concentrate on a utlitarian[1] function tempered by idealism. So in their Report on Standard of University Education the University Grants Commission stated that the universities should primarily provide training in professional skills although the inculcation of liberal values should be given due attention. Advanced technological courses and scientific studies become more meaningful when they are considered as an expression of the human spirit and not merely as an explanation of how the physical universe operates. It is significant that the Report on Standards of University Education in India agreed with the British Robbins Report and stated that there are four objectives for the higher education system: instruction in skills, promotion of the general powers of the mind, the advancement of learning and the transmission of a common culture and common standards of citizenship. The Report assumed as axiomatic that courses of higher education should be available to all those who were qualified by ability and attainment to pursue them and who wished to do so. But at present when the government is attempting to bring about far-reaching economic and social changes, it should be conceded that universities have to lay much greater stress on developing oriented education.

It is a fact that teaching has degenerated in many Indian universities into routine instruction, emphasis is given to mass lectures, students rely on ready-made notes and guide books. One of the main objectives to be achieved in order to transform teaching from imparting information to the acquisition of knowledge and changing memorization to the training of the mind and sharpening the intellect, are true roles for the teacher.

The Report was also concerned with university administration which they suggested ought to be more efficient. It stressed that research and teaching as the main function of the university, i.e. the expansion of postgraduate study, was a necessary development. What the Report did not point out was the important personal function of university education, it failed to pay proper attention to many real problems of the students such as housing and health.

The Education Commission of 1966 rightly stated that the universities should provide the right kind of leadership in all walks of life and train competent men and women in agriculture, arts, medicine, science, technology and various other professions.

The Indian university, the Commission pointed out, should have a twofold function. Firstly it is an institution of scholars engaged in lecturing and research. Teaching and research should to a great extent be related to the needs of contemporary India. The Report on Standards of University Education rightly stated that in the present situation, involving attempts to bring about far-reaching economic and social changes, it would be necessary for universities to place much greater stress on development-oriented education. But in so doing Indian universities should take care that the personality of the student as a cultured and responsible member of society was not lost sight of.

The transmission of exciting knowledge to new generations is of course one of the primary tasks of the university, but is never purely that. The development of scholarship and true research cannot be separated from studies of a moral and spiritual nature, an earnest desire for inquiry, a sense of purpose and intellectual integrity. Some of these are mentioned by the Education Commission in 1966 when it stated that Indian universities should foster in the teachers and students and through them in society generally, the attitudes and values needed for developing the 'good life' in individuals and society. In addition the Commission recommended that the universities should strongly develop programmes of adult education and evolve a widespread network of part-time and correspondence courses. High priority, it was suggested, should be given to the improvement in the quality and standard of education and research, the expansion of higher education to meet the manpower needs of national development and the improvement of organization and administration.

Conclusions

If we accept the Commission's suggestions then one purpose of the university should be to develop intellectual achievements relevant to contemporary India and another should be to provide the country with a sense of values.

Now we should ask how the Indian universities measure up to these criteria. It is not at all clear that Indian universities hold any precisely articulated values. For the most part they seem to cherish a rather superficial utilitarianism and operate as factories in which a particular craft can be taught. The lack of a feeling of fellowship and any real sense of community and an attitude towards members of the teaching staff as paid employees who should exert very little influence on the conduct of affairs, are symptoms of the malaise. In the contemporary situation the universities have not seriously attempted to make the intellectual and moral effort necessary to discover or recreate values which have so long rested on a cultural heritage. It is evident that university teachers have to think out their subjects anew and recast them so that they may be suitable to the educational and industrial needs of India since independence. The unprecedented and unplanned expansion of universities have led to the creation of intellectual 'unemployeds' – many of whom are confused, frustrated and rebellious. In India this crisis is more severe than anywhere else. Academic illusion and frustration are the main cause of the developing break-down in relations between the students and professors in India. The great expansion in the number of universities and in the student population, the subsequent social and cultural changes, the change in morals and values and the atmosphere of political uncertainty make it particularly difficult for the modern Indian universities to find their true role and functions. In addition the severe unemployment of graduates has aroused intellectual apathy with which earlier generations were unfamiliar to the same degree.

These problems show how necessary it is for the Indian universities to think out more positively and explicitly their true role and function and to proclaim it more clearly. Their main task must be to teach and develop research, but they must also accept social economic and cultural responsibilities. There is a big gap between the goal and ideals and reality. Indian universities can no longer dictate student morals, yet it cannot also ignore their anti-social and anti-moral activities. They must provide a philosophy of existence to the students, foster intellectual discussion to promote understanding and show concern in those vital matters which affect the students in their development of the whole man so that they are able to work out for themselves a meaningful and purposeful solution to life.

Again the most onerous responsibility which the Indian universities now have to do is to bring back the 'centre of gravity' of Indian academic life within the country itself. Sir Eric Ashby can rightly be quoted on this subject:

> Looking at Indian Universities a century after their foundation, one cannot but help feel that they have failed to adapt themselves sufficiently to the vast and unique opportunities which surround them; they seem to have lost enthusiasm and initiative under the crushing problems which have beset them. Despite three major commissions, they have not been able to extricate themselves from their own brief history. With a few notable exceptions they remain examining bodies and their students naturally regard success in examinations as the sole end of an undergraduate career. As universities multiply in number, their academic standards – relative to those elsewhere – do not improve. And something even more serious than this happens: the universities remain alien implantations, not integrated into the New India as the writers of the Radhakrishnan Report (in its brilliant second chapter) hoped they might be. This is one reason why to the observer from outside, the Indian intellectual remains a culturally displaced person; nostalgically treasuring his threads of communication with England. Notwithstanding the fact that the leadership of modern India is in the hands of statesmen more intellectual than perhaps are to be found in any other nation, there is in India (as Edward Shils recently wrote) 'no intellectual community'. This is due in part to the lack of a hierarchy of cultural institutions in the country: and this in turn is related to the fact that the universities have responded too weakly to the challenge of Asiatic culture.
>
> This failure of the university to meet the challenge of Indian society has many complex causes, but among the causes are undoubtedly the decisions made between 1835 and 1854. To exclude from university studies for half a century the whole of oriental learning and religion and to purvey to Hindus and Moslems a history and philosophy whose roots lie exclusively in the Mediterranean and in Christianity; to communicate the examinable skeleton of European civilization without ensuring that the values and standards which give flesh to these bones are communicated too; to set up the external paraphernalia of a university the warmth and fellowship of academic society.[2]

These are the handicaps against which Indian universities have to struggle because they prevent the university from becoming the centre and focus of India's intellectual life. These are also the challenges to the conscience of the Indian leaders and should be taken up in all seriousness.

NOTES

1. V. H. H. Green, *The Universities* (London: Penguin, 1967).
2. *The Bulletin of International Association of Universities*, November, 1962.

Bibliographic Review of the Literature on Higher Education

Thelma Bristow

Introduction

This is a selected bibliography on higher education based on the classification used for the organization of the articles in the rest of the volume.

Since there is a superabundance of material, items since 1960 only have been selected, except in exceptional cases. Books and articles are arranged in one sequence. Short annotations are given for books where the titles are not self-explanatory.

Bibliographies

There is a growing number of bibliographies on higher education appearing; the following selection covers a wide area.

P. Altbach, *Higher Education in developing countries: a select bibliography*. Cambridge, Mass.: Center for International Affairs, Harvard University, 1970.

P. Altbach, *A select bibliography on students, politics and higher education*. Cambridge, Mass.: Center for International Affairs, Harvard University, 1970.

American Association for Higher Education, *AAHE bibliography on higher education*. Washington, DC: AAHE – Annual.

Robert F. Arnove, 'A survey of literature and research on Latin American universities', *Latin American Research Review*, vol. 3, no. 1, Fall 1967, pp. 45–62.

W. C. Eells and E. V. Hollis, *Administration of higher education: an annotated bibliography*. Washington, DC: US Department of Health, Education, and Welfare. Office of Education, 1960.

P. H. J. H. Gosden, *Educational administration in England and Wales: a bibliographical guide*. Leeds: University of Leeds Institute of Education, 1967. Section I, Universities, pp. 40–4.

International Bureau of Education, Geneva, *The annual educational bibliography, 1955-1960*. Geneva: International Bureau of Education. Lists material on higher education for many countries.

M. Kendall, *Research into higher education: a bibliography*. London: University of London. Research Unit for Student Problems, 1964.

G. Miller, *Higher education research in Australia and New Zealand: a discussion of research literature and other studies*. London: Society for Research into Higher Education, 1970.

J. P. Powell, *Universities and university education: a select bibliography*. Slough: National Foundation for Research in England and Wales, 1966.

H. Silver and S. J. Teague, *The history of British universities, 1810-1969: a bibliography*. London: Society for Research into Higher Education, 1970.

University of Reading. Education Library, *Higher Education: a select list of recent publications*. January 1970 (Mimeo).

Centres for the Study of Higher Education

There is also a growing number of centres for the study of higher education, both within universities themselves and outside agencies. These produce publications and act as information centres for higher education.

Association of African Universities. University of Khartoum, Sudan. Founded, 1967. To encourage exchange and co-operation between African colleges of higher education.

Association of Commonwealth Universities. 36 Gordon Square, London. Founded, 1913. This body organizes conferences every five years and acts as a liaison and information centre.

Association of Southeast Asian Institutions of Higher Learning. Founded, 1956. To promote economic, cultural and social welfare of the people of Southeast Asia by means of educational co-operation and research programmes.

Committee for Higher Education and Research. Council of Europe, Strasbourg, France. Founded, 1960. Set up to promote co-operation between European countries in the field of higher education. Part of the *Council for Cultural Co-operation*.

Council on Higher Education in the American Republics (CHEAR). Institute of International Education, 809 United Nations Plaza, New York, N.Y., U.S.A. Founded, 1958. Has a programme of conferences, seminars, and research studies.

Educational Resources Information Centre (ERIC). Collects information on on-going research in education, including higher education, and distributes it on microfiche card. Mainly American but often gives information in other countries also.

Higher Education Research Unit. London School of Economics and Political Science, University of London. Founded, 1964. To promote research in higher education, with special reference to economic problems.

International Association of Universities. International Universities Bureau, 6 rue Franklin, 75 Paris 16e. Founded, 1950. Aims to provide services to university institutions throughout the world, to bodies concerned with higher education and scientific research.

Research Unit in Higher Education. Institute of Education, University of London. Began research in university teaching in the late 1960s and has held six significant conferences for members of the university.

Society for Research into Higher Education. London. Founded, 1964. Publishes monographs, research reports, reviews of research and reviews of literature, conference reports, a register of research into higher education, and research into higher education abstracts. It works in collaboration with other national bodies interested in research into higher education and seeks to establish contacts with overseas organizations.

Periodic Publications

There are various periodic publications on higher education which have a wide coverage, as well as national publications. The following is an indication of both types of material.

British Universities Annual. London: Association of University Teachers.

Commonwealth Univerities Yearbook. London: Association of Commonwealth Universities.

Home Universities Conference. Report of the Proceedings. London: Association of Commonwealth Universities.

Journal of Higher Education. Columbus, Ohio: American Association for Higher Education

Minerva (Quarterly). C.S.F. Publications.

Review on Educational Research. Washington, DC. Reviews the literature of higher education every five years.

Unesco. *World survey of education.* Paris: Unesco, 1966. Vol. IV: Higher education.

University Grants Committee. Returns from Universities and University Colleges in receipt of Exchequer Grants. Annual.

Universities Quarterly. London: Turnstile Press.

Section I. Changing Concepts of the University in Society

G. M. Addy, *The enlightenment in the University of Salamanca.* Durham, NC: Duke University Press, 1966. Bibliography pp. 394–9.

H. Anger, *Probleme der deutschen Universität.* Tübingen: J. C. B. Mohr, 1960.

W. H. G. Armytage, *Civic universities: aspects of a British tradition.* London: Benn, 1955.

M. Arnold, *Schools and universities on the continent.* London: Macmillan, 1868.

R. Aron, 'Some aspects of the crisis in the French universities', *Minerva*, Vol. II, No. 3, Spring 1964, pp. 279–85.

Sir Eric Ashby, *The academic profession.* The fourth annual lecture under the Thank-offering to Britain Fund, delivered by Sir Eric Ashby on 11 June 1969. London: OUP for the British Academy, 1969.

Sir Eric Ashby, *African universities and western tradition.* Cambridge (Mass.): Harvard UP, 1964.

Sir Eric Ashby, 'The future of the nineteenth century idea of a university', *Minerva*, Vol. VI, No. 1, 1967, p. 3.

Sir Eric Ashby, 'Universities under siege', *Minerva*, Vol. I, No. 1, Autumn 1962, pp. 18–29. This is the text of the first Chancellor's lecture at the University of Witwatersrand, Johannesburg, South Africa, 4 April 1962.

Sir Eric Ashby and M. Anderson, 'Autonomy and academic freedom in Britain and English-speaking countries in tropical Africa', *Minerva*, Vol. IV, No. 3, Spring 1966, pp. 317–64.

J. J. Auchmuty, 'The idea of the university in its Australian setting: a historical survey', *The Australian University*, Vol. 1, No. 2, 1963.

Australian Vice-Chancellor's Committee. *A symposium on the place of the Australian University in the community and postgraduate studies in the Australian Universities*. Melbourne: U.P., 1955.

J. Barzun, *The American university: how it runs, where it is going*. New York: Harper & Row, 1968.

M. Beloff, *The plateglass universities*. London: Secker & Warburg, 1968.

J. Ben-David, *Fundamental research and the universities: some comments on international differences*. Paris: OECD, 1961.

Bertram Vivian, Baron Bowden, 'The place of universities in modern society', *Comparative Education*, Vol. 1, No. 2, March 1965, pp. 45–62. Special reference to university systems in U.K., U.S., U.S.S.R., and Australia.

J. D. Brown, *The liberal university: an institutional analysis*. New York: McGraw-Hill, 1969.

J. S. Brubacher and W. Rudy, *Higher education in transition: a history of American Colleges and Universities, 1963–1968* New York: Harper & Row, 1968 (revised ed.).

Buenos Aires: Federación Universitaria, *La reforma universitaria 1919–1958*. Buenos Aires: Buenos Aires University, 1959.

N. Bullock, 'A theoretical model for university planning', *University Quarterly*, Vol. 22, No. 2, March 1968, pp. 124–41.

A. Busch, 'The vicissitudes of the Privatdozent: breakdown and adaption in the recruitment of the German university teacher', *Minerva*, Vol. I, No. 3, Spring 1963, pp. 319–41.

J. Caffrey (ed.), *The future academic community: continuity and change*. Washington, DC: American Council on Education, 1969.

A. M. Carr-Saunders, *New universities overseas*. London: Allen & Unwin, 1967.

Lord Chorley, 'Academic freedom in U.K.', *British Universities Annual*. London: AUT, 1963.

E. V. Chutkerashvili, *The development of higher education in the U.S.S.R.* Moscow: State Publishing House 'High School', 1961. [In Russian.]

K. G. Collier, *New dimensions in higher education*. London: Longmans, 1968.

Comitato di studio dei problemi dell'Università Italiana. *Studi sull'università italiana*, I–V. Bologna: Società Editrice Il Mulino, 1960–4. 5 vols. Detailed study of modern university education in Italy. The five volumes cover:
    I The University Population
    II Arts Faculties
    III Science Faculties
    IV Financing and cost of the Universities
    V Policy.

J. Conway, 'Styles of academic culture', *Daedalus*, Vol. 99, No. 1, Winter 1970, pp. 43–55.

R. Dahrendorf, *Bildung ist bürgerrecht: Plädoyer für eine aktive Bildungspolitik*. Hamburg: Die Bücher, 1965. Deals with the need for a rapid democratization of the German educational system.

H. W. Dodds, L. M. Hacker and L. Rogers, *Government assistance to universities in Great Britain*. New York: Columbia University Press, 1952. The first part of this book discusses the universities and the government, the second, the University Grants Committee, and the third, Government Grants-in-aid.

S. R. Dongerkery, *University autonomy in India*. Bombay: Lalvani Publishing House, 1967. Bibliography pp. 123–4. Chapter 5 deals with 'Osmania University's historic fight' for academic freedom.

B. Ducret and Rafe-Uz-Zaman, eds., *The university today: its role and place in society – an international study*. Geneva: World University Service, 1962.

E. Earnest, *Academic profession: an informal history of the American Colleges, 1936–1953*. Indianapolis: Bobbs-Merrill, 1953.

H. L. Elvin, 'Research in planning of higher education', *Paedagogica Europaea*, Vol. 11, No. 2, 1966, pp. 233–49.

Esprit, 'Faire l'université. Dossier pour la reforme de l'enseignement supérieur'. Numéro Spécial. *Esprit*, 32 année, No. 5–6, mai–juin 1964, pp. 705–1214. Articles and summaries of reports on the reform of higher education in France. Deals with research and teaching, teachers and students, pure science and human sciences, continuing education.

A. C. Eurich, *Campus 1980: the shape of the future in American higher education*, edited by Alvin C. Eurich and the staff of the Academy for Educational Development. New York: Delacorte Press, 1968.

A. Flexner, *Universities: American, English, German*. Oxford: OUP, 1930 (1968 reissued).

E. Z. Friedenberg, 'The university community in an open society', *Daedalus*, Vol. 99, No. 1, Winter 1970, pp. 56–74.

G. Gusdorf, *L'université en question*. Paris: Payot, 1964. After a historical survey, the author suggests the re-establishment of culture as the purpose of the university. Universities must be independent and establish co-ordination among themselves.

P. E. Hammond and others, 'Teaching versus research: sources and misperceptions', *Journal of Higher Education*, Vol. 40, No. 9, December 1969, pp. 682–90.

D. Heald, 'The transformation of the German universities', *Universities Quarterly*, Vol. 23, No. 4, Autumn 1969, pp. 408–19.

H. L. Hodgkinson, 'The next decade in higher education', *Journal of Higher Education*, Vol. 41, No. 1, June 1970, pp. 16–29.

S. Hook, *Academic freedom and academic anarchy*. New York: Cowles Book Co., 1970.

W. von Humboldt, 'On the spirit and organizational framework of intellectual institutions in Berlin', *Minerva*, Vol. VIII, No. 2, April 1970, pp. 243–50. Translated from the original German memorandum written some time between autumn 1809 and autumn 1810.

Z. Husain, *The dynamic university*. London: Asia Publishing House, 1965.

J. M. Hyslop, 'The university of East Africa', *Minerva*, Vol. II, No. 3, Spring 1964, pp. 286–302.

C. W. Inglehart, *International Christian University: an adventure in Christian higher education in Japan*. Tokyo: International Christian University, 1964.

International Association of Universities, *International university co-operation*, Paris: IAU, 1969.

International Association of University Professors and Lecturers, *The recruitment and training of university teachers*. Ghent: IAUPL, 1967.
  I Introductory chapters by Armand Hacquaert

II Country Studies. Study prepared for Unesco by the IAUPL and published in agreement with Unesco.

International Association of University Professors and Lecturers, University Conference, 14th, Jerusalem and Haifa, 1967. *Role and structural organization of the university in the modern world*: proceedings of the 14th University Conference. Ghent: IAUPL, 1968. International Association of University Professors and Lecturers. Communications, 59.

Japan, 'University and society', *Journal of Social and Political Ideas in Japan*, Vol. 5, Nos. 2–3, December 1967. [Whole issue.]

K. Jaspers, *The idea of the university*. London: Peter Owen, 1960. Re-statement of the classical academic tradition in Germany.

D. D. Karve, 'The universities and the public in India', *Minerva*, Vol. I, No. 3, Spring 1963, pp. 263–84.

Clark Kerr, 'Governance and functions', *Daedalus*, Vol. 99, No. 1, Winter 1970, pp. 108–21.

Clark Kerr, *The uses of the university*. Cambridge, Mass.: Harvard University Press, 1963. Supports the idea of the multiversity.

E. J. King, 'Universities in evolution', *International Review of Education*, Vol. 8, 1963, pp. 399–413.

J. Lawlor, ed., *The new university*. London: Routledge, 1968.

F. R. Leavis, *Education and the university*. London: Chatto & Windus, 1943. Supports the concept of the university as a centre of culture in the community.

J. Liwicka, *Polish universities*. Warsaw: Polonia Publishing House, 1959.

S. E. and L. Luria, 'The role of the university: ivory tower, service station, or frontier post?', *Daedalus*, Vol. 99, No. 1, Winter 1970, pp. 75–83.

A. Matejko, 'Planning and tradition in Polish education', *Minerva*, Vol. VII, No. 4, Summer 1969, pp. 621–48.

M. Nagai, 'The university and the intellectual', *Japan Quarterly*, Vol. 11, September 1964, pp. 46–52.

National Union of Students of France, *Manifesto for the democratic reform of higher education*. Prague: International Union of Students, 1965.

J. H. Newman, *The idea of a university, 1853 and 1858*. With an introduction by G. N. Shuster. New York: (Image Book), Doubleday, 1959.

W. R. Niblett, *Higher education: demand and response: the Quail Roost Seminar of December 1968*, edited by W. R. Niblett. London: Tavistock, 1969. Bibliography pp. 259–61.

Ortega y Gasset, *Mission of the university*. London: Routledge, 1946.

A. R. Oxenfeldt, 'Sketch of an innovative approach to higher education', *The Record* (Teachers College, Columbia University), Vol. 71, No. 4, May 1970, pp. 641–6.

Talcott Parsons and G. M. Platt, 'Considerations on the American academic system', *Minerva*, Vol. VI, No. 4, Summer 1968.

F. R. Paulsen, ed., *Higher education: dimensions and directions*. Tucson: University of Arizona Press, 1970. A collection of lectures on specific issues in higher education with a general consideration of roles and responsibilities of colleges in the future.

J. H. Perkin, *New universities in the United Kingdom*. Paris: OECD, 1969.

C. M. Ajo González de Rapariegos, *Historia de las universidades Hispanicas: origenes y desarrollo desde su aparición a nuestros días*. Avila: Centro de estudios e Investigaciones, 'Alonso de Madrigal', 1968. 7 vols.

Hastings Rashdall, *The universities of Europe in the Middle Ages*, edited by F. M. Powicke and A. B. Emden. London: OUP, 1936. (2nd ed.) 3 vols.

Recife Universidade, *Simpósio sôbre problemática universitária*. Recife: Imprensa Universitária, 1965. These papers, presented by university professors, on problems in higher education, examine, among other matters, the Brazilian university and regional development.

B. M. Remennikov, 'Economic problems of higher education in the U.S.S.R.', *Soviet Education*, Vol. 11, No. 9, Part 2, July 1969, pp. 3–49.

A. K. Rice, *The modern university: a model organization*, Foreword by Lord Fulton. London: Tavistock Publishers, 1970.

F. K. Ringer, *The decline of the German Mandarins: the German academic community, 1890–1933*. Cambridge, Mass.: Harvard UP, 1969.

Lord Robbins, *The university in the modern world and other papers on higher education*. London: Macmillan, 1966. These papers are concerned with organizational and administrative problems in higher education, including expansion and the binary system.

S. M. Rosen, *Higher education in the U.S.S.R.* Washington, DC: U.S. Department of Health and Welfare, 1963.

M. Shattock, 'A changing pattern of university administration', *University Quarterly*, Vol. 24, No. 3, Summer 1970, pp. 310–20.

E. Shils, 'The academic profession in India', *Minerva*, Vol. VII, No. 3, Spring 1969, pp. 345–72.

E. Shils, 'The implantation of universities: reflections on a theme of Ashby', *Universities Quarterly*, Vol. 22, No. 2, March 1968, pp. 142–66.

T. H. Silcock, 'The development of universities in South-East Asia to 1960', *Minerva*, Vol. II, No. 2, Winter 1964, pp. 169–96.

L. Soyer, 'Réflexions sur le rôle des universités dans les pays du tiers-monde', *Bull. Séances de l'Académie Royale des Sciences d'Outre-Mer*, No. 2, 1965, pp. 608–614.

C. F. Thwing, *The American and the German university*. New York: Macmillan, 1928.

E. K. Townsend Coles, *Universities and adult education, research and training: a survey*. Conference paper for the second World Conference of University Adult Education, 1970.

Unesco, *Formal programmes in international co-operation between University Institutions*. Report of an International Committee of Experts. Paris: Unesco, 1960. (Educational Studies and Documents, 37).

P. Van Duijn, 'Structural model for university self-rule', *Higher Education and Research in the Netherlands*, Vol. 14, No. 2, 1970, pp. 3–12.

Sir Peter Venables, 'Conflicting patterns and purposes in higher education', *Universities Quarterly*, Vol. 24, No. 4, Autumn 1970, pp. 375–91.

R. Veysey, *The emergence of the American university*. Chicago, London: University of Chicago Press, 1965.

Wang Chün, 'Current trends in the reform of higher education in Communist

China'. [English Summary.] *Chinese Education*, Vol. II, No. 4, Winter 1969/70, pp. 27–52.

M. Zweig, *The idea of a world university*; edited with a foreword by Harold Taylor. Carbondale, Ill., London: Southern Illinois University Press, Feffer and Simons, 1976.

Section II. Factors Influencing Change

M. L. J. Abercrombie, 'The work of a university education research unit', *Universities Quarterly*, Vol. 22, No. 1, December 1967, pp. 182–96.

P. G. Altbach, 'The international student movement', *Comparative Education Review*, Vol. 8, October 1964, pp. 131–7.

P. G. Altbach, *Student politics in Bombay*. New York: Asia Publishing House, 1968. (Indian Education Series, 3; Michigan University Comparative Education Dissertation Series, 14.)

Sir Eric Ashby and M. Anderson, *The rise of the student estate in Britain*. London: Macmillan, 1970. Deals with staff-student relations in an historical context.

Sir Eric Ashby, 'Some problems of universities in new countries of the British Commonwealth', *Comparative Education*, Vol. 2, No. 1, November 1965, pp. 1–10.

Sir Eric Ashby, *Technology and the academics: an essay on universities and the scientific revolution*. London: Macmillan, 1968.

R. P. Atcon, *The Latin American university*: a key for an integrated approach to the co-ordinated social, economic and educational development of Latin America. Bogotá: ECO Revista de la Cultura de Occidente, 1966. [In English and Spanish.]

K. Azumi, *Higher education and business recruitment in Japan*. New York: Teachers College Press, 1969. (Center for Education in Industrialized Nations, Teachers College, Columbia University.)

H. W. Benjamin, *Higher education in the American Republics*. New York: McGraw-Hill, 1965.

R. O. Berdahl, *British universities and the state*. London: CUP, 1959. Part I deals with the historical evolution of the relationship of the State and university. Part II deals with financial and constitutional issues.

S. Betsky, 'Universities in an industrial culture', *Universities Quarterly*, Vol. 24, No. 1, Winter 1969, pp. 7–28.

M. Blaug, *The causes of graduate unemployment in India*, Mark Blaug, Richard Layard, Maureen Woodhall. London: Allen Lane, 1969. (London University, London School of Economics, Studies in Education.) Bibliography pp. 299–306.

M. Blaug and M. Woodhall, 'Productivity trends in British university education', *Minerva*, Vol. III, No. 4, 1965, pp. 483–98.

D. C. A. Bradshaw, 'Diversifying colleges of education', *Universities Quarterly*, Vol. 24, No. 4, Autumn 1970, pp. 392–401.

V. B. Burke, 'Student participation in the government of colleges of education', *Universities Quarterly*, Vol. 22, No. 4, September 1968, pp. 398–403.

D. Burnett, 'Economics and the university library', *Universities Quarterly*, Vol. 24, No. 4, Autumn 1970, pp. 440–52.

J. Butterworth, 'Towards excellence', *Universities Quarterly*, Vol. 23, No. 3, Summer 1969, pp. 258–68.

A. M. Carr-Saunders, 'Staffing African universities', *Minerva*, Vol. I, No. 3, Spring 1963, pp. 302–18.

C. Carter, 'A programme for 1969–1989', *Universities Quarterly*, Vol. 23, No. 3, Summer 1969, pp. 305–19.

D. Chapman, *Industry and the role of the universities – collision or co-operation*. Inaugural lecture delivered May 1968, University of Sheffield. Sheffield: University of Sheffield, 1968.

N. E. Cohen, 'The university and social change', *School and Society*, Vol. 97, No. 2321, December 1969, pp. 479–84.

Comparative Education Society in Europe, *The university within the education system*; containing the papers read before the society at the third general meeting, Ghent, 1967. Ghent: The Comparative Education Society in Europe, 1968.

A. Curle, 'Nationalism and higher education in Ghana', *Universities Quarterly*, Vol. 16, No. 3, June 1962, pp. 229–42.

H. C. Dent, *Universities in transition*. London: Cohen & West, 1964.

R. Dershowitz, 'Higher education and the student: England, Germany, France', *Youth and Freedom*, Vol. 6, 1964, pp. 29–32.

D. S. Detwiler, 'The state and the university: the West German system', *Science and Freedom*, No. 18, March 1961.

R. A. Dungan, 'Higher education: the effort to adjust', *Daedalus*, Vol. 99, No. 1, Winter 1970, pp. 141–53.

B. Fletcher, *The universities in the modern world*. Oxford: Pergamon, 1968.

J. K. Folger and others, *Human resources and higher education*: staff report of the commission on human resources and advanced education. New York: Russell Sage Foundation, 1970.

B. Ford, 'The discipline of the curriculum', *Universities Quarterly*, Vol. 23, No. 3, Summer 1969, pp. 282–6.

A. Fortier-Ortiz, *Problems of university admissions in Latin America: a report to the Trustees of the College Entrance Examination Board*. New York: College Entrance Examination Board, 1963.

E. Fraenkel, *Universität und Demokratie*. Stuttgart: Kohlhammer, 1967. Includes a section 'Der Konflikt an der Freien Universität Berlin'.

W. D. Furneaux, *The chosen few*. London: OUP, 1961.

L. Gale, *Education and development in Latin America, with special reference to Colombia and some comparison with Guyana, South America*. London: Routledge, 1969 (World Education Series). Bibliography pp. 166–71.

N. Glazer, 'Student power in Berkeley', *Universities Quarterly*, Vol. 22, No. 4, September 1968, pp. 404–24.

R. A. Goldman, ed., *Higher education and modern democracy: the crisis of the few and the many*. Chicago: Rand McNally, 1967.

Great Britain. Committee on Higher Education appointed by the Prime Minister. *Report of the Committee . . .*; [Robbins Report]. London: HMSO, 1963. Chairman: Lord Robbins.

Appendices

I The demand for places in higher education.

IIA Students and their education.

IIB Students and their education.

III Teachers in higher education.

IV Administrative, financial and economic aspects.

V Higher education in the counties.

Evidence

Part I. Written and oral evidence received by the committee (6 vols.).

Part II. Documentary evidence submitted to the committee.

Great Britain. Council for Scientific Policy, *Enquiries into the flow of candidates in science and technology into higher education*. London: HMSO, 1968 [Dainton Report].

W. Hahn, 'Higher education in West Germany: reform movements and trends', *Comparative Education Review*, Vol. 7, June 1963, pp. 51–60.

S. E. Harris, *Higher education: resources and finance*. New York: McGraw-Hill, 1962.

R. J. Havighurst, *American higher education in the 1960s*. Columbus, Ohio: Ohio State University Press, 1960.

D. Heald, 'The transformation of the German universities', *Universities Quarterly*, Vol. 23, No. 4, Autumn 1969, pp. 408–19.

R. Hoggart, 'The academic community – (b) Its progressive development', *Universities Quarterly*, Vol. 23, No. 3, Summer 1969, pp. 274–81.

B. Holmes, 'Higher education in Britain: a review essay', *Journal of Higher Education*, Vol. 35, No. 7, October 1964, pp. 397–9.

J. Huddleston, 'German universities and adult education', *British Journal of Educational Studies*, Vol. 18, No. 1, February 1970, pp. 42–55.

M. Ikonikoff, 'Rôle de l'université et des étudiants dans le developpement de l'amerique latine', *Tiers Monde*, Vol. 11, No. 41, January–March 1970, pp. 169–182.

International Association of Universities. Proceedings of the 4th General Conference of the International Association of Universities held in Tokyo . . . 1965. Paris: AIU, 1966. Topics discussed: (a) university autonomy, (b) access to higher education, (c) the role of the university in economic and cultural development.

Japan, Ministry of Education. *Demand and supply for university graduates*. Tokyo: Ministry of Education, 1959. (Revised ed.)

C. Jencks and D. Riesman, *The academic revolution*. New York: Doubleday, 1968. A sociological and historical analysis of education in the U.S.A.

P. Kenyatta, *Economics of scale in African universities: a methodology with examples from the University of East Africa*. Paris: International Institute for Educational Planning, 1969.

A. Kettle, 'Books and the growth of higher education', *Times Literary Supplement*, No. 3,589, 11 December 1970, pp. 1439–40.

J. M. Kloysche, *The urban university*. New York: Harper & Row, 1966.

J. A. Lauwerys, 'Bases para a reforma da Universidada Federal da Bahia', *Revista Brasileira de Estudos Pedagógicos*, Vol. 49, No. 109, January–March 1968, pp. 27–52.

J. A. Lauwerys, 'Instalação e desenvolvimento das faculdades de educação no Brasil', *Revista Brasileira de Estudos Pedagógicos*, Vol. 51, No. 114, April–June 1969, pp. 305–39.

J. A. Lauwerys, 'The universities of Latin America', from: *Latin America and the Caribbean*: a handbook, ed. by Claudio Véliz. London: Anthony Blond, 1968.

Leningrad, State Pedagogical Institute. *University teaching in new directions*. [In Russian.] Leningrad: State Pedagogical Institute, 1961. (Research Studies, Vol. 201.)

J. B. Lon Hefferlin, *Dynamics of academic reform*. San Francisco, Calif.: Jossey-Bass, 1969.

J. R. Lukes, 'Concepts of excellence, 1969–1989'. A conference on higher education organized by Universities Quarterly, 1969. *Universities Quarterly*, Vol. 23, No. 3, Summer 1969, pp. 253–7.

R. Lynn, *The universities and the business community*. London: Industrial Educational and Research Foundation, 1969.

M. C. McCarty, *The employment of highly specialized graduates*: a comparative study in the United Kingdom and the United States of America. London: HMSO, 1968.

H. Marcuse, *An Essay on Liberation*. London: Allen Lane, 1969.

H. Marcuse, *One dimensional man: studies in the ideology of advanced industrial society*. London: Routledge and Kegan Paul, 1964.

W. B. Martin, *Conformity: standards and change in higher education*. San Francisco, Calif.: Jossey-Bass, 1969.

W. R. Niblett, 'Autonomy in higher education', *Universities Quarterly*, Vol. 22, No. 3, June 1968, pp. 337–43.

Organization for Economic Co-operation and Development, *Development of higher education 1950–1967*: statistical survey. Paris: OECD, 1970.

Organization for Economic Co-operation and Development, *Innovation in higher education*: reforms in Yugoslavia. Report prepared for the Institute for Social Research, University of Zagreb. Paris: OECD, 1970. (Case Studies on Innovation in Higher Education.)

Organization for Economic Co-operation and Development, *New universities in the United Kingdom*, by H. J. Perkin. Paris: OECD, 1969. (Case Studies on Innovation in Higher Education.)

P. H. Partridge, *Society schools and progress in Australia*. Oxford: Pergamon, 1968.

J. H. Petersen, 'Recent research on Latin American university students', *Latin American Research Review*, Vol. 5, No. 1, Spring 1970, pp. 37–58. Bibliography pp. 52–8.

C. M. Phillips, *Changes in subject choice at school and university*. London: Weidenfeld & Nicolson for London School of Economics and Political Science, 1969.

J. Porter, 'The democratisation of the Canadian universities and the need for a national system', *Minerva*, Vol. VIII, No. 3, July 1970, pp. 325–56.

A. R. Prest, *Financing university education: a study in university fees and loans to students in Great Britain*. London: Institute of Economic Affairs (Institute of Economic Affairs. Occasional papers No. 12).

K. F. Punch, *Some factors associated with the output of graduates from Australian universities: a survey and analysis of recent research*. Perth: University of Western Australia, Faculty of Education, 1966.

A. L. Pye, 'Higher education and politics in Singapore', *Minerva*, Vol. III, No. 3, Spring 1965, pp. 321–35.

A. K. Rice, *The modern university*. London: Tavistock, 1970. Deals with administration and shows ways for experiments in planned change.

Sir E. Richardson, *The changing pattern of higher education in Great Britain*. London: Association of Technical Institutions and Association of Principals of Technical Institutions, 1968.

M. Rivlin, 'Growth and change in higher education', *Academy of Political Science Proceedings*, Vol. 30, May 1970, pp. 66–74.

E. Rudd and S. Hatch, *Graduate study and after*. London: Weidenfeld & Nicolson, 1968.

C. Sanders, *Report on academic wastage and failure among university students in Australia and other countries 1928 to 1958*. Perth: University of Western Australia, Faculty of Education, 1958.

N. Sanford, ed., *The American college: a psychological interpretation of the higher learning*. New York: J. Wiley & Sons, 1962.

Sir Fred Schonell, *The university in contemporary society*. London: Association of Commonwealth Universities, 1968.

J. C. Sharma, *A comparative study of policies and practices in the administration of higher education since World War II: U.K., U.S.A. and India*. Thesis submitted to the University of London for the degree of MPhil (Education), 1969.

L. M. Sharp, *Education and employment: the early careers of college graduates*. Baltimore, Maryland: Johns Hopkins Press, 1970.

H.-A. Steger, *Die Universitäten in der gesellschaftlichen Entwicklung lateinamerikas*. Güterloh: Bertelsmann Verlag, 1967. Band I: Das lateinamerikanische Universitätswesen zwischen geschichtlicher Uberlieferung und geplarter Zukunft.

K. L. Stretch, 'Academic ecology: on the location of institutions of higher education', *Minerva*, Vol. II, No. 3, Spring 1964, pp. 320–35.

M. Trow, 'The academic community. (a) Its progressive collapse?', *Universities Quarterly*, Vol. 23, No. 3, Summer 1969, pp. 269–74.

M. Trow, 'Reflections on the transition from mass to universal higher education', *Daedalus*, Vol. 99, No. 1, Winter 1970, pp. 122–42.

Unesco, *The development of higher education in Africa. Report of the conference . . .* , Tananarive, 3–12 September 1962. Paris: Unesco, 1963. Deals with: I, the staffing of higher education in Africa: II, the financing of higher education in Africa: III, the choice and adaptation of higher education curriculum.

United Nations. Economic Commission for Latin America, *Education, human resources and development in Latin America*. New York: United Nations, 1968.

U.S.A. Commission on Higher Education, *Human resources and higher education*. A staff report to the Commission on Higher Education. New York: Russell Sage Foundation, 1970.

Sir Peter Venables, 'Technical and higher education: the changing pattern', Part I, *BACIE Journal*, Vol. 23, No. 4, December 1969, pp. 162–7.

Sir Peter Venables, 'The pattern of higher education', *Universities Quarterly*, Vol. 23, No. 3, Summer 1969, pp. 287–304.

E. L. Wheelwright, ed., *Higher education in Australia*. Melbourne: Cheshire, 1965.

M. Woodhall, *Student loans: a review of experience in Scandinavia and elsewhere*. London: Harrap, for the University of London Institute of Education, 1970.

Section III. National Policies for Higher Education

G. Aguirre Beltrán, *La Universidad Latinamericana, y otros ensayos*. Xalapa: Universidad Veracruzana, 1961. (Biblioteca de la Facultad de Filosofia y Letras.)

L. Aranne, *Government policy toward higher education in Israel*. (Preliminary study.) Jerusalem: Centre for Policy Studies, Israel, 1970.

Australian Universities Commission, *Report of the Australian Universities Commission on Australian universities 1958–1963*. Canberra: A. J. Arthur, Government Printer, 1960.

Australian Universities Commission, *Second report of the Australian Universities Commission: Australian universities 1961–1966*. Canberra: A. J. Arthur, Government Printer, 1963.

Australian Universities Commission, *Third report of the Australian Universities Commission: Australian universities 1964–1969*. Canberra: A. J. Arthur, Government Printer, 1966.

Australian Universities Commission, Committee on the Future of Tertiary Education in Australia, *Tertiary education in Australia: a report of the committee* . . . Melbourne: A. C. Brooks, Government Printer, 1964–5.

Harold R. W. Benjamin, *Higher education in the American republics*. New York: McGraw-Hill, 1965.

E. Boyle, 'Parliament and university policy', *Minerva*, Vol. V, No. 1, 1966, pp. 3–19.

Sir Sidney Caine, *British universities: purpose and prospects*. London: Bodley Head, 1969.

Canada, *Report of the Royal Commission on national development in the arts, letters and sciences, 1949–1951* [Massey Report]. Ottawa: Queen's Printer, 1951.

Carnegie Commission, *Quality and equality: new levels of Federal responsibility for higher education*. New York: McGraw-Hill, 1968.

Ceylon. Commission of Inquiry – Vidyalankara University of Ceylon, *Report of the Commission of Inquiry*. Colombo: Government Publications Bureau, 1968. (Sessional paper no. 23, 1968.) Chairman: V. C. Jayasuriya.

Council of Europe. Council for Cultural Co-operation, *Reform and expansion of higher education in Europe*. National reports, 1962–7. Strasbourg: Council of Europe, 1967.

W. S. Dillon, 'Universities and nation-building in Africa', *Journal of Modern African Studies*, Vol. 1, No. 1, March 1963, pp. 75–89.

V. P. Elyutin, *Higher education in the U.S.S.R.* London: Soviet Booklets, 1962.

A. B. Fafunwa, *Over a hundred years of higher education for Nigerians*. Lagos: Federal Ministry of Information, 1969.

France. Laws, statutes, etc. 'Enseignement supérieur, loi d'orientation' (Loi no. 68–978 du 12 Novembre, 1968), *Minerva*, Vol. VII, No. 1, Summer 1969, pp. 712–27. A translation in English of this law.

Germany (Democratic Republic). Staatsrat, *Die Weiterführung der 3. Hochschulreform und die Entwicklung des Hochschulwesens bis 1975*: materialen der 16. Sitzung des Staatsrates . . . am 3. April 1969. Berlin: Staatsverlag der D.D.R., 1969. (Schriftenreihe des Staatsrates der Deutschen Demokratischen Republik, Heft 8, 3. Wahlperiode.)

Great Britain, *Report of the Committee on university teaching methods* [Hale Report]. London: HMSO, 1964.

Great Britain. Department of Education and Science, *A plan for polytechnics and other colleges*. London: HMSO, 1966. (Cmnd. 3006, May 1966.)

Great Britain. Department of Education and Science, *A university of the air*. London: HMSO, 1966. (Cmnd. 2922.) A white paper which gives the case for a university of the air.

Great Britain. Department of Scientific and Industrial Research (DSIR), *Universities and colleges 1956–1960*. A report on DSIR support for research and training in universities and colleges. London: HMSO, 1962.

Great Britain. House of Commons, *Parliament and the control of university expenditure*; special report from the Committee of Public Accounts. Session 1966–7. London: HMSO, 1967.

W. Hahn, 'Higher education in West Germany: reform movements and trends', *Comparative Education Review*, Vol. 7, No. 1, June 1963, pp. 51–60.

S. E. Harris, *Higher education; resources and finance*. New York: McGraw-Hill, 1962.

A. D. Henderson, *Policies and practices in higher education*. New York: Harper 1960.

'Higher education in Spain: Part 1', *Minerva*, Vol. VIII, No. 2, April 1970, pp. 268–83. A slightly abridged translation of the Ministry of Education, Spain, report: *La educación en España, bases para una política educativa*. The present section deals with the existing situation in higher education. Vol. VIII, No. 3 deals with the proposed reforms.

Hochschulgesamtplan Baden-Württemberg, *Empfehlungen zur Reform von Struktur und Organisation . . .*; Bericht des Arbeitskreises Hochschulgesamtplan beim Kultusministerium Baden-Württemberg. Villingen: Neckar-Verlag, 1967. (Bildung in neuer Sicht, Reihe A. Nr. 5.)

India. Education Commission, *Report of the Education Commission 1964–1966: education and national development*. Delhi: Manager of Publications, 1966. Issued by the Ministry of Education. Chairman: D. S. Kothari.

India. University Grants Commission, New Delhi, *Report on standards of university education*. New Delhi: 1965. Produced by a committee; Chairman: N. K. Sidhanta.

India. Ministry of Education, *Education in universities in India: a statistical survey*. 1948–. Delhi: Ministry of Education, 1948–. Annually since 1948.

International Students' Conference. Research and Information Commission, *Report on higher education in Hungary, Oct. 1957–Jan. 1959*. Leiden: Co-ordinating Secretariat of National Unions of Students.

Japan. Ministry of Education, *Higher education in postwar Japan*. The Ministry of Education's 1964 white paper; edited and translated by John E. Blewett. Tokyo: Sophia University Press, 1965. (Monumenta Nipponica Monographs, No. 22.)

Japan. Ministry of Education, *The university establishment standards* [Ministry of Education ordinance 28, 1956]. Tokyo: Ministry of Education, 1965. Made under the provisions of the School Education Law.

Japan. Central Council for Education, 'Coping with student disorder in Japan', *Minerva*, Vol. VIII, No. 1, January 1970, pp. 116–35. An abridged translation of the Council's 'Report on measures to meet problems facing university education in Japan' (Tokyo: Ministry of Education, 1969). Includes a translation of Law No. 70 on provisional measures concerning university administration, 1969.

G. Kloss, 'University reform in West Germany: the burden of tradition', *Minerva*, Vol. VI, No. 3, Spring 1968, pp. 323–53.

D. S. Kothari, 'Higher education and national development', *Library Herald*, Vol. 11, Nos. 1 and 2, April and July 1969, pp. 18–31. Concerned mainly with the University Grants Commission's policy concerning the strengthening of university libraries.

R. Layard and J. King, 'The impact of Robbins', *Higher Education Review*, Autumn 1968, pp. 7–25.

J. R. Lukes, 'The binary policy: a critical study', *Universities Quarterly*, Vol. 22, No. 1, December 1967, pp. 6–46.

B. MacArthur, 'Who plans higher education?', *Higher Education Review*, Spring 1970, pp. 31–7.

J. B. MacDonald *et. al.*, *The role of the Federal Government in support of research in Canadian universities* [MacDonald Report]. Ottawa: Queen's Printer, 1969. (Science Council of Canada, Special Study No. 7.)

A. Matejko, 'Planning and tradition in Polish higher education', *Minerva*, Vol. VII, No. 4, Summer 1969, pp. 621–48.

F. W. Mitchell, 'The Hughes Parry Report and subsequent developments', *Australian Journal of Higher Education*, November 1961.

M. Moos and F. E. Rourke, *The campus and the state*. Baltimore, Maryland: Johns Hopkins Press, 1959.

R. Neuhaus, comp., *Dokumente zur Hochschulreform, 1945-50*. Wiesbaden: Franz Steiner, 1961.

New South Wales. Department of Education, *First report of the committee appointed by the Minister of Education to enquire into various aspects of higher education in New South Wales*. Sydney: Government Printer, 1961.

Nigeria. Commission on Post-School Certificate and Higher Education in Nigeria, *Investment in education*: the report of the Commission . . . Lagos: Federal Ministry of Education, 1960. Chairman: Sir Eric Ashby.

Nigeria. National Universities Commission, *University development in Nigeria*: report of the . . . Commission. Lagos: Federal Ministry of Information, 1963.

Organization for Economic Co-operation and Development, *Design for technological education*: the Escuela Técnica Superior de Ingenerios industriales of Seville. Paris: OECD, 1968.

Organization of American States, *Report . . . on inter-American co-operation for the development of higher education in Latin America*. Washington, DC: Pan-American Union, 1961.

F. G. Pearce, *Plan for education*: a descriptive and critical commentary on post-war educational development in India – otherwise known as the Sargent Plan. Bombay: OUP, 1948.

C. M. Phillips, 'Some changes in the factors affecting university entry', *Research in Education* (London), Vol. 4, November 1970, pp. 81–94.

'The Reform of Courses of Study in West German Universities', *Minerva*, Vol. VIII, No. 2, April 1970, pp. 250–67. A translation of 'Emfehlungen zur Neuordnung des Studiums an den Wissenschaftlichen Hochschulen verabschiedet in der Vollversammlung des Wissenschaftsrates am 14 Mai 1966'.

A. I. Richards, 'The adaptation of universities to the African situation', review article, *Minerva*, Vol. III, No. 3, Spring 1965, pp. 336–42.

G. Russo, *Università anno zero*. Rome: Armando Editore, 1966. The author gives the case against the Italian universities. The book includes a considerable amount of official documentation and comparison with higher education in other countries.

C. Sanders, 'A comparative review of three reports: Robbins, Martin and Hale', *The Australian University*, Vol. 4, No. 1, April 1966, pp. 66–94.

Spain, 'Manifesto for the establishment of a democratic university in Spain', *Minerva*, Vol. V, No. 1, Autumn 1966, pp. 82–8.

Spain. Ministerio de Educación Nacional, *Problemas de empleo professional de los graduados universitarios*. [Madrid?]: Ministerio de Educación Nacional, [1954?].

E. E. Stewart, 'The role of the Provincial Government in the development of the universities of Ontario, 1791–1964', *Notes and Abstracts in American and International Education*, University of Michigan School of Education, No. 31, Summer 1970, whole issue.

F. P. Thomassen, 'University education in the Netherlands', *Higher Education and Research in the Netherlands*, Vol. XIII, No. 2, 1969, pp. 3–55.

Unesco, *Access to higher education*: the international study of university admissions. Vol. I: [Director's report] by Frank Bowles; Vol. II: National studies. (The development of higher education.) Paris: Unesco and International Association of Universities, 1963, 1965.

Unesco, *Reform and development of higher education in Europe, France, the Netherlands and Poland*. Paris: Unesco, 1964. (Educational Studies and Documents, 49.)

U.S.S.R. Central Statistical Department of the Council of Ministers. *Higher education in the U.S.S.R.*: statistical collection. [In Russian.] [Moscow?]: Central Statistical Department, 1961.

University Grants Committee, *University development from 1935*. Series of reviews presented at five-yearly intervals. London: HMSO.

'University Reform in Japan', *Minerva*, Vol. VIII, No. 4, October 1970, pp. 581–93. Extracts from the publication of Central Council of Education (Japan) entitled: 'Draft outline of the preliminary report on the basic design of the reform of higher education in Japan'.

U.S. Office of Education, *Higher education in Poland*, Part II: Rules of admission, student activities and curriculum. Washington, DC: U.S. Government Printing Office, 1964.

Victoria. Committee for Development of Tertiary Education, *The development of tertiary education in Victoria, 1963–1972*. Melbourne: Ministry of Education, 1963.

E. L. Wheelwright, ed., *Higher education in Australia*. Melbourne: F. W. Cheshire for the Federation of University Staff Association, 1965.

V. Yelyutin, *Higher education in the U.S.S.R.* London: Soviet Booklets, 1959.

Section IV. Present-day Debates

M. B. Abram, 'Reflections on the university in the new revolution', *Daedalus*, Vol. 99, No. 1, Winter 1970, pp. 122–40.

E. Anrich, *Die Idee der deutschen Universität und die Reform der deutschen Universitäten*. Darmstadt: Wissenschaftliche Buchgesellschaft Darmstadt, 1960.

H. P. Bahrdt, *Die Universität: Kritische Selbstbetrachtungen*, by H. P. Bahrdt and others. Fünf Vorlesungen. Göttingen: Vandenhoeck & Ruprecht, 1964. (Göttinger Universitätsreden, 42.)

R. M. Beard, *Research into teaching methods in higher education*. London: Society for Research into Higher Education, 1967.

R. M. Beard, *Teaching and learning in higher education*. Harmondsworth: Penguin, 1970.

George Z. F. Bereday, 'Home thoughts from abroad', *The Times* [London], January 15, 1971. A special report: Universities and Polytechnics, p. viii.

Uwe Bergman, *Rebellion der Studenten; oder, Die neue Opposition, eine Analyse*, von Uwe Bergman, Rudi Dutschke, Wolfgang Lefèvre and Bernd Rabehl. Reinbek bei Hamburg: Rowohlt, 1968.

F. Bowles, 'American higher education in 1990', *Minerva*, Vol. V, No. 2, Winter 1967, pp. 226–41.

K. G. Collier, 'Syndicate methods: further evidence and comment', *Universities Quarterly*, Vol. 23, No. 4, Autumn 1969, pp. 431–6.

H. Crawley, *A degree of defiance: students in England and Europe now*. London: Weidenfeld & Nicolson, 1969.

D. K. Emmerson, ed., *Students and politics in developing nations*. London: Pall Mall Press, 1968.

H. S. Ferns, *Towards an independent university*: a view of the urgent need for establishing an institution of higher education free from government control. London: Institute of Economic Affairs, 1969.

R. L. Gaudino, *Indian University*. Bombay: Popular Prakashan, 1965.

N. Glazer, 'Are academic standards obsolete?', *Change*, Vol. 2, No. 6, November–December 1970, pp. 38–44.

H. Glennerster, S. Merrett and G. Wilson, 'A graduate tax', *Higher Education Review*, Autumn 1968, pp. 26–38.

R. Goodings, 'The B.Ed. – and after', *Higher Education Review*, Summer 1969, pp. 62–5.

F. M. Hechinger, 'Academic freedom in America', *Change*, Vol. 2, No. 6, November–December 1970, pp. 32–6.

International Student Conference. Research and Information Commission, *Report on higher education in East Germany*. Leiden: Co-ordinating Secretariat of National Unions of Students, 1959.

D. Johnson, 'Paris: city of thirteen universities', *New Society*, 10 December 1970, pp. 1038–41.

S. M. Lipset, 'American student activism in comparative perspective', *American Psychologist*, Vol. 25, No. 8, August 1970, pp. 675–93.

S. M. Lipset, 'University students and politics in underdeveloped countries', *Minerva*, Vol. III, No. 1, Autumn 1964, pp. 15–56.

M. Lowenthal, 'Unsanctioned projects for French university reform', *Universities Quarterly*, Vol. 22, No. 4, September 1968, pp. 371–84.

J. McLeish, *The lecture method*. Cambridge: Institute of Education, 1968.

L. A. MacManaway, 'Teaching methods in higher education – innovation and research', *Universities Quarterly*, Vol. 24, No. 3, Summer 1970, pp. 321–9.

D. Martin, ed., *Anarchy and culture: the problem of the contemporary university*. London: Routledge, 1969.

A. Matejko, 'Planning and tradition in Polish higher education', *Minerva*, Vol. VII, No. 4, Summer 1969, pp. 621–48.

O. Milton and E. J. Shoben, eds., *Learning and the professors*. Athens, Ohio: Ohio University Press, 1968. A collection of essays debating the status of American higher education.

W. Moore, *The tutorial system and its future*. Oxford: Pergamon, 1968.

National Union of Students, *Report of the Commission on teaching in higher education*; presented to the Liverpool Conference, April 1969. London: NUS, 1969.

W. R. Niblett, *All for the best?* London: Harrap and Co. for the University of London Institute of Education, 1970.

P. H. Partridge, 'The state of the universities', *Melbourne Studies in Education*, 1960–1, pp. 72–94.

P. H. Partridge, 'Universities in Australia', *Comparative Education*, Vol. 2, No. 1, November 1965, pp. 19–31.

R. Pieris, 'Universities, politics and public opinion in Ceylon', *Minerva*, Vol. II, No. 4, Summer 1964, pp. 435–54.

Gerald T. Rimmington, 'The development of the universities in Africa', *Comparative Education*, Vol. 1, No. 2, March 1965, pp. 105–12.

E. Rudd and S. Hatch, *Graduate study and after*. London: Weidenfeld & Nicolson, 1968.

N. Sanford, *Where colleges fail: a study of the student as a person*. San Francisco, Calif.: Jossey-Bass, 1967.

A. B. Shah, ed., *Higher education in India*. Bombay: Lalvani Publishing House, 1967. (Congress for Cultural Freedom.) Bibliography pp. 229–35.

Simpósio sobre problemática universitária, Universidade de Recife, 1965. Recife: Imprensa Universitária, 1965.

G. K. Smith, ed., *Stress and campus response*. San Francisco, Calif.: Jossey-Bass, 1968. (Current Issues in Higher Education.)

M. Trow, 'Binary dilemmas: an American view', *Higher Education Review*, Summer 1969, pp. 27–43.

M. Trow, 'Problems for polytechnics: an American point of view', *Universities Quarterly*, Vol. 23, No. 4, Autumn 1969, pp. 381–96.

University of London, Institute of Education. University Teaching Methods Research Unit. *Innovations and experiments in university teaching methods*: a report of the proceedings of the third conference . . . held at the University of London, Institute of Education, April 1968. London: University of London, Institute of Education, 1969.

H. Wöltge, *Student in the German Democratic Republic*. Berlin: State Secretariat, for Higher Education of the German Democratic Republic. 1966.

ADDENDUM

Centres for the Study of Higher Education

It may be helpful to readers to have a few additions to the list given on page 385 of centres doing significant work.

Center for Research and Development in Higher Education, University of California, Berkeley, U.S.A.

Institute for Studies in University Education, University of Copenhagen, Denmark.

Bureau for Research into Higher Education, Technological University, Eindhoven, Holland.

Department of Educational Research, University of Lancaster, England.

Department of Higher Education, University of London Institute of Education, 55 Gordon Square, W.C.1.

Tertiary Education Research Centre, University of New South Wales, Australia.

Higher Education Section, Direction des Affaires Scientifiques, O.C.D.E., 75-Paris (16e).

Department of Educational Research and Development, Office of the Chancellor of the Swedish Universities, P.O. Box 16334, S-10376, Stockholm 16.

Higher Education Group, University of Toronto, Ontario, Canada.

List of Contributors

Abu-Merhy, Nair Fortes, Dean and Professor, College of Education, Federal University of Rio de Janeiro; Member of the Federal Council of Education, Brazil; formerly Deputy Director, Department of Higher Education of the Ministry of Education, Brazil

Armytage, W. H. G., M.A., Professor of Education, University of Sheffield

Brick, Michael, B.A., M.Litt., M.A., Ph.D., Professor of Higher Education, Associate Director, Institute for Higher Education, Teachers College, Columbia University, and Director, Center for Community Colleges

Bristow, Thelma, Dip.Lib., F.L.A., Comparative Education Librarian, University of London Institute of Education; formerly Reference Assistant, Marylebone Public Library

Burgess, Johanna, M.A., M.Ed., Lecturer in Education (Philosophy), University of Sussex

Cerych, Ladislav, Ph.D., Counsellor, Directorate for Scientific Affairs, OECD, Paris; formerly Consultant to Unesco, Director of Studies, Atlantic Institute, Assistant Professor College of Europe

Cowen, Robert, B.Sc., M.A., Lecturer in Sociology, Furzedown College of Education, London

Cowen, Zelman, C.M.G., B.A., LL.D., M.A., D.C.L., LL.D., Vice-Chancellor, University of Queensland; formerly Vice-Chancellor, University of New England; Professor of Public Law and Dean of the Faculty of Law, University of Melbourne

Edwards, Reginald, B.Sc., M.Ed., Professor of Education, McGill University; formerly Lecturer in Education and Educational Psychology, Sheffield, Visiting Professor, University of Michigan

Ekgolm, Igor, Department Editor, *Journal of Soviet Pedagogics*

Froese, Leonhard, Dr.Phil., Professor and Director, Institute of Education, Director, Research Center for Comparative Education, University of Marburg

Furth, Dorotea E., Licenciada de Sociologia, University of Buenos Aires; Consultant, OECD; formerly Consultant to the Federal Council of Investments (CFI), Buenos Aires

Glowka, Detlef, Doktor der Philosophie, Research Officer, Institute for Educational Research in the Max Planck Institute, Berlin

Gumbert, Edgar B., B.S., M.A., Ph.D., Associate Professor of Education, Georgia State University, Atlanta, Georgia

Goldschmidt, Dietrich, Diplom-Ingenieur, Ph.D., Lehrbeauftragter in Industrial Sociology, Director, Max Planck Institute, and Honorary Professor of Sociology at the Free University, Berlin

Hecquet, I., Doctor of Law, Director for Scientific Affairs, Organization for Economic Cooperation and Development, Brussels

Hewett, Stanley, B.A., General Secretary, Association of Teachers in Colleges and Departments of Education in England and Wales

Hübner, Sibylle, Dr. Sociologie, Officer, Max Planck Institute, Berlin

King, E. J., M.A., Ph.D., D.Lit., Reader in Comparative Education, King's College University of London; formerly Assistant to Director of Extra-Mural Studies, University of London

Kobayashi, Tetsuya, Ph.D., Director, Unesco Institute for Education, Hamburg; formerly Associate Professor of Education, International Christian University, Tokyo

Limiti, Giuliana, Professore Inc. di Pedagogia Comparata, Professor of Comparative Education, Faculty of Education, University of Rome; Deputy, Italian Parliament

Michael, Ian, B.A., Ph.D., Vice-Chancellor, University of Malawi; formerly Professor of Education, Khartoum University

Mnthali, Felix W. J., B.A., M.A., Ph.D., Provost, Lecturer in English, University of Malawi

Montague, H. Patrick, M.A., Ph.D., Adjunct Assistant Professor, City University of New York; formerly Lt-Col., Royal Army Educational Corps

Mukherjee, K.C., B.T., M.A., Ph.D., Lecturer in Comparative Education, University of London Institute of Education

Nash, Paul, B.Sc., M.Ed., Professor of Education, Boston University

Pratt, John, B.Sc., Senior Lecturer in Educational Planning, North East London Polytechnic; formerly Research Officer, Higher Education Research Unit, London School of Economics

Scherer, Jacqueline, Ph.D., M.A., Research Associate, Department of Higher Education, University of London; formerly Director, Americanization Program, Syracuse, New York

Suchodolski, Bogdan, Dr.Philos., Professor, Warsaw University and Polish Academy of Sciences

Williams, B. R., M.A., M.A.(Econ.), Vice-Chancellor and Principal, The University of Sydney; Member Reserve Bank Board

Williamson, Ann, M.A., Lecturer in Comparative Education, University of London Institute of Education; formerly Principal Lecturer in Education, Garnett College, London

Woodhall, Maureen, M.A., Research Officer, Research Unit in the Economics of Education, University of London Institute of Education; formerly Associate Staff Member, International Institute for Educational Planning, Paris

Index